Blues Mamas & Broadway Belters

**Refiguring
American
Music**

A SERIES EDITED BY
Ronald Radano, Josh Kun, and Nina Sun Eidsheim
Charles McGovern, contributing editor

Blues Mamas

&

Broadway Belters

Black Women, Voice, and the Musical Stage

MASI ASARE

DUKE UNIVERSITY PRESS · DURHAM AND LONDON · 2024

2024 DUKE UNIVERSITY PRESS
Printed in the United States of America on acid-free paper ∞
Project Editor: Bird Williams
Designed by Matt Tauch
Typeset in Garamond Premier Pro and Archivo SemiCondensed
by Westchester Publishing Services

Library of Congress Cataloging-in-Publication Data

Names: Asare, Masi, [date] author.
Title: Blues mamas and Broadway belters : black women, voice,
and the musical stage / Masi Asare.
Other titles: Refiguring American music.
Description: Durham : Duke University Press, 2024. |
Series: Refiguring American music | Includes bibliographical
references and index.
Identifiers: LCCN 2024003296 (print)
LCCN 2024003297 (ebook)
ISBN 9781478030959 (paperback)
ISBN 9781478026730 (hardcover)
ISBN 9781478059967 (ebook)
Subjects: LCSH: African American women singers. | Women
singers—United States. | Voice types (Singing)—United States. |
Music and race—United States—History—20th century. | Blues
(Music)—History and criticism. | Musicals—New York (State)—
New York—20th century—History and criticism.
Classification: LCC ML82 .A73 2024 (print)
LCC ML82 (ebook)
DDC 782.0092/520973—dc23/eng/20240508
LC record available at https://lccn.loc.gov/2024003296
LC ebook record available at https://lccn.loc.gov/2024003297

Cover art: Eartha Kitt in the stage production *Shinbone Alley*, 1957.
Photo by Friedman-Abeles. © The New York Public Library for the
Performing Arts.

Publication of this book is supported by Duke University Press's
Scholars of Color First Book Fund.

FOR MY FAMILY

Contents

Contents

Warming Up

This section is not literally about warming up your voice. But it is a warm-up to the ideas in the pages that follow.

When I began writing this book, I was living in New York, working a day job, writing musicals and coaching voice whenever I could find the time. Now, as I finalize this manuscript, I commute between New York and Chicago, and work full-time as an artist, scholar, and teacher of musical theatre history, vocal performance studies, and musical theatre writing/composing. I think of my life as a flower that carries multiple blooms on a single stem. Sometimes the voice teaching, the theatrical songwriting, and the scholarly research appear to some people to be different undertakings, separate efforts. But for me they are all part of the same work, born of the same root. As a black woman and a mixed-race person living in the United States, holding multiple and simultaneous identities is simply part of the shape of my life.

The ideas I write about here are not purely theoretical; they are what I live with daily as an artist and practitioner. In my performance classes, students learn song repertoire by ear by singing along with the artists on recordings or in the room. I am also lucky enough to hear incredible singers rehearse and perform new musicals that I work on as a songwriter and dramatist. Some of these have scores where the full sense of the music really *can't* be written on the page, it can only be taught and learned through singing along with the voice of the composer or the music director. Often, that is also how my collaborators and I wrote it, voice to voice. Sometimes, learning the vocal music requires letting go of performers' prior experience of "training"—the music asks for less vibrato, different diction, adjusted tone colors. I witness singers retrain their voices in rehearsal for each new musical, bringing their own textures to the tune while also sonically citing all the voices that have taught them what the song is and how to carry it anew. The theories in *Blues Mamas and Broadway Belters* are absolutely part of my life in creative practice.

How should you read this book? I suggest that you at least skim the introduction, which has (toward the end) brief descriptions that are like a teaser of the chapters to come. This will give you a sense for which parts may interest you the most. Some parts of the book may be most fun for singers, some for people who love performance theory, some may be thought-provoking for voice teachers, and some especially meaningful to those invested in the history of US musical theatre, or in black female performance. In the appendix at the end of this book (and sprinkled throughout chapter 3) you'll find a set of whimsical vocal exercises to test out. They are not meant to be lessons per se, but more like invitations to sing along with the black women singers whose voices ring through the book. You could also think of these exercises as small poems or performance scores. Most of the book is written from my perspective as a scholar, singer, and voice teacher, but my background as a songwriter also inflects my analysis at times. And I do write directly about my experience as a musical theatre writer, in relation to the primary ideas of the book, in the closing section, the "Playoff."

Finally, I want to note that when I set out to do the research for this book, I knew very little about the blues. Yet nowadays when I teach courses in pop vocal styles for musical theatre performers, I begin with the blues. Writing this book has convinced me of how deeply the blues underlie American performance forms in so many styles, including vocal sound and technique for the musical theatre. Recently the blues have also called my name as a songwriter-dramatist, and I work on multiple new musicals that seem to have asked me, of their own volition, to write blues numbers for them. In the rehearsal room, the demo recording studio, the Zoom-bound virtual performance, and the songwriter's cabaret, I hear the blues come alive in the hands and voices of talented guitarists, pianists, and vocalists. I braid my own singing along the lines of these artists' voices and instruments, and my learning continues.

Thank *you* for bringing your own voice and presence to the work. Here we go. . . .

Note on Phonetic Transcription

Throughout *Blues Mamas and Broadway Belters*, in analyzing vocal performance on particular sung syllables, or particular vowel shapes and consonants within words, I employ the International Phonetic Alphabet (IPA), a standardized system of phoneticization. In addition to its usefulness for linguists, IPA is used widely among voice scientists and singers in classical- and musical-theatre traditions. Recognizing that this specialized alphabet may be of limited use to nonpractitioners or those approaching the text from a different musical perspective, I precede the IPA transcription with my own italicized phoneticization of the sound. For example: Consider the *ih* [ɪ] and *ng* [ŋ] sounds in the word "sing."

Acknowledgments

There are so many people who have poured love, and learning, and love of learning into me. This book is a testament to their faith in my work and their investments in the form of both ideas and care. I realize now that it was often when I felt least certain of my happiness that I was actually learning the most. I am thankful for the lessons and for the people who saw me through them.

I am truly grateful for the mentors who have guided this book, first of all my professors and advisors in the Performance Studies Department at New York University's Tisch School of the Arts. Alex Vazquez, whose critical precision, generosity, and elegance in prose and presence I have always admired, continues to guide me with patience, keen insight, and humor. Tavia Nyong'o has steadily encouraged me to believe there is a place in theatre and performance studies to engage the vocal practices I love. I remain inspired by Karen Shimakawa's rigorous and interdisciplinary approach to methodology, by the dialogic example of her pedagogy, and her reminder to always consider the exigency of the work. It was Deborah Kapchan who first introduced me to the field of sound studies and convinced me that the way I listen to the world really could make a meaningful contribution to scholarship. And I continue to be in awe of Fred Moten's mind, his courageous and gentle approach to teaching, and the way that he makes music of critical thought. At NYU I also learned so much in classes with Judith Casselberry, Barbara Browning, André Lepecki, Jason Stanyek, and José Muñoz, whose brilliance as a teacher still reverberates.

I am profoundly grateful to Daphne Brooks and Katherine Meizel for the inspiration of their scholarship and for reading the draft manuscript in full and sharing detailed, deeply helpful feedback. Nina Sun Eidsheim, whose work has helped me chart my own course since I excitedly read her doctoral dissertation the year it was completed, has been a kind and generous mentor and advocate in both intellectual and practical terms. I also thank the anonymous readers for their labor and for their warm, encouraging, and thorough feedback that has allowed me to think my ideas throughout more deeply and to streamline key aspects. At Duke University Press, I have had the good fortune to have Ken Wissoker's steadfast encouragement and thoughtful editorial guidance, and I am also grateful to Kate Mullen for her detail-oriented and kind follow-through.

Thank you to my colleagues at Northwestern University, where I have found a warm midwestern welcome and sharp interlocutors and mentors across a range of areas, especially in the Interdisciplinary PhD in Theatre and Drama faculty with the wonderful Elizabeth Son, Tracy Davis, Susan Manning, Thomas DeFrantz, Melissa Blanco Borelli, and Dassia Posner. Thank you to my Theatre Department junior faculty coconspirators, including Danielle Bainbridge, Roger Ellis, and Eric Southern, for the camaraderie and encouragement and the occasional, *necessary* text messages during pandemic-era Zoom faculty meetings. To the music theatre faculty, in particular Ryan Nelson, Amanda Dehnert, KO, Alexander Gemignani, and Kelli Morgan McHugh, you inspire me with your love for our art form and your tireless dedication to our students. In the Performance Studies Department, my brilliant NYU siblings Marcela Fuentes and Joshua Chambers-Letson have supported and advocated for me from the first time I set foot in Evanston. I feel lucky to know you and to be in your company. Thank you also to colleagues in the Sound Arts and Industries Program who sought me out early on and have always made me feel welcome—Jacob Smith and Neil Verma—and to fellow Radio/Television/Film Department faculty dynamos Miriam Petty and Thomas Bradshaw as well as my podcast buddy Ryan Dohoney in the Music Department. And I am grateful for colleagues in my pandemic-year junior faculty writing group who helped keep me sane and moving forward during an incredibly difficult year, especially Jen Munson, Sirus Bouchat, Ashish Koul, and Adriana Weisleder.

I also thank the wonderful students, graduate and undergraduate, research and teaching assistants, and advisees who have helped me move this project forward and think more clearly about this work. In particular, applause and flowers for Janine Chow, Jessica Friedman, Nathan Lamp, and Rachel Russell, and special thanks to Sunnie Eraso for bibliography and image permissions magic. So much gratitude to the students in my courses on Music Theatre Techniques: Vocal Styles, Vocal Sound and Performances of Race, Racial Histories of the Broadway Musical, and Black Women on the Musical Stage. Everyone promised that one of the best things about working at Northwestern would be the incredible students (smart *and* kind *and* talented!) and I have certainly found this to be true.

A deep thank you to Dean E. Patrick Johnson for his vibrant leadership of the School of Communication at Northwestern, and for supporting a year of leave at a critical juncture to enable me to complete revisions to this book project. Thank you also to the three Theatre Department chairs during my time at NU—Henry Godinez, Rives Collins, and Ramón Rivera-Servera—for the steadfast support and encouragement of my work. I am so grateful to Northwestern's Alice Kaplan Institute for the Humanities for supporting this book with a fellowship, and for the inspiring community of scholars I encountered there.

I thank the generous musical theatre studies colleagues who have invited my participation when I knew that I was a musical theatre practitioner and a performance scholar but wasn't quite sure if I was really a musical theatre studies person. Donatella Galella, Brian Herrera, Jake Johnson, Emilio Méndez, Stacy Wolf, Elizabeth Wollman, and Jessica Sternfeld, your cheerful welcome and encouraging emails—both the crisp and the effusive—have shown me that, in academia as in the rehearsal studio, I do love being with the people that love the musicals. The community of scholars working on sound and theatre studies that Patricia Herrera, Caitlin Marshall, and Marci R. McMahon fostered through an ASTR working group and curated "Sound Acts" panel, as well as the vibrant *Revolutions in Sound* symposium at the University of Maryland in February 2020 have spurred me on incalculably. I am so grateful for the thoughtful editing and feedback, the feminist example of how to do scholarship in community, and the chance to work through ideas in the joyful company of Katelyn Hale Wood, Kristin Moriah, Dylan Robinson, Jade Power Sotomayor, my wonderful NU colleague Shayna Silverstein, and so many more.

Thank you to the graduate students with whom I traveled through the NYU Performance Studies PhD adventure, for their collective example of lucid thinking, thoughtful feedback, and companionship on the road—in particular Ethan Philbrick, Nick Bazzone, Tara Willis, Brandon Rabbit-Masterman, and Henry Castillo. My writing buddy Charmian Wells, with her commitment to ethical scholarship and her joyful approach to combining scholarship and creative practice, provided vital encouragement for the last miles of graduate study. As the person who once sat in the "electrical closet" (it really was called that) in NYU's Department of Performance Studies working as an administrative secretary, I am thankful for the amazing staff and faculty of the department, who always supported me—whether as a receptionist coming in late because she was out writing musicals all night, or as a doctoral student with an unconventional timeline. Thank you to my former boss Noel Rodriguez and to my other former boss Jason Seth Beckerman. And I am grateful to the many graduate students who passed through the department while I was working there in the early 2000s—I have always regarded you as so many big siblings and remain inspired by your scholarship, persistence, and kindness. In particular I thank Sandra Ruiz for so many inspiring conversations, and for her brilliant example of weaving a life of poetry and critical theory and living courageously in the academy.

I also want to thank my own voice teachers, who lit a spark in me that has yet to be extinguished and helped me develop my love for this wild business of musical theatre singing—especially Jessica McNall, Thomas Jones, Joan Barber, and Robert Sussuma. Thank you for all your lessons, and for teaching me that two sets of ears are always better than one, and that the most important step to voice can be simply taking the time to lie on the floor and be present and deeply aware. I am also grateful to all the singers with whom I've had the pleasure to work as a voice teacher and coach in private lessons, who have taught me so much about what it means to listen together—thank you for your willingness to fearlessly explore and make weird sounds with me. And to the singers I have listened to, sung along with, and sung back—in addition to the artists in the pages that follow: Julie Andrews, Ella Fitzgerald, Astrud Gilberto, Lauryn Hill, LaChanze, Miriam Makeba, Audra McDonald, Joni Mitchell, Leontyne Pryce, Nina Simone, and Dionne Warwick, along with Evelyn Bartsch in my hometown church for her beautiful, self-taught soprano, plus Credell Coleman and Orchid Pusey from our days in Sisters of Kuumba at Harvard—thank you to these singers for the sounds, the recordings, the live performances, the rehearsals. Hugs to Nadiyah Dorsey, who from the time we were teenage acting majors at the Pennsylvania Governor's School for the Arts, has taught me so much about black elegance in the theatre, and who, along with Lacey Clark, first made me feel part of a proud tradition of black women in the performing arts. And I have learned so much from collaborators and performers on creative projects, the musicals I have worked on variously as a composer, lyricist, and bookwriter. Thank you in particular to those with whom I have worked on *The Family Resemblance*, *Delta Blue*,

Monsoon Wedding the Musical, and *Paradise Square*. Your voices astound me and give me hope for the future of our art form.

To my parents Fran and Kwadwo Osseo-Asare, both the first in their families to go to college, and who went on to earn PhDs—thank you for instilling in me an unshakeable belief in the value of education and the importance of creative practice and independent thought. To quote my father quoting an Akan proverb: *The bird is not stopped by the road! Ɔkwan nsi anomaa!* There are so many books this family has imagined (and is presently imagining) into existence; I know this commitment to writing and intellectual life has had a huge impact on me and, crucially, helped me to believe it was possible to add a title of my own to the bookshelf. To my siblings Abena, DK, Ernest, and Sam—all of whom hold graduate degrees and two of whom are also professors, you all inspire me in the dedication with which you pursue your passions and chart your own paths. Thank you (haha) for so many rapid-fire discussions. It was at dinner table conversations where everyone had a different (and strong! very strong!) opinion that this shy middle child learned to defend her ideas and hold her own. Abena, I have cited *Bitter Roots* but there are so many ways that your ideas have shaped mine, and your impact as one of the first voices I learned to sing along with in harmony, is indelible. DK, I am proud of you and though the worlds of design thinking and engineering, architecture, art biennials, and museum exhibitions are distant from my showtune-charged life, I travel alongside you in the practice of thinking deeply by making things. Mom, I am especially grateful for your courage in finishing your PhD and publishing multiple books while raising small children. I know I am a better writer because of the care you poured into editing my school papers years ago, and any success I am able to find in the academy is in large part because of the hard fight that you fought to prepare the way.

Although I can't precisely recommend this path, I completed my PhD, and the preliminary research for this book, while working full-time as a fundraising and development professional and simultaneously growing a career as a musical theatre writer/composer. I am truly grateful for the support and flexibility of leaders and supervisors in my day-job life who made it possible for me to study and research in this way—especially Carol Becker, Jana Wright, and Roberta Albert at Columbia University School of the Arts, as well as Lisa Yeh and the incomparable Elena Piercy at Columbia Business School.

To Inza Bamba, love and gratitude for all the laughter and companionship and perspective. What a joy to walk through the door after a day buried in my laptop to find you excitedly pulling off your headphones and inviting me to hear the latest music you are writing. It means so much that you have always believed in me and encouraged me.

Finally, to those who are not yet sure if it is even possible to be a singer, or a scholar—thank you for your questioning and your process. You are the reason we teach. I hope you will encounter something here that helps you to find your way, and to move forward knowing there is a full congregation of singers we are always, ever, singing along with.

Introduction

Citing the Vocal-Possible

This book dwells with the singing voices of black women in the context of US musical theatre in the early and mid-twentieth century. I argue that this vanguard of black women singers on the musical stage comprised highly trained, effective voice teachers who sounded and transmitted vocal techniques heard over decades in Broadway belting to the present day. My argument unfolds the ways that singing is citational practice, and that "singing along with" others is a viable method of vocal study—one that propelled the careers and secured the prowess of many of the black singers considered here. Throughout, I listen from the perspectives of the singer and the voice teacher, in a mode that might be considered listening by singing; that is to say . . . singing as an act of listening to black women.

What kinds of voices are thought to be possible for a black woman singer on the musical stage?[1] The urgency of this question arose from my experiences as a voice coach and composer-dramatist in the New York City musical theatre scene over two decades. As a performer, my own facility for navigating the Broadway audition circuit proved fairly limited. But I have remained the friend and confidant of many black women musical theatre performers over the years, increasingly those whom I coach and who perform my own musical theatre works. Among friends, the conversation about this or that audition often turns to the expectations of the producing team for whom a given actress recently auditioned. Regardless of the range of colors and styles borne in a singer's voice, time and again I have heard talented black performers lament having been expected to produce only one category of vocal sound. "Take us to church!" the casting directors demand, excitedly.[2] In this context, many a black musical theatre actress's worth has seemed to be determined purely by the degree to which she is able to use her voice to pave a smooth and familiar road, generally for white listeners, to what is often an imagined idea of black churchiness. This singer may be able to spin out, with equal ease, a breathy folk song, a husky jazz ballad, a golden-toned aria, a ragged rock scream. But often, none of these sounds are invited in the audition room, the liminal space through which the Broadway performer must successfully move if she is to earn a living with her art.

Of course, black people do not all sing the same way, and never have. I move beyond the presumed white audience of the early twenty-first century audition room and a theatre-going public still unreasonably invested in the idea of single-pointed black vocality to specify: What kinds of voices have *black women* thought and shown to be possible on the musical stage? This question has sent me in search of voice teachers, including those with whom black women singers might have chosen to study, historically. I pay attention to the way a series of voice instructors have posited the vocal-possible, for singers of any background and for black women singers in particular. Any teaching about the voice contains an inherent theory of voice and its possibilities.

In the literature on voice pedagogy, black women's voices are primarily understood as located within the realm of popular music, squarely in opposition to classical singing.[3] There is a pervasive narrative that black women singers of popular music such as the blues have always been "untrained," in possession of voices that sprang forth fully formed, just by the black churchiness of "feeling it." By contrast, I understand black women singers as not only voice students, but also voice teachers who taught and learned from one another. It is my aim to not only study early and mid-twentieth century black musical theatre performers, but to study *with* them. What do Sissieretta Jones, Ma Rainey, Bessie Smith, Ethel Waters, Pearl Bailey, Juanita Hall, Lena Horne, Diahann Carroll, Eartha Kitt, Leslie Uggams, and their contemporaries have to say and to teach about voice? I take the "singing lesson" as a key site of performance for analysis as I consider how performances of vocal sound replicate and transmit knowledge.

The Church Soloist and Her Voice Coaches

When I was a student at Harvard in the late 1990s, and not yet the lapsed churchgoer that I am now, for a time I traveled every Sunday from my dormitory in Cambridge to the Dorchester Temple Baptist Church, the better part of an hour's train ride on the T. In my zeal, I even sang in the church choir for a semester or two, inoculating myself against potential psychic illnesses of Ivy League life with regular doses of "black churchiness"—perhaps medium-strength in a church that had both black and white copastors at the time and where I recall once seeing a visiting Filipino dance troupe deliver an impassioned praise routine—but perhaps more potent than the dedicated if bookish Harvard Kuumba Singers gospel choir with which I also soloed and codirected a women's a cappella group.[4] At Dorchester Temple, I remember witnessing on more than one occasion a skinny, nervous young girl standing in front of the congregation to sing a solo. Often the unimpressive sound that came out at first was . . . not quite getting it done. But with the steady support of the congregation, so many firmly committed deaconesses clapping and invoking the Spirit ("Come on, baby. . . . Yes, Lord"), the scraggly first verses of the solo swelled in confidence, gradually rising to soar clean and strong above the choir in triumph, bringing churchgoers to their feet to celebrate this fresh evidence of the divine. The miracle of God was none other than the reworking of something inadequate, uncertain, not-quite-ready into the proud, representative voice of a God-fearing people.

Each time it happened, this miracle would strike me as proof that, even within the course of one song, a distinct progression in expressive ability is possible. Even if the singer is not sure how to "feel it"—or, perhaps, how to technically produce the sound needed to meaningfully deliver her song—through practice over multiple verses, with encouragement at key junctures, she is able to move into a stronger, more supple vocal sound. The lone singer in front of the congregation does not produce that powerful, rippling voice all on her own, but with the coaching of both the choir and musicians behind her and the congregation before her. She is audibly encouraged when her voice begins to soar, and so prompted to venture to soar higher. Thus even within the "take me to church" framework, it must be noted, singers encounter and must master particular kinds of singing lessons, of which this is just one example. Sometimes, singers' training in the church choir rehearsal allows technique in both classical and gospel traditions to flower—confounding essentialist assumptions that black church choirs always sing in precisely the same ways. As black Broadway and off-Broadway performers have commented to me meaningfully, "We do not all go to the same church."[5]

I also suggest that the myriad lessons given in this context are ongoing; coaching happens anew and in fresh ways with each singing of a song. The dynamism of voice coach and singer, the deaconess urging on the church soloist, is what calls up the sound that theatre producers are eager to hear from black singers at musical theatre auditions. And yet in that enclosed context the black musical theatre singer is expected to be both singer and congregation, producing a static, fully encapsulated blackness for the white ear. This "fixing" of blackness, reducing it to an isolated, set quality ("feeling it") disavows the ideas of progression, expanse, development, change, and vocal copresence—whether over the course of verses or decades. And it is this disavowal I critique in the chapters that follow. So the idea of ongoing vocal study is also central to this book, displacing the idea of singers who "can sing" or "have learned to sing" with the idea of singers who continue to grow and change in their sound over time and in differing sets of musical circumstances. And the singers I engage here trained their voices in a variety of settings, sometimes the studio of the private voice instructor, but also the vaudeville circuit, the nightclub stage, the Juilliard classroom, the concert hall, the dance school, and the television variety show.

Black Feminist Study and the Vocal-Possible

This book focuses on black women singers, not least because these are the performers whom I wish I had known about when I sought to imagine my own path into musical theatre as a singer-actress. I became a composer and writer for the musical theatre because the disjuncts of racialized perception and my own lived experience paved my path to the piano to write new songs and stories rather than try to wriggle into existing, ill-fitting parts.[6] It is not an accident that so many writers and composers of color presently working in musical theatre pen shows that are in some way autobiographical or, in Michael R. Jackson's preferred term, self-referential. We are working to literally write ourselves into a genre and industry that generally makes it quite clear we are welcome only in prescribed roles whose expressive contours are largely predetermined.[7] This study is a part of the larger project I am pursuing to write myself and people like me into the Broadway musical in positions of greater expressive possibility.

The black women singers studied in this book demand not just greater space but the deeper focus of intense listening. A photograph of Eartha Kitt in the 1957 musical *Shinbone Alley* (figure I.1) depicts her standing downstage center, arms flung up above her head, in a wide stance angled just so to reveal a glimpse of black tights-clad legs to one inner thigh beneath the fitted dress cinched at the left hip, skirt falling on the bias. It is

I.1. Eartha Kitt and ensemble in *Shinbone Alley* (1957). Courtesy of the Billy Rose Theatre Division, New York Public Library for the Performing Arts.

a moment preparatory to or just following singing, and there is a look of determination on her face, one of those fierce stares Kitt was famous for, a look of such intensity that it radiates outward into the space. A few steps away and upstage, the multiracial cast surrounds her, arms extended but lower to the ground, ceding space to the star. Telling the story or listening to the song with the black woman singer up front and center stage results in understanding the world according to quite different terms than those along which it is often represented.

The world that is sung into being by black women's voices is vast, collectively authored, and spun from the nuance of vocal details with seemingly small value—"a bent note, a throwaway lyric."[8] Yet, after Daphne Brooks, black women's singing is revolutionary because it is a practice "inextricably linked to the matter of Black life."[9] In singing, black women imagine futures and present realities into being—asserting and delighting in and conjuring possibilities where it has often been said that none exist. If your future is not possible, how can you imagine and live out your present? This is why the singing of black women is radical work that opens lesser-known avenues of understanding in both the world and the theatre. As Stacy Wolf argues in her feminist history of the Broadway musical, turning from a focus on heterosexual love stories in musicals to foreground women themselves and their relationships with one another in performance—whether as characters or, as I study here, as interpreters of song and character—allows for new understandings of Broadway.[10] Listening first and foremost to black women and moving through a black feminist approach enables new understandings of what musical theatre has been and what it may be. For these reasons, and in this way, I grapple with the vocal-possible that every singer seeks and fights for and immerses herself in and breathes out like fire across the stage.

In what follows, the discrete encounter of the singing lesson emerges as an important site and scenario of performance for analysis, also pointing up particular kinds of voice lessons that have gone unnoticed or negated. Teaching is often understood as a feminine and feminized activity, perhaps to the point that it seems uncomfortably appropriate to a book about women. The same has been said for the voice itself: "song is heard as naturally feminine, just as speech is naturally masculine."[11] Yet I am interested in thinking about the deeply theoretical contributions made by women who might otherwise be considered *just teachers* or *just voice teachers*.[12] Remember too that the classroom and other formal learning environments are spaces from which black people in the United States have systematically been excluded.[13] I attend to and reclaim a series of events that have not always been considered voice lessons as such. This involves taking seriously the sounds, statements, and listening practices of not only audience members, critics, and fans but also those of singers, accompanists, and voice coaches.

The scenario of the singing lesson as engaged here, if extrapolated to the broader category of music lesson, may well prove a useful frame for inquiry beyond the study of black women on the musical stage. But I want to be clear that the black feminist work of this analytic invites a particular mode of musical engagement—the practice of *singing along with*—that does not easily align with the valorized figure of the woodshedding, solitary horn player practicing for hours on end in a lonely room nor the competitive display of intertextual prowess in cleverly citing songs or phrases within one's own musical improvisation and/or composition.[14] By overtly invoking the notion of vocal technique in relationship to black women's performances, this book also enters into a conversation with formulations of technique in modern vocal pedagogy—both technique and vocal health, which this literature reveals as its de facto equivalent. To a much greater degree than for musicians whose technique does not rely as emphatically on the body as instrument, this precise link between (or collapsing of) health and technique is thrown into especially sharp relief by vocalists and voice practice.

Singing Techniques and Twice-Heard Behavior

Consider that the production of vocal sound is a learned technique of the body, even in circumstances where formal training in vocal technique named as such might seem to be absent.[15] Like other categories of bodily training, vocal instruction often takes place in informal settings, that is, not in classrooms, nonetheless transmitting techniques for learning to manipulate or play the body in specific, culturally prescribed ways. The notion of an array of embodied techniques also usefully displaces the concept of one monolithic "technique" as a territory to be policed. Nineteenth- and twentieth-century English-language voice pedagogy literature has much to say about what constitutes correct (read: "healthy") singing technique. Often, technique is figured as an idealized land to which one does or does not have access, and to which any access is conditional—the smallest misstep, repeated once too often, results in banishment. In this view, there can be no return to technique for the ruined voice, although the possessor of such a voice may be afforded the role of powerful border guard at the technical frontier. Manuel Garcia II, perhaps the most famous voice teacher in modern voice pedagogy, described his turn from singing opera to teaching opera singers as a pivot that resulted because early abuse had "ruined" his own instrument.[16] But this notion of the singing voice as stable territory that preserves the mythic (unruined) authentic self, the singular coherence of self and agency, has been shored up over centuries by the vocal pedagogy of European classical music. It is precisely this venerated belief that Katherine Meizel sharply critiques in her book *Multivocality: Singing on the Borders of Identity*.[17] For the present-day musical theatre, singers absolutely train in multiple vocal styles, invoking and maneuvering across music from varied expressive cultures and historical moments. It is also in contrast to this idea of a single-pointed technique that in chapter 4 I engage the Estill voice method as heterotopic pedagogy, instruction that posits vocal technique as a multiplicity of options from which a singer can formulate her sound according to her choosing.

Understanding voice practice as a technique of the body enables a move away from the fixedness that the term "technique" has sometimes called up when applied to music along with its cousins, style and genre.[18] The analysis here instead focuses on the specificity of technique within vocal sounds by attending to certain racial histories they carry. I am interested in the ways that styles are unstable or porous, and how certain performance techniques of voice have traveled across them. An overemphasis on musical style and genre might seem to obscure the ways certain vocal sounds are threaded through blues, vaudeville, "coon shouting," ragtime, torch singing, musical comedy song, nightclub performance, and Broadway belting. The work of this book is not to demarcate the particulars of styles of musical performance so that they can then be linked to markers of race, culture, or identity; rather, it is to consider what it might mean to track the flow of vocal sound across these various expressive categories.

Attending to the multiplicity and flow of techniques allows for an understanding of vocal technique as something that emerges over time. The contexts in which vocal techniques are strengthened—or clarified, or experimented with, or undone—are what I hear as singing lessons. What are the ways and routes by which the learning of vocal technique happens? Via the popular singing techniques of blues singers and shouters, whose "lessons" are rarely identified in the archive as such, I trace historical singing contexts and moments in which one singer taught a song to another. Through this work, I trouble the pervasive narrative around the black woman shouter or white woman belter whose "untrained" sound is deemed a marvel for seemingly having sprung forth from nowhere. And from these lessons of content, the transmission of sung repertoire, arises a theory about the dynamism of vocal sound as a citational practice.

The performance of song is a particular modality of what has famously been called "twice-behaved behavior."[19] At first impression, this would seem to be merely that of "twice-sung." No singer can fully claim for her song the status of firstness; even so-called new songs recombine longstanding elements. But in addition to this quality, more productively, the dynamism of song performance also calls up a *twice-heardness*. The twice-heard song is heard by both singer and listener, teacher and student. Its once-againness ensures that, even where singer and listener are one and the same, she nonetheless always also listens in to past singers. Attending to twice-heardness foregrounds the multivocality of song: in hearing variously, listeners produce various voices. Thus, in the case of the sonic, there is a dimension of critical distance produced by double-behaving vocal sound that can be felt not just between character and actor and not just between the racialized individual and the consciousness of white perception.[20] This critical distance exists also in the plurality of listenings and listeners; it is these distances which, as Nina Eidsheim theorizes, produce the polyvalent vocal sound itself via the act of listening.[21]

Every singer, by virtue of the sonic materiality of her song, is rendered both a teacher and student, both voicer and listener. So I listen to the blues shouter's lessons—those she teaches and those she attends—as well as the many colors of her sound, and the bleed of her shouting into and through Broadway belting, a twice-heard sound.

Sonic Citation and This Thing of Honor

In April 2021, barely a year past the onset of the COVID-19 pandemic, I Zoomed into a talk given by Fred Moten at the "Comparing Domains of Improvisation" series with Columbia University. This heady group of music studies scholars and musicians steeped in the practical urgency of ideas either esoteric or deeply theorized cut a swathe of intense reflection through my hectic Zoom schedule. (On the one other occasion I attended an event organized by this group, we sat in extreme concentration in a white, windowless room in upper Manhattan.) Sitting at the kitchen counter in my Chicago apartment, I paused my harried click-commuting through teaching, coaching voice, pitching for a Broadway writer gig, copy-editing a journal article, and planning a virtual residency for an international artist. And I arrived at the talk.

I arrive at Moten's voice, steady even when his camera image occasionally freezes: the measured thinking, understated delivery, rhythms of speech I can't hear as hesitance but instead as ongoing invitation to be and think together, a willingness to allow for complex thoughts that require careful unraveling, and to begin to do the work to unravel them in the moment, now, one strand at a time. After all, this lecture series is about improvisation. Tracing the lines of thinking along which he has traveled across his career, Moten speaks about a certain kind of corrective he is trying to move into these days in relation to his first book *In the Break: The Aesthetics of the Black Radical Tradition*.[22] He now realizes that at that time he was trying to critique modes of rationality that, incongruously, he still tried to leverage on behalf of the improvising musicians he studied. All this when really, he says, he needed to let go of being concerned with "the honor of black musicians." While as a performance scholar he did not want to position these players on the line between the animal and the human—and which of us in the academy today is comfortable saying that black musical artistry is simply part of the natural order? We know it inflicts the double violence of essentializing black people and disavowing black people's creative expertise—he can now concede, with some humor, that the musicians themselves were less worried about this. To take two hard-playing saxophonists, he continues: Charlie Parker was literally known as "Bird." Eric Dolphy would get up early in the morning to play along with the birds and birdsong. What mattered to them was the music, not the kind of recuperative honor the academy purports to be able to bestow. "I needed to get past this whole thing about honor," Moten said.[23]

But I stumble over this idea. In the Q&A I ask: "How did you get past that? Is there something that has to be sacrificed?"[24] Of note, this talk takes place two days after the conviction of George Floyd's murderer was announced. The national sense that the vindication of black life is something that must be fought for is just in the air. This despite the fact that it can never actually settle a score or bring true justice while a lynched man remains dead; or while women like Breonna Taylor who are slaughtered by racial violence remain largely forgotten and somehow perceived as less vindicatable. This despite the fact that all year I have been pleading with a loved one to abandon systems that, I believe, will never respect him (despite endless vacuous institutional statements to the contrary and time-wasting meetings to talk about black life instead of nurturing it), the hours I have spent pleading with this person to focus instead on stoking the fires of his own spirit. But I notice, in this moment at this talk, that I still feel: We have to fight for honor, don't we? Or if we are in the position to give it freely, shouldn't we do so? In the Africanist musical and poetic sense of giving appellations for a revered elder or leader, I have somehow internalized the belief that it is my responsibility if not to procure honor or respect, at least to give it freely where I can.

Moten explains: "The recovery of the honor of the black musician is another form of submission to a set of standards that I utterly repudiate. . . . I repudiate those opinions and standards," and forgo "whatever comforts I might derive from" them.[25] To give power to such standards, he teaches, comes at the cost of not fully engaging what black people are actually doing. Not actually listening to the music on the music's terms, and on the musician's terms. At this point in the conversation, in the heated tone, the recourse to blunt language, the affective charge and candor to admitting that it *does* hurt to be reminded "like eighteen times a day" of the subordinate place one is meant to have in this system, I hear in Moten's voice that the cost cuts deep. Refusing the imperative to seek honor and recognition for black musicians, then, requires sacrificing the seductive illusion that in doing so we will have escaped or defeated a racist system. On the other hand, simply acquiescing to the expectation that we must seek honors for black artists can only rob us of the more meaningful scholarship we could be bringing forth, if we paid full attention to what the artists are actually doing on their own terms. The primary aim of scholarship on black art does not have to be to prove that the art is honorable according to white supremacist frameworks. As Toni Morrison has counseled, in her own measured and unsparing speech, in an audio recording of a 1975 talk at Portland State University's Black Studies Center:

> The function, the very serious function of racism is distraction. It keeps you from doing your work. It keeps you explaining, over and over again, your reason for being. Somebody says you have no language and you spend twenty years proving that you do. Somebody says your head isn't shaped properly so you have scientists working on the fact that it is. Somebody says you have no art, so you dredge that up. Somebody says you have no kingdoms, so you dredge that up. None of this is necessary. There will always be one more thing.[26]

I move through this series of lessons, heard in Moten's voice and Morrison's voice, because I want to be clear that the sonic citations I write about in this book, in the full-flowering of their twice-heardness, do not necessarily afford avenues to greater honor in the conventional sense for these artists. In singing after and with them, sonically citing their voices, I cannot say that I am heaping flowers on their memories. Each citation is sonic memory in reiterated motion, after Eidsheim, "music in action," so where should the flowers go? [27] The nondiscursive nature of sound means that its citation does not come with a name attached in so many words. Its provenance, its evidence of origins, does not travel by means of the textual sign but rather, the *textural*, the timbral, the aspirated, and the released sound.

In her book *Bitter Roots: The Search for Healing Plants in Africa*, my sister Abena Dove Osseo-Asare, a historian of science, argues that the medical encounters between traditional healers and African and European scientists do not map neatly onto redemptive narratives of either scientific eurekas or ancient, originary knowledge located with one isolated ethnic group in one remote locale. She explains: "Narratives of discovery often fixate on singular inventors and original tribes, yet these accounts are often more mythic than historical."[28] Nonetheless, the ideas of property and ownership claims to novelty, to being *the first* to possess specific knowledge, have concrete implications for the economic well-being of individuals and rural communities, and certainly for the legal claims and financial gain of pharmaceutical companies. The concrete benefits that accrue to those who claim originarity can be felt both in medicinal practice, as my sister studies, and in musical-theatrical practice, as I study here. We are all globally entangled in what can also be understood as this settler colonial mentality of discovery and staking a claim. The very idea of appropriation is grounded in this way of understanding the world: that someone originally owned something and then it was stolen.[29] However, my sister's book traces "healing plant diasporas" that took shape as Africans have historically redistributed medicinal knowledge, recipes for healing, and herbal seeds across different geographic locations. The romance of the redemptive and honor-conferring claim to originary, stable knowledge remains strong. Yet, as my sister tells me, plants and the medicinal practices they occasion simply don't operate according to this logic. Seeds blow on the wind. And so does singing.

It is evidence of the tight-closed grip of settler colonial ways of knowing that it can feel overwhelmingly disrespectful to consider citing a black woman singer without accurately inscribing her name in the citation. In a logic mapped by the planting of flags and staking of claims, it is easy to be pulled along in the scramble to assert the value of sounds in terms of property and ownership. As Moten also testifies, certainly there is a felt cost to forgoing the scrambling and the asserting. But what if, in the compact aphorism-lyric from a song by punk vocalist and Inuk throat singer Tanya Tagaq has it, in fact, "Money has spent us."[30] As xwélmexw artist and scholar Dylan Robinson (stó:lō/Skwah) teaches, it is possible to exist and move as a theorist and listener by means other than the extractive, settler colonial approach that too often forms the unmarked baseline of scholarly or musical inquiry. Beyond the circuits and mindsets of starvation, Robinson deftly articulates, exist perceptual logics with the potential to call forth more resurgent ways of understanding and living.[31] It is in this spirit that I offer not only the theoretical concept of sonic citation, the twice-heardness of vocal sound, as a tool for the interpretation of performance. Sonic citation also presents an invitation to creative practice, a recipe to sing in the clear and joyful knowledge of voices one is ever *singing along with*.

Listening to Black Women on Broadway

In the chapters that follow, I listen to and invite new ways of singing along with black women singer-actresses in US musical theatre between 1900 and 1970. When the black woman singer on Broadway is invoked in the present day, she is most often heard in terms of iconic roles such as Dorothy in *The Wiz* (1975) and Effie in *Dreamgirls* (1981), with repertoire built on musical styles from popular music which had, by that time, had long histories outside of vaudeville and musical comedy.[32] *The Wiz* was one of the first successful shows on Broadway by a black creative team since the days of Eubie Blake and Noble Sissle's *Shuffle Along* (1921). Indeed, the early decades of the twentieth century saw a flowering of black talent on the US musical stage; the 1900s and 1920s have been called the most important decades for black musical theatre.[33] The 1970s ushered in an equally vibrant decade for black musicals on Broadway, in part because artists sought to reclaim and historicize the work of early black musical theatre such as that of the 1920s heyday.[34] Of course, the precise definitions of what counts as a black musical have been articulated according to a range of differing criteria at different times.[35] Suffice to say, the goal of this book is not to further delineate and isolate the so-called black musical but rather to focus on black women performers themselves. The singer-actresses I study move through various performance spaces including those for primarily black audiences and those for primarily white audiences. The musical stages that interest me most during the 1900s and 1920s are those beyond Broadway, not the celebrated cakewalking and charlestoning black Broadway shows of the era but the vaudeville-blues stages where black women blues singers honed powerful vocal techniques.[36] This approach is useful for my black feminist project of augmenting existing work that hails unrecognized "fathers of black musical theatre."[37]

The 1970s birthed several highly successful musicals showcasing black talent that, in addition to *The Wiz* and Harlem Renaissance–fabulous revues such as *Bubbling Brown Sugar* (1976), also included two musical versions of plays by black playwrights, adapted by white authors: *Purlie* (1970), after Ossie Davis's *Purlie Victorious*, and *Raisin* (1973), after Lorraine Hansberry's *Raisin in the Sun*. The decade also birthed *Don't Bother Me, I Can't Cope* (1972), written and composed by the pathbreaking black singer-actress and composer/writer Micki Grant, choreographed by George Faison, and directed by Vinnette Carroll, who became with this production the first black woman to direct on Broadway. When *The Wiz* arrived on Broadway in 1975, the composers of its score, led by Charlie Smalls, a Juilliard-trained jazz musician and nightclub pianist who would go on to win Tony and Grammy awards, also included Timothy Graphenreed, whose previous credits were principally as a dance arranger; Harold Wheeler, who was Burt Bacharach's hand-picked music director for *Promises, Promises* (1968) and later became a legendary Broadway and Hollywood orchestrator; choreographer George Faison, a former Ailey dancer; and R&B artist Luther Vandross.[38] Appearing six years later, *Dreamgirls*—written and composed by white writer and composer Tom Eyen and Henry Krieger, respectively, and profoundly shaped by the white director-choreographer Michael Bennett—was explicitly about Motown. Having failed to nurture a generation of black songwriters and librettists, Broadway sourced the composers and the sound for later Broadway musicals showcasing black talent from the worlds of pop, Motown, soul, and R&B.

The scope of opportunities available to black performers who appeared on Broadway from the 1930s through the 1960s was necessarily impacted by the dearth of black composers, lyricists, and producers working in the industry during this period. Black tunesmiths appeared disinterested in writing for the musical theatre in these decades, drawn by the greater allure of Hollywood, and midcentury Negro Theatre groups tended to focus on dramas rather than musicals.[39] Earlier decades saw a marked shift away from black musicals produced by African American impresarios in the 1920s, whose proof of concept only resulted in their being edged out by white producers who sought to cash in on the success of shows like *Shuffle Along*.[40] In this context, the vocal and character type of the weary-bluesy mammy that Ethel Waters inhabited in the 1930s, as discussed in chapter 2, arose in direct relation to the shift away from black leadership in the arena of musical theatre producing.

As a result of these combined factors, and the definitive performances by Stephanie Mills, original Dorothy in *The Wiz*, and Jennifer Holliday, original Effie in *Dreamgirls*, the voice of a black woman on Broadway has become indexed in the American imaginary by a pop sound with a lineage that is heard as flowing through recorded popular music rather than the sound of what is often called the "Golden Age" of Broadway.[41] The title of chapter 3 is drawn from Diahann Carroll's felt experience of this dichotomy, what it meant to be a black woman vocalist who did not come up through the recording industry but knew instead that she sounded, as she put it, like "a little singer on Broadway." This split can also be understood as part of a trend, long decried, of Broadway music that has largely become, after the 1940s, its own separate genre that diverges from the popular music of the day. My goal here is not to delineate what constitutes Broadway music, but to acknowledge that the shift effected during the 1970s and 1980s by shows like *The Wiz* and *Dreamgirls* in ushering in a period with long-running, box office smash hits starring black women has tended to obscure what came before, in particular the performative and sonic contributions of black women who starred in Broadway musicals at midcentury.

There is also a certain erasure of the performances of black women on Broadway during the so-called Golden Age of musical theatre (1940s–1960s) that is enacted in the way that musical theatre histories are generally told. From *Show Boat* (1927) to *Oklahoma!* (1943) to *West Side Story* (1957) to *Cabaret* (1966) to *Hair* (1968) and *Company* (1970) to *Miss Saigon* (1991) to *Rent* (1996) and *Hamilton* (2015)—to trace one possible articulation—historians and musical theatre aficionados thrill to the cult of hit shows, a line of beloved works held up as exemplary and/or groundbreaking, even if taken to be mildly flawed in interesting or provocative ways. Thus the story of Broadway is narrated in terms of successful shows, in a broadly accepted litany of "great works." If in retrospect certain shows are deemed unsuccessful, or worse, embarrassingly out of date, even racist, the performances of the actors who starred in them are excised from the narrative regardless of the acclaim they may have received in their time.[42] Although it is the star who sells tickets, and so functions as the gem in the producer's crown, historians of musical theatre have tended to prioritize those gems with long-running careers in the form, that is, the stars who sparkled on the stages of one after another of the "great shows." This elite circle has rarely included black women stars on Broadway, in any era, each of whom has typically had one or at most two "great shows" to her name.[43] The extent to which Broadway writers and composers were simply not writing star vehicles for black women is perhaps a subject for another book. Certainly, I take note in chapter 3 of the rapidity with which Diahann Carroll and Leslie Uggams, on the heels of their 1960s Tony wins, shook the dust of Broadway from their feet and built the bulk of their careers in television and film where performance opportunities were far more forthcoming. In any case, when the shows in which black women starred are erased from the narratives of "great shows," so too go their performances, as their presence and voices are reduced to mere anecdotes.

Within this context, I position myself as a scholar, listener, and voice student. In addition to studying singing lessons given and attended by black women and their contemporaries on the vaudeville-blues circuit and in early Broadway musicals, I focus on a set of black women singers in Broadway's "Golden Age," primarily those who won its most coveted prize, the Antoinette Perry Award for Excellence in Theatre, or the Tony Award.[44] Listening closely to black women belters on Broadway and their contemporaries, I draw out aspects of their performances as a legacy of coachings and vocal exercises for the aspiring singer-theorist in the present day.

In the Scholarly Interdisciplines

By bringing vocal sound into hearing along with theories on race and gender as well as research on health, music studies, and musical theatre history, this project moves across several scholarly fields. I am indebted to the works of scholars at the intersection of performance studies and popular music studies that trace genealogies of US musical performance by artists of color, engaging the politics of race, queerness, gender, and sexuality in the nineteenth and twentieth centuries.[45] Where scholars of performance have engaged blackness and nineteenth-century performance forms such as minstrelsy, burlesque, vaudeville, and early musical theatre, they have rarely considered the legacy of these performances for the twentieth-century musical stage. This is my project. And despite a marked interdisciplinarity, the field of performance studies has not often troubled the distinction between high and low art that continues to police certain disciplinary boundaries within the academy. Scholars working on music and sound from a performance studies approach have often located their work in proximity to popular music studies and ethnomusicology—reinforcing the unspoken assumption that bodies of color are confined to these fields— or else aligned with the avant-garde. Fred Moten and George Lewis have eloquently critiqued the notion that the avant-garde is necessarily white; without denying the particular claims to the popular that black expression may make, blackness is not always, nor only ever, heard in popular song.[46]

This book directly engages the ways that musical theatre stages a rupture in the boundary between elite and popular art at the level of multivocal singing practice. My project enacts a certain sonic bleed of popular music studies into critical vocal pedagogy, and music studies more broadly, listening to the concert voice in counterpoint with, for example, the jazz voice. This work addresses a vital question raised by Loren Kajikawa, "How can popular music studies help to overcome ongoing racial inequality within schools and departments of music?"[47] The extant voice pedagogy and voice science literature, within which popular singing training is a relatively new topic, stands to gain a great deal from a more thoughtful engagement of the historicity of race and vocal sound—a topic I examine in detail in chapter 4, especially vis-à-vis the problematic rubric of "Contemporary Commercial Music" posited by voice teacher and researcher Jeannette LoVetri that is now widely in use. The analysis of musical theatre performers and performances here also invites a greater focus on musical and embodied sound within scholarly analysis of Broadway musicals, extending the work of writers such as Jake Johnson, Ben Macpherson, and Elizabeth Wollman.[48] As a field, musical theatre studies has the opportunity to gain a great deal from more supple theorization of vocal sound, and an understanding of the indebtedness of this sound to multiple musical influences—including popular vocal performance.[49]

The account of musical theatre history that I give is revisionist in the sense that I consider it primarily from the perspective of women singer-actors. The chapters that follow throw into relief the ways that attention to black women singers and their vocal practices across time can augment, frustrate, or reroute well-worn accounts of historical musical theatre performance in the United States. I am especially interested in considering the sounds of musical theatre history as *experience* rather than *narrative*.[50] Understanding singing as citational practice means we are dwelling with and reanimating history whenever we open our mouths to sing. In the Africanist sense: ancestors and the ancestral past are ever with us. The Akan principle of sankofa teaches, via the symbol of a bird reaching its beak backward: *Go back and get it. It is not bad to go back for what you have forgotten.*[51] "Go back" means crane your neck and reach behind to know what you already carry. And so the history I write about is always carried in the mouth, called forth and reanimated in its re-expression. Singing produces history in that it brings the past into the air, enabling attention, witnessing, and copresence.

In disciplinary terms, my purpose is less to correct the official historical record than to open conditions of greater expressive possibility for musical theatre artists, and especially black musical theatre artists. Instead of seeking primarily to fill in the gaps in incomplete histories, I grapple with Tracy Davis's evocative question for theatre and performance historians: "What might the unseekable be?"[52] By confounding ocularcentric beliefs that what is knowable is limited to what is seen, and proffering a richly opaque site of nondiscursivity—performance ever-elusive to textual capture—the history of vocal *sound* in musical theatre performance may be unseekable precisely because it is *already here*, already heard, sonically cited and present in performance today. Thus, the revision I hope to make to musical theatre history is in fact a revision to musical theatre's present and possible future—one that allows for hearing black women artists as always manifest in the song and in the singing, then as now.

Performance Analysis via Creative Practice

The approach to performance analysis in this book leverages my more than two decades as a musical theatre artist, in particular as a singer turned voice coach. I have been working with the building blocks of the Estill voice method, studied in chapter 4, from the time I was a child; its theory of the voice as multiply configurable has had a significant impact on my own understanding of what it means to be a singer, voice student, and voice teacher in myriad ways.[53] Challenging widely accepted yet vague terms such as "bright" and "dark" timbre, or "head" and "chest" voice, Estill practitioners make the case that the ear can be deceiving. The sound that seemed to be "nasal" may not in fact resonate in the nose. The "loudness" of a bright voice may actually be an aural illusion, an acoustical trick that the savvy singer uses to her advantage. A key focus of my study is to explore how listening alongside singers and voice teachers allows for particular kinds of rigor and precision in the critical discussion of vocal sound and embodiment. At the same time, the instructions given by Estill teachers that "your body should be louder than your voice, "or that singers should seek to "hallucinate the feeling of your bones" to produce specific vocal sounds may be understood as theoretical or metaphysical ruminations.[54] I engage voice methods including Estill not simply as a practice or performance that is illustrative of theory, but as theoretical assertions in their own right.[55]

This project also draws obliquely on my positionality as a musical theatre composer and lyricist to deepen my work as a performance scholar. While musical theatre history is the material through which my argument moves, the method by which I move as a performance analyst is one that delves into modes of musical-theatrical expression, and particularly, the shapes and effects of theatre song. In my practical approach to writing a scholarly book, I draw inspiration from the form of the musical itself. One thing that musicals can do beautifully is use songs to "telescope through" narrative time and space, as Broadway lyricist and mentor Lynn Ahrens once explained to me.[56] Musical theatre songs enable multiple access points to an overarching story beyond the constraints of everyday temporal logics or even linearity.[57]

In this vein, my argument proceeds by the primary means of analysis anchored in individual songs, even while I construct performers' training biographies within sociohistorical contexts.[58] It is as a voice coach who thinks in terms of songwriting and musical dramatism that I conjure up the sonic doings of theatrical songs and the voices that realize them in this book. In a musical, the song is a metonym for the whole show. It is a world unto itself. Although this deep focus on performances of specific songs as documented in audio and televised recordings—the discrete turn of phrase, release of a note, attack and grain of minute sounds—yields insights certain to be relevant to the larger frame, for the most part the analysis of the broader musicals as dramatic and literary works falls outside the focus of this book. I attend to the vocal actions that the singer is scripted and scored to produce (song in the sense of the road she must travel) as well as the interpretive choices she makes about how to do so (song in the sense of the way that she travels that road).[59] This attunement to the black singer and her "book" of songs makes possible a version of musical theatre performance history that moves beyond the well-established trend of reifying the contributions of white musical theatre songwriters.[60]

Structure and Scope

Structurally, this project arcs through four chapters that each focus on a different aspect of voice practice and teaching—voice lessons, coachings in how to listen, vocal exercises, and the critical theorizing of voice pedagogues. The first three chapters unfold in loosely chronological order, examining the transmission of various vocal techniques that may be considered under the capacious canvas tent or proscenium arch, as the case may be, of musical theatre belting. These are studied via a parade of types of singers—vaudeville-blues singers and shouters in the 1900s to 1920s, black torch singers and character singer-actresses in the 1930s and 1940s, on to nightclub vocalists, television variety performers and black Broadway glamour girls in the 1950s and 1960s. The final chapter addressing voice pedagogues spans the long twentieth century, from the late nineteenth century advent of modern, clinical voice teaching up to late twentieth and early twenty-first century voice training methods.

Chapter 1, "Vocal Color in Blue: Learning the Song with Blueswomen, Shouters, and Belters" counters the suggestion that black women singers of popular song in the early twentieth century were untrained. Examining the influence of the blues shouter's vocal sound on what became the Broadway belter's technique, the chapter invokes a line of historical singing lessons, the contexts and moments in which singers taught particular songs to one another and in which, I contend, vocal technique was also part of what was being transmitted. In addition to Gertrude "Ma" Rainey and Bessie Smith, I listen for lessons attended by white ragtime vocalists also known by the distasteful term "coon shouters," including Jewish star Sophie Tucker, to whose sound Broadway belting is often linked. Here I discern lessons both acknowledged and disavowed. Through Ethel Waters, Sophie Tucker's voice teacher, and renowned in her day as both a blues mama and a Broadway performer, I point out the multiplicity of vocal colors in which blues music has been sung. Via the voice, I argue for the blues as not only an antecedent of jazz but also a vastly underacknowledged protogenre of the Broadway show tunes belted out by the likes of Ethel Merman.

In chapter 2, "Beyond the Weary-Bluesy Mammy: Listening Better with Midcentury Character Divas," I take care to heed the black woman singer's directives and instructions for how she should be heard. When blues tonality was taken up by Broadway songwriters, I note, much of the form's earthiness, humor, and self-determination was lost. The watered-down result from Tin Pan Alley was the sad, sad torch song of the weary-bluesy mammy, a type Ethel Waters was repeatedly called upon to voice, despite the sharply different musical-theatrical aspirations Zora Neale Hurston had for her. I complicate this figure through Juanita Hall and Pearl Bailey—and briefly, Lena Horne via her outright refusal to appear on Broadway in the 1940s. In character roles leveraged to maneuver around the vocal type of the weary-bluesy mammy, these singers taught audiences to, as Bailey put it, "listen better." The understudied case of Hall, original Bloody Mary in *South Pacific*, is particularly generative, as she negotiated a path from the concert stage to the nightclub and, via vocal acts in what I term "high yellowface," convinced listeners to hear her voice as representative of Vietnam or Chinatown. Where the book's initial chapter traced lessons in how and what to sing, this second chapter collects a series of coachings in how to listen around the edges of racialized expectations for voice.

Chapter 3, "'A Little Singer on Broadway': Exercising American Glamour with Golden-Age Starlets" analyzes how 1950s and 1960s black women performers sang as stylish black ingénues and sex kittens previously unimaginable on Broadway. I begin with a study of Lena Horne and just why it was that she *didn't* headline on Broadway as a young starlet. Despite her refusals and the ways she was refused on the Jim Crow-era musical stage, Horne established—by different means from her carefree, white contemporary Mary Martin—strategies for performing girlhood that reverberated for the young black women who sang in her slipstream. Revising expectations for who could belt out show tunes and who could be a dewy-eyed ingénue in a mainstream musical, these performers included the first black women to win Tony Awards in the category of Best Performance by a Leading Actress in a Musical—Diahann Carroll and Leslie Uggams. I examine how these ingénues built vocal sounds that both aligned them with and distinguished them from their white counterparts in the 1950s and 1960s, in conversation with pop music ingénues of the time. Following Horne/Martin and Carroll/Uggams, in a third duet between Japanese American belter Pat Suzuki and self-styled international cosmopolite Eartha Kitt, I study how each deployed the sexiness of her singing in unexpected ways to secure and elide claims around national belonging. My analysis further considers these singers' legacies for the Broadway stage in practical, ongoing terms. After Alexandra T. Vazquez's methodology of listening in detail, I linger with details and contours of these singers' performances and revoice their particularities as a set of "vocal exercises" that remain available to and relevant for aspiring singer-scholars today.

Finally, chapter 4, "Secrets of Vocal Health: Voice Teachers and Pop Vocal Technique" takes voice teachers and their training methods as objects of analysis, locating black women stars of the musical stage within the continuum of historical voice pedagogy in the United States. I analyze the way that US vocal pedagogy has constructed singing technique as bodily healthfulness, such that popular singing voices employed in blues shouting and Broadway belting are deemed unhealthy, even abusive. I argue that modern voice teaching is characterized by a Foucauldian medical regard predicated on the notion that the bodily interior is possessed of dangerous secrets to be divined by the expert ear. In this analysis, singers and voice pedagogues emerge as thinkers advancing distinct theories of race and vocal sound, pathologizing or fetishizing the black popular singing voice, as the case may be. I revisit the turn of the twentieth century with African American vaudeville star and operatic singer Sissieretta Jones, and her theory of the voice as that which is flexed in collectivity. Through Jones, and the preceding chapters' studies of and with black Broadway singers, I propose an alternate theory of ongoing singing study—learning to sing by *singing along with* . . . the possibility of technique as the pleasure in sharing an open secret. Via Abbey Lincoln and Hortense Spillers, I consider what the act of *singing along with* proffers for the black woman and her vocal-possible.

The limited scope of this project has rendered it impossible to include every single blues singer and black singer-actress who graced Broadway from 1900 to 1970. I feel keenly the absence of a detailed study of Florence Mills, the shining breakout talent of *Shuffle Along* (1921). How fortunate we are to have such a dazzling array of talented black women singers across Broadway history whose legacy is, I hope, refracted and extended in some small measure through this project. Another book entirely could be traced in terms of the artists who walked through the doors opened by the performers I study here—such as black actress Norma Mae Donaldson, Leslie Uggams's understudy for *Hallelujah, Baby!*, and Filipina actress Vi Velasco, Diahann Carroll's standby for *No Strings*. Additionally, the decision to close this study with the decade of the 1960s prevented the inclusion and analysis of numerous remarkable black women singer-actors who appeared in Broadway musicals from 1970 to the present day. This luminous roster includes Melba Moore, Stephanie Mills, Jennifer Holliday, Nell Carter, Lilias White, Armelia McQueen, Gretha Boston, Lonette McKee, Vanessa Williams, Heather Headley, LaChanze, Tonya Pinkins, Audra McDonald, Anika Noni Rose, Cynthia Erivo, Denée Benton, Nikki M. James, Renée

Elise Goldsberry, Kenita Miller, Rebecca Naomi Jones, Patina Miller, L Morgan Lee, Ariana DeBose, Danielle Brooks, Adrienne Warren, and Joaquina Kalukango—and the list goes on. Keeping the focus primarily to New York and the Northeastern United States has meant forgoing study of black women singer-actors who held forth on stages in Chicago, Detroit, and Los Angeles. The project also bears the distortions that come with a US-specific and Anglophone focus—in addition to the dynamic tradition of black British singer-actresses in the West End, would that I could have included the zarzuela performances of Cuban vedette Rita Montaner and Puerto Rican star Ruth Fernández, and the appearance of South African legend Miriam Makeba in Johannesburg jazz opera. May this book open up many more opportunities to study and learn from the vibrant sounds and vocal techniques that black women singers call forth in the artful practice of musical theatre singing.

1 Vocal Color in Blue

Learning the Song with Blueswomen,
Shouters, and Belters

The Twice-Heard Voice of Broadway

Broadway belting is a much-mythologized vocal sound, one whose force flows in no small part from beliefs that it is both natural and dangerous. In my experience, students who seek to learn how to belt out show tunes often come to lessons with the strong fear that singing in such a powerful way may damage their voices. Certainly many voice teachers within the classical tradition impress this idea upon their students. By contrast, rising dancers may study ballet, jazz, and modern dance, as well as tap, yoga, and African dance forms, for example, without confronting the unforgiving assertion that using one's body to express certain genres will ruin it forever for others. In music conservatories, it is quite a different story; classical singers and jazz singers train in segregated tracks that remap the lines of racialized genre and style. Young classical singers are fiercely protected from the potential contamination of pop music vocalization on the grounds of preserving vocal health. Within this context, musical theatre has the potential to be a productive zone of miscegenation where singers train and perform in multiple technical modes. Professional musical theatre singer-actors sustain proficiency in both belt numbers and light classical repertoire, the latter referred to, in a telling phrase, as "legit" songs. But the flourishing of interleaved vocal styles in Broadway music is secured, I submit, by the narrative that the quintessential Broadway belter is, and always has been, a white woman. In fact, listening to a performer such as Ethel Merman has been touted as no less than "listening to the voice of Broadway itself."[1]

My project with this chapter is to complicate the premise of the implicit whiteness of the Broadway woman belter's voice, and further, to attend to the racial histories borne in vocal sound. In this chapter, I trace a line of historical singing lessons that locate blues singers Gertrude "Ma" Rainey, Bessie Smith, and Ethel Waters in the lineage of Broadway belters. Contesting the pervasive notion that black women who sang the blues and performed on the musical stage in the early twentieth century possessed natural and "untrained" voices, I argue instead that singing is a particular form of sonic citational practice. In the act of producing vocal sound, one implicitly cites the vocal acts of the teacher from whom one has learned the song. And, I suggest, if performance is always "twice-behaved," then the particular modes of doubleness present in voice point up this sonic citationality, a condition of vocal sound I name the "twice-heard."[2] I listen across this profoundly underacknowledged lineage of musical theatre vocality for the ways that early twentieth-century singers' voices are twice-heard, across racial lines, up to and including Ethel Merman's Broadway belt.

The Listening Singer

For singers, the acts of both listening and producing sound are conjoined. One listens to one's own sound, and to the sounds of others; within and across this field of listening, one's own voice takes sonic shape.[3] Nina Sun Eidsheim has argued for a move away from thinking sound as a fixed, external object to be apprehended, and rather, sound as practice experienced multiply at the level of the apprehenders' material experience.[4] Consider the various ways that bodies cradle sound beyond the curl of the ear. Singers' listening encompasses the awareness of how vocal sound vibrates in the bones of the breastplate and the skull; how the muscles in the abdomen, the neck and across the back ripple into motion as the voice climbs; the textural feel of subtle shifts in one's throat, nose, and mouth; the pressure of air rushing past the vocal folds as they draw close and draw apart. All of this is listening that, like the performance of a responsive pianist, accompanies vocal sound. It is typically said that a piano accompanies a voice and not that a voice accompanies a piano. Similarly, the act of voicing is generally understood as the main attraction beyond the singer's multiple acts of listening that underscore it.

And so the singer may not be circumscribed by the overemphasis on listening and reception that has been detected in sound studies scholarship by Patricia Herrera, Caitlin Marshall, and Marci R. McMahon.[5] In fact, the practitioner-driven voice science and voice pedagogy literatures manifest an attunement more likely to privilege the production of sound, articulated in anatomical terms, with *less* attention to singers' acts of listening. Within this literature, there is also a pervasive narrative that black women singers of popular music such as the blues have always been "untrained," that is, in possession of voices that sprang forth fully formed, just by "feeling it." This dismissive view—even when cloaked in tones of admiration—reduces black women singers to the category of vocal production only, making no provision for the ways in which such artists have listened to and studied with one another, sculpting their voices over time. This chapter offers a double intervention by engaging black women singers of the musical stage as highly trained producers of vocal sound as well as voice teachers in their own right. In so doing, I refute the assessment of such black voices as "untrained" and assert that, beyond personal, musical, or cultural *style*—often a euphemism for racial essence or the celebrated aestheticization of black suffering—early twentieth-century blues singers possessed and deployed robust vocal techniques.

The following analysis draws on archival sources, close readings of recorded and documented performances, and my more than two decades as a singer, voice coach, and songwriter in the musical theatre. As I consider how performances of vocal sound replicate and transmit knowledge, I take the "singing lesson" as a key site of performance for analysis. Unlike the stories of classical singers, the archive is largely silent on lessons or training that early twentieth-century popular singers, in particular black women singers, used to gain their technique.[6] What it does present, by contrast, are lessons of content—the ways and contexts in which singers learned particular songs. Thus the singing lessons I examine are largely occasions having to do with the shared experience of learning repertoire. It is these singing lessons and their implications I wish to consider here. By singing lesson I mean, primarily, a particular scenario in which a singer learns a song and polishes its delivery by working with another singer or voice coach. Thus, I engage the learning of song repertoire as a specific scenario of both listening and vocalizing by which the transmission of technique registers in the archive.[7]

Ma Rainey's Singing Lesson

Let's begin with Gertrude "Ma" Rainey. Rainey is widely regarded as the "Mother of the Blues." And yet, it is difficult to claim full maternal rights to the form for Rainey when she herself spoke of learning her first blues number from a young woman in 1902 while working the tent show circuit in Missouri. In her one known interview, Rainey shared the anecdote with the black musicologist and choir director John Wesley Work, Jr., who later related, "She tells of a girl from the town who came to the tent one morning and began to sing about the 'man' who had left her. . . . The song was so strange and poignant that it attracted much attention. 'Ma' Rainey became so interested that she learned the song from the visitor, and used it soon afterwards in her 'act' as an encore."[8] Almost a century earlier, white performers such as T. D. Rice were described by contemporaries as having drawn material from the "peculiarities" of street and stable-yard performances by black men to craft blackface minstrelsy.[9] Rice is said to have taken up the song that would make him famous for the number "Jump Jim Crow" as the result of a simple hearing, a chance encounter with a street performer, and the reported decision on the white listener's part to elevate a performance by taking it to the stage. In Ma Rainey, by comparison, we have an example of study in which the soon-to-be Mother of the Blues studied and learned a particular song, taught by one black woman to another, with all its strangeness and poignancy.

What does it mean to learn a song? What does it mean to share a repertoire between teacher and student, between an originary singer and the one who listens and sings back, in a process of learning to put the song into her own body and voice? In descriptors such as "strangeness" and "peculiarities," I detect gestures toward the notion of technique; specifically, techniques thus far unfamiliar to the listeners in question, whether Rainey or Rice. From my own work as a voice teacher and songwriter, I know that any song makes certain technical demands of the singer. One must be able to sustain this note, execute that leap, navigate such and such a rhythm. At the same time, the standout performer has the facility to justify the technical demands of the song, even as she may finesse them. There must be a reason why the singer chooses to hold this note so long, a more meaningful reason than simply "This is how my teacher taught it to me," or "That is how it is written on the page." There must be a good reason for why she holds this note or bends it—because the singer is still waiting for her lover to return, or she's given up and her heart is on the edge of breaking. There is a reason for this space between the phrases, and the way she exhales into it, because she's warming to her theme, building in intensity, or winding down to a quiet ending. She throws away this note, tosses it away, because who needs money when I have your love? Money? Throw the word-note away, the second syllable a mere shadow of the first. Or she may add a little lilt, a half-suppressed laugh to the sound, the sonic equivalent of a wink and a shrug, because everyone knows this lyric is rife with double entendre. Thus, while the song with its particular configuration of pitches, intervals, and rhythms may provide a map to technique, the singer must animate this map in performance and imbue it with a series of choices about how to deploy the breath and flesh of the vocal mechanism. A singer brings her own technical choices and feelings to the project, but much of how to do this is learned from other singers, by putting their songs into one's own throat and voice.

Learning Technique by Learning Repertoire

A collection of songs, and often songs in a particular genre of music, is generally understood to be a repertoire. As I explore here, there is value in examining what happens in and with song repertoires not just to pinpoint, for example, "how black people sang" or "how white people sang." Karl Hagstrom Miller has usefully contested the construction of folklore that implied a certain cultural isolation between Southern black and white people, observing that folklorists and the subsequent recording industry used this artificial distinction around racially bounded folklife to justify drawing a fixed musical color line between blues and country singers. Miller's analysis does not compare performance practices and styles. He asserts, "I instead emphasize repertoires—what songs musicians played rather than how musicians played them."[10] He identifies this strategy as a contrast to that of late twentieth-century folklore scholars whose influential work shifted focus from texts to practices, cautioning, "While a focus on performance might be best for identifying a core musical vocabulary or group identity formation, I hope *Segregating Sound*'s emphasis on repertoire helps to identify interracial and transregional conversations."[11]

There is much I find generative about Miller's work, not least for helping to identify and engage a performativity of song repertoire.[12] If performativity engages what words, and works, *do* in addition to simply what they *mean*, it enables the critical examination of the ends to which song repertoires have been put by various deployers, whether individual per-forming artists or larger forces. Such worthwhile efforts are, however, not the primary focus of my study. I argue here for an extension of Miller's position in order to suggest that an engagement of technique can also con-tribute to a conversation about racial dynamics and cross-racial cultural expressions. Listening for vocal techniques can be much more than the search for an imagined, authentic point of origin. In any case, the existence of Ma Rainey's singing lesson makes clear that such a project will only be futile; everyone has "learned the song" from someone else. What's more, learn-ing a song is, for the learner, an exercise in both repertoire and technique. Again, the dynamism of song repertoire calls up a twice-heardness such that even where singer and listener are one and the same, she nonetheless always listens in to past singers.

In theorizing embodied performance, Diana Taylor is to an extent in accord with Karl Hagstrom Miller, considering that ways that the actions of folklorists have to do with how repertoires can be archived and how this act of curation necessitates a certain violence. Yet she is also attentive to the ways that performances are replicated themselves—revised, reinvented, or in other ways mediated. The repertoire, with all its dynamism, cannot be made to stand in pure contrast to the violent, flawed archive. And the site of the singing lesson is a key space where its mediation—whether rep-lication, reinvention, or loss—is performed. John Wesley Work, Jr., makes the same point regarding the singing of a given blues song by a particular singer, a process he refers to as "taking over," noting "the individual singing it almost always gives her own coloring to the song by modifying, omit-ting, and adding lines."[13]

In the following section I consider how a singer such as Bessie Smith learned to put her own "coloring" on the blues repertoire she sang, not just in terms of its text but in her very vocal sound. The full volume of the legendary singer's theatrical savvy and star power emanate from a public-ity photo that looks to be from the late 1920s (figure 1.1). The bright-eyed Smith stands in a long gown, one foot placed slightly before the other, gazing directly at the camera. There are jewels in her ears, at the neckline of her dress just at the collarbone, and at the waist. She seems to have just parted the dark curtains behind her, making an entrance, and looks to be in the midst of a song, or a peal of laughter. Here was a singer who clearly knew how to hold stage with her persona and with her voice.

1.1 Bessie Smith in a 1920s publicity photo. Courtesy of the Music Division, New York Public Library.

Bessie Smith's Shout
Learning the Vaudeville-Blues

Listening to "Poor Man's Blues," a song Bessie Smith authored herself and whose lyrics Angela Davis has lucidly analyzed as containing an incisive social protest, I take in the slides in Smith's voice, each a caressing or easing over the many surfaces of a given pitch with all its curves. I hear the gravel in her sound, the majestic, muscular ripple of vibrato, and the ring to her tone. There is a sweetness underneath the grit and growl that comes, as the metaphorical landscapes of anatomy and acoustics would have me believe, from a particular technical posture, holding the throat in the position of a laugh, or a sob, or both simultaneously. The affective arrangement of body for voice is a performance in its own right. The shape contains an ambivalent multiplicity that in itself evokes the blues. As theologian James H. Cone writes, "The blues were living reality. They were a sad feeling and also a joyous mood. They are bitter but also sweet. They are funny and not so funny."[14] I hear this doubleness in the color of Smith's voice itself, the physiology and sonic materiality of double entendre, an enfleshed performance that means more than one thing at once.

The way that Bessie Smith delivers a song has to do with more than just the timbre of her voice, and more than its grain, understood as a kind of frictive beyond-timbre—what Roland Barthes calls "the body in the voice as it sings."[15] Although, as far as grain is concerned, Steven Connor cautions usefully that the body does not "upload" cleanly into voice, and voices may also ventriloquize the rooms in which they resound.[16] Further, in the crack of the voice, the cut of the grain, as Fred Moten teaches, a black singer's vocal sound may thwart both the accusation of incompleteness and assumptions around "the soft, heavy romance of a simple fullness."[17] Beyond timbre, consider also Bessie Smith's phrasing, consider improvisation, consider her stage presence, reportedly commanding, and the fact of the songs she penned herself. Ethel Waters once commented, "I was as crazy about her shouting as everyone else, even though hers was not my style."[18] Of note, the term in use was not *belter* of blues, although in contemporary parlance this phrase does not sound wrong per se, but instead *shouter* of blues. In any case, I am after the vocal *sound* and what it bore, what it continues to bear. How did Bessie Smith learn to shout, and with her particular sound?

It has been suggested, and sometimes refuted, that the Tennessee-born Smith learned to sing from Rainey, and certainly they did perform together early in Smith's career. Smith's entrée into show business came when she was hired to work mainly as a dancer with a traveling company in 1912 at the age of eighteen, and soon after she appeared in a troupe with "Ma" and "Pa" Rainey. Yet Maud Smith, Bessie's sister-in-law, commented, "Ma and Bessie got along fine, but Ma never taught Bessie how to sing," and Smith's biographer Chris Albertson insists, "Ma Rainey may well have passed on to the younger singer a few show business tricks, and she probably taught her some songs, but Bessie was, by all accounts, a good singer before she left Chattanooga."[19] What is interesting about these comments is the way in which they seem to suggest that learning to sing is an on/off switch— you've learned or you haven't—when, in practice, technique develops over time. There is also a sense of defending Smith's legacy, as if having learned anything at all other than "a few show business tricks, and . . . some songs" robs Smith of her authenticity, somehow diminishes the force of her talent. The antitheatrical investment in the authenticity of blues performers, as Paige McGinley has documented, disavows the technique—whether theatrical or, as I discuss, musical—that such artists developed and displayed.[20] Of course, the impressiveness ascribed to black singers often flows from the mysterious and magical sense in which they are supposed to be those who are never taught, but just "feel it" all along.

However, in contrast to the on/off switch model of singing training, where "on" perpetuates the myth of authentic, unlearned, natural black talent (and off is, well, just *off*), I contend that learning to sing, or learning to sing in a certain way, generally has a slow rise to it.[21] To the above assessments, then, I argue for the importance of *continuing* to learn. Even once a singer has grasped the basics of vocal production, even if she knows "how to sing" she can continue to learn and grow in her technique. It is impossible that Smith could have learned nothing from Rainey as they shared a stage. The assertion that Smith would not have studied and in some aspects emulated the more successful singer eight years her senior is, far from preserving her legacy, only an insult to any self-respecting performer who aspires to be a star. Sharing a stage, singing together, and learning songs from another singer certainly constitute listening scenarios that fall within the category I consider here as "singing lesson." But even more deeply, if the learning of repertoire is what we are after, what is to be made of two singers who write a song together?

The song "Don't Fish in My Sea" was cowritten by Rainey and Smith, as documented by Davis, and recorded by Rainey in Chicago in 1926. The tune is a straightforward twelve-bar blues that works up to a woman's assertion of the boundaries, value, and territory of her body over and against the actions of a philandering man: "If you don't like my ocean, don't fish in my sea . . . Stay out of my valley and let my mountain be." There is a smoothness to Rainey's sound, a forswearing of overexertion. This is an easy sliding over notes, with pickups, those quick notes between phrases thrown away almost to the side instead of straight ahead. Her sustained tones are burnished with warm vibrato, the low notes sound as though she's leaning right in to make her point. It's as if a blue note sounds blue because she can't be bothered to reach all the way up to it . . . the way a queen should not be expected to work too hard, with a languid elegance that calls up hot and humid air. The recording consists only of Rainey's voice and Thomas Dorsey's upright piano playing, which prances along behind her, lilting and dipping into tremolos at every occasion. After the second verse, however, there is a brief spoken line before the sung melody resumes:

> He used to stay out late, now he don't come home at all
> He used to stay out late, now he don't come home at all
> [Spoken] Won't kiss me, either
> I know there's another mule been kickin' in my stall.[22]

Angela Davis speculates, "The speaking voice sounds to be that of Bessie Smith, who may very well have been present at this recording session on an informal basis."[23] It's hard to tell. The line comes close on the heels of the last sung note and it could have been difficult for Rainey to have finished singing and managed to spit out the line as quickly and casually as it sounds; I can understand why Davis hears this as the voice of a second woman in the room. And it does have some of Bessie Smith's inflection: "Won't kiss" as two dotted quarter notes of emphasis, like two firm shakes of the head with a certain flash of indignance; affect aside, the rhythm, bend, and articulation of such a two-note phrase reverberate throughout Smith's own recorded repertoire. What I enjoy about this acoustic riddle are the generative implications of the two interpretations that seem most likely. If the spoken line is Rainey herself, then the fact of its being mistaken for Smith's (whose body of recorded work is more extensive than Rainey's and thus more familiar to the listening historian's ear), only points up a strong similarity between the two women's voices. In this event, the case for the younger Smith's having learned a hefty portion of vocal technique from the older Rainey is strengthened. And if the interjection is in fact Smith's voice? Imagine her scenario of listening, envision her sitting silent in the room next to Dorsey's piano while Rainey sang into the recording horn, taking it all in and perhaps holding her cowriter accountable to sing the song in the way the two had agreed.

The scene of collaboration reimagines the scene of teacher-to-student repertoire learning as one of shared repertoire creation, in which a new song is borne out in the voices and embodied performances of two black women as they sang and wrote the blues together. I picture the two bent over a hot piano and a fresh sheet of paper, backstage at one of the theatres at which they performed together, companions in song and in travel on the black theatre circuit of their time. Singing the tune back to each other, ensuring its viability in its twice-heardness.

Blues Shout as On-the-Road Show Tune

The blues singers were traveling women and, as I discuss below, traveling theatre artists. Plenty of ink has been spilled on the topic of travel as a theme of blues lyrics. The spread of the blues coincided with a time of sweeping migration as black people moved in increasing numbers from the rural South to northern cities. In the wake of slavery and the oppressions of its aftermath, travel and sexuality were markers of a new era in black identity: "The experience of freedom is sought in the journey itself—it is mobility, autonomously constructed activity that brings with it a taste of liberation."[24] Davis identifies a kind of radical openness that the road provided to a Southern black woman migrating to the North or claiming the uncertainties of the road as a means to escape a man who had done her wrong, for example, despite the fact that the open road promises no certain resolution. But what the listener must reconcile with this interpretation is the harmonic closedness of the twelve-bar blues; in a way it is an incredibly circular form that never dances too far from harmonic resolution. The singer states the theme over the one chord (I), which is like the hard ground, and then maybe hops up briefly to put the song on a shelf, on the four chord (IV), then back down to the one. Then, in the second phrase, which restates the same words, she hops back up on that four-chord shelf, and then comes tumbling back down to earth to the one. Then (third phrase) she blows it wide open with the five chord (V), new harmony to the ear matched with new words, before being pulled back, and it's like the tide, inevitable, to the familiar shelf of the four chord and then all the way to the ground of the one. But if the blues sound the radical possibility of the road the blueswomen traveled, perhaps this can be heard in the openness of its repetitions, the refusal to ever arrive for the final time. In this way, the circularity of the blues' harmonic rhythm simply promises that heading out on the road will always end in nothing less than being back on the road again.

Sonically and structurally, the usefulness of this repetition, when there are words to work with, is that the blues lyric becomes radically open to interpretation and new meaning in its second statement. It's a basic tenet of musicality, as my childhood music teachers taught, that when the same phrase is repeated twice, you cannot do it exactly the same way each time— the second time through the phrase has to mean something different, be somehow changed, whether in volume, articulation, phrasing, tone color, or combination of these and more attributes. The eloquence of this tenet is built into the structure and poetry of the blues form itself. When the first phrase is repeated the second time, in the throat of the consummate singer, the words do not just mean the same thing they meant before, in simple constative state, instead they *perform* something new in their twice-heardness. Here is another way that the blues form's very circularity creates a space for its discursive openness. As a result, the blues teach the listener to listen in a certain way—to listen more deeply into the second phrase for what is new. And it's well known that blues lyrics, in the pens and voices of their creators, often personify the blues themselves. The blues can wake a person up, set her to shaking, run around her house, and hold up their end of a conversation. The blues are plural and inclusively gendered, known as they rather than he or she. One might feel blue at a particular moment in time, but the blues are a repetitive condition and repeat visitors—they come around again and again; of themselves they articulate and embody once-againness. In the distinguished cohort of singing teachers under consideration here, as sculptors of the vocal sound produced by Ms. Bessie Smith in particular, the blues themselves call out for recognition and clamor for their rightful seat.

As blues singers, Smith, and Rainey before her, are widely and deservedly credited as pathbreakers who prepared the way for the traditions of (recorded) jazz that would follow them. But the two women's connections to the theatre world deserve consideration as well. Of note, in the 1930s, Rainey owned and operated the Lyric and the Airdrome Theatres in Georgia after retiring from her own career as a performer.[25] These were theatres on or adjacent to the famed TOBA circuit whose acronym, officially the Theatre Owners Booking Association, was also said by black performers of the day to stand for "tough on black asses." In the first two-and-half decades of the twentieth century, Smith and Rainey performed for black audiences across the circuit at many of its nearly eighty theatres, which ranged in size from the 500-seat American Theatre in Houston to the 1,800-seat Lyric Theatre in New Orleans. [26] What's more, in the 1920s, Smith was lauded in the black press as "one of the greatest colored actresses" of the day.[27]

What kinds of shows were performed for black audiences across the country, in particular at Southern theatres, on the TOBA and other circuits at the time? Certainly such shows built on the tradition of all-black minstrel troupes whose touring productions dated from the 1860s. In the 1870s, two black stars known as the Hyers sisters had a hit with their musical play *Out of Bondage*. But it wasn't until 1898 with the unfortunately named *A Trip to Coontown*, by Bob Cole and Billy Johnson, that more traveling groups began expanding their repertoire to include musical comedy that broke increasingly with minstrel form conventions. Even then, many groups retained the word "minstrel" in the company name, such as the Rabbit Foot Minstrels with which both Rainey and Smith toured in 1915.[28] By the 1920s, in the heyday of the TOBA circuit, its theatres were booking vaudeville acts. Musicologist Eileen Southern aptly observed that singers like Rainey and Smith were vaudeville artists, noting that scholars "have found it difficult to describe adequately the quality and style of the blueswomen's voices, which ranged from lilting soprano to deep contralto, from expressive, soulful wails to abrasive, gut-bucket groans and moans."[29] Southern refers to the music these singers sang as "vaudeville-blues," an important intervention in prevailing narratives of musical theatre history. Tracing a history of musicals that listens through black women's voices requires a rethinking of the dominant narrative of blackness via minstrelsy that is subsequently coopted into white vaudeville innovated by European immigrants and then, via a dash of European operetta, arrives at (white) musical comedy, from which black musical comedy is a separate and "parallel" strain.[30] The black vaudeville-blues artist, by her very existence, complicates this articulation.

Bessie Smith is known to have performed in at least two early musicals. The first was *How Come?* by Eddie Hunter (a black comic actor who also starred in the production in blackface) and Ben Harris, in which she performed during its tryout run at the Dunbar Theatre in Philadelphia in January 1923. Following an altercation with the show's star, Smith was subsequently replaced by Alberta Hunter when the production was presented at George White's Apollo Theatre on 42nd Street for forty performances in the spring of 1923.[31] In any case, in its Philadelphia incarnation, Smith sang five blues songs in this musical, under her own name, and the production was well received. The second was the musical *Pansy*, by Maceo Pinkard and Alex Belinda, which opened at the Belmont Theatre in New York in 1929. While no script for this show survives, playbills indicate that its opening scene unfolded at a commencement at a southern university and that the plot subsequently moved through various locales including a sorority house, the university campus, a farm, Penn Station, and the front of a skyscraper. Once again, Smith starred as herself.[32] Her contributions to musical theatre as one of the great vaudeville-blues artists did not end there. Her sound and style inspired numerous subsequent musicals that graced the Broadway stage. Not the least of these was the revue *Me and Bessie*, coauthored by Linda Hopkins (who also starred in an acclaimed performance) and William Holt, which opened on Broadway in 1975 following successful runs in Washington, DC, and Los Angeles, and ran for 450 performances—holding the record for decades for the longest-running one-woman show to play Broadway.[33]

As theatre artists, Smith and her cohort of black women blues singers were performers on the same vaudeville stage that is widely accepted as an antecedent of musical theatre. But hearing a blues singer like Bessie Smith and her vaudeville-blues sound in the lineage of Broadway belters puts pressure on the oft-stated assumption that white Broadway belters such as Ethel Merman deployed a vocal sound traced to another great lady of show business, the Jewish "coon shouter" Sophie Tucker. Tucker's success as a singer brought her the finer things in life, starring appearances for impresario Florenz Ziegfeld and the finest jewels and furs to suit. In an early career photo (figure 1.2) she is draped in the voluminous collar of a leopard-print coat, a wide-brimmed hat tilted fashionably atop her head and covering her face partially in shadow as she looks into the camera with the aloof not-quite-smile of the talent who knows her star is on the rise. The opportunities and financial success available to Tucker were, however, beyond the reach of the black women contemporaries whose sound she studied.

Sophie Tucker's Lessons
The Ghost in the Tin Pan "Coon Shout" Rag

Sophie Tucker grew up in Hartford, Connecticut, in the last decade and a half of the nineteenth century, and first sang vaudeville numbers for diners in her family's delicatessen and restaurant, before hitting the road to New

1.2 Sophie Tucker in a 1910s publicity photo. Courtesy of the Billy Rose Theatre Division, New York Public Library for the Performing Arts.

York City to pursue a career in show business. Her early years included stints in a Manhattan beer garden, then traveling burlesque and vaudeville companies, where she performed in blackface before moving on to the Ziegfeld Follies and international renown. Known for her stentorian delivery and great comic timing, Tucker was famous as "The Last of the Red-Hot Mamas" and "Queen of Jazz." But before all that, in the 1910s and 1920s, she was billed as an expert in a form of popular song known as "coon shouting." Listening to the sounds, and the personal accounts, of blueswomen alongside those of "coon shouters" brings into hearing a singing lesson that is often uncredited. Here, one shouter remains audible if invisible, ghosting the voice of the second with her undeniable, twice-heard sound.

I must interrupt the narrative here to address the fact that the term *coon shouting* is in and of itself an awful and racist phrase. The word *coon* was and is deployed as an epithet, perhaps less charged than the n-word that is, for good reason, studiously avoided in scholarship today, but an epithet nonetheless—a derogatory term for a black person. The word has bestial origins, likening black people to raccoons and continues to animate the nineteenth-century racist stereotype of the minstrel figure Zip Coon. Here in the twenty-first century it carries the nuances of not only Zip Coon, a ludicrous figure with overblown pretensions to intelligence and "high-class" white culture, but his many fellows among the minstrel types—overall a lazy, stupid, untrustworthy buffoon. Among black audiences and critics the term *coon* is also applied nowadays to a given black person deemed to be acting the fool in front of white people, denigrating the race for selfish, personal gain.

Notwithstanding—and of a piece with—all this painful racial history, in the same way that savvy black artists donned blackface as the price of entry to access some portion of the financial rewards of early US musical-theatrical performance, black artists at the turn of the twentieth century reclaimed the moniker "coon" in performance, song lyrics, and titles. An example is the significant 1898 black-authored musical *A Trip to Coontown*. And in addition to white artists like Sophie Tucker and her predecessor May Irwin, there were also celebrated black "coon shouters," their performances described in the black press with the specific modifier "up-to-date." Carrie Hall, Bessie Gillam, and Rosa Scott led the ranks of black women known to black audiences as *up-to-date* "coon shouters."[34] But the fact remains that the perpetuation of the word and the music to which it was attached dismayed many black listeners, such as Ethel Waters as noted below, and the author of a 1909 article in the African American newspaper the *Indianapolis Freeman* titled "Coon Songs Must Go!" The twenty-first-century poet Tyehimba Jess has worked an exquisite polyvocal poem from this outrage in newsprint, speculating the view of the one who performs the "coon song" in counterpoint with an excerpt from the 1909 essay: "Believe this: ain't no way I'd take a / insult if I weren't getting paid. Yes, I sing /—it keeps a belly full."[35]

I do not take lightly the fact that writing extensively about the "coon shout" in this book means having to read and hear, repeatedly, a racist phrase. But a central part of my argument is that it is precisely because the term has been removed from circulation that it is often forgotten how the ragtime music on which Broadway singing is built flowed from vocal practice explicitly affiliated with black performance in multiple ways. In that spirit, and in the spirit of the ancestors who strategically reclaimed the phrase for artistic and literal (food-in-the-belly) survival, I have chosen to print the term in full throughout *Blues Mamas and Broadway Belters*. But in my own writing I mark it with quotes to throw into relief, each time, the reality that despite the vocal techniques it denotes, the term is predicated on a false and violent depiction of black life. May the quotes remind us, each time, just how limited the vocal possibilities have been for black vocalists seeking to make a living in US musical-theatrical performance in every era.

By the turn of the twentieth century the "coon shout" was, as Lori Brooks has traced, a form that offered white female comediennes access to comic arenas previously dominated entirely by men. A late-breaking offshoot of blackface minstrelsy, this style of shouting featured lyrics generally written from the perspective of black men—or, more accurately, violent and incompetent caricatures of black men. With this repertoire, singers like the Canadian star May Irwin, famous for her "Bully Song," captured the white national imagination and built highly successful careers for themselves. In her lucid analysis, Brooks observes, "Literally taking form as the sign of the presence of blackness through her voice, the 'coon' becomes disembodied and ghostly, simultaneously present and not present. Audible but not visible, blackness emanates sonically from within the white coon-shouter, as she gives him presence and voice."[36]

At the level of the sound itself, however, there is little about this mode of singing that seems ethereal. This is evident in the voice of one of the stars whom Tucker describes, later in life, as lighting up the world of show business when she herself was a girl who longed for the stage. Listening to a recording of Irwin's signature song made in 1907, I note that the vocal sound is forthright and full-bodied. It is a bright, forward-placed sound with a bit of a wail to it. And there's an uptempo marching feel to the number, not dreamy or floaty at all. The "when" of "When I walk that levee road" is kicked out—a sustained, powerful note. By today's standards, this is hardly a good-time show tune lyric: "I'm a Tennessee n—r and I don't allow / No red-eyed river roustabout with me to raise a row. / I'm lookin' for dat bully and I'll make him bow."[37] The uncomfortable reality is that, from a songwriter's perspective, the epithet sings well, a high vowel launched by a gently voiced "n" right in the front of the mouth, flipping easily to the "g" with a flick of the tongue to the back of the hard palate—and plus it fits cleanly with the quick catch-step rhythm of the song, the frequent double eighth-note figure sprinkled throughout. There's also the sob of vocal retraction to Irwin's sound. Even accounting for the distortion of the early phonograph recording, my voice coach ear cannot deny that her voice sounds quite healthy; it sounds like a voice that could sing this way for days without tiring. And yet, the attentive listener will hear that there is a fadedness within Irwin's sound, a sonic ghost in the "coon shout"; this is the ghost of the blueswoman's shout. She's heard just at the end, as Irwin blues up a note a bit—"when I *walk* that levee"—in a melodic variation that skips up higher than before. It's just a hint of blue, a light blue, perhaps a sound with a translucent, ghostly tone.

For at least one early twentieth-century listener, "coon shouting" was a technique under whose cavernous umbrella a range of musical styles could be categorized, from blues to cabaret and beyond. In a 1930 article titled "Shout, Coon, Shout!" musicologist John J. Niles pens a sweeping ode to the vocal technique in which he effuses about the thrills of listening to great "coon shouters"—in whose ranks he lists Irwin and Tucker as well as Fanny Brice, Mistinguett, Alice Carter, "the five Smith sisters," Ethel Waters, Helen Morgan, and Josephine Baker, among others.[38] While Niles asserts that "native American blues material is an inspiration to any aspiring shouter," he contends that "coon shouting" is a longstanding and wide-ranging, even international vocal technique.[39] In addition to blues singers, he professes to have heard "coon-shouted" performances by European and US Civil War soldiers, southern Appalachian mountaineers, Negro stable men and jockeys, cowboys, as well as in English music halls, Chinese operatic music, and at the French opera in a performance of *Carmen* by a diva of Spanish descent. Such an expansive understanding of the "coon shout" was surely uncommon for his time, yet what it points up is that the sound to which

Niles attended is a particular technical configuration of the voice. While I would not go so far as to say that this vocal sound is fully isolable from the body, throat, and lived experience of the woman, of whatever race, who gives voice to the shout, the technical configuration by which it is produced emerges as, at the very least, describable. And if he does not fashion himself explicitly as a teacher, Niles certainly writes as an expert, the authoritative listener.

Despite his fetishizing of what he clearly hears as an exotic sound, the essay is notable for Niles's detailed analyses of singing technique. He argues that the "coon shout" lies not in the song itself but in the act of the singer. Any number of songs, whether popular tunes or operatic arias, may be "jazzed" or "shouted." For example, he recounts the case of one singer whom he accompanied at the piano, whose "trick" was to have him transpose a given song up an interval of a fifth; situated in this higher zone of her vocal range, she was well positioned to produce her signature, powerful shout. He speaks to the technical demands of this mode of singing, and the specter of vocal unhealth does not diminish his raptures about its appeal:

> The coon-shout is of ancient origin. It is rasping on the voice. Some native southern Negro blues are perhaps the best musical vehicles for shouters, but the method of "putting over" a song with energy and noise and voice-breaks is universally understood. In every singing nation on earth it happens. [...] The coon-shouter who knows her technique can be thrilling, and I dare say she must be thrilling or she will soon be forgotten. The fact that she will quickly wear out her voice matters not at all to the modern audiences who are becoming more and more addicted to speed, noise, voice-breaks, energy and inuendo [sic] in the singing of popular music and native blues.[40]

As a collector of songs and a devotee of "folk" performance styles, Niles was an observer and a listener more than a teacher or a generator of new vocal material. His role is that of accompanist and audience member. By contrast, the pianists and songwriters whom "coon shouters" like Tucker claimed as voice coaches were a different set entirely—the denizens of the Manhattan-based song publishing machine known as Tin Pan Alley.[41]

Tin Pan Alley and the much-lauded ingenuity of songwriters like Irving Berlin feature prominently in histories of musical theatre. They also feature prominently in Sophie Tucker's self-penned autobiography, in which she depicts herself as a self-made woman who worked hard to make her way in show business, winning the favor of theatrical impresarios like Tony Pastor and Florenz Ziegfeld, as she pounded the pavement armed with the latest songs from "the Tin Pan Alley boys."[42] These songwriters, including Berlin, were by her account her voice coaches and the source of her extensive repertoire. Tucker's comments about all the things she learned about how to make a name for oneself in show business are, in large part, quite savvy and hold up for performers today—make sure your makeup is flawless and your costumes are high quality, shape your act with a mix of uptempo and slow songs that build and peak in energy, don't be snotty with the theatre staff, tip the stage hands and the orchestra leader, get to know the publicists, and of course—always have new repertoire.

Among the singing lessons I wish to examine in the case of Sophie Tucker is the lesson she herself offers to others who would follow in her footsteps: "For all the years I have been in show business, to singers who have asked my advice I have said: 'Get new songs. Pay a writer to write them for you. Get songs that you can make your own. Don't copy other singers. Don't sing their songs. Don't do their stunts. Don't make your act a carbon copy of someone else's. Not if you want to succeed.'"[43] In this lesson, I discern a distinct emphasis on originality, a curious claim for a shouter of "coon songs" to make, particularly one whose career was launched on her abilities to render imitations of black dialect that delighted the white ear. The twice-heardness of the "coon shout" comes with its own distortions. Yet where the figure of the songwriter might seem to justify claims to a certain originality—the song originated with the writer and so it is a "new" song—as we have seen with Ma Rainey, no vocal sound is fully original. Listening to Tucker means simultaneously listening in on May Irwin, the caricatured "coon" whom she sought to voice, and the ghosts of blues singers, as well as listening in to the "original" ragtime of songwriters like Irving Berlin. [44]

A dirty secret of musical theatre history is that the celebrated ragtime of the Tin Pan Alley songwriters whose tunes came to define Broadway was, in fact, the same thing as "coon song."[45] "Coon songs" *were* ragtime songs.[46] White, turn-of-the-century singers of this kind of music—Irwin and her contemporaries including Stella Mayhew, Clarice Vance, and Artie Hall—were described in the popular press of their time as both "coon shouters" and ragtime vocalists, the two terms used interchangeably. From the late twentieth century on, ragtime in the popular imagination has seemed to be synonymous with instrumental music along the lines of the elegant piano rags of black composer Scott Joplin. Yet, contrary to this impression, as Edward Berlin notes, the hit rags of the era were not instrumental music but rather, vocal. While popular myth ascribes the origins of the word "ragtime" to the less than dapper clothes worn by its early, black proponents, its use primarily connotes rhythmic innovation; ragging a number meant syncopating its rhythms. Further, it's notable that "rag" in the musical sense was employed variously as noun, verb, and adjective in its day. A song could be a rag, or a song in any style from a Sousa march to a waltz could be ragged, or its syncopations could be described adjectivally as rag time in a phrase later hyphenated and then collapsed entirely.

Since ragtime is, etymologically at least, about ragging time and not voices, as a musical-historical category it emerges more easily detached from racialization than the "coon shout." Taken up by white and Jewish songwriters, the blackness of its vocal origins became increasingly glossed over. Of course, when "coon song" as a genre faded from general usage, black entertainers and audiences were hardly disappointed to see the distasteful term removed from circulation. Yet its subsumption into ragtime by the 1920s obscured the extent to which the vocal techniques that characterized the delivery of "coon songs" were in fact derived from black cultural expression, even as these techniques were carried forward on a tide of ragtime songs into the age of musical comedy singing.

Consider Tucker's performance in a recording of Irving Berlin's 1913 song "The International Rag," with Al Jolson.[47] This is a song built for dancing— again the prancing piano, but here backed up by a full orchestra complete with the swoon of strings and the brassy wail of trombones. Tucker's voice has a conversational lilt, with a mostly straight tone (only a small quiver of vibrato), and strong sustained notes. There is the sense of a wink and a laugh in her husky sound; here the songwriter has forgone the use of "Negro" dialect for clever rhymes and syncopations. The sound is placed with a lowered larynx, which gives it a grandness and warmth. The center of her voice likes to sit lower than Smith, in a tessitura perhaps closer to Rainey's, which means that it sounds that she is powering through, exerting more when she goes up high. She blues up a few notes, singing about "*dukes* and lords," and drawls through the release of phrases. But overall, the song is fast-paced (like Irwin's "Bully Song"), here invoking city life and cosmopolitanism rather than the sweep of a rural landscape. Its cause célèbre is ragtime itself, positioned as the music of choice of sophisticates worldwide, in a litany from which blackness and black people are conspicuously absent:

London dropped it's [*sic*] dignity
So has France and Germany
All hands are dancing to

A raggedy melody
Full of originality
[...]
Italian opera singers
Have learned to snap their fingers
The world goes round to the sound
of the International Rag.[48]

The lyrics clearly convey that Berlin, if not also Tucker and Jolson, felt they were making something entirely new with the ragtime songs, Tin Pan Alley, and the "coon shouting" style. Certainly for Jewish artists with immigrant backgrounds who sought access to mainstream Americanness, ragtime-infused musical theatre presented an important platform for acculturation and reinvention.[49] Part of the fabric of which this Americanness was fashioned, however ingenuously, was in fact sublimated black cultural expression. Tucker's is a voice with heft, not sunlit gossamer like the voices of the vaudeville ingénues who were her contemporaries. Hers is an immigrant voice, encrusted with a foreignness that cannot be fully disguised by Negro dialect or ragtime rhythms.[50] Like the "coon shouters" who paved the way for white comediennes, there was something in the blueswomen's sound that allowed a different kind of white female singer access to commercial success on the musical stage. The ethnically marked sign of Tucker's voice is a complex one; scholars have also noted the ways that her repertoire was predicated on and engaged Jewish audiences, who responded with great emotion to the songs she sang in Yiddish, both in the United States and abroad.[51] Yet, despite the decided originality that she and her Tin Pan Alley songwriters claimed for themselves, it would have been difficult for a singer like Sophie Tucker to be as legible and widely embraced by her audiences without the figure of the blues singer who ghosts her sound. Regardless, the black women blues singers who were her contemporaries, among them Smith, Rainey, Alberta Hunter, and Ethel Waters, appear nowhere in the pages of her autobiography.

Clearly, these singers crossed paths, as the blueswomen's accounts confirm. Alberta Hunter narrates an encounter with Tucker as follows:

[White performers] studied us so hard that you'd think they were in class.... The white shows used to come in from New York and everybody else was there to see us work, the stars, the chorus girls, Al Jolson, Sophie Tucker, everybody. One night I was doing "A Good Man Is Hard to Find" and they handed me a little note from Sophie Tucker. She wanted that song, and that's how they were, always trying to get something out of us, always trying to pick up on our little tricks. And what could *we* do? Only thing we could do was to do those numbers even better—which we did.[52]

The above anecdote sheds fresh light on Tucker's assertion that securing new, original repertoire was the key to success for the aspiring performer; clearly the goal was to discover material that would be a novelty to white ears, a longstanding approach of business-minded musicians throughout the history of US popular song. In a related anecdote, the celebrated singer Ethel Waters offers up another scenario of study involving Tucker that stands as a rare example of a lesson explicitly focused on vocal technique rather than, or in addition to, repertoire. Waters recalls encountering Tucker during the late 1920s when Waters performed regularly at the venue Rafe's Paradise in Atlantic City:

> Sophie Tucker was playing at the Beaux Arts that year and she, too, came several times to catch my act. This Last of the Red-Hot Mammas was then called a "coon shouter," an expression whose passing from the common language none of us laments. Miss Tucker paid me a little money to come to her hotel suite and sing for her privately. She explained that she wanted to study my style of delivery.[53]

It remains an open question as to how conscientious Miss Tucker really was in her requested studies; the written and recorded archive attests that her vocal sound was quite different from that of Ethel Waters. This singing lesson taught by the early career blues singer to the renowned "coon shouter" supports the assertion that even skilled, established singers seek to grow in their own technique. At the same time, this lesson could be heard to constitute a ghostly encounter between "coon shouter" and blues singer. And yet, here is a ghost whose voice one pays to study, and who refuses to remain in the shadows. As I address below, Waters made her way from the vaudeville circuit and dive cabarets in Harlem to the Broadway theatre and international renown on stage and screen. Along the way, she even took a singing lesson, of sorts, with her contemporary Bessie Smith. A 1920s publicity photo (figure 1.3) presents an angelic-looking Waters gazing serenely upward. Against a shaded background, a white circle halos her face and close-cropped hair, her slim bare shoulders and long neck accentuated by the dangle of a long, art deco earring and fingers spread delicately at her collarbone. Hers was a sweet but powerful vocal sound that

1.3 Ethel Waters in a 1920s publicity photo.

gave new meaning to what it meant to sing the blues, and where the blues could take a singer.

Ethel Waters's "Low Kind of Singing"

Of the singers considered thus far in this chapter, Ethel Waters is the one most readily associated with the musical theatre; her Broadway shows include *Africana* (1927), *As Thousands Cheer* (1933), and *Cabin in the Sky* (1940) and she remains known for her definitive performances of several iconic songs from stage and screen musicals such as "Supper Time," "Am I Blue?" and "Stormy Weather."[54] Conceived in violence and born into poverty to a single mother in Philadelphia in 1896, the Queen of the Blues was just two years younger than Empress Bessie Smith. Yet no matter how poor her family was, they kept an organ, and music was much loved by the matriarch, her grandmother Sally Anderson. On her seventeenth birthday, Waters went onstage on a whim at the South Philly venue Jack's Rathskeller and, on the strength of that performance, was booked by a vaudeville company once her mother agreed to cosign the lie that Waters was twenty-one. Even at that time her voice had, by her own account, a "sweet, bell-like" tone.[55] Waters toured with the company as a member of the Hill sisters group and under the stage name "Sweet Mama Stringbean," then performed at the famed Harlem dive bar Edmond's Cellar, and in the recording studios and touring company of Black Swan Records before going on to new heights across Broadway, Europe, and Hollywood. Yet while a famed blues singer in her own era, today she lacks the prominence and reputation of Smith and Rainey and does not easily map onto the narrative of blues mama as protojazz singer.

The signature blues song of the young Waters's vaudeville days offers a productive site through which to hear and assess some of the reasons why her voice has proved difficult to categorize. Astutely navigating the early structures of music licensing, she wrote the publishers of composer W. C. Handy's "St. Louis Blues" soon after its publication in 1914 and received permission to be one of only two acts, and the first woman, then allowed to perform the song. Despite the facts that the published sheet music identifies it as both a blues and ragtime composition, and that the song's opening section strategically incorporates the tango rhythm all the rage at the time of its writing, "St. Louis Blues" is now considered one of the great blues numbers of all time.[56] Listening to a recording of the song made in

1942, I hear in Waters's voice a liquid tone, not without blues viscosity but with some lift to it.[57] She floats out high notes in octave leaps ("to-*mor*-row") but has deep low notes as well and isn't afraid to show them off, vibrato melting the ends of phrases into warmth. She sings through the voiced consonants, the final *n*'s and *ng*'s ([n], [ŋ]) of things like trains and rings gaining new, extended lengths of expression. When she heads up high ("*Saint* Louis," "*When* you see me leaving") the sound remains clear but gets thinned out and a bit brighter, maybe nasalized (in the best of senses), the voice's taffy texture stretching out thinner and thinner as it wisps to new heights. She adds in a growl and flutter here and there ("*I'll* be gone") but overall this is a warm, smooth sound with a lot of lift to it. Lighter in terms of heft and mass of vocal folds engaged, this sound feels less earthbound than those generally employed by Smith, Rainey, or Tucker. It is true that the recording clips along at faster tempo than many of Smith's and Rain-ey's early twentieth-century blues—no doubt a result of its reshaping for popular (white) consumption in the 1940s. And the accompanying pianist and bassist from the RKO Studio Orchestra just don't swing very hard, the whole number sticky with the cloying vocals of a backing trio. But to the extent that the arrangement allows, Waters still uses the beat as something to alternately hit hard and rappel off of. This blues singing comes with the Northern accent of the Philadelphia-born singer, not elongated southern vowels that seem to go on for days. And yet it's still a blue sound, with back-phrasing and the bluing of notes true to style, and that sense of throwing notes away, tossing them away, common to all the blues singers.

Around 1918, Bessie Smith and Ethel Waters shared a stage at the No. 91 Theatre in Atlanta. By this point, Smith was already a high-earning star on the vaudeville circuit who called the shots wherever she performed. A respectful Waters deferred to her status, calling her "Miss Bessie" and trying to stay on good terms, later recalling:

> Bessie, like an opera singer, carried her own claque with her. . . . [She] was in a pretty good position to dictate to the managers [and] told the men who ran No. 91 that she didn't want anyone else on the bill to sing the blues. I agreed to this. . . . And when I went on I sang "I Want to Be Some-body's Baby Doll So I Can Get My Lovin' All the Time." But before I could finish this number the people out front started howling, "Blues! Blues! Come on, Stringbean, we want your blues!" . . . Before the second show the manager went to Bessie's dressing room and told her he was going to revoke the order forbidding me to sing any blues. He said he couldn't have

another such rumpus. There was quite a stormy discussion about this, and you could hear Bessie yelling things about "these Northern bitches." Now nobody could have taken the place of Bessie Smith. People everywhere loved her shouting with all their hearts and were loyal to her. But they wanted me too. There had been such a tumult at that first show that Bessie agreed that after I took two or three bows for my first song I should, if the crowd still insisted, sing "St. Louis Blues."[58]

This encounter between Smith and Waters can be understood as a kind of failed voice lesson. In another scenario, the story could have gone differently: had Waters's fans proved less enthusiastic, the theatre manager less intrepid—or Smith more territorial—the singer could have been forced to migrate away from blues to a different repertoire (light popular song) that would hardly have launched her career so successfully. Instead, the restriction Smith attempts to place on the repertoire Waters may perform does not hold; the lesson is not attended to. Consequently, Waters establishes herself as a skilled blues singer even in comparison with the greater star whom she herself concedes was "undisputed tops as a blues singer."[59] In this way, Waters models the student who defies the teacher—here, with the backing of theatre manager and audience—to assert her own technical approach in contrast to the performance that is held up as definitive. It is not that her performance recreates or supersedes Smith's shouting but rather that she presents a vocal sound with an effective but contrasting mode of delivery. To the voice teacher's assertion that, literally, "It must be done the way I do it or not at all," the student counters with, "What if I do it this way?" According to Waters, the two singers made peace after the incident and struck an amicable tone for the rest of the engagement. They had much in common: both were statuesque, powerful women who lived the blues life, collecting female lovers as well as male, and not afraid of a knock-down, drag-out fight if they thought their rights were being trodden on. But Smith continued to maintain that Waters had the lesser voice. For her part, Waters recognized the value in her own sound, what she called "my low, sweet, and then new way of singing blues."[60]

It was this blues sound that carried Waters to cabarets and clubs of New York, where, as her contemporary Elisabeth Welch later recalled, "She had a reputation as a tough lady. She sang in nightclubs, not the nightclubs we knew with white tablecloths, but dives and cellars, where you took your own bottle of drink."[61] While performing at the cramped, dingy Edmond's Cellar in Harlem in the 1920s, Waters sang the blues songs she had performed in traveling vaudeville shows up until that point. In his well-known essay evoking performances in Harlem clubs before the incursion of white audience members in the late 1920s, the black physician Rudolph Fisher remembered the ways that Waters distinguished herself there with not only her voice but the self-confidence that shaped her sound.

> Other girls wore themselves ragged trying to rise above the inattentive din of conversation, and soon, literally, yelled themselves hoarse; eventually they lost whatever music there was in their voices and acquired that familiar throaty roughness which is so frequent among blues singers, and which, though admired as characteristically African, is as a matter of fact nothing but a form of chronic laryngitis. Other girls did these things, but not Ethel. She took it easy. She would stride with great leisure and self-assurance to the center of the floor, stand there with a half-contemptuous nonchalance, and wait. All would become silent at once. Then she'd begin her song, genuine blues.[62]

At Edmond's Cellar, Waters took a set of lessons in learning repertoire from the piano player there, Lou Henley. Henley argued that learning popular ballads and Tin Pan Alley songs in addition to the blues would build up Waters's career and create new performance opportunities for her. She resisted, citing her dislike of the stories contained within many of these songs, but the pianist was persistent and Waters eventually agreed to work with him on the new material. Arriving early to her gigs at Edmond's for sessions with Henley, she learned a range of popular ballads and worked out ways to interpret these songs in her own style. This mode of study—rehearsing and developing new repertoire with a trusted accompanist—was repeated throughout her career and later during her decades-long collaboration with pianist Pearl Wright. With Wright, Waters stated that the key to their partnership lay in the fact that Pearl was a singer herself. "An accompanist who can sing knows the effects you seek, and you can feel understanding and help coming out through her fingers, through the piano, to you."[63] Wright, the black woman singer-as-accompanist, proved an able coach for Waters when she was presented with material by white songwriters that had the potential to transform the blues singer's career. At an audition for Broadway's Plantation Club to replace Florence Mills, star of the hit, all-black Broadway musical *Shuffle Along*, as a headliner, Waters was asked by Tin Pan Alley songwriters Harry Akst and Joe Young to learn one of their songs. When they performed it for her, "doing it fast and corny," Waters was dubious.[64] The songwriters encouraged her to work up the song in her own (blues) style. Waters went away and rehearsed the song with Wright and discovered she liked it after all. Returning to the songwriters and producers to perform the number "in her own way" got her the job and her first big hit. The song was "Dinah," which she recorded for Columbia Records in 1925, a recording inducted seventy years later into the Grammy Hall of Fame. It is notable that where Sophie Tucker claimed Tin Pan Alley songwriters as voice coaches, Waters learned and restyled her new repertoire at the elbow of the black piano accompanist who was also a skilled singer. This pattern is repeated with Akst and Young's song "Am I Blue?" and Harold Arlen's "Stormy Weather." In each case the learning of new repertoire is framed by the singer's suggestion, "Let me take the lead sheet home . . . I'll work on it with Pearl."[65]

But if the extension of her repertoire began in coaching sessions with Lou Henley and Pearl Wright in New York City, the extension of the vocal range Waters was able to show off with her expanded repertoire also had to do with lessons and medical treatment undertaken during her European tour at the end of the decade. When she stood at the microphone to perform "St. Louis Blues" in her midforties as described above, it is impossible that aspects of her sound and interpretation would not have shifted since she first sang the number on the vaudeville stage in her late teens. As the radio announcer introduces her on the broadcast, she has now become "a famous lady with a famous song." Listening, it does seem to me that the ring and palette of colors in Waters's voice remain largely consistent with that heard on her early recordings. But I do notice a change in the lift she is able to achieve at this later point in her career. Specifically, Waters seems to have gained more ease with the higher part of her register. This technical ability may be credited, at least in part, to the coaching of Louis Drysdale, a black voice teacher with whom Waters studied in London in 1929. During this period, Waters battled several vocal problems that ultimately resulted in surgery to remove a node from one of her vocal cords. The delicate procedure was conducted by a renowned European throat specialist and surgeon variously reported to have been either a Dr. Wicant in Paris or a Dr. Horsford in London. In her 1951 autobiography *His Eye Is on the Sparrow*, Waters attributes the surgery to Cyril Horsford, a distinguished British laryngologist who regularly treated singers at the Royal College of Music, as follows:

> With two of his colleagues looking on, he prepared me for the operation, warning me not to move or sneeze. Then he held his right hand straight

out in front of him for a long time to make sure it was steady enough. Next he applied the local anesthetic and got out his long instruments. Finally he put those long, thin scissors deep down into my throat—and snipped. It took only a split moment, and then he brought up the nodule. It was about the size of a grain of rice.[66]

However, a November 1929 issue of the *Baltimore Afro-American* newspaper published a photograph of Waters in the reception of room of "Dr. M. Wicant, noted French throat specialist in Paris, who removed a growth from the vocal chords [*sic*] of Miss Ethel Waters."[67] In any case, following her surgery, Waters observed that the results of the operation were that a certain huskiness that had been in place for several years was gone, and that she was able to sing in a higher range. In the same section of her autobiography, she devotes one sentence to her studies in London with vocal coach Louis Drysdale. It was his coaching that enabled her to continue performing, even while she was losing her voice in a certain tessitura, so that she could earn the money to pay for her throat operation: "The treatments of Professor Drysdale, a colored voice coach, who showed me how I could lift my voice, enabled me to sing in another range."[68]

Drysdale was born in the late 1800s in Kingston, Jamaica, and came to London in 1906 where he studied at the Royal College of Music with distinguished teachers of the *bel canto* tradition. These included Gustave Garcia, son of the famed nineteenth-century voice pedagogue and laryngologist Manuel Garcia who invented the laryngoscope, and whose legacy I examine further in chapter 4. In the 1920s, Drysdale's studio welcomed students of different races, singers from the worlds of Broadway, cabaret, opera, and British musical comedy in the West End. Florence Mills, the star of Broadway's *Shuffle Along* and the internationally touring revue *Lew Leslie's Blackbirds of 1926*, studied with him in London and was a great advocate of his teaching methods until her tragic, untimely death a year later. Just nine months before her passing, the *New York Amsterdam News* reported that Mills would sponsor a scholarship for voice study with Drysdale for "two colored girls" from the United States.[69] While studying voice abroad in 1928, the young contralto Marian Anderson also received coaching from Drysdale in the *bel canto* tradition and enthused about the efficacy of his methods.[70] Even Waters's fellow blueswoman Alberta Hunter is known to have taken a lesson or two with the maestro. Certainly, the black press lay nearly all the credit for the improvements to Waters's voice at Drysdale's feet: "While in England Miss Waters studied with Louis Drysdale, eminent

English singing teacher, and it is said that the throat trouble which threatened to cut short her singing career has been entirely eliminated."[71]

From Blues to Broadway

I recognize that there is a risk implicit in figuring a black woman singer as a student of her vocal style, as one in a line whose voice was sculpted by study with teachers—whether those teachers and coaches were black women and men, or white men.[72] It would seem to suggest that she is disempowered, "only a student," and thus not the site of true vocal authority. Fierce belief in the on/off switch of vocal study—if you've learned to sing, you've learned to sing—persists. Accordingly, the period of learning from which the fabled black woman singer emerges is generally taken to be discrete, brief, and largely indiscernible, during a few short years of a not-quite-childhood. Yet while it may cement her reputation, the significant disservice that this narrative does to the artist is eliminate any tolerance for or understanding of her exploration of new aesthetic directions, timbres, or expressive devices. It romanticizes the untutored singer and fixes her in a time warp of talent that denies any development of her technique over time; instead, any exploration or study is seen as a dilution of that talent's purest form. Worse, in the case of black artists, such exploration may be seen as the betrayal of assimilation. Ethel Waters has often been the target of censure from black listeners who surmise that she turned her back on her own race and sought to sound "white." Like the upper middle-class black people Langston Hughes critiques in his seminal essay "The Negro Artist and the Racial Mountain," her too-sweet vocal sound is heard as self-loathing, the prim rejection that says, "We don't believe in 'shouting.'"[73] Similarly, in pitting Bessie Smith and Ethel Waters against each other, Angela Davis valorizes Smith as the singer who, with her blues singing, authentically represented her race and heritage, while Waters "consciously cultivated a sound from which many of the unfamiliar and inaccessible elements of black culture had been purged."[74] Dwandalyn Reece takes Davis to task for this assessment of Waters's voice and blues sound, pointing out that aesthetic styles and their expression have varied forms and modes; black performance cannot be understood in static, essentialist terms.[75] I would note that, further, paying attention to the ways in which singers studied and shifted their technique over time enables us to, as Shane Vogel has elucidated, understand musical performance in historical terms "as both an object and a process."[76] Without the acknowledgment that singers not only produce but also *learn* technique and repertoire, adjusting their sound over time, their performative contributions are certain to be denied. In such a situation the singer emerges merely as the hollow symbol of the race, composer, or genre she is seen to represent.

I submit that this is a key reason why Waters has been so undercelebrated in the pantheon of blues, jazz, and popular songstresses. Her movement from blues to Broadway simply doesn't align with the more familiar blues-to-jazz or blues-to-gospel trajectories of popular music histories. And the blues are not seen as a protogenre of Broadway in the way that they are in the case of jazz and gospel (and the rock'n'roll these spawned). It is true that at the end of her career, Waters found acclaim as a performer of the gospel hymn "His Eye Is on the Sparrow" with tele-evangelist Billy Graham on his Crusades. But first, she herself considered the costs of trying to rearticulate herself as a jazz singer, observing, "I could no longer think of myself as just a blues singer . . . Away back in 1929 I'd done a lick in *I Got Rhythm*. But if I returned to that kind of singing I realized audiences would think I was imitating Ella [Fitzgerald]."[77] Waters knew well the risk this would entail. If she appeared to be a "student" of Fitzgerald, a singer more than two decades her junior, she would have to forget about star billing. The student can never be the exemplar of the genre. Popular opinion rewards those who perpetuate the mythology that their talent is so innate that it sprang forth from nowhere; this narrative was certainly espoused by Broadway belter Ethel Merman, and loudly.

Ethel Merman's Show Tune
The Held Note as Knockout

Born in Astoria, Queens, just six years after Ma Rainey learned her first blues, Ethel Merman lives in collective memory as the archetypal Broadway belter—possessor of a loud, brassy voice that cut clear to the back row of the theatre, carrying over a full orchestra without the need for anything so mundane as amplification. Merman, who shortened her family name of Zimmerman to a more marquee-friendly length, grew up in a family of German and Scottish ancestry. She was not Jewish, although often thought to be, a misidentification that she alternately railed against and took as a compliment, since there were so many successful Jewish women in showbiz from Fanny Brice to Sophie Tucker and beyond. Merman's middle-class upbringing took her from singing at church events and her parents' Republican Club in Queens to working as a secretary in Long Island City while she moonlighted as a nightclub and radio singer until a series of breaks led to her career-defining appearance in the Gershwins' 1930 musical *Girl Crazy*. Merman attests that during the intermission of that show's opening night, composer George Gershwin ran up three flights of stairs to congratulate her on her performance of the song "I Got Rhythm." Merman reports of this performance:

> When I held the C note for sixteen bars, an entire chorus, while the orchestra played the melody, the audience went a little crazy. I don't think they were responding to the beauty of it. I think it was the newness. Nobody had ever done it in a Broadway show before. Thank God I was blessed with a strong diaphragm and lungs. Because I had to sing I don't know how many encores. And that was the song that made me.[78]

Gershwin was so taken with Merman's voice that, as she recalls, he counseled her, "Make me a promise . . . Never go near a singing teacher. Because you have a natural talent. And if you ever go near a singing teacher, then you'll become conscious of breathing . . . and you're going to lose all the naturalness that you have."[79] The great composer's advice not to let conventional voice teachers tamper with the vocal technique she had apparently developed on her own is one that reverberates throughout the archive, repeated again and again in the Broadway star's interviews and biographies. Merman wore the alleged "naturalness" of her mighty voice as a badge of honor.

In viewing and listening to footage of the young Merman performing "I Got Rhythm" at a benefit the year after *Girl Crazy* opened on Broadway, the first thing apparent to me in the vocal sound is that this is a voice that carries.[80] Her long notes are simply leveled at the audience, with wide open vowels—almost every vowel sound emerges as "aw" as she drops her jaw and pours out sound. The lyric, "Who could ask for anything *more*" becomes, "Who could ask for anything *maw* [mɔ]." There are a couple of bluesy growls here and there ("*Old* man trouble, *I* don't mind him"). Occasionally she adds a bit of a laugh to her sound, as if she is finding the fun in a phrase, but this is short-lived and for the most part the sound is not as warm as that of Rainey, Smith, or Waters; it's a bit like the difference between listening to the blare of a trumpet versus the warm buzz of saxophones, respectively. And where the blues singers often throw in vibrato at the end of the phrase, for accentuation, or to make a sustained note shimmer a bit, Merman's vibrato on long notes is compulsory, extended, and wide. The wobble of vibrato is the only motion away from fixity on the powerful, sustained notes she delivers, and even that has the effect of seeming to stabilize her claim to a particular held note. I notice that this is unlike the movement through bent pitches that characterizes the blues sound of Rainey and Smith when they are shouting high. It seems Merman's voice is mostly sharp angles where the blues singers are comfortable with all the curves in their sound; in this context, Merman's signature grace note, a skip-hop attack from above, seems a kind of unblue note. The grace note is almost an impulse toward a slide, bent succession of pitches, but this is a slide from which some of the connective tissue has been removed. The implications of gentleness in the term "grace note" belie the sound itself, its high-pitched, bullet-like incision of a rupture before it cuts down to the shouted note it adorns. Lower pitches (the verse's "I'm *chipper* all the *day*") seem harder for Merman—perhaps this is why she often uses the grace note to sparkle up some of the lowest notes of phrases—while her strength lies in the mid and high notes that she can power out.

I am struck by her stance in staking her claim to sound. While her feet are planted—she was known for her marked preference to stand squarely facing the audience—her upper body remains active. She gestures and waves her hands about, and I can see that part of her strategy for hitting those money notes is the way she braces with her upper torso: a quick dropping of the shoulders like a decisive, inverse shrug. Making this sound requires a certain looseness, almost casualness with the upper body, even while the lower half of the body is well anchored, still but for the occasional, assertive shift of weight. Clearly, the singer's whole physicality is engaged in a sound that calls to mind the shouted, battle-ready cry to which John J. Niles thrilled.

Listening, I am surprised to notice that Merman's sense of time is fantastic, she really punches the syncopations and swings hard. It is notable that during this time period, Merman was considered to be not only a torch singer but also a "rhythm singer."[81] The term connotes a vocalist who knows how to swing and play with rhythmic effects generally to the accompaniment of a big band.[82] Today, Merman is remembered best for her iconic performance as the larger-than-life, Jewish stage mother Momma Rose in the 1959 musical *Gypsy* with a score by Jule Styne and Stephen Sondheim, and book by Arthur Laurents. There are syncopated elements to that score, but the drag triplets and straight eighths of a song like "Everything's Coming Up Roses" do not cast her in the role of rhythm singer—a term that was jazz legend Ella Fitzgerald's preferred designation for her own vocal style, and that has also been applied to Ethel Waters. But beyond her swing and her grace notes, what Merman delivers overall is the sense of an abundance of sound, a luxuriating in volume: this is a sound that keeps on coming at you. Perhaps it is this, her durational performance in the epic sustaining of long notes, that is the key to her virtuosic appeal.

In her reading of Merman's "direct, aggressive, and physically tough" vocal presence as a performance of butchness and Jewishness, Stacy Wolf details how the singer's bravura and attention-seeking style merged with that of the character she played in *Gypsy* to create a star turn out of the character's failure.[83] It is, in fact, Momma Rose's failure to believe she has failed that produces the dramatic space for the show's powerhouse finale "Rose's Turn." Part of the quintessentially Broadway approach to failure is a doggedly unrealistic optimism; during the point at which Momma Rose sings "Everything's Coming Up Roses," absolutely everything in the plot is going wrong and looks to continue in that vein for the foreseeable future. Nothing at all is coming up roses, but with her sound the singer negates that reality, enabling the character to forcefully assert her vision of the world. As Ethel Merman comes to define it, the Broadway number emerges as repertoire that is not about the expressiveness with which one bends or throws the note away, the way that blues singers do, but the tenacity with which one holds on. A 1938 photograph of Merman (figure 1.4) shows the forthright posture in which she was known to sing—body facing squarely forward. Flowers in her shoulder-length hair, head tipped slightly the side, she looks cheerily out of frame. Both elbows angled away from her torso, with one braceleted hand she gestures airily skyward; with the other she clutches the stage curtain behind her.

If George Gershwin told Ethel Merman to never take a voice lesson, he did, however, teach her his own songs. So did Irving Berlin and Cole Porter, who both wrote shows expressly for her voice—and it is this learning of repertoire I wish to consider. Songs by these master tunesmiths moved Merman's voice through melodic contours that, for all their rhythmic elements, privileged the sustained note. By comparison, the declamatory structure of the blues does not invite sustained notes at the ends of phrases in such a way. To make sense of its oratory, the would-be blues singer must learn to throw away the first phrase in order to come back to it a second time, again, and again. But in the "coon shout-," blues-, and ragtime-influenced popular song of the 1930s, this structure is not to be found. Here there are no breezy, open repetitions that prompt a throwing away because of the inevitability

1.4 Ethel Merman on the cover of *Sunday News,* July 1938. Courtesy of the Billy Rose Theatre Division, New York Public Library for the Performing Arts.

of one more return. By contrast, the AABA structure of a Gershwin popular song, such as "I Got Rhythm," varies its first two A-sections with different lyrics and keeps them on such a tight loop that they feel of a piece; it is only after moving through the B-section and coming to the third A-section that one feels the sense of return. In a structure that allows for only one return, the song and singer are positioned to celebrate by song's end the satisfaction of a final arrival. The inserted choruses where Merman holds the same C for sixteen bars (an extended "Oh"), far from invoking the blues' circular sweep, merely prefigure the arrival of the song's ending—regardless of a few interruptions of the held note, it is the holding that matters and lives on in memory. And if Ira Gershwin's lyrics seek to evoke the simple, carefree experience of the imagined black subject who ghosts the song (any lyric about "Old man trouble" is a dead giveaway), consider that they do so by tallying items of possession. The things being tallied may be as simple as rhythm, music, daisies, green pastures—the imagined elements of romanticized, pastoral black life that hearken back to the plantation—and, of course, "my man." But the overall sense is not one of grappling with loss, as in the open returns of blues poetry, but rather, an assertion of the sum total of what "I got." In both the music and lyrics, what matters vocally is what is held. And Merman deployed showstopping vocal technique to hold a note.

As much as the early Broadway songwriters ghosted their songs with the imagined black woman, drawing on their own hearings of rhythm, imagery, and harmony within black expressive culture, they relied on a singer's infusion of vocal sound to invest their songs with meaning on the stage. What is evident with Merman is that the instruction provided by the song (and the songwriter) does not allow the white belter to perform a simple ventriloquizing of the blueswoman. This is, not least, because to the songwriters' scenario of listening must also be added the belter's. How did Merman learn her sound? To whom did she listen and sing back? Little information is available about Merman's childhood and teenage years. Although she was taught by her father and in high school classes to read music, she is not known to have sung in the school choir or glee club. At the same time, her Queens background must have had a hand in her diction, rendering words like "more" as the full-throated "maw" [mɔ] in the example above. She roundly denied assertions by the pianist Al Siegel that he coached her into her own particular vocal technique. But she admired Sophie Tucker, to whom her sound has often been compared, and who was in turn complimentary of Merman's delivery. Reviewers also detected in

Merman's voice echoes of torch singer Libby Holman, another Jewish star whom she also respected and whose signature song "Moanin' Low" was a staple of Merman's nightclub repertoire. While scholars have deemed it unlikely that Merman would have listened to recordings of blues singers aimed at black audiences, it is known that Holman was an avid student of the blues and modeled *her* voice on singers such as Bessie Smith and Ethel Waters. A millionaire who lived a life full of scandal—in between Broadway engagements, she was tried (and acquitted) for the murder of her late husband, and she openly cultivated a string of lesbian relationships—Holman found a trusted voice coach in the black guitarist Josh White, a blues musician who became her longtime accompanist.[84] But despite what she learned from Tucker and Holman, the luminaries whom Merman claimed as responsible for her career time and again were the composers—in particular Gershwin, Berlin, and Porter—of the hit songs she belted out.

The word "belter" itself discloses a scenario of listening. The origins of the word "belt" in reference to singing can be traced to boxing.[85] Correlated with the idea of the "knockout" performance, the image of the singer-as-boxer adds an oppositional dimension to that of the singer-as-shouter by figuring the listener (or opponent) in the word for the act of singing itself. In order for the belter to belt, there must be one who is belted. Thus, the belter is so named because of the way her song is received, the leveling reaction that her powerful sound produces. Accordingly, the scenario of listening that the descriptor evokes is one that is forward-facing rather than back-formed, foregrounding lessons taught rather than lessons learned. The singular contribution of Ethel Merman, with all the singers her voice carries, is that her belt voice makes such an impression on many a listener who, once recovered from shock, picks herself up off the ground, dusts herself off, and seeks to learn to make just such a sound herself. In contrast to this oppositional encounter, the blues singers who precede Merman teach another way—by activating listening scenarios in which sound takes shape via the studied act of *singing along with* another's voice.

Conclusions

I have argued here against listenings that would filter out the frequencies and impact of black blues singers on the musical theatre belt sound, attending to the specific bodies through which its shouted tones resounded in historical context. My goal has not been to merely catalogue performance traits (blues shouting) that signal blackness and detect them within white performance modes (Broadway belting) where they may have gone previously uncredited. This would be an oversimplification not least because, as the sounds of Bessie Smith and Ethel Waters show, there is no one "pure" way to sing the blues. The essential signifier of blackness in the voice proves impossible to locate. But I have contested the idea that black women who sang the blues and performed on the musical stage in the early twentieth century (and beyond) possessed "untrained," spontaneously formed voices. Against this notion, I have examined a series of singing lessons that variously map the ways that black women singers learned from and taught one another and their white contemporaries.

The lessons taught and attended by the blues mamas in this chapter also invite revised understandings of US musical theatre history broadly writ. Their voices sing through an array of musical-theatrical genres, the careful and illusory separation of which belies longstanding racial anxieties. Specifically, Rainey, Smith, and Waters can help us hear how flawed it is that musical comedy song should be traced to ragtime, (white) vaudeville, operetta, melodrama, and (white women's) burlesque, but not generally to blues—and certainly not to black women's blues. Unsettling the narrative that "the black influence" on the early Broadway musical was confined to white male-authored minstrel song and, later, (white appropriations of) jazz music innovated by black male instrumentalists, these women's performances teach the vexed way that black female vocality travels unacknowledged within the innocuously titled "ragtime" celebrated as foundational to the Broadway sound. Further, the fact that singers learned and studied with one another, shifting their sound and repertoire over time and in differing musical contexts, resoundingly refutes notions about the ahistoricity of black talent as that which exists only and perpetually in the present.

I have examined several kinds of singing lessons here. One kind is the lesson that occurs in the context of the professional singer's ongoing practice, challenging the notion that learning to sing can be understood as a sort of on/off switch. Another kind is the lesson in which two women write a song together and teach it to one another. Others are lessons that are disavowed, unacknowledged, ghosts of lessons, denied in some archival accounts and revealed in others. There is also the failed lesson—that in which the student refuses to attend to the teaching and instead goes her own way. Beyond the lesson taught by the teacher who defines himself as a proper voice teacher, there is the one given by the teacher and coach who calls herself a piano accompanist. And in addition to the lesson that the singer disavows, there is the lesson that the Broadway songwriter-as-voice-coach helpfully disavows on her behalf, solidifying a cult of the white belter and her so-called natural sound. This last must be attended to, in sifting through the echoes of all the lessons that precede it, because it perniciously recasts the so-called untrained voice as nothing short of miraculous, never minding the ways in which its sounds, for all their seeming offhandedness, are already studied, already citational, already twice-heard.

Sung vocal sound is modeled on previously heard vocal sounds, and neither voices nor singers are ahistorical magical objects. Regardless of the extent to which proponents of new musical genres proclaim their decided originality, the sound of the voice itself resists such assertions. Singing is a citational practice. And certainly, the singers who followed the early twentieth-century blueswomen, shouters, and belters were to take up and discard blues vocality in various ways, as they revoiced "the Broadway sound" on the musical stage into the 1940s and beyond.

2 Beyond the Weary-Bluesy Mammy

Listening Better with Midcentury Character Divas

Casting and Vocal-Affective-Racial Type

Where popular opinion has long held that the idealized Broadway belter is a snappy, brash-voiced, white woman singer in the mold of Ethel Merman—an ideal I questioned in chapter 1—the expectations of who and how a black woman singer-actress should perform on Broadway pose a stark contrast. Setting aside the white Broadway belter's sonic citation of black women blues singers, perhaps the kind of role most widely assumed to be overtly the province of the black Broadway singer-actress in the early twentieth century is one in which that other showstopping Ethel, Ethel Waters, shone in the 1930s—a type I term the "weary-bluesy mammy."

In the musical theatre then as now, perceptions of voice and affect shape key aspects of character type by which actors, and certainly racialized female actors, are measured and pronounced either a good fit for the part or somehow lacking. Performers are required to deliver not only particular voice ranges and vocal qualities, but also specific emotional configurations that such sounds are understood to mandate—whether in the bright tone and timing of the comic actress or the sweetly unthreatening treble of the ingénue. The intricacies of casting practices for the professional theatre continue to be shrouded in a certain degree of mystery, despite the valuable impact of present-day initiatives, such as the annual reports conducted by the Tony-winning Asian American Performers Action Coalition (AAPAC), which shine a light on the racially disproportionate outcomes of casting in the twenty-first century US theatre industry.[1] In recent years, scholarly conversations around theatrical casting and race have also increased. As Brandi Wilkins Catanese reminds, theatre practices built around ideals of colorblindness or multiculturalism are deeply grounded in particular ideologies. Daniel Banks observes, "Unless a person is playing herself in an autobiographical performance, all theatre is cross-casting of some sort."[2] However, my focus here is not on perceptions and implementation of race-appropriate (or race-transgressive) casting in the late twentieth- and early twenty-first-century US theatre but rather the vocal and affective trappings of the kinds of roles that black singer-actresses have historically been asked to play in the musical theatre from the 1930s on. While this question of racial type has prompted meaningful study among film historians, it has gone largely untheorized among scholars of the musical stage.[3]

In this chapter, I first propose the character type of the weary-bluesy mammy for which white artists and audiences enthusiastically celebrated Ethel Waters in her stage performances during the latter part of her career. I compare this figure to two others—the dynamic blues mama persona for which Waters was applauded by black contemporaries such as Zora Neale Hurston, and the elegant, world-weary white torch singer. I then listen for how two black singer-actresses who came to prominence on the Broadway stage in the 1940s sounded and operated in relation to that racial and vocal type in shows such as *St. Louis Woman* (1946) and *South Pacific* (1949) as well as in performances on nightclub stages beyond Broadway. Where the previous chapter attended to lessons with Bessie Smith and Ethel Waters and their contemporaries, this chapter moves through Waters—and, obliquely, Lena Horne—to focus in on Pearl Bailey and Juanita Hall and the ways they maneuvered around racialized expectations of vocal and character type.

I consciously claim the mantle of divadom for Bailey and Hall even though at the outset of their careers both were lauded for performing not as leading ladies but in secondary, comic roles—as character actresses. Hall remained in that category through her career following *Pacific* with both *House of Flowers* (1954), in which she appeared opposite Bailey as a rival bordello madam, and in her appearance as a cheongsam-clad auntie in *Flower Drum Song* (1958). Decades after her Broadway debut Bailey pivoted to the category of leading lady with her star turn in the title role of the all-black revival of *Hello, Dolly!* (1967), but she was perhaps best known for her humorous performances as a nightclub entertainer, an ethos that permeated her appearances in musical theatre.

Bailey and Hall both studied their lessons, so to speak, performing in the wake of Smith and Waters as documented in their own testimony and in the hearings of contemporary reviewers. At the same time, the radically open, nondiscursive nature of sonic citation allows hearers to pronounce—or ignore—interpretations of twice-heardness at will. This is, after all, what enabled Ethel Merman to staunchly assert the naturalness of her Broadway belt, despite her deployment of a sound imbued with the vocal shout innovated by black women blues singers. In such a context, a valuable component of the singing lesson is the teacher's instruction for how she should be heard. For even as Bailey and Hall sonically cited and called back to Smith and Waters, they also became voice teachers for singers who followed them. With this chapter, I amplify Bailey's sharp rejoinder to those who would hear her signature comic mumble as nothing more than plantation dialect: take care to "listen better."[4]

Enter the Black Torch Singer

In 1933, nearly two decades after introducing the showstopping "St. Louis Blues" on the vaudeville-blues circuit, Ethel Waters delivered not one but two legendary performances of torch songs: "Stormy Weather," and "Supper Time." Four years earlier, her performance of "Am I Blue?" in her debut film *On With the Show* (1929) had established her finesse with this kind of song. In *The Cotton Club Parade of 1933*, Waters gave the premiere performance of "Stormy Weather," a number by Harold Arlen and Ted Koehler that she had rehearsed with her accompanist Pearl Wright. This Cotton Club performance was one that Waters strategically self-directed away from the spectacle of stage-designed lightning and thunder to center her own emotive performance.[5] I contend that this conscious shift from the elemental and the natural to the singer's expressive performance can also be understood as a clear move to access the realm of the torch singer—a type of performer whose skill in unadorned vocal pathos is what sells the song. At the Cotton Club, Waters leans against the lamppost casting cool light around her, a painted log cabin in the background. In her warm, sweet tone, she sings the "gloom and misery" of the lovelorn woman whose spirits are caught in what feels like everlastingly overcast weather, and it seems every other note she sings has a slide or a bend to it. Listening to her May 1933 recording, I conjure the vocal scene.[6] There is the low throb of a sob in the voice that sounds like it would be as at home on a Follies stage in midtown

Manhattan as up here in Harlem, and Waters even rolls an "r" in one spot ("evrry"); she has added some Tin Pan Alley popular stylings to her sound since her days on the vaudeville-blues stage. When the melody leaps up and then drops an octave on the repeated word "love," we get something like a blues shout, and then in the very last line, on the descending phrase sung to "Keeps raining," there is the catch in the voice that also aligns with singers like Fanny Brice and her cohort of white torch singers, those for whom being overcome by emotion in song was an opportunity more readily available.

From the 1930s on, Waters is referred to in both the black and white press as a torch singer, although that term does not seem to be applied to her prior to then, and surely "Stormy Weather" had much to do with this change.[7] As various scholars have noted, during the 1920s, the torch singer as a figure was decidedly a white female performer.[8] Fanny Brice's performance of "My Man" in the Ziegfeld Follies in 1921 is considered by many to be the first rendition of a torch song. "My Man" was an adaptation of a French chanson, "Mon Homme," made famous by French music hall performer Mistinguett—whom, it may be recalled from chapter 1, was included in John J. Niles's eclectic, expansive compendium of "coon shouters" published in 1930. The French version of the song was grittier and harsher, with more sexual energy and even sadomasochistic vibes that were written out of the English rendition that Florenz Ziegfeld contracted for his Follies. Sonically, Mistinguett's version emerges brighter and with an almost entirely straight tone (that is, no vibrato), with much less of the sense of a suppressed sob than in Brice's rendition.[9] Brice was the great Ziegfeld Follies star whose story would later serve as the basis for Barbra Streisand's breakout Broadway musical *Funny Girl* (1964); it is notable that, for all her comic expertise, by her own account she got her start on the New York vaudeville stage with an early performance of vocal pathos, as a "spectacle of a scrawny thirteen-year-old girl with a Jewish face singing a heartbreaking ballad."[10] In writing about Jewish torch singers including Libby Holman who, like Irish American artists such as Helen Morgan, occupied a certain "racial borderland" and exotic proximity to blackness, Jon Stratton notes the extent to which Eastern European vernacular and Jewish cantorial music sustained a reputation for sadness and melancholy. This attributed ethos of melancholy aligned with the emergent genre of the torch song and was thought to typify the music created by Jewish immigrant songwriters who propelled the music publishing machine of Tin Pan Alley.[11] As a song of unrequited love, sung by a female vocalist who carries a torch for a man who has done her wrong, the torch song has gone on from its early twentieth-century origins to incarnations in a range of popular music genres including country and soul. But in the 1920s it was the lament of the blues that overlaid musically with lamentative elements from Jewish, Eastern European music as well as French chanson to produce what was celebrated as the novel American sound of torch singing.

Teasing apart the strands of what is blue and what is torchy may be ultimately a futile project. Again, the search for the defining marker of blackness in the music can be a directive to—led by the circular harmonic rhythm of the blues—end up ever returned once again to the open road, in pursuit of a thing just out of reach. If bluesy torch songs did not precisely follow the blues' harmonic rhythm and structure, certainly there were discrete rhythmic and harmonic elements—the delays and surprises of syncopations and the ache of seventh chords with their bent-blue notes—that inspired white and Jewish Tin Pan Alley songwriters to infuse bluesiness into their tunes. I am struck, for example, by the elegant asymmetry to Harold Arlen's opening melody in "Stormy Weather," an eight-bar verse that is not evenly subdivided but feels like a three-bar phrase, a two-bar phrase, and another two-bar phrase with an extra bar tacked on just to let it breathe. This is a melody that follows the rhythms of informal speech, not the strictures of a lyric's tidy meter. It has some bright wildflowers winding in and blooming in what could have been simply a pleasant, well-tended musical garden. Compare it, for example, to the Akst and Young song "Am I Blue?" that Waters performed in the 1929 film *On With the Show*—a very tidy garden into which Waters had to freely improvise over the closing verses to really allow the blues to creep in . . . there's more than one reason that song title lives as a question. The recorded version of her performance of "Am I Blue?" is all kinds of ways different from what is written in the pretty sheet music.[12] And the staging of the filmed number, how she has been directed to walk onstage at a theatre (before an onscreen audience of white faces) with a full basket of laundry and a big ruffled-and-polka-dotted dress with a matching kerchief on her head speaks volumes about the way the torch singing black woman was imagined differently from the torch singing white woman. In short, she sings her torch song as a mammy. Although, she does so with as much artistry as the song will allow—with sensitive phrasing, rhythmic and melodic adjustments to excavate the blues feel and project a disarming sense of candor. Film historian Donald Bogle has taken note of Waters's heroic efforts to recuperate this type and assert the humanity of the mammy characters she played onscreen.[13] Within this context, Waters's self-directed performance of "Stormy Weather" at the Cotton Club in 1933 has even more significance. There, beyond the catch in her throat, and the torchy suppressed sob, even the fact of Waters's stillness and pose of rest, her body leaning against the lamppost within its pool of light, lives in relation to Fanny Brice's flickering streetlamp-lit performance of her torch song "My Man" a decade prior. But despite Ethel Waters's best efforts, in the roles and songs she was offered, the emotive world-weariness and urbane sophistication that characterized white torch singers was swapped out for a different kind of weariness—that of the long-suffering, laboring and bluesy black mammy.

Coachings with Zora Neale Hurston
Talking Back to the Negro Folk Opera

A part that Ethel Waters *almost* played, in a show whose production never came to pass, was that of Big Sweet in Zora Neale Hurston's 1944 musical *Polk County*, a writing credit shared with white author Dorothy Waring. In this unproduced show, the character of the young northerner Leafy Lee arrives in a sawmill camp in southern Florida and literally seeks blues-singing lessons, which are arranged for her by a woman named Big Sweet, the de facto community leader and a skillful singer in her own right. As Eric M. Glover has beautifully detailed, it is the mode of blues singing that creates space for friendship and song-teaching between the two women, a joyful black feminist space that Hurston celebrated and advanced in her musical theatre writing. Glover also observes that Leafy's aspirations to sing blues in the style of Ethel Waters, explicitly stated in the script, belonged to a character who functioned as a "thinly veiled" stand-in for Hurston herself.[14] In the singing lesson she posits, Hurston locates a version of herself in the spot of voice student studying with Ethel Waters, for whom the part of Big Sweet was written. Glover understands this onstage dynamic between blues singing novice and expert as manifesting the female pedagogical duet, a Broadway song form studied by Stacy Wolf.[15] I also feel that in the broader context of the show it is a vocal scenario that, as discussed in chapter 1, was iterated time and again in the history of black women on the US popular musical stage. The relation between Big Sweet and Leafy Lee reproduces a listening scenario that enables the vocal sound to be passed on, sonically cited, and carried across geographic space, for example from rural, Southern performance spaces to the New York venues where *Polk County*'s Leafy dreams of going on to secure her financial future as a singer.

What is to be made of Hurston's writing herself, via the alter ego of Leafy Lee, into the presumptive position of voice student to a blues mama of Ethel Waters's stature? Daphne Brooks puts it to us plainly: "While no scholar in her right mind would dispute the fact that Zora Neale Hurston revolutionized and revitalized the voices of Black folk in her beloved fiction, her less feted drama, and her still influential anthropological scholarship, you'd most likely be hard pressed to find anyone who would call her a 'great singer.'[16] In the audio recordings of songs collected in her ethnographic practice, Hurston sings fearlessly; her ethnographer's voice a wide open, shaky treble that often dips down to a bright, harder-edged sound in the realm of her everyday speech.[17] For the most part, her pitch is clean, although the attacks and releases of notes are sometimes uncertain, and her rhythms are generally locked in and clearly articulated. It strikes me that Hurston tosses her voice out into the world as the proud repository of, as the subtitle of *Polk County* puts it, "Authentic Negro Music." Her sole aim seems to be authenticity, such that her voice is the blank canvas for its capture, for the expression of "Negro culture" broadly writ rather than expression of the individual self. In this sense her vocal delivery can be heard as striving for and achieving a kind of neutrality that enables voice to gesture toward (conjure up?) the collectivity of black experience. Hurston seeks to deliver the authentic Negro song, not necessarily to interpret it. Is it the cold frame of the ethnographic recording scene that produces this quality in her sound? Typically there does not seem to be any audience other than the white man operating the recording apparatus, for whom she skillfully explicates the provenance of each tune just before she breaks into song. But I submit that a singer who is a performing artist by trade, different from a trained ethnographer, will always imagine an audience even if the room is empty. The singer who must sell a number to the demanding audience of the vaudeville tent or the cabaret venue cannot afford, or is quickly trained out of, the relatively flat affect serviceable enough for the singing ethnographer collecting material relevant for her next musical play. It is notable that in *Polk County* the character of Leafy enters the sawmill camp with the stated aim of learning to sing the blues in order to make money as a blues singer in New York. Both Leafy and Hurston, then, share the goal of coming to a community to learn "authentic Negro music" from the rural source and take it back to New York to earn a living—Hurston as a writer of musical plays, Leafy as a singer on the musical stage.

From the first moment the women of the Lofton Lumber Company encounter her, the fair-skinned Leafy is racially identified and evaluated by her vocal sound. The women are at first concerned that she is a white woman invading their space, but as soon as she says simply "Hello," the women reassess: "Seem like she colored from the sound."[18] However, it isn't until Big Sweet passes judgment that they are quite sure what to make of her. Big Sweet, she who "has the quality of leadership" as Hurston puts it, announces her entrance with her own offstage singing. Soon Leafy Lee and Big Sweet are staring each other down. Leafy breaks into a grin. And although she tries to suppress it at first, it is the sound of Big Sweet's chuckle that indicates her approval of the newcomer, as their friendship forms fast and strong:

BIG SWEET: I see what you come here for. You come here for a reason, and not for a season, and Leafy, you done come to the right place. Me and my man sings them blues every night at our house. And we got a friend man that cold picks 'em on a guitar. [...]

LEAFY: Well you all the very people I want to meet up with. I wants to sing the blues. [...]

LAURA B: And Big Sweet sure can sing them blues. When she gits hold of a good one, she turn it every way but loose. She's the one can help you out a lot.

As it turns out, the scenario of the singing lesson, as mapped in Scene 4 of the play, reveals that Big Sweet has distinct ideas about just what kind of "sure enough blues" should be taught to Leafy.[19] She promptly quashes the first three selections the menfolk try to teach the younger woman. There will be no singing of a song called "Nasty Butt," or a song about gals that "rocks their hips from wall to wall," nor a song about someone named Angeline and her rocking and reeling behind. Not on Big Sweet's watch. "Stop it!" she exclaims. "Don't you sing nothing like that in front of Leafy. She's a lady." Big Sweet's man, Lonnie, is injured: "Good Lord, baby, how we going to teach the girl if you won't let us sing?" Led by Big Sweet, the women on the scene retire to the kitchen to teach Leafy the song "Careless Love." The best song to teach Leafy, it is determined, is a song that is specific to women singers.

Ethel Waters's rendition of "Careless Love" survives in recorded form, and in the 1947 recording I am listening to, I hear that her voice sits in that treble range that Hurston favors, but the sound is much more stable than Miss Zora's.[20] There are artful bends as she sings through those voiced consonants, and the general feeling has a kind of quietness. In Waters's performance, the song calls up an intimate sound, more a croon than a holler. It is less strident and seemingly the result of less exertion than the watery soprano heard throughout Hurston's recorded oeuvre. Perhaps it really is a song suited to the intimacy of the kitchen, as Hurston has set it in the play. There, Hurston/Leafy as the speculative voice student of Waters/Big Sweet might best learn how to voice the quiet sound and affective conviction that an artist of Waters's caliber can bring to such a song: "Love is like a hydrant / it turns off and on / Just like friendship / when your money's gone."[21] But if sung in the space of domesticity it is not, however, a song having to do with the laboring (for white folks) of the weary-bluesy mammy. Instead it is a song that, staged by Hurston, black women sing for their own recreation, comfort, and enjoyment.

Hurston's closeness to and admiration for Waters, to the point that she envisioned a starring role for the artist as a blues-singing character in her new musical play, also speaks to the extent to which Waters was celebrated by black audiences as a legit blues singer even as she moved fluidly across styles. From her days as Sweet Mama Stringbean on the vaudeville-blues circuit, to Harlem jazz clubs, to what Amiri Baraka called her "torchy, 'pop' style" and what I discuss here as deliberately torched-up interventions in the bluesy Tin Pan Alley material she was given on Broadway and in Hollywood, Waters engaged a kind of multivocality, to use Katherine Meizel's term, that *South Pacific*'s Juanita Hall would later emulate to different ends.[22] Brooks writes of Waters, "Like Hurston, she mastered the art of multilingual colloquialisms and phrasings, assumed multiple personas in her vocal performances, and finessed the art of deeply performative storytelling" via blues aesthetics.[23] Brooks finds much to make of the productively contrary way Hurston's singing relays something other than the virtuosic vocal sound for which black women are so often celebrated. For me, Hurston's less-than-polished vocal delivery points up the fact that no, not all black women can magically sing as powerfully and sensitively as our great stars. This fact denaturalizes and celebrates the significant artistry of singers like Waters, with whom Hurston essayed a wish to study in the form of her scripted alter ego Leafy Lee. As Broadway performer Zonya Love Johnson wisely reminds me, if we did not take talent and effort into consideration alongside, for example, a singer's vocal training in the church—or in the vocal collective of the blues joint—then "my sister's singing would be as good as mine."[24]

With Waters's voice in *Polk County*, Hurston hoped to talk back to and replace portrayals of black folklife on the musical stage that she considered misleading depictions of black lived experience—specifically those in the 1935 opera *Porgy and Bess* and the musical play *Show Boat*, originally staged on Broadway in 1927 but with many tours, revivals, and films from the 1920s to the 1940s and beyond that kept it active in the public imagination during the time Hurston was writing. In advance publicity for the never-realized *Polk County*, the white press understood the planned Hurston show as a "Negro folk opera," which is of course how *Porgy and Bess* was billed. As I will examine, the specter of the Gershwin opera, understood by many to be the ideal vehicle for black talent on Broadway, loomed so large for over a decade that even 1946's *St. Louis Woman*—in which Pearl Bailey and Juanita Hall appeared—faced unfavorable comparison for deviating from the celebrated model. But it is *Show Boat* that solidified the arche-typal mammy character in musical theatre. She persists in the Broadway canon, despite heroic recuperations by performers such as the regal Gretha Boston, who won a Tony for her performance in the 1994 Broadway revival, in the role of Queenie.

Blues Mama to Bluesy Mammy

In the original Broadway cast of *Show Boat*, the role of Queenie—smiling, bandana-wearing, ship's cook counterpart to Jules Bledsoe as "Ol' Man River" warbler Joe—was played in blackface by Italian American vaude-ville star Tess Gardella. Known for a hefty voice that matched her impressive girth, and for the white dress and head kerchief with red polka dots that she sported as part of her blackface vaudeville persona Aunt Jemima, Gardella hailed from a coal-mining family in Wilkes-Barre, Pennsylvania—just fifty miles north of the Keystone State coal town where Pearl Bailey would launch her career as a nightclub performer. Gardella went on to perform in *George White's Scandals* as well as *Show Boat*. In 1936 she sued Log Cabin Syrup and NBC for presenting another singer as Aunt Jemima as part of a radio promotional campaign after she had turned down the low-paying gig; in the end she was awarded $115,000 in damages. Of the producers who sought to do her dirty, a *Variety* author contextualizes: "This was nothing more than a revival of the 'copy act' practice of vaudeville, widely used not so many years ago. When they didn't wish to pay a good act its proper salary, some vaudeville managers hit upon the bright idea of booking replica acts, not as good but not as expensive."[25] Like Sophie Tucker's insistence on the originality of the songs she sang and yet sought to lift from black singers' acts, the pretensions to authentic originarity of white female artists who performed in blackface remain suspect—although clearly these claims secured financial rewards. Todd Decker has assessed the way that Gardella's recorded vocal interpretation of "Can't Help Lovin' Dat Man," the song that cues the character Queenie to the secret, racial origins of white-passing tragic mulatta Julie, featured fully swung rhythms as well as scooped and blued notes. By contrast, Irish torch singer Helen Morgan's rendition of the tune as Julie in the show's cast album sounds to Decker "resolutely white."[26] In *Show Boat*, the vocal types of the mammy and the torch singer can clearly never be one and the same. Even though Julie's mixed-race origins ultimately preclude happily-ever-after chances with her dashing white male lover—and the torched-up "coon song" is the racial tell—Julie's unblue vocal performance in the mode of a 1920s white torch singer reveals the character's tragic obliviousness to her foregone conclusion of racially thwarted, requited but impossible love.

For Ethel Waters to inhabit the torch song in the years following *Show Boat* required yoking torchiness to the mammy by maneuvering around the ways that torch singing required performing weariness and sadness. The white torch singer as a type cut an image of the languid sophisticate; as John Moore observes, torch singers such as Libby Holman, Fanny Brice, and Helen Morgan enacted personas that were "deliberately contrived to convey the impression that these women are urbane, worldly-wise, but hence rather world-weary, and possessing a deep sadness edging toward despair."[27] Moore takes note of filmed press photos in which these singers are often resting on one leg, head flung back or tilted over a shoulder with pouty lips ready for the sad consolation of the next cigarette. These are positions of repose, and although the torch singers were hard-working showbiz women, the illusion was that they did nothing more than lounge all day feeling listless and despairingly lovelorn.[28] The lyrics to "My Man" and "Can't Help Lovin' Dat Man," vehicles for white female torch singers, are generally disconnected from any sense of spirituality and do not contain the word "weary." But weariness is splashed all over the lyrics of the torch songs that Ethel Waters made famous, along with the kind of "Christian stoicism" that Bogle identifies as central to the type of the mammy.[29] In "Stormy

Weather" she is "weary all the time, all the time, so weary all the time." In "Am I Blue?" she is "waiting on the weary shore." In "Supper Time," discussed in more detail below, she worries about how to ensure her children will be prayerful and thankful to God even in the absence of a lynched father. The primary action of the song is one of being too exhausted to perform the domestic labor she knows is required of her: "Supper time / I should set the table / 'Cause it's supper time / Somehow I'm not able."[30] A photograph from the 1933 Broadway show in which she sang this song (figure 2. 1) depicts the singer with a mournful expression, hands clasped prayerfully to her breast, lips just parted. Beads of sweat dot her face as she casts her eyes heavenward beneath furrowed brows. The diamond-shaped earrings from an earlier publicity photo (figure 1. 3) reappear here, but the bare shoulders and self-assured half-smile are gone. A scarf taut over her hair, upper body swathed in a garment that reveals only her muscular throat, Waters has transformed from stylish blues mama to a tragic, worn-down woman.

In encompassing the weariness of the mammy's laboring body, the bluesy torch songs Ethel Waters introduced pronounced the bluesy aesthetic as endless sadness, effectively removing the blueswomen's humor and self-determination from the sound and the scene. As Samuel A. Floyd has assessed:

> The blues, as they emerged during or after Reconstruction, were a way of coping with the new trials and realizations brought by freedom. There were blues songs about voodoo, estrangement, sex, protest, bad luck, deceit, war, joblessness, sickness, love, health, evil, revenge, railroading, and a variety of other life experiences, some sad, others not.[31]

Yet when blues tonality was taken up by Tin Pan Alley songwriters, this breadth was massively curtailed. No longer a repository for open-ended, lived philosophy, the black torch singer as weary-bluesy mammy was required to be only ever achingly sad—about her missing man, about the evils of racism, or as conveniently packaged in Irving Berlin's "Supper Time," about both.

In August Wilson's immortal speech for Ma Rainey, the depth of what blues can mean and do, separate from the distortions of white perceptions of bluesiness, rings forth in full clarity. [32]

> The more music you got in the world, the fuller it is. . . . White folks don't understand about the blues. They hear it come out, but they don't know how it got there. They don't understand that's life's way of talking.

2.1 Ethel Waters in *As Thousands Cheer* (1933). Photo by Alfredo Valente via Billy Rose Theatre Division, New York Public Library for the Performing Arts.

You don't sing to feel better. You sing 'cause that's a way of understanding life. . . . The blues help you get out of bed in the morning. You get up knowing you ain't alone. There's something else in the world. Something's been added by that song. This be an empty world without the blues. I take that emptiness and try to fill it up with something. . . . I ain't started the blues way of singing. The blues always been here. . . . They say I started it . . . but I didn't. I just helped it out. Filled up that empty space a little bit. That's all. But if they wanna call me the Mother of the Blues, that's all right with me. It don't hurt none.[33]

For Wilson, the blues mama type, different from the bluesy mammy, understands her music as the very fact and action of copresence: "You get up knowin' you ain't alone." Singing the blues is also *singing along with* the blues. And, as Wilson's Rainey knows, it is not a kind of singing that she invented but belongs to a practice that long precedes her.[34] By contrast, in Irving Berlin's "Supper Time" it is overwhelmingly the profound sense of loss, a debilitating loss in the face of racist violence, that animates the music. The very lyric is about the desperation of having to carry on living in the absence of the lynched loved one, singing along *without*.

It is reported that Irving Berlin saw and heard Waters perform "Stormy Weather" at the Cotton Club in Harlem and was so enraptured by her performance that he insisted she appear in the Broadway musical revue for which he was writing the score, *As Thousands Cheer* (1933). The concept for the revue was a series of twenty-one numbers based on newspaper headlines, covering a range of themes with commentary and satirical treatments of the White House and president and Mrs. Hoover to Gandhi and Rockefeller. The weather segment was musicalized into the sexy "Heat Wave," which Waters also sang. "Supper Time" accompanied the newspaper headline of a woman whose husband has been lynched. In his Ethel Waters biography, Bogle draws a link between this song and Billie Holiday's race protest song "Strange Fruit," recorded in 1939. Without question, the song made tangible to white audiences the personal cost of racism to a woman whose husband has been lynched, and the pathos of the winding blue melody. Waters's expressive range lent humanity to what may have seemed like just another headline of violence against one more black man.[35] Unable to bring herself to set the table knowing how "that man o' mine / ain't coming home no more," the unset *ta*ble is blue, the fact of being not *a*ble to set it is blue, the anticipated *yell*in' of kids for their dinner is blue, the impossibility of *tell*in' them what has happened is blue. And although at first acknowledgment the certainty of her man coming home *no more* is consonant and diatonic, bright three upswinging to the fifth note of the scale, the second time it arrives it blues down, a flattened, sliding third that can only make recourse to the tonic. What brings the song home is Waters's voice on the edge of breaking, the way she exploits the tender edge between the shout and the sob. When the song builds as she imagines her children as they "start to thank the Lord, Lord!" we move into a full belt on the final "Supper Time," although it blends soon into what Waters called her low, sweet sound. We get a crack in the voice, the voice so thick with emotion she can barely get the words out, and then after the word *ain't* she simply breaks off entirely. There is only the sound of wordless sobs as the final chord in the accompaniment arpeggiates out beneath her.[36]

Part of the appeal of torch songs was the sense audiences had that the singers themselves were in fact singing from autobiographical, felt experience about carrying a torch for a brutish man—the knowledge that Fanny Brice might very well have been singing about Nicky Arnstein, or Mistinguett about Maurice Chevalier.[37] It is striking that Billie Holiday is often listed in the line of torch singers given that, as Nina Sun Eidsheim has pointed up, the extent to which she is understood by listeners to be singing the pathos of her own experience undervalues the richness of her technique and interpretation.[38] In the case of Ethel Waters and "Supper Time," she herself spoke at length about what it cost her emotionally to perform this song, the harrowing toll of reliving frightening and painful memories. In her words, "I was so emotionally moved when I first let myself go at the dress rehearsal, that I sobbed uncontrollably for 10 minutes after the number was finished."[39] What may be dismissed in popular music as just singing from lived, autobiographical experience can also be admired in the theatre for the actor's technical skill in accessing such affective depth and emotional honesty. I do want to be sure to applaud Waters's musical and vocal technique alongside her skill as an actress, the combination of both the desperate, blued shout and the mournful, more classically inflected sustained tones. But the fact remains that the weary-bluesy mammy on the musical stage is required to serve up her own affective labor—it is expected that she will suffer and make music of her suffering. In 1954, Waters spoke about her reluctance to continue to perform sad or "serious" material in an interview with Ed Murrow on the television show *Person to Person*: "It's too closely related to my past life. I mean, I don't act, I relive unhappy experiences that right along through here I'd like to forget. And I also want to laugh and, you know, sing again. . . . I want to be gay. I constantly can't live in my tragic past, and it has been tragic, if night after night you have to pour out your soul. And people. . . . it reaches people, it affects people, it's good sometimes. What I'm. . . . I'm grateful to God for the blessing and the comfort that I can give people. I don't resent that. But I have to get away from it at times, because it undermines *me*."[40] Ever in the position of being asked to labor in the act of providing comfort for the (white) audience member, the weary-bluesy mammy is at risk, as Waters's comments throw into stark relief here, of losing herself in the process. As well as comfort, the "blessing" Waters speaks about that "affects" listeners, the black woman singer is also, as Farah Jasmine Griffin has elegantly theorized, expected to provide healing for others via her voice.[41] Yet clearly there is both technique at play as well as a personal cost to the performer. The sleight-of-hand that masterful songwriter Irving Berlin managed with "Supper Time" was to switch out the no-good man, whose love the pouty white torch singer ever craved, for the undeniable villainy of racism itself. The song's love object was a black man who left his woman not of his own untrustworthy accord but, simply, because he was murdered by white people. The fact that there is no humor and self-determination to that tune is a big part of what turns the blues bluesy. In being moved by the performance, white audiences secure the solace—the "comfort" Waters speaks about—of knowing that they are decidedly unvillainous because they have been affected by and empathize with the black woman's song of suffering. But this is a tricky absolution. Film scholar Miriam Petty has written about the way that white audiences' celebration of the mammy type, particularly as performed by Oscar-winning Hattie McDaniel in *Gone with the Wind* (1939), only shores up white supremacy. Petty notes that individualized applause for a black woman performing a show-stealing turn as a mammy "is of a piece with the ideological work that the mammy icon performed so prominently in this era of American culture; white people's love for their individual mammies did not obligate them to see or oppose racism at work in its myriad forms."[42]

Despite Ethel Waters's many turns on stage and screen as the long-suffering domestic servant, the good Christian woman, and the weary-bluesy mammy, accounts from her black contemporaries attest to a side of her that was sharply different from this all-enduring figure. In Hollywood, while shooting the 1943 all-black film *Cabin in the Sky*, an adaptation of the 1940 Broadway musical, Waters is said to have maintained a vicious rivalry with her younger costar Lena Horne. Horne was cast in the role of sexy "bad girl" Georgia that Katherine Dunham had originated three years earlier in the stage musical; Waters reprised her performance as Petunia, the devout, long-suffering wife-of-a-gambler. As one cast member attested, "Ethel was religious, yes. But she would call Lena every name, like 'bitch' or whatever. I remember Ethel going off into the corner many many times and she'd be mumbling 'mother fucker' and she would be looking up at the sky and talking to Jesus."[43] Waters was also reportedly jealous of Horne's style of delivery and insisted that the younger artist had copied Waters's vocal approach. In these testimonies I detect echoes of a lesson in vocal rivalry Waters may have picked up from Bessie Smith back on the road in her vaudeville-blues days. It could not have helped that the same year *Cabin in the Sky* was released Lena Horne performed the now-famous torch song "Stormy Weather" in another all-black Hollywood musical that was literally titled *Stormy Weather* (1943). I examine Horne's impact for the Broadway musical stage briefly below and in more detail in chapter 4. On the Hollywood film set of *Cabin in the Sky* in the early 1940s, the young woman who had been a chorus girl at Harlem's Cotton Club when Waters first performed the song a decade earlier was now a rising starlet. Yet Horne and the black women singers who rose after her encountered and fought for a range of options on the musical stage that extended significantly beyond those available to Waters as a path-breaking black woman torch singer.

Coachings on How to Listen
Lena Horne and the Character Divas

When the curtain rose on *St. Louis Woman* on March 30, 1946, at the Martin Beck Theatre on West 45th Street in Manhattan, Lena Horne was not, to the producers' dismay, onstage. During the musical's tempestuous journey to Broadway, Horne had withdrawn from the project, once considered a sure bet for a Hollywood transfer with its enhancement funding from MGM's Arthur Freed and a budget to the tune of $200,000.[44] But after reading the script Horne had reportedly declared she could never play such a part that would "bring discredit to her race."[45] The black press alternately amplified the critiques of leading black intellectuals that the musical was a throwback to demeaning portrayals of African American characters and bolstered counterarguments that the musical, based on Harlem Renaissance writer Arna Bontemps's 1931 novel *God Sends Sunday*, would represent finely drawn characters.[46] Walter White of the NAACP railed against the show and wired the head of MGM in defense of Horne's decision; actress Fredi Washington, via her platform as entertainment editor of the African American newspaper *People's Voice*, agreed with him. The acclaimed poet Countee Cullen, who was cowriting the musical's book with Bontemps, passed away tragically at the age of forty-three just two days before rehearsals were scheduled to start. The producers scrambled to find a replacement for Horne and cast one actress, the star of Broadway's *Carmen Jones* (1943), Muriel Rahn, and then replaced her after only two performances with another, newcomer Ruby Hill. Even director Rouben Mamoulian could not rescue *St. Louis Woman* when called in to doctor the show out of town, despite his sparkling Hollywood resume and aspirations of recreating a theatrical credit with the stature of his earlier success, none other than *Porgy and Bess*. Mamoulian restructured the show and cut unwieldy numbers by composer Harold Arlen and lyricist Johnny Mercer. But when he aimed to fire the second Lena Horne stand-in, Ruby Hill, he met with objection from multiple fronts, likely due to the beleaguered company's fatigue from an exhausting, disorganized rehearsal process. Pearl Bailey, the breakout performer who was saving the show nightly rallied the cast and, with the threat of an all-out strike, Hill stayed in the show. She did not, as it turns out, get particularly good notices—"pretty but that's all," as one reviewer put it in the black press.[47] The real plaudits for *St. Louis Woman*, such as were to be had, went not to the performer in the leading female role but to the actress in the character role who had championed her, one Pearl Bailey.[48] Lena Horne would not appear on the Broadway stage until a decade later, and then decidedly as a leading lady, in *Jamaica* (1957).[49] Horne's refusal to appear in *St. Louis Woman* in a role she deemed an outdated and disreputable portrayal of black female personhood can also be understood as a directive for possible listening—improve the parts if you want to hear this star on the Broadway stage!

Perhaps part of *St. Louis Woman*'s difficulty lay in that its creators were not quite sure how to present black people onstage in a musical in 1946. The celebrated black-cast shows of decades past that aimed to stage black musical folklife and took pastoral black vernacular song and language as a point of departure, such as *Show Boat* and *Porgy and Bess*, were no longer in step with the times—as Zora Neale Hurston, via her own musical theatre writing, asserted in her own way.[50] In a subsection of its review of *St. Louis Woman* titled "Casting Important," the critic for the African American newspaper *New Journal and Guide*, John Lee, asserted:

[I]t would be an excellent idea for Mr. Gross and other producers who are contemplating Negro productions on Broadway to give a lot of thought to the business of casting. It also might be wise to give some thought to the kind of play they want to unveil to an increasingly critical audience. It is no longer profitable to exhibit Negro performers as versatile curiosities.[51]

Black audiences were on the alert to critique roles that harkened back to mammy and Uncle Tom stereotypes and that used dialect. The role originally intended for Horne, that of Della Green, was described variously in the press as a "shady lady" and a "mighty loose woman."[52] The presence of gamblers and ne'er-do-wells generally offended the sensibilities of those intent on uplifting the race via black performance in popular entertainment such as the musical stage. In the *New York Times*, white critic Lewis Nichols also observed:

No doubt the basic trouble is that "St. Louis Woman" never fully decides what it wishes to be. Presumably the original design was to make a folk play of it, something on the order of "Porgy and Bess." The scenes, being largely of saloons, cakewalk, and carnival, take it away from folk opera and put it into the classification of musical comedy. . . . It is a hybrid affair, and unfortunate.[53]

Against the folk- and minstrel-derived types that overdetermined expectations for black performers on the musical stage, during the 1940s black singer-actors such as Pearl Bailey and her fellow *St. Louis Woman* castmate Juanita Hall, soon-to-be styled as *South Pacific* islander, carved out success for themselves with character roles that attested to the power of the black diva in midcentury Broadway musicals. The exoticism that Juanita Hall insisted listeners hear in her voice was of a different variety than that of the Irish and Eastern European Jewish torch singers whose proximity to blackness aligned with orientalist fantasies of alluring femininity. But it was nonetheless a sound cast very far afield from the terrain of the weary-bluesy mammy.

Juanita Hall
Blues in High Yellowface

When I began this project, I intended to begin my study of Tony Award–winning black women with Diahann Carroll and Leslie Uggams, who hold the focus for much of the following chapter, and their 1960s Best

Performance by a Leading Actress in a Musical wins. Midway through my research I realized that somehow, I'd overlooked the fact that more than a decade earlier, Juanita Hall was the first black actress to ever win a Tony Award. This honor was bestowed upon her in 1950 in the Best Performance by a Featured Actress in a Musical category for her showing in the role of Bloody Mary in the original Broadway cast of the Rodgers and Hammerstein musical *South Pacific* (1949).[54] There are ways that, for all her achievements, Juanita Hall's performance and trajectory as a singer-actress present an embarrassing, conveniently overlooked hiccup to any impulse toward heralding a glorious tradition of black women stars on Broadway. She was, after all, cast as a middle-aged Vietnamese woman living in the Pacific Islands during World War II.[55] Hall instantiated with her celebrated performance in *South Pacific* a long and fraught yellowface tradition of fair-skinned black women actresses—often referred to by the less than complimentary racial designation "high yellow"—cast in this role.[56] It is tempting to launch here into an aggressive critique of the classic musical *South Pacific*, calling attention to its blatant Orientalism and setting askew its seemingly untouchable title as yet another "great show" of the Broadway musical canon.[57] But what is of greater interest to me is the fact that Hall followed this role with another yellowface turn when she played Madam Liang in Rodgers and Hammerstein's musical adaptation of C. Y. Lee's San Francisco Chinatown-set novel *Flower Drum Song* in 1958. It is said that the producers faced significant challenges trying to cast race-appropriate singers and dancers in Broadway's first attempt at a modern Asian American musical comedy.[58] In any case, the distinctly non-Asian American Juanita Hall was the first actor signed to the original cast of *Flower Drum Song*.[59]

It is likely due in large part to the uncomfortable fact of her reputation as a yellowface performer that Hall is underacknowledged both in Broadway history books and in celebrations of African American singers. No substantial biographies exist chronicling her achievements and she fades easily from hearing as yet another relic of another time. The photographs of her that regularly circulate typically show her in costume as *South Pacific*'s grass skirt-peddling Bloody Mary. But a deeper dive into the archive reveals her as a doyenne of black entertainment culture, the smartly dressed star feted at society dinners and the choir director of respected vocal ensembles—groups of women in neat matching dresses with bows at the neck and men in sharp suits, pocket handkerchiefs just so. In a publicity photograph from the 1950s (figure 2.2), an elegantly coiffed Hall is shown looking dreamily up from the low-cut cowl of fabric draped around

2.2 Juanita Hall in a 1950s publicity photograph. Courtesy of the Billy Rose Theatre Division, New York Public Library for the Performing Arts.

her shoulders. Her eyes sparkle in a carefully made-up face, wide hoops at her ears, her fingers entwined in the edge of a loosely crocheted shawl that evokes netting and the island theme of her most famous show. How did the Julliard-trained soprano and conductor turned blues singer from New Jersey convince audiences to hear her voice as that of characters imagined in the islands of the South Pacific and San Francisco's Chinatown?

Juanita Hall, of mixed Irish and African American heritage, was born in Keyport, New Jersey, in 1901, thus a contemporary of Bessie Smith and Ethel Waters.[60] In encyclopedic entries it is often noted that at a young age Hall commuted to Manhattan to study at Julliard, taking courses in orchestration, harmony, theory, and voice.[61] By her own account, Hall was trained as a high dramatic soprano, and worked extensively in choral and concert venues before moving to Broadway.[62] In the 1920s she performed with the renowned Hall Johnson Negro Choir, which took its moniker not from her surname but from director Hall Johnson, for whom she served as an assistant conductor. This was the choir that, in 1929, backed up Bessie Smith in her only known film appearance, *St. Louis Blues*.[63] Hall also appeared with the choir singing spirituals in the 1930 Pulitzer Prize–winning Broadway play *The Green Pastures*. She went on to direct her own ensemble, the Juanita Hall Choir and Negro Melody Singers, heard regularly on WNYC Radio from 1937–1939 on Works Project Administration broadcast programs showcasing renditions of spirituals that she arranged and conducted. A concert program from a "New Masses Concert" in 1938 lists Hall as a performer sharing the bill with Count Basie, Marc Blitzstein, Aaron Copland, Lehman Engel, Harold Rome, Anna Sokolow, and Virgil Thomson, among others, singing excerpts from Paul Bowles's never-completed opera *Denmark Vesey*.[64] In 1939 she served as the director of musical activities for Negro Week at the New York World's Fair, where she conducted a three hundred-voice choir. Additional Broadway credits came earlier in the decade with the short-lived plays *Stevedore* (1934), *Sailor, Beware!* (1936), and *Sweet River* (1936). Then, in 1946 Hall was cast in her first Broadway musical, *St. Louis Woman*. In 1947, she had a small part in a second Broadway musical, perhaps better termed a musical that wanted to be an opera, *Street Scene*, with lyrics penned by Hall's friend Langston Hughes and music by Kurt Weill.[65] But in 1948 her big break came along. In a private revue presented by the Stage Manager's Club, "Talent '48," Richard Rodgers and Oscar Hammerstein II heard Hall perform the song "Lament Over Love," a blues lyric by Langston Hughes set to music by composer Herbert Kingsley, and promptly invited her to audition for her career-defining role of Bloody Mary.

During the years in which she performed in eight shows a week of *South Pacific* on Broadway, Hall also maintained a busy schedule as a nightclub singer. A journalist from the *New York Post Home News* enthused, "Evidence of her energy is this: When the curtain rings down on 'South Pacific' every night, she rushes away from the Majestic Theatre and hops a taxi to fill her night-club engagement at Cafe Society, down in the Village. It's nearly dawn before she finally gets home."[66] In her set at Cafe Society, she regularly sang quite a different repertoire from the spirituals and operatic works for which she had trained. A *Variety* reviewer lauded "her excellent voice, a deep and powerful alto which she parlays with fine diction and phrasing into top results," before going on to document her song choices, noting:

> Emphasis is on blues, which she fashions into soulful laments with her dramatic overtones. She tees off here with a dramatic tune, "Anyplace I Hang My Hat" and then heads into the blues idiom with "From Now On." Best number is "Lament Over Love," into which she injects a maximum of pathos, following with a sock job on "Am I Blue?" Closer (routine encore) is the surefire "Bali Ha'i," which she created in "Pacific."[67]

Where other black Broadway divas of the period such as Pearl Bailey, Diahann Carroll, and Leslie Uggams began their careers on nightclub stages before arriving on Broadway, Hall's trajectory is distinctive in its movement from beginnings in classical singing into a subsequent shift to blues. In particular, I note that with the change of material she asks us to attend to the way her vocal register *registers* differently, two decades after her first Broadway show. In a 1949 interview she put it very clearly: "It's been a wonderful life. . . . I was a dramatic soprano when I was in 'The Green Pastures' and hit high Cs every night at the finale. Now I sing contralto." Fascinatingly, it was on the strength of a Langston Hughes blues number that she landed the major dramatic vocal role of her career in which she continued to sing in a more classical idiom—certainly Rodgers and Hammerstein aspired to the realm of high art with their "Golden Age" musical drama, and the exoticized themes of *South Pacific* tended toward the operatic. The show's male lead, bass-baritone Ezio Pinza, was a bona fide opera singer, which contributed to the effect. While I will return to Hall's performances of blues repertoire later, I turn here to listen to the sound of her singing in her signature song from *South Pacific*, the haunting "Bali Ha'i," as heard on the original cast album.[68]

A rolled chord on the harp, then Hall's voice comes in with a statement in a warm, liquid sound, low and heavy. The orchestra answers, a sound weighted with low brass. Another vocal statement, arcing up, supple with vibrato, as the orchestra answers. The harp rolls. Hall's voice leads the orchestra upward, reaching for something out of sight before pausing, dropping to a series of slower repeated pitches before it is carried on a gentle swell into the main part of the number. This is a song of longing, of an otherness meant to bewitch. The central melody, in the key of C, is launched by a dramatic octave jump on its first two syllables: "Bali Ha'i may call you." There are so many open vowels—*ah* [ɑ], *ai* [aɪ])—and Hall makes the most of them, serving them up with a rolling shimmer. Her voice has a strength to it, this must be what the music critics are calling "dramatic." Something about it is no-nonsense, primarily in the pitch register of spoken language rather than the stratospheric heights, although the tumble of vibrato on sustained tones sets it clearly apart from actual speech. This is the sound of a grounded, assertive woman, one who uses dialect, incidentally ("lak" for "like," "dey" for "they," "anudder" for "another"), and one with the power to wield an incantation.[69] In her schema of operatic voice types (*fachs*) and corresponding character types, Catherine Clément considers the contralto a "voice from beyond the human world," the site of spiritual power associated with earth and sky, a hearing that seems provocative here.[70] Listening to Hall, I would say there is molasses in this sound, but that seems wrong somehow, too American, when the whole effect is trying to evoke something not-American, something tropical, an island shrouded in mist and mystery. Maybe the viscosity in her voice is more akin to the swirl of thick, dark ocean waters. And then the melody, for all its long tones, is full of octave jumps and chromatic dips. It's a melody that seems to come at you sideways, despite the directness of the octave leaps. A melody not to be trusted, obscured by spirals of woodwinds that eddy around its edges. This orientalist stereotype is borne out in the fact that, lyrically, in the process of singing about the allure of the island Bali Ha'i, the singer shiftily slips into the voice of the island itself, as a geographic formation becomes personified in her voice: "Here am I, your special island / Come to me, come to me." The slippage evokes another Vietnamese musical theatre character who embodies her "foreign" land musically, lyrically, and symbolically, and whose passions are mobilized as fanatical maternal devotion to her child via unswerving loyalty to a white American officer. Of Kim in *Miss Saigon* (1991), Karen Shimakawa writes, "Kim does not merely embody Vietnam-eseness or even Vietnamese femaleness—she *is* Vietnam."[71] In *South Pacific*, "Bali Ha'i" constitutes a seduction that Hall-as-Mary is performing on behalf of the island, and, within the context of the musical play, on behalf of her daughter who resides on the island, whom she has picked out as the chosen mate of the white American naval officer to whom she sings. Neither the island (perhaps not surprisingly) nor her daughter Liat (surprisingly, even appallingly) ever utters a sound in the musical. Both are ventriloquized through Bloody Mary in this song. At times, such as at song's end, Hall's voice glides out of its speech register sound into a lighter, softer quality, almost melting from presence, fading from view ("Bali Ha'i, Bali Ha'i").

New York Times critic Brooks Atkinson does not fail to single out Hall for praise in his review of Rodgers and Hammerstein's new musical, and yet the terms on which he does so are stark and revealing: "Since 'South Pacific' is not an assembled show, but a thoroughly composed musical drama, you will find high standards of characterization and acting throughout. Take Juanita Hall, for example. She plays a brassy, greedy, ugly Tonkonese [*sic*] woman with harsh, vigorous, authentic accuracy; and she sings one of Mr. Rodgers' finest songs, 'Bali Ha'i' with rousing artistry."[72]

Ultimately it is the musical play that is heralded, for its "high standards" as elite entertainment, and Hall's "artistry" consists of the fact that she does justice to "one of Mr. Rodgers' finest songs." Atkinson was not the only newspaper writer of his time to comment on the supposed authenticity of Hall's performance as "ugly" Asian woman. Hall herself related to interviewers the impact of the crude ethnographic research she undertook in preparation for the part.

> Professional or otherwise, audiences are constantly astonished by the complete mastery of mannerisms Juanita acquired to play this unusual character. The first time she read the stories, she rejected Mary as a real horror. On re-reading, she concluded the character was an invincible mother and a real person, and a role well worth playing.
>
> Then she began studying Orientals, using as her first model her Chinese laundryman. "They are perfectly relaxed people," she says, "and if they don't want you to get at them, you don't. . . . The Chinese use a hiss to show surprise," she continues, "and the women never cry but give an embarrassed laugh when their dignity is gone. I wanted to play the part so no Orien-

tal would think I was embarrassing his race. Chin Yu, a girl in the show, helped me with these customs. She is teaching me to use chopsticks, but I can't get enough to eat."[73]

Clearly Hall embraced stereotypical information about the Asian American character she embodied—uncomfortable, imperialist generalizations about how all "Orientals" and "the Chinese" behave en masse, and clearly vying for laughs in bemoaning her failures with the strange mechanism—and, the joke implies, supposed inefficiency—of chopsticks. At the same time, the perspective attributed to Hall that her character could emerge as "an invincible mother and a real person" offers the possibility that she approached the racist role with some degree of warmth and humanity. These contradictions—the uncomfortable racial typing and the attempt at a redemptive, compassionate effort on the part of the singer-actress—are knit together in Hall's contention that, "I wanted to play the part so no Oriental would think I was embarrassing his race." Black folks of Hall's time certainly knew what it was for one's race to be embarrassed and misrepresented, as the Lena Horne-led conversations around *St. Louis Woman* serve as just one example. Hall's statement indicates that she knew she carried a responsibility for the racial representation she was undertaking and had some sense at least of the stakes.

Juanita Hall's identification with the part of Bloody Mary did not end with the Broadway stage production of *South Pacific*. In 1958 she reprised the role in the movie musical version, filmed in Hawaii.[74] Yet, by this point at least one listener considered her singing to have changed, and composer Richard Rodgers insisted that her signature song, "Bali Ha'i" be dubbed by Muriel Smith, who had performed the role (again, in high yellowface, as has become the expected way to cast the role of Bloody Mary) in the London production. As director Joshua Logan recalled, "Juanita Hall had her own style of singing and it seemed a shame to miss its special quality in our picture. Still . . . in spite of my misgivings, I was forced to say okay."[75] In listening to the outtake recording of Hall's performance of "Bali Ha'i" that was not used for the film, the main thing I notice is that the texture of her voice is a bit choppier than before. She sounds comparable in the opening section, even warmer than in the original cast recording. But as the song continues, the hard edges between the different qualities of her voice—the classical, airborne sound and the dramatic alto from the nightclub scene—seem to emerge more sharply than before. The different colors of her voice are chipping away, chipping into one another. Her pitch seems slightly unstable, especially at the ends of phrases. But then her voice, even in the earlier rendition, always had that sense of being a little on the edge, between being shouted and crooned, the shout taken up high to its edge and covered over with wave of vibrato. Overall, I wonder if what I am hearing is the classically trained singer who has found success in singing a register that was not quite her own to begin with and found her way there by a means that has left things a little rough around the edges. In correspondence with Eugene Thamon Simpson, classically trained singer, pianist, voice teacher and biographer of Hall Johnson, about Juanita Hall, he observed that in his own experience, "typically, classical singers who migrate to Broadway suffer vocal change from the style of singing required and the 8 performances per week."[76] Then, too, what is to be made of the classical singer who comes to Broadway, sings eight shows a week, and follows this up with a full schedule singing blues in Greenwich Village nightclubs? It seems to me that a voice would have to be almost superhuman to endure such a schedule and emerge unchanged.

Lessons with Juanita Hall's Grandmother

The rough-around-the-edges aspect of Hall's voice nearly a decade after she first took the stage as Bloody Mary calls to mind Richard Middleton's hearing of the "tightened throat" in rock music, discussed in chapter 4, seeming to imbue the sound with a certain kind of unvarnished honesty.[77] This is a quality that, if it has less currency in the world of Richard Rodgers' Broadway musical drama with classical aspirations, certainly plays well in the nightclub scene. Reviews from this era of Hall's performances singing blues show clearly the different set of standards according to which her voice was also being judged beyond the domains of Broadway and Hollywood musicals:

> Singer opens with a trio of pop numbers, and her Juilliard and Broadway backgrounds never get in the way. She has a true, resonant set of pipes and sends over a lyric with solid artistry, tallying particularly with the ballad "How Deep is the Ocean."[78]
>
> Miss Hall is an unusual song stylist who registers most effectively on special material numbers. Her workover of a ballad such as "How Deep is the Ocean" is also impressive but her heavy vibrato is too pronounced. She scores strongly on a couple of blues numbers.[79]

In the performance space of the nightclub, a singer's classical and Broadway backgrounds, lumped together, are—in the best of scenarios—something to be overcome. Jazz critic Leonard Feather, who wrote the liner notes to Hall's 1958 record *Juanita Hall—The Original Bloody Mary—Sings the Blues*, enthused about her vocal talents, while also admitting his initial surprise on learning that Hall could creditably sing the blues.[80] The same year, Hall gave an interview to the *New York Herald-Tribune* at her Fifth Avenue apartment after the *South Pacific* film adaptation was released. She wore a mu-mu she had brought from shooting the film in Hawaii and coolly interposed, "I don't know just why they're shocked when they learn that I can do other roles besides Bloody Mary. . . . Leonard Feather said, 'I didn't know you could do this,' when he heard me singing the blues one night. I told him, 'Nobody gave me a chance.'"[81]

Feather's liner notes map the way that conversations with Hall revealed for him the fact that a blues sensibility had been, as he terms it, "latent" during her time on the musical theatre stage. What follows is quite a different narration of Hall's musical development from the one I've outlined here, a coming into her own that is marked not with the glamour of a hit on the Great White Way but in a conversation with a black male music director on her first Broadway musical. Feather writes: "Not until around 1945, when she was in *St. Louis Woman* on Broadway, did the question of singing with a beat begin to bother her. Asking conductor Luther Henderson what she should do about it, she was flattered to be told that she already had the beat and might as well stop worrying about it."[82]

In powerful contrast to this masculinist assessment, Hall offers a different origin story in her typical straightforward style. Her words emerge as guidance to hear her voice and the sounds it carries as based in lessons from her grandmother: "My grandmother was the cause of it all. My home town was Keyport, N.J. and I was raised by my grandmother who always made me get up and recite and sing. She gave me that certain sense of rhythm, and I've been supposing ever since that the whole world is based on rhythm. Without rhythm, there's nothing very important in life."[83]

On *Juanita Hall—The Original Bloody Mary—Sings the Blues,* with a sextet of musicians led by Coleman Hawkins on tenor saxophone and Doc Cheatham on trumpet, Hall sings several songs recorded by Bessie Smith, including "Baby Won't You Please Come Home," "Downhearted Blues," and "Gimme a Pigfoot." It is a performance that, according to Feather, the presumptive authority, "evokes the gaudy, rowdy, rugged colors of the blues era." The liner notes also feature a prominent quote from Hall, with the respectful statement, "In singing these songs, I have tried to keep the authenticity and flavor of the real folk blues, and in no way do I claim to imitate Bessie Smith." A few years prior to the record's release, Hall had taken the stage in a revival of *Cabin in the Sky* at Sea Cliff Summer Theatre in Long Island, in the role originated by Ethel Waters. In 1966, just two years before her passing, Hall's nightclub repertoire included tributes to Bessie Smith, Billie Holiday, Dinah Washington, "and even 'Am I Blue,' which has practically been copyrighted by Ethel Waters, and which Miss Hall sings as a salute to that great lady, also."[84] Listening to her statements and her vocal performance in counterpoint enables a hearing of Juanita Hall as a midcentury Broadway singer whose classical and blues voices chipped into each other, cracked at the edges, refusing to present as the stable, pure voice in either one or the other form. Taking seriously what she has to say about her voice—irredeemable performances in high yellowface notwithstanding—enables a hearing of Hall's vocal sound according to her own directives: as both soprano and alto, as bearing musical gifts bequeathed by an encouraging grandmother, and borne out via nightclub repertoire that manifests as singing along, respectfully, with artists including Ethel Waters and Bessie Smith. And also, don't be shocked "that I can do other roles besides Bloody Mary." But where Hall's voice was characterized by its multivocal articulations of wide-ranging racial and musical types, Pearl Bailey, the big-voiced character diva who appeared alongside Hall in 1946 in *St. Louis Woman*, found one expressive mode that worked for her and sustained it throughout her career across performances at nightclubs, on television, and on Broadway.

Pearl Bailey
Singing Along with Waters, Tucker, and Channing

In February 1955, on an episode of the hit television game show <u>What's My Line?</u> a tall black woman enters the frame, smartly dressed, and signs her name on a chalkboard in sweeping script for the benefit of viewers: *Pearl Bailey*.[85] She wears a tailored two-piece ensemble, jacket with a wide collar and plunging neckline, three-quarter length sleeves, and a full skirt. There are pearls at her neck; large earrings dangle on either side of her face. She has an elegant bracelet on her wrist, and a flat, wide-brimmed hat set stylishly atop her head. Bailey is a "mystery celebrity" on this episode, soon seated next to host John Charles Daly while four blindfolded panelists ask her questions and try, from the answers, to divine her identity. Apart from Bailey, all on the show are white. Asked if she would be considered a leading lady, Bailey gives a tiny, smothered laugh and demurs. Daly answers readily on her behalf, "Actually, I would think, in the broad category of leading players, we would have to say a big, resounding Yes." In responding to the panelists' questions, Bailey pitches her voice high, emitting a falsetto sound that is almost like a child's voice—a very small sound. She keeps her answers short. Throughout, she clutches at her throat and silently makes faces at Daly to show how much effort it takes to make her voice come out in this particular state, and Daly looks away, trying to keep from laughing aloud so as not to give her away to the blindfolded contestants. One panelist, Arlene Francis, perceptively asks, "Are you having a little trouble disguising your voice?" The audience laughs while Bailey just smiles a pursed-lip half-smile, tilts her head, wide-brimmed hat and all, and adjusts her dress as if she knows she is done for. Francis hones in and soon determines that this mystery celebrity is currently appearing in the lavish musical *House of Flowers* on Broadway, for which this panelist has only glowing words. What a "beautiful commercial" this is, Bailey peeps out, comically, in her tiny voice. Francis deduces that the mystery celebrity is Pearl Bailey, star of stage, screen, and the nightclub world. Removing her blindfold, she asserts, "You can't disguise that voice, I'm sorry." For her part, Bailey sighs, shaking her head good-humoredly, and answers in her usual tone, several octaves lower, "I knew it was useless." And yet when she appears on the show a decade later, she tries the same tiny-voiced tactic.[86] The panelists wrack their brains, "Since you're saving your voice, is it that you usually sing? . . . Well, now, let me think. Who sings that softly?" The studio audience roars, and the questions pivot: "Who's the biggest-voiced singer I know? Ethel Merman. Are you Ethel Merman?" It is determined that she is not. And yet, Bailey is a singer in a time when to be a Broadway singer with a big voice necessarily meant falling in the shadow of Merman.

A tremendous star in her own time, if often forgotten today, Pearl Bailey was born in 1918—that is, seventeen years after Juanita Hall—in Newport News, Virginia. She spent her early years in Washington, DC, where her father was a reverend at the sanctified House of Prayer church, a shouting congregation where churchgoers regularly "got happy" with the power of the Holy Spirit. There she learned early that shouting could be a money-making enterprise, later recalling wryly: "When the older folks shouted, sometimes their money would fall out of their pockets; that was the children's cue. We got extremely happy, started to shout, fell under the Power but on top of the money."[87] While Bailey was quite young, her parents separated and her mother moved to Philadelphia where Pearl's older brother Willie soon had a job in show business as a tap dancer. One night, teenage Pearlie Mae performed in the Amateur Night talent competition at Willie's theatre and, to her surprise, won the show with her singing and dancing. She was offered a contract that led to a series of short-term bookings, more Amateur Nights, and then, what seemed like the big time—the chance to be a nightclub performer in the then-booming coal mining town of Pottsville, Pennsylvania. This was not, however, the most refined of entertainment venues.

> There were four or five singers and dancers, a comedian, and an M. C. Each performer would take his turn, and in between the girl singers did "ups." "Ups" meant going from table to table singing the same song. Sometimes the customers put money on the table and you took it off. No! my sweet, not with your hands but with your thighs. You pulled up your dress to a certain height and grabbed the money off the corner of the table.[88]

After the coal-mining circuit, Bailey played the Savoy Ballroom and the Apollo Theatre in Harlem with Edgar Hayes's band, and then toured with the Sunset Royal Band, Cootie Williams and His Orchestra, and in 1944 was booked as a solo act at the Village Vanguard in New York. Her big break came soon after, when bandleader Cab Calloway picked her as the last-minute replacement for Sister Rosetta Tharpe in a national tour with his celebrated band. Following that engagement, she secured her Broadway debut, in the musical *St. Louis Woman* as the zingy barmaid Butterfly, for which she won the Donaldson Award (a precursor to the Tony Awards) for best newcomer to Broadway. The *New York Times* attested, "A young lady named Pearl Bailey can sing a song so that it stays quite sung; although she is not imitating, her style is roughly on the order of Ethel Waters."[89] Bailey's six Broadway shows include *House of Flowers* (1954), Irving Berlin's *Call Me Madam* (1966), and the all-black revival of *Hello, Dolly!*—she starred in this last both in 1967–1970 and again in 1975, and it was surely the catalyst for the Special Tony Award she received in 1968.[90] With multiple appearances on television and film (she shares with Diahann Carroll the Hollywood credits *Carmen Jones* and *Porgy and Bess*) and in nightclubs across the country, Bailey was also invited to perform for presidents, served as the special ambassador to the United Nations, recorded more than thirty records, wrote six books, and earned her bachelor's degree from Georgetown University at age sixty-seven. By her own estimation, she was an entertainer before a vocalist: "When I'm called a great 'singer' I always disagree. I think of myself as telling stories to music, in tune, and the words become very important. That I love. And it doesn't hurt if you've lived a bit too."[91] In a 1965 publicity photo (figure 2.3), Bailey strikes a dramatic pose, her upper body in profile in a backless gown and her face turned toward the camera as if she has just been caught by surprise. Eyebrows arched, her direct expression is full of flash, confidence, and verve—with no trace of conciliatory smiles or beaten-down weariness.

Where Juanita Hall's choir sang backup for Bessie Smith, Bailey was the recipient of career advice from another star of the blues era, Sophie Tucker. In 1948 the two met for the first time, when Bailey sought out Tucker while both were performing in London, and they remained friendly thereafter. Bailey greatly respected the artist she termed "Lady Tucker," who was thirty years her senior. On one occasion after Bailey had performed at a nightclub in Las Vegas, Tucker, who was in the audience, sent for Bailey to join her at her table, where black people were not generally permitted to enter. As Bailey put it, "It was such a laugh. . . . Though you had worked the club, you were not welcomed as a guest in the main room."[92] But management couldn't refuse Tucker's request and, escorted by three men, Bailey came to sit and chat with the senior star.

> We had a nice long talk. . . . By now I had some jewelry, so I asked her if I had on too much for the stage. She said, "No, honey, if you got it, wear it." I said, "What if folks say I'm getting too fancy? 'I knew you when . . .'" She replied with a hearty laugh. "Tell them it ain't what it was; it's what it *is*. . . . Miss Tucker said, "If you can hold the fort and last long enough, they're going to need you. It ain't how good you are, it's how long you can last."[93]

Bailey herself "lasted" quite a long time in show business (and repeated this anecdote in multiple interviews), her performance career extending more than five decades. Similar to Juanita Hall, whose breakout role in *South Pacific* arrived when the singer was forty-eight years of age, Bailey did not perform her landmark Broadway role, the title character in *Hello, Dolly!* until she was fifty. The all-black cast version of *Hello, Dolly!* opened on Broadway a scant few years after Carol Channing originated the role of Dolly Levi in the show on Broadway in 1964.

The specific performances of race and voice that Carol Channing contributed to midcentury Broadway merit at least brief mention. Channing abruptly found out as a teenager that her fair-skinned African American

2.3 Pearl Bailey in a 1965 publicity photo, via Getty Images.

father had been passing for white throughout her whole life. In her auto-biography, she relates:

> When I was sixteen years old, packing for leaving home alone for the first time to go to Bennington College, my mother announced to me I was part Negro. "I'm only telling you this," she said, "because the Darwinian law shows that you could easily have a black baby." Anyway, she went on to say that that was why my eyes were bigger than hers (I wasn't aware of this) and why I danced with such elasticity and why I had so many of the qualities that made me me.[94]

Channing also recalls learning from her father what she thought were hymns but later realized were actually gospel songs that most well-brought-up white girls did not know how to sing. Here we have a real-life answer to the tragic mixed-race woman of *Show Boat*, in a plot that also turns on who is expected to know, or not know, certain kinds of songs. With her trade-mark mix of wide-eyed obliviousness (see figure 2.4), Channing quips, "I thought every father had two accents. I was surprised to find out how one-cylindered other people's fathers were."[95] Both Carol Channing and Pearl Bailey sustained long careers on the nightclub circuit on television, which, as I will discuss, contributed to a certain breeziness of stage presence, comic timing, and ethos of familiar intimacy with the audiences that served a role like Dolly well.

At the 1968 Tony Awards, the first time the definitive award ceremony of the Broadway theatre was ever televised, the cast of the hit, all-black production of *Hello, Dolly!* takes the stage to perform a montage of two numbers, after having been introduced enthusiastically by Channing.[96] When the chorus exits on the musical playoff after their number, the train set piece rolls off upstage, emitting a puff of "steam" from its smokestack. Behind it, by a scenery flat of a train station, is revealed Pearl Bailey sitting upright atop a pile of luggage. In a blue dress and white blouse with turn-of-the-century puffed sleeves, her hands are folded demurely in her lap as the audience applauds and applauds. She hasn't done a thing but already they can't get enough of her. She raises a hand and the orchestra insinuates a chord. With an introductory string of sung "Goodbyes" as she waves a languid hand, she is off and running. The orchestra picks up in tempo and she climbs down, unhurried, from her perch on a steamer trunk to claim center stage. This is not a blues, it's an uptempo show tune by songwriter Jerry Herman, but despite having been written in the 1960s (for a story set in the 1900s), it has a similar premise to many classic blues, that of waving

2.4 Carol Channing in a 1965 performance. Courtesy of the Billy Rose Theatre Division, New York Public Library for the Performing Arts.

off a no-good man. "Wave your little hand and whisper so long, dearie, / Dearie, should have said 'So long!' so long ago!" And in Bailey's vocal texture I hear much of the blueswomen, in the throaty alto shout, the bare shimmer of vibrato, the words thrown away at the ends of phrases, the strategic addition of growl ("Oh, you treated me so rotten and rough"). Bailey is a class act, with a sense of elegance and restraint, but she also throws in a couple of well-placed hip bumps that evoke the burlesque—perhaps moves she picked up in her Pottsville days—and bring ripples of laughter from the audience.

When I watch and listen to Pearl Bailey, I am not inclined to talk about her raw voice as an instrument, I want to talk about her whole presence, that twinkle in her eye, that half-smile ready to overflow into a laugh at any moment, the line she walks between the classy and the down-to-earth. She moves beautifully. Midway through the number on the Tonys she picks up a hat and cane and gives some old-school Broadway realness. This is what when I worked as a singer-actor we used to call "star dancing," because she's holding the stage and giving some moves without kicking up her heels or ever really breaking a sweat. A star only has to dance a little bit in order to be adored, to show she's not above it, to show that she can dance at all in addition to hitting money notes, that she can cut loose a little. Yes, Bailey has a big voice, but it seems to me that many of the colors to the voice are in her movements, and in her timing. Her comic timing is impeccable, and she lands a spoken aside in the middle of the song with ease: "And on those cold winter nights, Horace" [Strides away and then turns back dramatically], "Snuggle up to your old cash register." [Sashays on and then shifts and plants the cane emphatically.] "It's a little lumpy, but it rings." [Gives a split second, open-mouthed grin to the audience, eyebrows raised, as if even she is surprised at how funny she is. Big laugh.] Bailey is a statuesque black woman who by this time in her career has switched from a character diva to a leading lady but remains a far cry from the weary-bluesy mammy type. To really hear her sing, it occurs to me, you have to see the quick gestures of her eyes, up, to the side, the tilt of the head. It's not eye-rolling but more a precise choreography of the performer's gaze. She looks so comfortable onstage it's as though she were a plant that sprang from the wooden floorboards, utterly in her natural habitat. She oozes star quality. At the number's close, she forgoes the Mermanesque long held note in favor of a tossed away half-spoken lyric "So long!" and a series of quick steps and cane-twirling dance moves across the length of the stage. She ends with her arms spread wide as, still in character, she shouts a few unintelligible words directed at the absent no-good man over the breaking wave of applause. The camera pans briefly across the audience. It's a sea of white faces, men and women in black-tie attire, clapping wildly.

Mumbled Asides: A Performance for the Self

Across her extensive career in nightclubs and television in particular, Bailey was known as, if not a comedienne, at least a humorist as much as a charismatic singer and entertainer. In the 1960s, Broadway overall began to make more space for musicals that placed a showstopping leading lady in the spotlight, as Stacy Wolf has analyzed in her schema of the "Single Girl" musicals.[97] This was a trend that not only gave center stage to youthful characters like Sally Bowles in *Cabaret* (1966) and Charity Hope Valentine in *Sweet Charity* (1966), but also to fabulously independent, quirky leading ladies of midlife in *Hello, Dolly!* and *Mame* (1966). Kelly Kessler notes the way that a background in nightclub work served both Bailey and Channing well in their television variety work, charismatic performances that translated on Broadway into roles of this kind, also described by Ethan Mordden as "big lady" shows. Kessler writes:

> Both Channing and Bailey had been regulars in Vegas and other nightclubs alongside their theatrical work. In the late 1950s Channing appeared at the Dunes with George Burns and later took her act to the Riviera, whereas Bailey signed a three-year, twenty-four date, $360,000 contract with the Flamingo in 1958. The type of interactive repartee the two women parlayed into successful club acts served them nicely as both big ladies and variety hostesses. These big ladies carried the show, *their show*, in the palm of their hands.[98]

The thought of snappy stage banter effused by a skilled nightclub performer calls to mind comments made, for example, in between numbers in a set. But Bailey's reputation as a humorist has much to do with the hilarious spoken asides through which she drawls *during* many of her numbers, in between sections of singing. In the midst of one of her best-known songs, "Tired," for example, after singing a set of lyrics about all the things that exhaust her, including (black) women's work of "washing and a-tubbing / cleaning and a-scrubbing . . . a-mending and a-mopping / a-starching and a-shopping" as well as a man who doesn't treat her right, she launches into a long stretch of spoken text while the orchestra takes a chorus.

I guess by now, brother, you have the general idea. I am tired. There's no need in me kidding myself, "Maybe you're all right, but—" I'm just tired. Think I'll go to a psychiatrist, one of them rich people doctors, you know? And I guess he'll tell me a lot of big words all about "psychiatrics" and metaphysics and, oh, a whole lot of stuff I don't understand. Wonder how much he'll charge me for that? Whatever he charges he'll probably end up saying the same thing, "Pearl, you're just tired." I . . . I guess I better go to a plain doctor, so he can tell me what I need. In fact, I know what I need, I need a little change—[99]

And smoothly she is right back into the sung lyric. She always seems certain of exactly where she is in the tune, carefully tracking the passage of time in the instrumental music that underscores her speaking, but without calling attention to doing so. What makes the aside sparkle so much is that it really does feel like she's making it up on the spot, her delivery is that conversational, the pauses, stops and starts of everyday speech. You feel like she's confiding in you. Yet contrary to the assumptions of many audience members, these comments are not purely improvised, but in fact carefully and thoughtfully prepared.[100] Bailey also had zero patience for journalists who rendered her words in dialect, interviews that quoted her as saying not "the manager" but "de manager," and so on. "I'm not the lord of all the English language," Bailey comments, "and I use my hands for words sometimes, but I certainly do not talk in dialect"; I note this because it is important to recognize that those who would hear her comic, mumbled asides as bumbling dialect should rather, she directs, "listen better."[101] In this way, although the song positions her as being tired, she differentiates herself from a singer caught in the type of the weary-bluesy mammy—let alone the high yellowface performer whose exoticized Asianness is couched in imagined black dialect penned by a white lyricist.

Bailey carried this aspect of her performance to Broadway with her in *Hello, Dolly!*, in a turn that was, as reviewers commented, essentially an extension of her nightclub persona: "Miss Bailey settles into her Dolly characterization with complete ease, using her own gestures, inflections and phrases to bolster it."[102] This 1967 production, in which Bailey starred opposite her old friend Cab Calloway, was an all-black rendition of the hit musical scored by Jerry Herman that had appeared on Broadway starring Carol Channing only three years prior. Initially, opinion was divided as to whether this kind of casting was a regressive approach, an outdated throwback to the segregationist politics of yesteryear. The show was such a hit, however, that such critiques largely subsided, producer David Merrick was heralded for his brilliant showmanship and critic Clive Barnes, so overwhelmed with the high level of talent on display, raved in his *New York Times* review that "Maybe Black Power is what some of the other musicals need."[103] Yet, as *Ebony* magazine reported, not all in the cast shared his view: "Among the performers themselves, viewpoints differ. Pearl Bailey does not want the racial angle played up and refuses to discuss the issue."[104] After running for three years and touring nationally, yet another production was mounted in 1975, again helmed by Bailey, but this time with an integrated cast. This production was less well-received. In summarizing the critical and audience response, Angela C. Pao assesses that Bailey's persona had grown to "overshadow" the role of Dolly she was ostensibly playing. "Apparently, the ad-libbing and direct audience engagement, which had been lightly sprinkled through each performance in the 1960s, had now evolved into a more pronounced breaking of character."[105] For some, Bailey's asides were symptomatic of a highly unprofessional production; for others, they were the highlight in an otherwise lackluster production, the best thing in the show.

Perhaps the most surprising thing about Bailey's understated asides is the audience for whom she asserts she is actually performing when she utters them:

> Reviewers say I have a clever way of delivering asides (mumbling words). Well, it's one of my trademarks. I'm amused that no one has ever reasoned why. (Maybe they don't care, Pearl.) People yell to me sometimes, "We didn't hear you." I answer, "When I say something worthwhile, you'll definitely hear it. *The reason I mumble, friend, is that I'm not talking to anyone but me.*" The question-and-answer game inside—"Should I or shouldn't I?"—makes me come up with those things you think are ad libs.[106]

Bailey's quiet insistence on protecting the (not merely) subvocalized voice puts me in mind of writing by Elena Elías Krell that points up the stakes around which internal voices are or are not audible to others. Krell theorizes "the performance of being oneself as a matter of internal listening," in writing about transmasculine musicians who recognize the manifestation, post-T, of the subvocalized voice now made audible.[107] This understanding of the subvocalized voice, the voice one has always heard in one's head, aligns with Jacques Derrida's notion of voice as vital to self-presence: "the voice is the being which is present to itself . . . the voice *is* consciousness."[108] Where Derrida might reduce voice to meaning, Mladen

Dolar and Adriana Cavarero have instructed that the sound of the voice itself must be accounted for, beyond the symbolic or the logocentric. The subvocalized voice Krell invokes is generative for me in writing about vocal sound because it is the *sound* of the voice heard inside the head—not the thought formulated inside the head, but vocal sound itself in the process of being thought. What is radical about Pearl Bailey's claiming her asides as a performance *for the self* is that they posit a black woman for whom the most important aspect of vocal performance is hearing the sound of her own flow of thoughts. The most celebrated aspect of her voice is not shaped by the demands of the audience; regardless of the audience's expectations for how Bailey should perform her gendered and racial identity, here is a singer who has the audacity to voice her own thoughts while performing for others. And yet this audacity goes largely undetected—the audience assumes these comments are for *them* ("We didn't hear you," they yell). Bailey refuses to keep her thoughts and musings subvocalized—she brings them into vocal sound as interruptions heard aloud in the flow of song. It is the very fact of their sound, particularly when just loud enough for her to hear but not loud enough for the audience to understand, that produces satisfaction for her while not necessarily for other listeners. Here is a black woman who attends, first and foremost, not to the needs of others but to her own. *"The reason I mumble, friend, is that I'm not talking to anyone but me."*

Claiming the Character Diva

I claim the artists studied here as character actresses who attained, and in fact demanded, the status of divadom. It is notable that the roles in which black women first earned widespread acclaim on the Broadway stage were those of the character actress—the comic, quirky, feisty secondary lead. This casting category stands at some remove from that of the leading lady, a category Lena Horne exemplified from her successes onscreen even if the Hollywood industry practices long deposited her into the "character actress" bucket. As film historian Pamela Wojcik has documented regarding Hollywood's casting types dating from 1928, "race and ethnicity figure heavily in the category of 'character' roles, which seems to refer back to the categories of light comedy and eccentric business and generally includes actors who play distinct ethnic types, roles in uniform or other elaborate costumes, and roles in heavy make-up."[109]

The notion of a character diva is perhaps a contradiction in terms—containing something not unlike the tensions that, as chapter 3 will address, inhere in the notion of a black Broadway ingénue. A character actress is thought to be a bit to the side, a performer in a supporting role who cannot fully claim the center stage sparkle that exudes from a show's main star. Nonetheless, I find the term *diva* generative because of the ways that black character actresses like Bailey and Hall—and yes, even Horne, if she is deposited in this category—insist on being heard on their own terms. I engage the word diva separate from its contexts in the worlds of opera and contemporary pop music, in a way that is more closely aligned with the work of Deborah Vargas, for whom it is useful distinct from nuances of camp and the uncomplimentary application to overdramatic women of color. For Vargas and for me, the word diva is useful "to acknowledge the creative strategies too often misread or misrecognized that draw upon . . . racialized gender epistemologies for cultivating representations and cultural productions."[110] The diva insists on having a say about how she should be heard. When you are listening to us, these singers teach, you must "listen better."

Conclusions

I wish I could say that the casting type of the weary-bluesy mammy is located squarely in the past. But black singer-actors today are still called upon to perform—and wildly applauded by predominantly white audiences for such performances—vocal roles showcasing virtuosic displays of suffering. In the preprofessional realm, educators would do well to think twice before asking young black musical theatre singer-actresses to don a head kerchief and sing uncritical tributes to Waters that reify this problematic type, making no provision for the ways that songs like "Supper Time" were personally difficult for Waters and may be similarly wrenching for performers today. The work of this chapter further reveals how certain, widely accepted vocal types on the musical stage such as "torch singer" can have vastly different forms and implications for performers of different races. Indeed, the ways that race, voice, and affect play out in gendered character types for musical theatre have implications beyond what I address here, constituting an area for fruitful further study. And, in considering how black women on the musical stage impact the arc of US musical theatre history, Hurston's *Polk County*, unproduced in her lifetime, offers a meaningful cautionary note. The power that the "negro folk opera" has held in the white imagination as the pinnacle of black expression on the US musical stage has surely foreclosed opportunities for other possible expressions to come forward. A work like *Polk County*, were it as well-known in its time as *Show Boat* and *Porgy and Bess*, could have done much to combat the pervasiveness of the weary-bluesy mammy type and create musical-theatrical space for celebrating black female friendship and the singing of blues music.

Where chapter 1 of *Blues Mamas and Broadway Belters* traced lessons given and sounds cited by blueswomen, shouters, and belters, in this chapter I have attended to the ways that black women singers on Broadway navigated the imperative to perform the type of the weary-bluesy mammy and, in the case of Hurston, Hall, and Bailey, gave alternate directives for how their voices should be heard. Not all of these performances can be neatly classified as redemptive or empowered in simplistic terms. Yet part of the discipline of listening to black women singers and of striving, as Pearl Bailey directs, to "listen better" means being able to celebrate such singers' artistry and technique without having to justify them as being exemplary or magical Negroes. I have tried to listen to these singers' directives and their voices without insisting that they earn an honored place in history by voicing particular kinds of politics.

Broadway is commercial entertainment—hardly the avant-garde—and not known for inciting revolution, regardless of how many banners may be waved or military waistcoats paraded on its stages in recent years. In the midtwentieth century, as the United States was moving from the era of Jim Crow segregation toward dreams of civil rights liberation, musicals distinctly lagged behind the times. And yet given the abject history of "coon shouters" and weary-bluesy mammies, a particular expression of the radical took shape—as I unfold in the following chapter—in the sounds of singers belting out new terms for glamorous, young black womanhood on the Great White Way.

3 "A Little Singer on Broadway"

Exercising American Glamour with
Golden-Age Starlets

Critical Duets in the Girlish Art of Yearning

The middle of the twentieth century brought hard-won space and widespread acclaim for black women singers performing as stylish black ingénues and sex kittens in ways heretofore unimaginable on the Great White Way. This chapter addresses how black musical theatre singers and their contemporaries voiced the young, glamorous American girl for the Broadway stage in the 1950s and 1960s. The voice of girlhood, Gayle Wald has posited, can be understood as "the art of yearning," yielding singing that is "tethered to a set of presumptions about what girlhood can or cannot be, what girls can and cannot want, and *how* or *how not* girls can want."[1] Wald is writing about girls' voices in popular music more broadly, but the description aptly conjures the young heroines of musical theatre, a genre littered with starry-eyed, wishful "I Want" songs. I am interested in how this art of yearning played out for black girls and young women on the midcentury musical stage, those who when judged by white America's standards for beauty and femininity were often found wanting—and who frequently found that they themselves were unwanted in rehearsal rooms, afterparties, and subsequent seasons at the theatre. Attending to the voices of young black stars on the Broadway stage of this time disrupts conventional narratives about who belts out hopeful, youthful show tunes and foregrounds a set of contours along which singers of any background may follow in their vocal example today. My approach draws inspiration from the sonic and dramaturgical telescoping enabled by musical theatre song as well as from the fragmentary texture of exercises for voice practice. The chapter is structured as a series of critical duets intercut with a collection of vocal exercises inspired by the singer-actresses included here. In differing terms from the notion of *singing along with* that is developed in chapter 4, these critical duets function as comparative and contrapuntal means to listen to two singers through and against each other.

I contend that the figure of the dazzling Lena Horne exerts a distanced but powerful force on the vocal formations and cultural legibility of the Broadway singers performing young black womanhood in this era.[2] This has much to do with the fact that Horne herself was almost entirely absent from the Broadway stage as a young black starlet; the reasons for this absence—both her refusals and her being refused—speak volumes about the singer's lived experience of unforgiving expectations for black girlhood under segregation. Despite the loneliness she later admitted feeling as a pathfinding black musical starlet in the 1930s and 1940s, as I hear her Horne sings in an overarching series of duets with all the other black women for whom she prepared the way—studied in this chapter are Diahann Carroll, Leslie Uggams, and Eartha Kitt. In a more discrete critical duet, I also listen to Horne's voice and career reverberating through and against that of her Jim Crow-era contemporary, the tomboyish white ingénue and Broadway headliner Mary Martin. A second critical duet features Diahann Carroll and Leslie Uggams, ingénues who in the 1960s became the first two black recipients of the Tony Award for Best Leading Actress in a Musical. And a third duet with starlets Eartha Kitt and Pat Suzuki foregrounds how access to the terms of national belonging were far from guaranteed for black and Asian American girls in the United States during World War II and the Cold War. Together, these duets call attention to how young Broadway belters of color at midcentury were conscripted—or refused conscription—to the project of extolling the virtues of Americanness in the voice of the glamour girl.[3]

Distinct from the statuesque vaudeville-blues singer, the weary-bluesy mammy, or the charismatic character diva who hits her stride late in life, the women of different races studied here navigated a complicated set of expectations around what it meant to be a charming young woman on Broadway. In what follows, I examine the contours and vocal means by which each of these women exercised girlish allure while sounding, as Diahann Carroll framed it, "like a little singer on Broadway."[4]

Vocal Exercises: Singing in Detail

Locating the voices of these youthful belters within a dynamic continuum of singers past and present requires tracing their biographies in terms of how they acquired their vocal training over time, via the singers, institutions, and constraints that shaped their sound, and the impact such studies had on the contexts in which they then performed. And it invites the question: *What do these artists have to teach today's singers about both vocal technique and expectations of racialized and gendered performance?* To formulate a response, I linger with details or gestures of sound and movement in the performances of the singers studied here and revoice these particularities as a set of "vocal exercises." In this way I engage directly with the voices of the women artists in this chapter to not only study these singers but also to study *with* them. By claiming Horne, Martin, Carroll, Uggams, Suzuki, and Kitt as my own teachers, I locate my voice, and those of the singers whom I coach, in the lineage of their vocal artistry and in relationship to their specific, lived social histories. With the vocal exercises gathered here, I find, in the Audre Lordean clinging of my voice to hers, of yours to mine, a means of stretching into pleasurable new possibilities for the exercise of vocal sound and racial politics.

A vocal exercise, however, need not be the regular intervals of a scale or arpeggiated chord on a set of vowels, nor the medically informed manipulation of palates, arytenoids, cartilages. Beyond narrow, European-derived definitions, a vocal exercise can be a single word or phrase spoken. An unfamiliar and unintelligible sound repeated back. A two-note melodic phrase, with syllables attached. A physical stretch or movement. And a vocal exercise can also be understood as a sung performance of imperfect unison, of adhering to the curves of another's voice, following in another singer's vocal slipstream. The figure of the vocal exercise I offer here fails to give guidance about secret, hidden dangers of "incorrect" technique; instead, these exercises are grounded in pleasure and shared experience.

My formulation of the vocal exercise also draws inspiration from Alexandra T. Vazquez and her injunction to the scholar to "listen in detail," proposing a vibrant method that engages popular music as experience rather than account.[5] Details evoke both the sense of too muchness, the possibility of "getting lost in the details" and also of the precious few, the impulse toward gathering together a sparse collection of details about Cuba disclosed by immigrant parents, for example. For Vazquez, a detail is often an interruption of sorts, something that gives pause, that "catches" the listener, a thing that both troubles notions of cohesive narrative and gestures to all the many details that are out of sight or out of hearing. This practice of invoking and lingering with musical details calls up for me the singer's practice of dwelling with vocal exercises. Like Vazquez's details, many of the vocal exercises I love give too much attention to things that are too small. They ask for overemotiveness and even childishness, abandon in service of precision.

I hope that you will sing along with at least some of the exercises included in this chapter. They serve to remind that the histories detailed below are not just intellectual narrations but are lived, received, negotiated, and carried *in the body*. The point is not for you to "take on" the body of any of the singers in this chapter nor even necessarily to "sound like" them. The exercises interspersed below are meaningful for me not as opportunities for us to compare and judge our voices and bodies in relation to others, but simply as opportunities to *be present in voice* in relation to the black women singers considered in this chapter. It is my hope that you, the singer-scholar, find this practice more generative and creatively rewarding than trying to tamp down or contort your expressivity to fit racialized and/or appropriative stylistic expectations. Instead, this practice allows for something like the sonic breakthrough of a Barthesian punctum. I invite you to experience what the vocal details collected here spark in your own sound, in the ever-evolving vastness of your own vocal-possible.

Lena Horne and Singing from the Double Bind

Although this chapter focuses on black girls and young women and their vocal expressions of youthfulness on the Broadway stage, truthfully this book has been about black girlhood all along. The idea of voice as the unfolding process of learning to sing necessitates an awareness that, throughout musical theatre history, black women singers did not simply arrive on the scene fully formed women artists. I am interested in how these singers grew up and what they learned about what it was possible to do with one's voice as they grew and sculpted their sounds. One thing a singing voice enabled for the performers studied across these chapters was the ability to earn a living. Again and again the tune is one of black girls who leveraged showbiz singing voices to secure financial well-being as they grew into adulthood. Barely turning the page on a childhood that included singing and dancing for coins on the streets of Chattanooga, Bessie Smith got her first vaudeville gig at age eighteen.[6] After being married off in the sixth grade, the teen Ethel Waters imitated vaudeville performers in the mirrors of New Jersey hotel rooms she cleaned before, by her own account, booking her first professional job on the vaudeville circuit at age seventeen.[7] And although my studies of Juanita Hall and Pearl Bailey focus primarily on how their singing revised expectations of mammified matronliness, they too entered the biz at young ages. At age fifteen, Bailey won an Amateur Night talent competition that led to her first contracted work as a performer.[8] Throughout her life, Hall repeated a story perhaps apocryphal only in part—of graduating from high school at fourteen and heading directly into work as a performer, "drawing on her slender savings" from earnings as a Broadway actress to pay for music lessons at Juilliard.[9] And Lena Horne was sixteen when, her mother and stepfather in dire financial straits, she left high school studies behind to work at the Cotton Club in Harlem. Initially hired as a chorus dancer, within a year she parlayed this into billing as a featured singer—in addition to dancing in the chorus five shows a day, seven days a week—with an attendant increase in pay.

As girl singers, these artists operated from within what LaKisha Simmons powerfully theorizes as the "double bind" of white supremacist restriction and the imperative to respectability that definitively shaped the lives of so many black girls in Jim Crow America.[10] A black feminist historian, Simmons eloquently reconstructs the experience of black girls growing up in segregated New Orleans; her conclusions are also meaningful for understanding the lived experience of black girls in other Southern cities at this time as well as their sister-peers in the Jim Crow North where legal enforcement of racial segregation began long before its enactment in the South. Lena Horne, who traveled across the country as a child in the 1920s trailing her itinerant actress mother and then in her early career performing with the orchestras of black bandleader Noble Sissle—Broadway songwriter of *Shuffle Along* (1921) fame—and white bandleader Charlie Barnet, knew well that the bitterness of discrimination was hardly contained south of the Mason-Dixon line.[11] Throughout the nation, this double bind required black girls to move cautiously through the world in order to avoid predatory white men and boys and preserve the chastity that middle-class black communities expected of them. Bear in mind that in a number of Southern states the law had long held that "it was impossible for white men to rape black women" because of white male lawmakers' certainty that by their tween years black girls were already promiscuous and oversexed, thus the question of consent was irrelevant.[12] And so the double bind of black girl-hood mandated living in relation to white supremacist beliefs that black girls and women were always, already sexually available objects for white men. At the same time it meant protecting a ladylike respectability that, despite being negated by white lawmakers, was deeply valued by upwardly striving black people. A major part of growing up as black girls in Jim Crow America was learning where one could safely exist within this complex geography. This was the case whether in the South navigating a maze of "whites only" signs and country roads terrorized by lynching parties, or in the North amid a sequence of dimly lit alleys and politely but firmly closed doors to opportunity. Simmons observes, "Geography influenced black girls' subjectivities, bodily comportment, and sense of place. . . . Black girls sometimes walked the city streets carefully, figuring out where they belonged."[13] In her first autobiography, Horne describes learning a new spatiality as a girl-child freshly arrived in Miami from New York: "At every turn, something or someone showed me that Negroes have 'their place' and white folks have 'their place' [and] if you're smart, you'll stay in your own place or you'll get in trouble."[14]

To study how the voices of mid-twentieth century black singer-actresses expressed girlhood on the musical stage, I find it necessary to address the ways that the double bind of black girlhood has also related to silences and performances of disguise or concealment. This approach augments the work of scholars such as Simmons and ethnographer Aimee Meredith Cox who have considered in spatial and choreographic terms the ways that black girls maneuvered around the constraint of racism in different time periods.[15] As Hazel Carby sharply asserts, "the institutionalized rape of black women has never been as powerful a symbol of black oppression as the spectacle of lynching."[16] In addition to the unequivocal devaluing of black women and the integrity of their lived experience, this reality has much to do with the silences that black women are encouraged or required to maintain. Writing on black women and sexual vulnerability, historian Darlene Clark Hine articulates this silence-keeping as a function of the "culture of dissemblance" that secures black women's safety. She specifies, "By dissemblance I mean the behavior and attitudes of Black women that created the appearance of openness and disclosure but actually shielded the truth of their inner lives and selves from their oppressors."[17] I extend this line of thinking by considering the sonic, vocal, and musical-theatrical implications of the double bind of black girlhood.

The vocal performances of Lena Horne call out to be understood via the spatial geography and the dissembling comportment of this double bind. Unlike Bessie Smith, who came of age performing vaudeville-blues in front of black audiences, Lena Horne performed in front of white audiences from the time she was sixteen and developed strategies to maintain psychic space to protect against the indignities expected of her. Horne and Pearl Bailey were born just one year apart, but the effusive nightclub-and-Broadway vocal mode mobilized by Pearl Bailey was markedly different from that of Horne. Yet although the younger Bailey provided white audiences with the sense of intimate access to her, as discussed in chapter 2, she too found ways to preserve the integrity of her own self-defined interiority. The appendix to this book includes an exercise ("Listen to Yourself") inspired by the virtuosic fluidity of Bailey's subvocalized voice. By comparison, Horne carefully renders her voice as one that if not literally silenced is affectively distanced, what Shane Vogel calls a symbolic "voice throwing." Vogel experiences Horne's vocal mode as one of strategic aloofness, her voice functioning as a calculated withholding of the self when she could not agree to the only terms on which her presence as a black woman would be accepted. In this analysis, Horne emerges as the theorist-performer who clearly understands yet refuses the assignment to perform as either the oversexed whore or the docile servant:

> In suggesting that all available images of black women were ultimately readable in one of two frameworks of sexual interpretation, Horne identified the representational trap faced by black women performers. Her response to this forced legibility was to position herself outside any formal plot by which her audience—or even, she notes, herself at the time—could narrate her. As a racialized body performing against racialized entrapment, Horne sought a way to elude this policing of the black woman's body, even while standing center stage.[18]

Vocal sound is the means by which she eludes such bodily policing, resulting in a performance that Vogel terms Horne's "impersona." This is a presence that manifests sonically but nonetheless declines to deliver affective closeness. Ultimately, Horne refuses to perform her sexual availability on the terms allowed to her. In her smooth, elegant vocal delivery, I hear her deploying what Licia Fiol-Matta has called, in reference to Puerto Rican women singers of popular music, the slippery nothingness of a "thinking voice."[19] Lena Horne sings from the double bind. Her voice is a testament to the way that, as Houston Baker has put it, black artists have found elegant

3.1 Lena Horne in a 1944 publicity photo, via Getty Images.

ways to produce a "voice crafted out of tight places."[20] A 1940s publicity photo (figure 3.1) has her in full movie star glamour: off-the-shoulder gown, jewels at her ears, wrists, and finger, and hair pinned up in a sleek pompadour. Horne looks to be sitting low to the ground and resting her elbows on the cushioned bed of a piece of furniture. The light falls in such a way as to cast smoky shadows at the eye line, throat, and left side of her torso. Arms just crossed, her manicured figures spread at her bosom in a gesture that seems somehow protective, she looks into the camera with an unsmiling expression that remains open to interpretation—sultry or secretive.

What does Horne's vocal impersona *sound* like? Below I consider her performance of the song "Can't Help Lovin' Dat Man" in the film *Till the Clouds Roll By* (1946), a biopic vaguely based on the life of composer Jerome Kern.[21] The film opens with a montage of excerpts from Kern's most famous musical, *Show Boat* (1927), and Horne sings the already iconic torch song of the white-passing black character Julie. A simple song with a simple AABA form and a simple message—I will love my man no matter what—in the context of *Show Boat* the song is sung at various moments by different characters, even accelerating to become a feel-good, cakewalk-ready ensemble dance number. But it is introduced by the character Julie, a woman destined by racial circumstances to sing wistfully through beautiful melodies of unrequited love.[22] It is a role that both Horne and I wish she could have had the chance to perform onstage, but MGM Studio denied her the opportunity to perform in both the 1946 Broadway revival and the 1951 film adaptation.[23] In her view, these opportunities were foreclosed through the retaliatory moves of MGM executives angered by her refusal to play a "loose woman" in their pet project, the stage musical *St. Louis Woman*. Of her regrets about not being able to play Julie, Horne asserted:

> I asked to do it. But I was having a difficult time at the studio at the moment. They didn't like it because I had refused to do a Broadway show they wanted to do . . . the only thing I can say about it [is that] I was paid the supreme compliment. Mr. Kern, before he died, when they did the Broadway revival, asked MGM if I could play the Julie part, and I think to finish the punishment they were giving me they refused.[24]

But here she is onscreen in Technicolor, swathed in the sheen of a pale lavender gown of what looks to be jacquard chiffon, a V neckline that remains demure—not too much revealed—puffed gigot sleeves gathering at the elbow before fanning out in filmy pleated bells to her wrists.[25] There is a deep purple bow and flowers in her sleek updo, and on her right shoulder is pinned a bouquet of purple hydrangea blooms. Everything is pulled back, pulled up. A bright orange-red lip, compact white earrings. The orchestra swoons into sound with utter sexiness, lush revelry, but she merely glides to one side and clasps her hands in front of her. She comes into voice looking over her shoulder; it's unclear who she's addressing. Seated alone on the supposed river dock, she sings, "Oh listen, sister," but she gets no sister on set to sing to. And her gaze avoids the camera, so the audience cannot be her scene partner. She drops her eyes often, and her sound is contained, careful; she doesn't have the luxury of abandon or knows its consequences. Still she doesn't seem tremulous or naive. This voice is sensitive, smooth, flowing. For the most part, her face is still, as if she knows she is expected to be decorative. Yet her phrasing is evocative, revealing how much is at work underneath that placid exterior. In this song about a beloved man, she imbues "man" and "can't" with extra vowels—elongated diphthongs. "Why" has a little puff of air before it: *hhhwhy* [hwaɪ]. And there is velvet in the low-voiced consonants *v* and the soft *th* [ð] of "love that." (She steps carefully around the dialect lyrics, softening each *d* of "dat" into a gentler, voiced consonant.) She lays down the gauntlet: "*Tell* me," and eases her torso upward. But completing the phrase with "he's lazy" she steps off the accusation with speed; hurrying on to the next "*tell* me." Although the lyric scripts the singer's love object as "he's slow," she is quick to fade out that *low* [loʊ] after a slight hiss, but that's the wrong descriptor, it's more an emphatic sibilance—just for a second. She is trafficking in tiny shifts and pressures. She emphasizes the culmination of this phrase: "*maybe* I know" and there seems more behind that, somehow, than she's willing to share. On each "day-*ee*," rain or shine, when she waits for her man, her voice rises through the paired pitches and slips into lighter tone as she ascends to the brief higher perch. Arriving upon "that day is *fine*" she shifts her shoulders just a tiny bit, and the sound rings out clear, strong, belted. But then she eases off of this forthright sound, softening the *n*. She has to be careful. "The sun will shine" is placed small, in the space of the nose. The briefly blooming sound has folded up again. In the declaration of love's depth, "til I die," there is a half-moment of ferocity, but only if you listen for it, a blink-and-you'll-miss-it flicker of tension/resolve in her brow. She has power but she can't really use it. She must smolder demurely, for the time being.

An Exercise from Lena Horne:
Self-Knowing Smolder

Holding your torso upright, lean against a wall and clasp your hands in front of you, elbows away from your body. Pick a pitch that is comfortable and sing the words "maybe I know" on one pitch at the pace of regular speech. Linger on the voiced consonants: the m of "maybe" and the n of "know." Keep your mouth small (don't open too wide) on the word "I" and see what this does to your sound; it may help to put a y in front of it: "maybe yi know." Finally, when you sing the word "know" give it more belted power but then ease off, soften the volume, almost as if the sound comes out of your mouth strong and then gets sucked back into it.

Lena and Mary
Jim Crow–Era Girlhood in Two Timbres

Born just four years apart, performers Mary Martin and Lena Horne rose to heights on the strength of their singing, acting—and sometimes dancing—by sharply different paths. Where in her early career the polished Horne sang demurely from within the double bind of black girlhood, throughout her career Martin was associated with an energetic, tomboyish youthfulness encapsulated by what one 1950s journalist described as "the hoydenish type."[26] Among the eleven Broadway shows to Martin's credit, she is known for originating the canonical musical theatre ingénues Nellie and Maria in Broadway megahits *South Pacific* (1949) and *The Sound of Music* (1959) as well as the title role in *Peter Pan* (1954) onstage and in multiple televised versions. All three of these roles secured Tony wins for Martin as Best Leading Actress in a Musical. Where Horne's voice is typically heard as guarded and aloof, steeped in the culture of ladylike dissemblance, Martin's is often described as projecting a guileless boyishness. Stacy Wolf notes, "Martin's style as a performer is aggressive—not graceful, not careful."[27] Horne's long-awaited star turn on the stage, some time after two brief appearances on Broadway in the 1930s, was the calypso musical *Jamaica* (1957); an ill-fitting show conceived as a Harry Belafonte vehicle with which she nonetheless became the first black woman nominated for the Tony for Best Leading Actress in a Musical. Her only other credit in a leading role on Broadway was the celebrated revue *Lena Horne: The Lady and Her Music* (1981), for which she won her sole Tony, a special award that season. By differing means, both Martin and Horne emerged as models against which subsequent performers have been measured as musical theatre ingénues and black glamour girls. Below, I briefly survey their growing-up years and the singing lessons that shaped each's voice along different routes to sounding the part of the American musical-theatrical girl.

Martin was born in 1913 in Weatherford, Texas, to a mother who had been a violin teacher at Weatherford College and a father who was a respected judge. Horne came into the world in 1917 in the Bedford-Stuyvesant neighborhood of Brooklyn, New York, born to the rich-boy-turned-gambler son of one of Brooklyn's elite black families and an actress mother who did not conform to her in-laws' social expectations. Descended from plantation owners and prior to that, of Scottish and Irish ancestry, young Martin was ensconced in the home of a venerated family, her carefree singing secure in the legal contours of the Jim Crow South and the warm regard of the wealthy residents of oil and cattle country where she grew up. The musical theatre writer and fellow Texan Harvey Schmidt commented, "Everyone loved her because she was 'the judge's daughter. . . .' Mary told me that when she was growing up, she just loved going around the town square, where the courthouse was, singing loud and so proud, knowing that her father was inside."[28] Horne, whose well-to-do paternal grandparents are often cited as a source of a well-resourced upbringing, in fact was shuttled around to various caretakers in her childhood years following her parents' split, with differing levels of financial security. On the road with her glamorous mother, who performed ingénue roles in plays, and always underfoot in the bustle of a touring theatre troupe, according to family lore one night young Horne "crept into the fireplace on the set, just out of sight of the audience, and hummed audibly all through the performance."[29] Yet despite such charming stories, during her childhood years in the Jim Crow South, Horne also learned, as noted above, that black people needed to stay in "their place" to be safe. This meant no strawberry ice cream sodas for little black girls on hot days when drugstores were reserved for whites only, and it meant turning back from a fun trip with friends and family to see the Silas Green variety show upon hearing that the roads were not safe for black folks that night—white people were out on a killing spree.[30] Meanwhile, in wealthy Weatherford, when her sister was crowned the year's "Princess of the Cotton Palace" in local festivities, eight-year-old Martin played dress-up in her finery. She also sang at civic events including the firemen's ball and the ladies' Garden Club as well as Saturday night concerts at the bandstand in the center of town. The degree to which each young singer was or was not able to move freely through her childhood landscape can be heard to contribute to later vocal modes of careful dissembling versus guileless innocence.

Both girls' mothers looked out for their daughters' performance education. Horne's mother coached her in diction and script analysis and gave her dancing lessons, teaching from a book of exercises ordered from a correspondence school. Martin's mother took her to study voice in Fort Worth with Helen Cahoon, an opera singer and Texas Christian University instructor. Cahoon later praised Martin's strong innate sense of pitch and "adorable stubborn nature," insisting modestly that, "Nobody can claim credit for making Mary Martin sing."[31] Horne's mother, after her daughter starred in a musical revue at Girls High in Brooklyn, leveraged connections in New York's black theatre community to secure an audition for her sixteen-year-old at the Cotton Club. She also signed her up with "the best singing teacher she could find," a certain Mr. Jerrahol who had toured Europe performing in concert venues and was now "teaching singing on a side street in Harlem."[32] Martin's mother ensured that her daughter attended a finishing school in Nashville where she was able to study voice with a credentialed operatic baritone, Dr. Stetson Humphrey. However, the sixteen-year-old Martin wasn't quite "finished" when she left the Ward-Belmont School for Girls a year later to marry and give birth to a son.[33]

At the Cotton Club, Horne came into consciousness as a black working girl employed by white management. She learned the exhausting, exploitative rhythm of performing five shows a day at a midtown theatre from 11 a.m. and 7 p.m., then three evening shows in Harlem (8 p.m., 10 p.m., and 2 a.m.) plus frequent unpaid, after-hours performances at the managers' discretion—all for white clientele; black audience members were turned away at the club door. The teenage Martin's marriage did not last long, and her mother raised her baby when the disconsolate girl turned to teaching dance to recapture a sense of drive and purpose. A neighbor recalled, "She said to her father, 'I want to have a dancing school. . . . So he gave her one.'"[34] Martin rapidly became a successful small business owner. In three years, she expanded her dance teaching operation from five students to three hundred across three locations in the region, employing an assistant, a bookkeeper, and an accompanist. From the age of nineteen, she traveled to Los Angeles several times to briefly study dance and later voice at the Fanchon and Marco School, a legendary training ground for Hollywood's song-and-dance talent.[35] These educational excursions, and a zippy yellow convertible in which she commuted from Texas to California, were funded by her father. In Los Angeles Martin again encountered and studied with her voice teacher Stetson Humphrey whose scientifically informed vocal credo was, "Be yourself."[36] Meanwhile, Horne was excited to triple her salary when an audition at Mr. Jerrahol's voice studio won her a contract touring as a vocalist with the gracious bandleader and Broadway songwriter Noble Sissle of *Shuffle Along* (1921) fame. From Sissle she learned much about showmanship and how black artists navigated white patronage on the road. Juggling a brief marriage and motherhood, Horne commuted between coasts as a featured performer in the musical film *The Duke Is Tops* (1938) and the one-week run of Broadway revue *Lew Leslie's Blackbirds of 1939*, plus nightclub performances at New York's Cafe Society downtown and Savoy Plaza, and Los Angeles's Little Troc.

Both Horne and Martin engaged in career-defining vocal studies in Los Angeles. Once she established a home base in Hollywood at the onset of World War I and negotiated a historic, seven-picture contract with MGM— unheard of for black performers at the time—Horne found an able voice coach in Kay Thompson, the fearlessly chic head of MGM's Voice Department. "Kay had been known to have her students sing along with Ethel Merman records," Horne's daughter remembered. This new voice coach "got her to open her mouth and let it rip. Belting, I guess you'd call it."[37] A fascinating figure in her own right, Thompson was a vocal arranger, actress, and irrepressible personality who ignored Jim Crow-era conventions of her time by assembling mixed-race choral ensembles at will and listed Judy Garland and Frank Sinatra among her not-too-shabby coachees.[38] Under her tutelage, Horne—the singer whose respectability game did not allow for singing blues songs—began to bring forth glimpses of a powerful sound that still remained mostly concealed.[39] For her part, Martin was spurred on by the advice of her finishing school voice teacher Stetson Humphrey, now considered a leading vocal authority, who catered to the Hollywood actor crowd while preaching the latest in vocal determinism: "It is the study of the cranium enclosures, by means of the X-ray, that enables us to determine vocal range, for the pictures point out the singer's limitations."[40] Humphrey advised Martin to take six months to focus on voice study, "if you can afford it," which she did with her father's sponsorship.[41] A breakout vocal performance in 1938 at the Sunset Strip nightclub the Trocadero earned her an agent and, shortly after, a part in the Broadway musical *Leave It To Me!*

Martin's showstopping number in her Broadway debut was the mischievous "My Heart Belongs to Daddy," a song later associated with Eartha

3.2 Mary Martin in *Leave It To Me!* (1938). Courtesy of the Billy Rose Theatre Division, New York Public Library for the Performing Arts.

Kitt as well as Marilyn Monroe. She sang this number while coyly perched on a suitcase at a Siberian train station, wearing a fur coat and little else. A production photo from the musical (figure 3.2) shows a lingerie-clad Martin cheerfully peeking out from behind a curtain, one bare arm and one long, bare leg visible below her beribboned tap shorts and camisole, the fur coat thrown off to one side. Offstage, her daddy back home in Texas really was paying the bills for her big city lifestyle at the time, covering the cost of her Manhattan penthouse. Martin was seen by audiences and journalists as an innocent, giggling, "tall slender girl from a Texas town" who had never even seen a striptease before she was asked to do a tame version in this show.[42] Sophisticate songwriter Cole Porter assumed she simply didn't understand the double entendre in his song, commenting, with the verbal version of an eyeroll, "Mary Martin, you know, is probably the most basically naive person I've ever met."[43] But at least some of the young singer-actress's success with this song may be chalked up to the valuable coaching she received from no less a castmate than Sophie Tucker. Whenever you're delivering a dirty lyric, Tucker coached—and the veteran singer, now in her fifties, certainly had experience with putting over risqué, comic numbers—don't look at the audience. To bring the song home, she directed, "Look straight up to heaven, fold your hands, and sing."[44] With this guidance, Martin brought the house down. Yet the ability to do a striptease, naively or not, relies on an act of withholding that does not presume a girl's sexual availability. And so it was a role that in 1938 could only, ever have been as funny and charming as it was because the singer was not, like Lena Horne, required to sing from the double bind of black girlhood.

Mary Martin
Jazzing the Aria for Fun

Mary Martin is without question one of the great musical theatre stars of "Golden Age" Broadway, and with her trademark "hoydenish," carefree style she sustained opportunities to play ingénues and youthful characters for more than two decades. Yet Martin's voice is rarely discussed to the degree of fellow white Broadway divas like Ethel Merman or Barbra Streisand; while respected, she does not incite the same level of idol worship. Reviewers and contemporaries describe her as possessing a winning onstage magnetism of the kind that is difficult to conjure from cast albums and photographs. I would argue that this is in fact what defines a theatre voice as not (just) a sound that sparkles in the recording studio—a vocal performance woven from the singer's onstage ease and her delighted rapport with the audience. Stacy Wolf has written thoughtfully about the way that Martin's short hair, manspreading, and tomboyish persona bucked expectations of musical theatre femininity. Where Horne broke new ground in creating access for black movie stars, Martin struggled to find her footing in Tinseltown not least "because the studio could not successfully mold her into a Hollywood starlet"; she hated the awkward glamour photographs Paramount executives pushed her to take.[45] Yet she thrived on Broadway even while the ageist attitudes of filmmakers prevented her from bringing her stage successes to the screen. Although considered too old to play World War II nurse Nellie in the movie of *South Pacific* in 1958, the following year Rodgers and Hammerstein came running back to her to star as the ingénue in the original stage production of *The Sound of Music* at age forty-five. I find it fascinating to listen to Martin's early career in duet with Horne's. Building on Wolf's study, the fact that Martin became the quintessential, wide-eyed Broadway ingénue regardless of her actual age and her boyish embodiment seems even more remarkable. Listening to her alongside Horne makes it clear how much her whiteness secured not only her "freedom to play around with gender" but also, I argue, her freedom to crystallize the Broadway ingénue type on her own terms.[46] This crystallization not only led to her own career longevity but also provided the template for later young women singer-actors. A primary way she accomplished this was with her vocal sound.

As I have listened to Martin's singing while writing this chapter, revisiting long-familiar show tunes, it occurs to me that her a-little-bit-unremarkable voice is absolutely remarkable for the fact that every musical theatre singer nowadays is expected to have the facility with multiple vocal styles that she deployed. If her voice doesn't stand out as strongly in memory, it surely stands out vividly in practice. Perhaps different from an Ethel Merman, in Martin's case avowing her twice-heard sound and the extent to which it is resung by many singers today, far from dimming the shine of her vocal reputation, only bolsters her voice's renown.

In the original cast recording of "My Heart Belongs to Daddy," Martin has a very sweet and yet bright sound. She has a "legit," classically inflected upper register and then she intercuts it with that wonderful, nasalized twang, right in the front of the face, maybe aided by her Texas roots. She moves back and forth easily between these sounds with a playful energy. True to her voice teacher Cahoon's testimony, she is always precisely in the center of the pitch (a composer's dream), with a smile. It may be that her voice gets it done because there is something quirky and funny about her performances, her gawky onstage awkwardness, but I cannot overstate that her voice *swings* while also remaining elegant. She emerges as both down to earth and refined at the same time, approachable and fun. From Martin's perspective, the work of musical comedy was simply a fun thing to do—unlike the eight-show-a-day working-girl slog that young Horne lived. On this theme, an article claiming to be her first-ever interview, during the Boston tryout of *Leave It to Me!*, summarized her vocal coming of age in Los Angeles:

> After six months Miss Martin was doing so well in her study of classical music that one day she tried a little relaxing, in the form of adapting a well known aria to modern swing. Everybody who heard her in the studio declared the number was delightful. And when Mary was asked to appear for one of those "professional-amateur" Sunday night shows at the Trocadero, she decided to include the swing adaptation. She started her act with one of the "blues" songs to which the public was accustomed, having heard her on the radio. Then she began a bit of opera, to the amazement of the patrons, who hardly expected such music. Right in the middle of the aria, she changed suddenly into a swing song, and finished it out in Benny Goodman tempo. And it was then that the patrons . . . got up and yelled and stamped. [She realized] "At last I know what I want to do the rest of my life. I want to stay in musical comedy, getting better all the time. No, I shan't get married. A career is more fun."[47]

Throughout her career, Martin repeated this story of delivering the operatic aria "Il Bacio" in jazz waltz form as an on-ramp to musical comedy and a way to move beyond singing blues songs on the California radio.

One of Martin's most famous songs is "I'm Gonna Wash That Man Right Outa My Hair" from *South Pacific*, whose creation she is said to have inspired with an idea she had in the shower one day. Soon enough she was washing her hair onstage at eight shows a week while hopping around and flinging soap suds at a gaggle of cheery American nurses stationed on a wartime island base. I listen to her performance of this song on the original cast album and a televised performance of the 1952 London production.[48] The number situates her in the context of the female ensemble that backs her up, securing her girlish status. Clear and well-projected (she despised the microphones that would later come to Broadway), she maneuvers her bright sound through short percussive phrases and the occasional, Mermanesque skip-hop ornament. Similar to the way she hops around the stage barefoot in a bra and shorts, sometimes marching energetically or offering up akimbo moves with gangly arms, her singing is bouncy, forthright, full of glottal-stop vowels "*out*a my *arms*" and to the point. She leaves most of the vibrato out of this tune. Maybe she is saving it for shared numbers with her costar, Metropolitan Opera bass-baritone Ezio Pinza in the original production, where she is a credit to her operatic voice teachers in holding her own despite a comparatively lighter, less formal sound. Here in "I'm Gonna Wash," sometimes she adds a shimmer of vibrato at the end of a phrase, "on his *way*." She has a fantastic sense of time, holding fast to the rhythmic groove throughout. While her singing is light and easy, she is not afraid to belt it out: "*send him*." The number doesn't feel particularly sexy but in the London performance she does throw in a couple of goofy pelvic thrusts and a growl on "ride that man / right *off that range*." This number has been described as failed, unblue blues (white songwriters doing their best), but she gets an actual blue note on, "If the man don't under*stand* you," it's just that she doesn't lean on it. [49] She slides in and out of a few notes expressively ("make a butterfly *strong*"), which gives it some blue energy, and soon she is brandishing a towel and, via a half-suppressed laugh, gleefully delivering childlike delight that she has in fact "washed that man / right outa my hair." The end of the song has plant-your-feet-and-power-it-out belter energy but she remains bouncing in her little march-step as she sings and maintains her vocal ground.

An Exercise from Mary Martin: Shower Bounce

Stand in the shower and sing. Massage your scalp as you hold your elbows out at sharp angles. Sing a song you think you *should* like and when you get to the middle of it, switch styles. You could go from opera to jazz, or try things like country to soul, gospel to folk, pop rock to metal. Consider that the possibilities can be endlessly fun. Keep moving, bouncing in place (okay, please do not slip in the shower!) while you sing. Optional variation: Wear a chic shower cap while vocalizing as above.

Diahann Carroll and Leslie Uggams
Black Broadway Musical Ingénues

In 1962, for her starring role in the musical *No Strings*, Diahann Carroll became the first black performer to win the Tony Award for Best Leading Actress in a Musical. Six years later, in 1968 Leslie Uggams followed

suit, accepting a Tony for her leading role in the musical *Hallelujah, Baby!*
And so in the persons of Carroll and Uggams, Broadway introduced at
midcentury its first widely celebrated black ingénues—feted by black and
white theatregoers alike—since the 1920s. During that long-gone decade
the "trilling voice" of the beloved Broadway talent Florence Mills had, as
Jayna Brown notes, "affirmed the light-hearted right to an independent
young womanhood" for Jazz Age black audiences.[50] But in general, the
ingénue as a character type has often been understood by white arbiters
of culture as operating outside the category of blackness, a role applicable
primarily to young white women.[51] (There's a reason all those black girls
in movies are cast as the best friend.) Stanislavsky's terse characterizations
of the general requirements of the type remain apt: the cheerful, somewhat
naive young girl "who is of slight build . . . is, of course, the *ingénue*," she who
"goes around being charming."[52] As such a definition makes clear, however,
the ingénue is one whose innocence is sustained by the way that she moves
freely and hopefully through the world. Despite the honors accorded to
them, this freedom of movement was only granted to civil rights-era ingénues Carroll and Uggams via a provisional reprieve from the double bind
of black girlhood. No matter how skillfully they wielded the "girlish art of
yearning" in their singing, each was still required to reckon in different ways
throughout her career with being unwanted in the musical theatre business.

In writing on the confounding geographies of black girlhood under
segregation, Simmons notes that there is a stark "difference between 'being
allowed' [into a space] and 'being wanted'" there. She recounts a telling
exchange between young black girls and the white social workers who led
a field trip to a part of New Orleans the girls had not previously been to
and where they were unsure about their welcome: "A younger girl asked
if 'colored people' were allowed in the space. The social worker reassured
her: yes, colored people were allowed. Another girl chimed in, 'Suppose
they don't want us here?'"[53] While this trip occurred in 1946, when Carroll and Uggams would have been a tween and a toddler respectively, thir-
teen hundred miles northeast in their middle-class New York homes, this
poignant question is nonetheless one they grappled with as ingénues and
indeed throughout their lives in relation to the musical stage.

A 1962 rehearsal photo from *No Strings* (figure 3.3) vividly portrays the
pressures on a young black woman singer working within a theatre industry defined by white men at midcentury. Carroll stands beside a pianist in
what looks to be the lobby or interior room of a theatre, a piano-vocal score
in her hands, her mouth open in song. I note the smart suit she wears, its

3.3 Diahann Carroll sings at a rehearsal for *No Strings* (1962). Courtesy of the Billy Rose Theatre Division, New York Public Library for the Performing Arts.

three-quarter length sleeves and neat bow at the waist, the single strand of pearls at her neck, and the way her entire physicality is contained, elbows held at her sides and eyes carefully trained on the pages of music she holds. Her pressed hair, always so immaculate in her publicity photos, is slightly windswept. She is the only black person in the room, one of only three women, and the only person whose voice is heard in the moment the photo was taken; twelve others cluster around listening intently, mostly white men. Composer Richard Rodgers stands just behind Carroll, a look of concentration on his face, and her costar Richard Kiley is seated to her right, gazing downward as if reviewing his own copy of the score. The pressure this young black woman carried to present herself impeccably on this day in 1962 reverberate from the image like waves of heat from a city sidewalk in summertime.

After winning her landmark Tony at age twenty-six, Diahann Carroll returned to Broadway for only one other production, to perform in the play *Agnes of God* for short engagements in 1982 and 1983. Subsequently, her sole major musical theatre credit is the role of Norma Desmond in the Toronto iteration of *Sunset Boulevard* (1995), a role she earned despite the reluctance if not outright disdain she detected composer Andrew

Lloyd Webber had for the idea of casting a black actress in the role.[54] This felt experience of disrespect from a famous white musical theatre composer is one that in her autobiography she connects to a painful and perfunctory conversation with Richard Rodgers decades earlier.

> It happened in Detroit. I was working extremely hard in 1962 for the out-of-town opening of the Broadway-bound *No Strings*. And the night before we opened, Mr. Rodgers came to see me in my dressing room. In a voice that was something between avuncular and condescending, he told me he had something he needed to discuss with me: the hostess of our opening-night party did not want me in her home. She felt that it would confuse her children to see a black woman who was sophisticated and elegant because they didn't exist.[55]

Clearly, in the shift away from the weary-bluesy mammy, black women performers who did not align with the character diva and her larger-than-life comic persona found a limited welcome in the circles of the musical theatre elite—onstage and off. Like Carroll, Uggams also left Broadway after her Tony win and built the bulk of her career in television and film; she is best known for playing Kizzy in the miniseries *Roots* (1977), as well as more recent roles in Marvel's *Deadpool* films (2016, 2018) and the series *Empire* (2016–2020). But, different from Carroll, and although she remains underacknowledged within twenty-first century musical theatre communities, the silver-voiced Uggams holds seven additional Broadway credits. Five of these are musicals; they include the revue *Jerry's Girls* (1985) and stints as Reno Sweeney in *Anything Goes* (1989) and Muzzy Van Hossmere in *Thoroughly Modern Millie* (2003). Even as I celebrate these singers' artistry and delight in offering analyses of their path-clearing work, I want to be clear that the opportunities and welcome available to Carroll and Uggams as glamorous artists on the musical stage were, notwithstanding the early acclaim they garnered, plainly circumscribed.

At the same time, despite insistence on and precedent for the idea that ingénues must be white women, in the years around 1960, as Daphne Brooks has argued, US popular culture began to create space for and recognize black ingénues in popular music.[56] The girlhood and early careers of Carroll and Uggams coincided with the rise of the figure of the girl singer and girl groups in popular music; their voices and personas as black Broadway ingénues of this period must be heard in relation to those of early black pop ingénues such as Aretha Franklin and Tammi Terrell and girl groups like the Ronnettes and the Chanteles. Jacqueline Warwick makes the startling point that despite their race and working-class origins, many of the black girl singers in pop music of this era became national models of ladylike behavior for white teen girls as well.[57] The national and international reach of these pop singers' voices and stylish personas constituted a remarkable escape from the restrictive geographies to which black girls were so often subjected. I submit that the steady beat and careful diction of this sound treaded a fine line between carefree innocence and strategic dissemblance. In operating as both "straightforward" and "polished," the sound itself proffered the possibility of a truce between the conflicting demands of the double bind of black girlhood. This was, like that brought to Broadway by Carroll and Uggams, a hard-won image of girlish innocence. Performers such as Diana Ross and the Supremes were carefully coached by the strict Mrs. Maxine Powell, who operated her own kind of finishing school in the Motown Artist Development Department, teaching singers "elegance, ladylikeness, grace—crucial components of respectability" subsequently marketed to listeners of different races.[58]

At Motown, Powell and Berry Gordy, a black woman and a black man, may have called the shots on appropriate black femininity. But on Broadway at midcentury it was white men, whether producers, directors, or audience members, who were the chief decision makers on the point of who should be considered an ingénue.[59] Theatre-going white men have not always found self-assured, powerful women to be charming.[60] In fact, the idea of the black ingénue in the musical theatre may well serve as a political statement in itself, venturing a contradiction in terms. For the theatre ingénue's defining feature is her vulnerability, a characteristic that historically has not been associated with black women in the United States. Naive and overly trusting, the musical theatre ingénue may misstep, slip and fall in love—of course, she must be delicate so that she can be protected in the arms of a man. Onstage, she is charged with entrancing not only her love interest but also the straight male audience members and producers. And it wasn't until midcentury that Broadway's overwhelmingly white audiences, and composers like Richard Rodgers, were remotely willing to admit to falling in love with black women stars of the stage.[61]

For black girls and young women, then as now, the requirements to be charming, happy, and guilelessly innocent can present difficulties for would-be musical theatre ingénues. These preconditions for positive affective display are often fraught for black girls, as musical theatre scholar Jordan Ealey examines.[62] Put another way: the guardedness required by the double bind of Jim Crow-era black girlhood and its afterlives does not easily translate to naive charm, and the presumption of sexual availability works to spatialize black girls beyond notions of innocence.[63] In terms of vocal sound, in my own work as a voice coach and performer I have long been familiar with the challenges that face the black girl ingénue in musical theatre. It is a landscape in which the options can seem profoundly limited, and if wide-eyed, cutesy, and bright voiced is not how you want to go, the path forward is not always immediately obvious. In today's era of so-called colorblind or even color-conscious casting, those who make choices about who should or should not appear in a given production may expect a black ingénue to be nothing less than a white ingénue with black skin. I have met many an actress beginning her career who seems outwardly to align with the contours of the ingénue—young, hopeful, full of life and optimism, a bit awed by the wideness of the world but determined to face her fears and pursue her dreams. But when this hopefulness does not come packaged in the bright-voiced, even saccharine sound that is expected of the (white) ingénue, the actress in question can encounter challenges in being cast. I fervently want the black women singers I coach to know there are many ways to express the black ingénue in voice. I wish I felt certain that the casting directors whom these singers will face in their auditions, and the composers, writers, and producers presently generating material in this genre, have listened to singers like the young Diahann Carroll and Leslie Uggams, and considered the specific and differing ways that these black women stars performed a black woman's ingénue sound on Broadway at midcentury. In their musical-theatrical singing, Carroll as Ottilie in *House of Flowers* (1954) and Barbara in *No Strings* (1962), and Uggams as Georgina in *Hallelujah, Baby!* (1967) voiced the ingénue according to contours just as viable, if distinct from—for example—the Marias of *The Sound of Music* (1959) and *West Side Story* (1957).

. . . .

Eight years apart, the two ingénues-to-be were both raised in middle-class black families in New York City; Carol Diann Johnson was born in 1935 and grew up in Harlem, and Leslie Uggams, born in 1943, one neighborhood north in Manhattan's Washington Heights. Young Carol began studying voice while still in elementary school and gained acceptance to the prestigious High School for Music and Art, to the great pride of her family. But her first break in show business came not through music but through modeling—at age fifteen, after sending a photograph of herself to *Ebony* magazine, she was hired as a model for catalogue work by *Ebony*'s parent company. That same year, 1950, the precocious seven-year-old Uggams landed her first TV spot, playing Ethel Waters's niece in an episode of the television comedy *Beulah*. Waters, now an elder star, treated the young talent kindly; as Uggams later recalled, "They wanted me to wear my hair in those terrible little pickaninny braids all over my head, and Ethel Waters said absolutely not, and she combed my hair long with two tiny bows."[64] A year later, Diahann Carroll jettisoned her family name, Johnson, and crafted a more glamorous stage name from an inversion of her first two names, when she successfully auditioned for the television variety show *Arthur Godfrey's Talent Scouts*. Carroll's big break came at age eighteen when she won a televised singing competition and "rocketed to overnight fame as the new 'Cinderella Girl' of New York night clubs," with bookings at the celebrated Café Society and Latin Quarter venues.[65] Journalists took note of her credentialed voice noting, "Although she is featured as a pop singer, Diahann is equipped with a thorough classical background. She combines the song-selling charm of Lena Horne and Dorothy Dandridge with the enthusiasm of youth."[66] Carroll briefly attended New York University, intending to major in psychology, but withdrew after one term to pursue her modeling and singing career. Hollywood soon came calling; in 1954 she flew to California for a small role in the film *Carmen Jones*, appearing as a friend of the lead character played by Dandridge. When she returned to New York she auditioned for Truman Capote and won the role of Ottilie in her Broadway debut musical *House of Flowers*, with a book [script] by Capote and a celebrated score by Harold Arlen, an elaborate production in which both Pearl Bailey and Juanita Hall also appeared. Meanwhile, during this time, little Uggams worked steadily on television "kiddie shows" and attended the Professional Children's School in Manhattan. From age nine to sixteen, she performed regularly at the famed Apollo Theater in Harlem, mothered by the likes of Ella Fitzgerald and Dinah Washington, and brought onstage by Louis Armstrong to sing impromptu duets. Watching the performances of these musical greats from the wings was, she later asserted, "a great, great education. . . . You couldn't pay enough money at a school to learn what they did."[67] Both in the formal, more classically oriented vocal studies supported by their middle-class parents—Uggams later went on to study at Juilliard—and in the informal arenas of black music venues and nightclubs, Carroll and Uggams honed their vocal talents and sparkling personas.

In the case of both singers, the emerging space of television afforded a degree of access and attention that had eluded a previous generation of young black performers; this was a medium in which both were pathbreakers as well. In the early 1960s, the teenage Uggams was a regular on the NBC show *Sing Along with Mitch*, curated by a top executive at Columbia Records, Mitch Miller. With this show she became a "household name" nationwide, and the sole African American performer featured on network television at that time.[68] For her part, Carroll nabbed the leading role in the Broadway show for which she would win her Tony, *No Strings*, after composer Richard Rodgers saw her appear in 1961 on Jack Paar's *The Today Show*, which he confessed he "often used as something of a talent audition."[69] Carroll would go on to star in *Julia* (1968), the first sitcom to feature a black woman in a leading role that was not a stereotypical, servant character. Both actresses also hosted their own televised variety shows on CBS, *The Leslie Uggams Show* (1969) and *The Diahann Carroll Show* (1976). Breaking ground in these ways was cause for celebration throughout black communities. Uggams recalls how African Americans would phone one another excitedly to be sure to tune in when she was appearing on *Sing Along With Mitch*—the only black face in sight.[70] And when Carroll saw success on Broadway, the black press proudly celebrated the new musical that had been "tailor-made" by the famous composer, Rodgers, for the young black star, with recaps of all the raves from critics in the major New York papers.[71] But being vanguard performers, whether in television or the theatre, was only one way that these singers have been accountable to black audiences throughout their careers. While I do not seek to argue here for some ineffable black "essence" that these singers retained and manifested even while singing white songwriters' material, what interests me is how they themselves conceptualized and articulated racial identity in the ways they navigated multiple sets of expectations for their varied audiences. Although both operated within the category of the young black ingénue, Carroll and Uggams performed this role in differing ways, and with differing understandings of what was expected of them in doing so.

Diahann Carroll
Disarming Elegance

In her performances from the 1950s and 1960s, the svelte Carroll evinces a self-possession and composure that would later register as closer to hauteur, but in her early years seems merely disarming. By contrast, Uggams brings a fresh-faced sense of down-to-earthness, coming across as the (at least moderately) righteous, middle-class girl-next-door, as I discuss further below. For her part, Carroll has spoken about how her upbringing came with the trappings of racial uplift that characterized many upwardly mobile black middle-class families of the time. Visiting her grandmother in North Carolina while a child, for example, she learned that her grandmother's dream "was to allow me to have the kind of education that would separate me from, I don't think she realized that she was separating me from the [black] community, but she certainly was."[72] And her mother's perspective on what kinds of music were acceptable was made clear:

> Very early in life . . . I studied voice, and this career that I was pursuing was extremely important, particularly to my mother. But my mother always said, "Oh, please, don't ever sing the blues. Please. I'm so tired of people believing that the blues belongs to black people, because the blues represents unhappiness and people who are not gracious towards each other, and it teaches . . . the unkindness between men and women, and . . . I don't want you to sing about that. Please. Don't do that. *Don't bring the blues to my home.*" Well, she said it with a smile, as she said everything, but . . . she really meant it.[73]

The roles in which Carroll was cast were increasingly those of elegantly dressed, proper characters—a model in *No Strings*, a schoolteacher in the film *Paris Blues* (1961) opposite Sidney Poitier, and a respectable nurse on her sitcom *Julia* (1968). When in 1974 she appeared, in an Academy-nominated turn, as a single mother on welfare in the film *Claudine*, black audiences were no longer so enamored of her. A few months after its opening, *Jet* ran a short item with a quote from Carroll in its "Words of the Week" section:

> Diahann Carroll, actress, in answer to those who refer to her as the "white Diahann Carroll": "There is no confusion in my mind that I am Black. And if confusion exists—and it obviously does—in the minds of some Blacks, then I ask them: 'What makes one Black more Black than the next?' Even if I were the kind of Black who turned her back on present-day pressures, that still wouldn't make me any less Black. Just uninvolved. And that is one's choice. Whether I am or am not involved is no one's business. I refuse to discuss what I do or do not do for Blacks. I will not appease anyone to prove that I am Black."[74]

If to at least some African American audiences Carroll's race card was in danger of expiring, creative producers of stage and film also seemed to view her as racially somewhat nonspecific—perhaps more nonwhite than "black" per se. In a mind-bending passage from his autobiography, composer Richard Rodgers effuses about the "stunning Diahann Carroll, a singer whom I'd greatly admired ever since seeing her in Harold Arlen's musical *House of Flowers*. I had even tested her for the lead in *Flower Drum Song*, but we were never able to make her appear Oriental."[75] And when her Broadway hit musical *No Strings* was being developed into a film (an adaptation that was ultimately never completed), Carroll was incensed when she heard secondhand that "her" part would be played by an actress of mixed Asian and European descent: "One day you win the Tony Award and are performing the lead in a Broadway musical that Richard Rodgers wrote for you. The next day you pick up the morning paper and read that an actress named Nancy Kwan has just been hired to play your role in the film version. I was furious."[76] Certainly, Carroll's path as an ingénue (and later a leading lady) was not a straightforward one, once the luster of youthful aspirations had worn a bit thin. At the star-studded "House of Flowers" dinner honoring her in 2013, an event honoring groundbreaking women of color in the entertainment industry, and themed around the Broadway show in which Carroll made her debut, the seventy-eight-year-old actress confessed, "I certainly don't feel like an icon. . . . I've had long stretches of unemployment. This is not an easy game."[77]

Carroll's trajectory of vocal study in some ways mirrors that of Juanita Hall, with early classical study followed by opportunities to develop her skills through singing in nightclubs—both their live and televised forms. She has also reflected on the ways that her particular vocal sound was one that did not align with expectations of the recording industry at the time she was coming of age as a young black singer:

What happened to me was that when I recorded I sounded like a youngster that only wanted to do theatre. It was a theatre voice, it was a theatre interpretation. It had nothing to do with the music that was coming out of the black community. And *that* was where the money was generated; the money for the young black artist was primarily about the recording industry. I never really wanted to record (but then again I was very young and I didn't understand what the recording industry meant at that time). . . . I was wrapped in this confusing, complex "I want to be an actress, I want to be a singer." But in the recording studio, I was a dichotomy, a black girl that sounds like a little singer on Broadway. It began to frighten me because I really felt I had to settle on one or the other. And then, as my life emerged,

I recognized that I could have more than one. I could really have more than one way of expressing what I felt as an artist.[78]

In this 2013 interview for the Oprah Winfrey Network, Carroll speaks haltingly at times, as if she is not sure what words to use for herself and her voice: "I sounded like [pause] a youngster that [pause] only wanted to do theatre. . . . In the recording studio, I was a dichotomy, a black girl that sounds like a little [pause] singer on Broadway."

In listening to Carroll's vocal performances, I note this blending of vocal sounds, a melding of the belted sound and the more "legit" head voice. Both her speaking and singing voice are, especially in her younger years, warm—it seems like she is smiling and just excited to be there, sharing this moment with the listener. At times—I notice especially in the original cast album of *No Strings*—she has an impulse to whisper, a leaning toward overdrama. The pacing and texture of vibrato sounds similar to that of other musical theatre singers of this era for the "little singer on Broadway" that Carroll knows herself to be in the quote above. At first hearing, I wonder if the vocal range in which she sings her repertoire is pitched lower than those typical of this style and period, but upon close comparison is actually quite comparable—and yet somehow Carroll seems to have more weight, more ground than lift in her voice than, for example, a singer like Mary Martin.[79] She does have a liquid sound in the upper register, the smoothness of the "legit" head voice, although it is noticeably lighter in heft than in a singer like Juanita Hall. And her high, belted money notes feel powered out, requiring significant effort. Her warm speaking voice has some breathiness mixed in with the sonic equivalent of smiling. It occurs to me that she sings as if she knows she is seen as beautiful, and as if she believes she is living in a beautiful world. These colors and contours are specifically audible in Carroll's vocal performances connected with the 1954 musical *House of Flowers*, which I analyze below via one of her solo numbers from the show as heard on the original cast recording and in televised performance.[80]

The musical's plot concerns two rival bordello madams (played with gusto by Pearl Bailey and Juanita Hall) in a romanticized Haiti, with Carroll in the role of a young sex worker named Ottilie who, against all obstacles—including the madams' various machinations—falls in love and eventually runs off with a boy of modest means who has stolen her heart. As might be expected, this "opulent and earthy musical" as black theatre critic Miles Jefferson put it, was not to the tastes of a number of middle-class black theatregoers; Jefferson himself was generally positive and cited newcomer

Carroll as an actress "to be watched," however, he did concede some "flaws in good taste—was it necessary to show young [black] boys working up a sexual lather in a house of ill-fame?"[81] Carroll's character, however, some-how must be a wholesome, wide-eyed version of the hooker with a heart of gold. The particular demands placed upon the black ingénue are in full evidence here—no Maria from the *Sound of Music* or Nellie from *South Pacific* is asked to conjure up the ingénue's optimism against the backdrop of the whorehouse.

....

In the first of her solo numbers from *House of Flowers*, "A Sleepin' Bee," Ottilie, after asking "But how does a lady know if she's really in love? Ain't there a sign, some magic sign that can tell a lady for sure if she's in love?" reflects on the advice of the local voodoo authority. He has counseled her that if you catch a bee and it doesn't sting you, then you'll know for sure the love you have is the real thing. Despite the somewhat belabored lyric by Truman Capote ("When a bee lies sleepin' / in the palm of your hand / You're betwitched and deep in / love's long looked-after land"), Carroll delivers the lyric with convincing commitment, emitting a smooth, con-nected sound, with warm, bubbling vibrato on the word "hand." In the sec-ond phrase, we get the belt, a brighter sound, but at phrase's end this melts into the warm tone again on "land." As the melody unfurls, she takes her time, sliding in and out of notes. Her back vowels (*oo* [u]) are also warm, and even her classic belt vowels on words like "passed" (*ae* [æ]) are more warm than bright. I am struck by the shading of colors, the way one vocal quality transforms into another, the low and midrange powerful notes and the velvety smoothness at the top. In the televised performance, the verse ends with her smiling, just beaming, the notes seeming to radiate from her smile. It seems significant that this is the song of a woman in love, not a woman whose man has left her. As the lyric conveys, serviceable if less than eloquent—"I'm so happy at last"—it seems radical to have a black woman singing a lyric about happiness, something that, I reflect, does not often happen on Broadway to this day. At the song's end, there is a sense in which her sound is covered over, on the final lyric about having found her true love. She sings in a buttery tone through the voiced consonants of the *n*'s and *l*'s of her "one true love" and on "I have found" there is both the low-larynx warmth of the woman, not just the girl—a sound beyond her years somehow delivered with a smile. Despite the openness required for the vowels of "I" (*ai* [aɪ]) "have" (*ae* [æ]) "found" (ow [aʊ]), she manages it all with a smile.

An Exercise from Diahann Carroll:
Smiling Open Vowels

Make an *ah* [ɑ] sound and exhale on a yawn. Do it again and, while making the sound, place a cupped hand at the front of your throat and feel how the larynx drops down. We are going to use an interval of a perfect fourth (the "Here comes the bride" interval . . . the notes on "Here comes"). Keep the low larynx, yawn shape and, on the first lower note, use the vowel *ah* [ɑ] moving to the second higher note, on *ow* [aʊ] (*ow* as in "ouch"). Put a *y* [j] sound in between: *ah-yow* [ɑ-jaʊ]. Coming up from *ah* to *yow*, think of laughing while you are singing, until at note's end you wind up in a smile. Repeat it again and, if you like, walk up the scale with the same exercise: *ah-yow; ah-yow*.

Leslie Uggams
Righteous Ingénue

If Diahann Carroll and Juanita Hall both followed trajectories of vocal training that began in the conservatory and then migrated to the nightclub, Uggams's studies followed an arc similar to that of Ethel Waters. Uggams honed her skills at the Apollo Theatre, perhaps the 1950s equivalent of the black vaudeville circuit and the televised family entertainments that were the direct descendants of the stage variety show, before studying classical singing formally—in her case, at Juilliard rather than, as did Waters, in London with a Jamaican-born instructor. Uggams herself came from a family with musical and theatrical connections; her father was at one time part of the Hall Johnson Choir and her mother a former Cotton Club chorus girl.[82] As well, she reported, "My grandfather, who's a minister, he sang, and my Aunt Eloise sang, so music ran in the family."[83] Unlike in Carroll's family, there was no desire to separate her from the black community for the purpose of upward mobility. True, the first song she ever sang along to, when her mother first noticed the three-year-old's nascent singing ability, was the song "Nancy" as performed by Frank Sinatra—hardly a song that emerged from the center of the black talent in the 1940s recording industry—although we must remember that Sinatra claimed Billie Holiday as *his* greatest voice teacher, and perhaps we can hear the line carrying through as he sings along with Lady Day.[84] At the same time, as Uggams has articulated, even as a child she knew herself to be a leader and vanguard artist in terms of race relations in the entertainment world and felt keenly the responsibility that came with that: "I realized I was breaking barriers, absolutely."[85] She also cites the confidence her parents instilled in her that enabled her to refuse to be intimidated regardless of the contexts in which she found herself at a young age. Rather, her mindset was one of, in her words, "Hello world, here I am! And aren't you lucky?"[86]

In his book *Black Music*, LeRoi Jones/Amiri Baraka hears Uggams as located on the politically charged continuum of black popular music's connection to African spirit worship, what he terms Afro-Christian "churchified" singing. Baraka places Uggams at the extreme of the continuum, farthest from the source (with soul duo Sam and Dave closest to it, and pop diva Dionne Warwick in the middle), but still located in its arc before the influence fades completely. Other leading artists of Hollywood, the nightclub, and the stage, such as Lena Horne, Pearl Bailey, and Diahann Carroll are absent from his text entirely. But Uggams is, for Baraka, integral enough to the black popular music of the moment to rate mentioning, and he cites her specifically as representative of the yearnings of the black middle class. Recalling Langston Hughes's 1926 critique of the upper-class Negro clubwoman's antishouting stance in "The Negro Artist and the Racial Mountain," Baraka argues in his 1968 text, "The middle-class Negro wants a different content (image) from James Brown, because he has come from a different place, and wants a different thing (he thinks). *The something you want to hear is the thing you already are or move toward.*"[87] Yet if Uggams's family in their middle-class aspirations wanted their daughter to train her voice at Juilliard, they nonetheless raised her in the shadow of great black artists performing at the Apollo Theatre, where she was invited into Ella Fitzgerald's dressing room for postshow snacks and encouraged to eat heartily, and advised by "Aunt Dinah" Washington on what it meant to act like a lady.

Where Carroll admits she felt uncertain in the recording studio of how to bring her "theatre voice" to terms with the sound expected of black artists, Uggams appears to have emerged with fewer qualms. Her close association with Columbia Records, starting from her appearances on *Sing Along with Mitch* during her teen years, meant that she recorded her first album *The Eyes of God* (Columbia, 1959) while still in high school. Moving smoothly from the tremulous innocence of religious songs drenched in sweeping sentimentalism to tremulous seductiveness of standards and ballads, still drenched in sentimentalism, in her follow-up album *So in Love!* (Columbia, 1963), she comes across in these recordings as anything but uncertain. And in a 1965 televised performance of the Harold Arlen/Ted Koehler standard "I Gotta Right to Sing the Blues," despite her dainty dress and put-together, auburn bouffant wig, she growls and swings with the best of them—those early years spent listening backstage to Ella Fitzgerald clearly paid off.

The musical in which Uggams starred, when she was twenty-four years old, which landed her the Tony Award, was *Hallelujah, Baby!*, a show whose white authors (Arthur Laurents, Betty Comden, and Adolph Green) undertook, clumsily, to tell six decades of the history of black people in America. The authors originally intended the role for Lena Horne, and when she declined to participate, for reasons similar to those for which she declined *St. Louis Woman* two decades prior—a clichéd role—the door was open for Uggams.[88] In any case, Horne didn't need to star in a white-authored musical that sought to capitalize on a civil rights movement ethos, for she was front and center with the civil rights movement offstage, participating in the March on Washington and singing at events held by the Student Nonviolent Coordinating Committee (SNCC). The young Uggams, while respectful, was quick to differentiate herself from Horne in an interview the year the show opened. Yet these comments in and of themselves indicate how much she knew that she was singing, in this case literally, in Horne's slipstream.

> I never thought of Lena at all. I mean this was a very big thing and I had enough to worry about without worrying how Lena Horne would do it. I had met her, of course. There is no Negro woman in the world not aware of her, but I'm not like her. She smolders and sets you on fire; I use more comedy—and the voices are not the same. We are sorority sisters—when I joined the Negro sorority, Delta Sigma Theta, she pinned me. She's great, but I don't want to be another *anybody*. If you are Negro, they love to label you. Diahann Carroll was called another Lena too, at first. In this business you're automatically either another Dorothy Dandridge or another Lena. But times are changing for us all.[89]

The story of *Hallelujah, Baby!* concerns the various obstacles a young woman named Georgina encounters in her rise to becoming a nightclub star. These obstacles include the practical outlook of her mother, played by Lillian Hayman, who advises her to keep her job as a maid and give up her dreams.[90] Hayman also won a Tony Award that year for her role in this show, the Best Performance by a Featured Actress in a Musical. Musical theatre historian Ethan Mordden refers to *Hallelujah, Baby!* as a "civil rights musical."[91] However, that designation is misleading given that the show was more of a response to the civil rights movement than a creative expression that grew directly out of the movement itself. Black critics of the day felt it was ludicrously out of step with the times.[92] A production photo (figure 3.4) shows the clear-eyed Uggams poised midsyllable. In a short mod wig and with an open umbrella coolly slung over the shoulder of her 1960s minidress, she appears much more the part of the upbeat musical theatre heroine than riot-ready activist. In the course of the musical, Uggams is called upon to sing in a variety of musical styles, including numbers like "Smile, Smile, Smile," a minstrel-style shuffle that, as Uggams carefully announces to the audience at the 1968 Tony Awards, is intended to "poke fun at the attitude that society expects of us." The extent to which its parodic nature hits home with the audience is unclear, given the enthusiastic round of applause that swells up when, after a brief introduction, the shuffle rhythm kicks in. Other numbers include the show's title song, a gospel number that, if a bit stilted in its arrangement, allows Uggams the chance to riff and swing and show off additional range. In general, regardless of the decade in which a given number is set, Uggams's character is one who, as Mordden observes, "goes about the usual musical-comedy heroine's business."[93] This is evident in two songs "My Own Morning," a fairly typical musical theatre "I Want" number in the form of a wistful tune about young Georgina's hopes, and "Being Good Isn't Good Enough," the first act closer, a powerhouse belt anthem of self-empowerment and resolve.

In the original cast recording of *Hallelujah, Baby!*, Uggams sings "My Own Morning" in a pronounced, somewhat affected Southern accent, about her dreams of leaving behind her current life and having "a morning that really belongs to me."[94] It's a compact number that starts slowly and then ambles along listing all the things the character dreams of having on such a morning—a bed, a floor, a chair, a ceiling, the knowledge that her time is her own. This list leads up to a series of extended notes as she imagines how "on that day that belongs to me / I'll have the man that belongs to me" with whom to share all these other dreamed-of possessions. The bright, forward color of her voice—that buzzing right in the front of the face, closer to the nasal than the yawned—reminds me, I suddenly realize, of the distinctive timbre of Uggams's "Aunt Dinah" Washington. At the verse's conclusion, Uggams takes a deep breath and warms up her tone a bit

3.4 Leslie Uggams in *Hallelujah, Baby!* (1967). Courtesy of the Billy Rose Theatre Division, New York Public Library for the Performing Arts.

with a glottal attack-launched *oh* [oʊ] in a wide-open "and my own morning," shimmering with an even vibrato. These are the Broadway belter's long notes, not tossed away but held steady as the ripples of vibrato break over them; as with Merman's performance of "I Got Rhythm," this is a song primarily about material possession that enacts, at its height, the vocal possession of long notes. There is also the subtle addition of the theme of self-possession, that of the black maid who wants to own her own time, but this nuance is easily lost amid the contours of the otherwise typical show tune construction.

The number "Being Good Isn't Good Enough" offers up even more of the belter's long notes; I attend to Uggams's performances of this song on both the original cast album and in a televised performance of the number from the *Ed Sullivan Show*.[95] Supported by a web of low strings, the song begins pitched low in her voice, still full with the shimmer of vibrato, but with come-hither warmth. In the televised performance, the belter's chest rises and falls as she takes high breaths in contrast to an opera singer's low diaphragmatic breaths—something else Uggams surely didn't learn at Juilliard. Her vowels are beautifully loose, there is not a hint of tension at all in her jaw or face, she drops her jaw and the sound is open and clean whether the vowel is in the word "*enough*" (*aw* [ʌ]), "*below*" (*oh* [oʊ]), "*best*" (*eh* [ɛ]), or "*all*" (*aw* [ɔ]). Once it gets going, this is a profoundly difficult song to sing—one, long, high-belted note after another, with some tricky chromatic shifts in the melody. Uggams's intonation is rock solid—no "pitchiness" here. And then there is this move she does with her shoulders that has me fascinated, the way she's bracing to get those powerful notes out. Again, with a belter such as Merman one clearly sees the singer square her shoulders and sing with her chest square to the audience, using those upper body muscles to brace the sound. This is a song not about holding, but about flying high enough to reach one's dreams: "Being good won't be good enough / I'll be the best or nothing at all." Each long note from Uggams is triumphant and yet it has a tiny decrescendo at its close, a tiny easing out, easing off, with vibrato that feels like a shower of confetti. This is a decrescendo stabilized by the shoulders. In fact, the way she powers into those high notes to begin with has to do with, I notice, the way she eases her shoulders up through the course of the long note, ("Should I try, am I strong enough?") or drops them down like a quick inverse shrug before a power note. Especially at the song's close as the number slows down and there are more and more high, sustained notes, she makes use of this technique: "Being good just won't be good enough" [*shoulder* drop] / "I'll be" *[shoulder drop]* "the best" *[shoulder drop]* or nothing *[drop]* at all!" What this means is that when she is belting those money notes, she is almost always singing in the position of a shrug, and the inverse shrug or shoulder drop is both a release and a preparation for essaying the powerful belted voice.

An Exercise from Leslie Uggams: Shoulder Drop

Let's use the words "the best of all," mostly on the same pitch, but you could use the word "the" as a pickup on a lower pitch of your choosing (I like to use a fifth down) as you prefer. Start somewhere in the middle of your range. Sing "the best," and while you are singing the word "best"—stretch it out—let your shoulders ease up slowly in a shrug. Then drop your shoulders down in a release, suddenly letting go of the shrug. Now sing "of"—a fairly long note again, the same pitch as before, and let your shoulders ease up a bit again. Then drop your shoulders and hold them down, dropped, bracing, and sing the word "all." Try the whole sequence: "the best" *[shoulder drop]* "of" *[shoulder drop and hold it]* "all!" You can edge up chromatically if you like, going up to belt higher and higher in your range. Make sure to keep the "st" short, so it doesn't get in the way of your vowel. What we are interested in here are vowels and shoulders.

Pat Suzuki and Eartha Kitt
The Sexy Sound of Citizenship

Where Carroll and Uggams were hailed on Broadway for their performances as ladylike ingénues, Pat Suzuki and Eartha Kitt negotiated their leading roles as American glamour girls on the strength of their sexy singing. For both, the option to seduce on the musical stage as the quintessentially alluring American girl was by no means guaranteed; below I examine the strategies by which each managed this feat during the Cold War period. In the case of Suzuki, this involved appearing in a musical that, as Anne Anlin Cheng assesses in her magisterial analysis of *Flower Drum Song*, operated as "a morality play about national identity" with a plot centering on a beauty contest for the most desirable (read: most Americanized) bride.[96] I argue that, unlike in the musical's film adaptation in which she did not appear and where the singing for her character was dubbed by a white artist, onstage Suzuki's vivacious vocal performance secures her claims to Americanness in the part of the showgirl vixen. By all accounts a serious talent who lit up the stage, *Flower Drum Song* is Suzuki's only Broadway credit. Kitt, despite having ten Broadway shows to her name—more than any other black female Broadway star of her generation—remains markedly understudied as a musical theatre singer-actress. The globetrotting cabaret performer was already building her repertoire of novelty songs in ten languages in the 1950s and 1960s when her outspoken comments against the Vietnam War at a White House ladies' luncheon in 1968 essentially blacklisted her in the United States and led her to take her cabaret act even farther afield transnationally. I contend it was Kitt's internationalism—and vocally, her multilingualism—that allowed her to set the sensual terms for playing the part of the cosmopolitan American sex kitten—a far cry from her childhood in a southern sharecropping family. She leveraged the French-language songs she sang on Broadway in the revue *Leonard Sillman's New Faces of 1952* and the early concept musical *Shinbone Alley* (1957) to this end, caressing consonants as she finessed musical theatre characterizations in which she reinvented herself as simultaneously innocent and worldly wise. Before going on to study (with) each singer individually, I arrange a duet of their girlhoods and performance training.

....

Eartha Kitt was born in 1927 and Pat Suzuki in 1930 in the towns of North, South Carolina, and Cressey, California, respectively. Kitt grew up poor, and—the defining feature of childhood, prominent in her multiple autobiographies—unwanted. Abandoned by her mother, taunted, and abused by other children for her fair skin, Kitt's rejection by her community stemmed from the fact that she was the product of her mother's rape by the wealthy white heir to the plantation where her family worked picking cotton. "This act of violence not only marks Kitt racially—as 'yella gal'—but also, it is implied, as sexual outsider, the inheritor of her mother's supposed sin."[97] At the age of seven she departed the southern chapter of a girlhood marked by food insecurity and hard work to live with her aunt in Harlem. This too was a hardscrabble existence with an adoptive mother figure who alternately cared for Kitt and resented her presence and was by turns welcoming and abusive. Meanwhile, in central California Suzuki grew up in a Japanese American farming family who nicknamed her "Chibi," Japanese slang for a short person or "squirt" since she was the youngest of four siblings and the smallest in the family.[98] She acquired another name when her hometown grocer, who could not pronounce her given name, Chiyoko, insisted on calling her "Pat." During World War II, Suzuki and her family were incarcerated in the Grenada War Relocation Center, also known as Camp Amache, in Colorado, part of the 120,000 people of Japanese descent whom the US government viewed as national security threats and forced into "internment" during the war. In later interviews she spoke about this time with a mix of candor and diplomacy, "[I]t was not exactly the kind of home life I'd recommend for a growing girl. I had a sense of inferiority for a while after the war, but no hatred. Hatred is like war itself. Nobody can win."[99] If Suzuki downplayed the impact of her time at Camp Amache to the press, the fact remains that her girlhood was marked by the trauma of being considered an "enemy alien" in the country of her birth. The experience of living in army barracks surrounded by barbed wire, her entire family confined to one room and forcibly required to swear allegiance to the US government, can only have convinced a young Suzuki of the stakes of appearing appropriately American to white evaluators. In different ways, both Suzuki and Kitt had girlhoods marked by the trauma of being unwanted, whether at the level of the wartime nation or of the family crushed in the double bind of white supremacy and respectability.

During her early teens in Spanish Harlem, Kitt was accepted by a set of Cuban and Puerto Rican friends and, at evening jam sessions and weekend dances, picked up skills in the rhythms of Afro-Cuban social dance as well as Spanish language. She briefly attended the Metropolitan Vocational High School, the precursor of New York's renowned High School of Performing Arts, where she studied elocution with Edith Banks and was taken to audition (unsuccessfully) for the Broadway show *Carmen Jones* (1943). By age fifteen, Kitt had dropped out of school, been kicked out of her home, and was working in a factory as a seamstress. On a dare, in borrowed clothing, she auditioned for the Katherine Dunham School of Dance and was awarded a scholarship at age sixteen. It would be difficult to overstate how significantly this opportunity transformed Kitt's life and paved the way for a career in dance, theatre, and music. Kitt bore the scars of childhood rejection and abuse into adulthood. The radical nature and virtuosic craft of her performance strategy arises from the way that, nonetheless, "she insists on the importance of pleasure and sensuality as a means of survival."[100]

Following her time in the Japanese internment camp, which included a period in which she worked on a sugar beet farm in Colorado, Suzuki returned to California. There she went on to study art and education at Mills College and San Jose State University with the occasional nightclub singing gig. Of her years in college she later commented: "Musical training? I signed up for an opera workshop once in college and they wouldn't let me sing, so I said the hell with it."[101] She made her way to the East Coast, planning to travel to Europe but when cash ran out she auditioned for and secured a role with the touring company of the 1953 hit Broadway play *Teahouse of the August Moon* ("I was understudy to a walk-on . . . that's really starting at the bottom").[102] The tour's schedule included a stop in Seattle. While in that city, she sang on a whim at the Colony nightclub and was such a hit that the club owner persuaded her to stay in town and headline at the venue, which she did for three years. When Washington state-born star Bing Crosby happened to be in town he stopped by and was impressed with her chops. Crosby's endorsement helped open doors for Suzuki at RCA Victor where she soon landed a recording contract, and he penned the liner notes for the album that resulted: "There's a girl up in Seattle named Pat Suzuki, sings anything from jazz to light opera. Great bet for the big time. I mean that."[103] Suzuki appeared on television on the famous *Jack Paar Show* (*The Tonight Show*), on television specials with Frank Sinatra and Lawrence Welk. When Broadway came knocking, Suzuki's star was rising so high that the savvy performer turned down the gig until the producers returned with a more generous offer.

Pat Suzuki
All-American Vixen

Like Carroll, Uggams, and Kitt, Suzuki stands as a Broadway singer-actress of color who belted beyond limiting expectations about what kind of voice was appropriate for a young woman of her race. "Song belter" Pat Suzuki was cast in the role of vamp Linda Low, the coquettish nightclub singer in the lavish Rodgers and Hammerstein musical *Flower Drum Song* (1958).[104] In step with the black women in this chapter who were her contemporaries, she disrupts the idea that the classic Broadway belter is only ever a white woman, and that women of color must then be consigned to lesser roles. In addition, unlike Latina star Chita Rivera whose acclaimed performance as Anita in 1957's *West Side Story* was leveraged by that show's producers to reinforce mainstream assumptions about the fieriness and sexiness of Latina women, Suzuki's appearance as a brash Broadway belter directly contested pervasive narratives around Asian American women as quiet, restrained, and submissive. Some of her predecessors include Chin Yu who played Liat in international productions of *South Pacific*, a character who, as noted in chapter 2, does not speak at all throughout the entire musical, and the Japanese American performer Sono Osato, featured in another all-American girl role in the wartime musical *On the Town* (1944). Remarkably, during the height of World War II, while her Japanese-born father was detained indefinitely in her hometown of Chicago, Osato performed on Broadway as the literal winner of a New York City beauty contest, Miss Turnstiles. But Osato's was a dance role in which she did not speak or sing onstage.[105] As *Blues Mamas and Broadway Belters* arcs toward an understanding of the citational practice of singing, and how the blues shouters' sound wound up on Broadway, Suzuki presents a valuable example of how one particular belter found her way to the musical theatre stage by way of the jazz nightclub.

It is true that fair-skinned black actress Juanita Hall, discussed in chapter 2, also appeared in the original cast of *Flower Drum Song* in high yellowface as the cheongsam-clad Madam Liang with an (I think I can say) abomination of an upbeat show tune entitled "Chop Suey."[106] This is a group dance number that feels like a bizarre mash-up of musical theatre songs from *West Side Story* and *Oklahoma*! set in Chinatown. ("Chop suey! Chop suey! / Living here is very much like chop suey!") The film version even includes rumba and square-dancing sections before turning to a rock'n'roll dance break. Of this dance mélange, Anne Anlin Cheng astutely observes, "Such an insistent celebration, in a changing ethnic enclave of America in the fifties (and in light of those styles' own ethnic origins) can only announce an anxiety over the very idea of 'an American style.'"[107] Yet with the premiere of *Flower Drum Song*, Suzuki and her showstopping pipes were pronounced "Broadway's new vocal sensation."[108] Compared variously to Ethel Merman and Mary Martin, critics described the force and entertainment value of her "captivating" performance with words such as "verve," "earthiness and gusto," and "brashness"—this last understood as a high compliment for a Broadway belter whose sound must have a certain edge and power to carry a show tune to the back of the house.[109] In December 1958, Suzuki and her *Flower Drum Song* costar, sweet-voiced ingénue Miyoshi Umeki, were featured on the cover of *Time*.[110] Broadway's first star Asian American belter had arrived.

Suzuki was not invited to take the role of Linda Low for the 1961 film adaptation, which was given to Chinese-Scottish actress Nancy Kwan on the heels of her box-office success in the 1960 film *The World of Suzie Wong*, with Kwan's voice dubbed by white actress B. J. Baker.[111] The role of the Chinese American showgirl Linda has been considered what film scholar Juliana Chang summarizes as "the fantasy of the postwar American woman. . . . Scholars such as Robert G. Lee, David Palumbo-Liu, and Anne Anlin Cheng interpret Linda as the modern ethnic woman who is hyperassimilated and Americanized and even figures racial whiteness."[112] But where onscreen the Americanness of the character is secured by her literal proximity to whiteness—the casting of the mixed-race Kwan, bringing her European ancestry to attest to her acceptable beauty under the close scrutiny of the camera—this is not the case in the stage musical. On Broadway, what attests to Linda's all-Americanness is not only the pinup girl's bold striptease she performs in her nightclub act but also the force of her belted voice singing after what audiences and critics heard as such indisputably American talents as Mary Martin and Ethel Merman. Perceived as "singing along after" these white women Broadway stars, Suzuki's talent was celebrated onstage in a way that the cinematic genre did not support—there the strategy was to literally affix the voice of a white singer to the onscreen mixed-race, Asian feminine body.

Suzuki's is not the sound of a naive or powerless woman. A photo from the stage production of *Flower Drum Song* (figure 3.5) depicts her standing alone on set in a satin cocktail dress, her hair pulled back in her signature ponytail with bangs fringing her forehead. Unlike so many of her cheerfully smiling press photos, in this image Suzuki looks like she sounds when she belts—a woman not to be trifled with. True, the dubious source of her confidence, as imagined by the writers of her hit song from *Drum*, "I Enjoy Being a Girl," may feel somewhat ridiculous by today's standards. The song has however sustained multiple valences beyond its place in the original show, as evidenced by its place in the 1950s repertoire of white transgender cabaret singer Christine Jorgensen.[113] It is also worth noting that with this number Suzuki charts vastly different vocal and emotional terrain from that navigated by defenseless, self-sacrificing sex worker Kim in *Miss Saigon* (1991), and her sister character, victimized concubine Tuptim from *The King and I* (1951), two of the best-known examples of Asian women characters in the Broadway musical theatre canon.

My goal here is not to unreservedly commend the authors of this deeply flawed 1950s musical for making supposed great strides toward racial equity. Certainly the stage and film versions of *Flower Drum Song* have been justifiably critiqued by Asian American scholars and artists, even while celebrating the visibility both provided for Asian American performers.[114] Playwright David Henry Hwang even persuaded the Rodgers and Ham-

3.5 Pat Suzuki in *Flower Drum Song* (1958). Courtesy of the Billy Rose Theatre Division, New York Public Library for the Performing Arts.

merstein estate to allow him to rewrite the libretto entirely for a 2002 revival; this is the version most often performed today. It must also be noted that the accepted casting conventions of the 1950s required Suzuki to share the stage with multiple actors in yellowface—not only Juanita Hall, but also her character's love interest, played by white actor Larry Blyden in the role of slick nightclub owner Sammy Fong. In writing about what it is to witness yellowface in contemporary musical theatre, mapping her felt experience "of Asian American affect under white supremacy," Donatella Galella unsettles the idea that cheery, toe-tapping musicals are always ever destined to produce happiness for all audience members.[115] Galella also details the discomfort of witnessing "I Enjoy Being a Girl" sung by a white singer-actress in a 2015 concert at New York City Center that completely elided Suzuki's presence from theatrical memory—no Asian Americans or indeed performers of color of any background were included in the concert. Yet because vocal sound is twice-heard, any subsequent performances of the song Suzuki originated must be understood in some sense as citations of Suzuki's voice—even when, as in this instance, such a citation travels uncredited.

In 1958, despite the limitations of script, score, staging, and casting, in the effervescent voice of Pat Suzuki, an Asian American Broadway singer changed the definition of who could belt out show tunes to great effect in a "Golden Age" musical. In later years, Baayork Lee, the veteran Broadway performer and choreographer who appeared in the original cast of *The King and I* (1951) as a child and *Flower Drum Song* as a teen, and went on to originate the role of Connie Wong in *A Chorus Line* (1975), put it this way:

> Thank God in 1958 there was Pat Suzuki, who was the new girl on the block, who was fashionable, who sang jazz, and she really put us on the map in terms of bringing us into the twentieth century. It was Pat Suzuki who had her straggly bangs with a long pony tail, and she was brassy. Everybody looked up to her character. She was strong, and there was the contrast.[116]

The song "I Enjoy Being a Girl" from *Flower Drum Song* is starkly revealing about perceptions of 1950s femininity even if present-day listeners feel that it has not necessarily aged well. As the lyric essays, "When I have a brand new hairdo / with my eyelashes all in curl, / I float as the clouds on air do, / I enjoy being a girl!" The bouncy tune goes on, in what reads now as near-caricature, to extol the virtues of curves, frills, pearls, flowers, cold cream, candy, dancing, and bikinis, and 1950s femininity generally imagined as delightfully high-maintenance and objectifying in the breeziest of senses. One verse of Hammerstein's lyric that plays especially poorly today: "When I hear a complimentary whistle / That greets my bikini by the sea / I turn and I glower and I gristle / But I'm happy to know the whistle's meant for me!" Yet it was declarative text like this that enabled Suzuki to clearly locate herself and her character in the position of sex symbol. Here I also find especially valuable the discipline of listening closely to the sound of Suzuki's voice beyond the content of what she is singing about. I am listening to her performance of the number on the original cast album in tandem with footage of footage of a live performance she gave on the *Ed Sullivan Show* in a sequence of selected numbers from the show performed by the original cast.[117]

There is a confident smoothness to Suzuki's tone. In her live performance, she has a bright, glowing smile, she radiates star power. There is a crunchiness to her sound, she uses her consonants well. And then there's a little scratchiness that comes from the glottal attacks she uses on certain vowels at the starts of phrases (the glottal attack being that stop of the vocal cords that comes with a sound like *Uh-oh* [ʔʌʔoʊ] heard here on words like I, at, on, or, eyelashes, in) which give them that extra kick, and makes the voice seem more conversational since that is something that classical singers generally don't do. In the middle of phases or at their ends, she has so many back vowels in this song—the *er* [ɜr] / [ər] sounds of girl, curl, whirl, pearl, flow*ers, cur*vy—these are hard vowels to sing but she makes them sparkle, resonating right in the front of the face. Even when she has the classic belter vowels—high vowels such as "a" in "hat" [æ] or "ey" in "hey" [eɪ]—she covers them over a bit, as a word like "race" comes out with more of the second half of the diphthong than the first, which makes it a bit warmer and, in a way, less formal.[118] It sounds like she's always midway into a laugh. She's comfortable when the song goes up higher, moving smoothly between the power notes and a lighter quality that still has an even fullness. Sometimes when a belter slips into the top part of her register it feels like something has been lost, but not for Suzuki. She alternates notes without vibrato, words bitten off for expressive purposes, with long notes where the vibrato just rings, fast and steady. But the thing that strikes me most is a certain kind of lilting slide she adds in multiple places. She finds extra notes where they're not written, accentuating the syncopated rhythm of a repeated note by dropping down a third and then swinging back up to hit the second note in the set.[119] She mines the voiced consonants, singing through the *r*'s of couplets like hairdo/air do, the *n*'s of funny/honey, candy/brandy, and the *l*'s of smolder/shoulder. I am struck, in accounts of the rehearsal process of *Flower Drum Song*, by Suzuki's recollection of how she struggled to learn this song, so different from her nightclub repertoire, when composer Rodgers demanded precise delivery of the rhythms: "He always had a very definite idea about the timing because it was important that the words were emphasized in a specific way. . . . It's hard to sing because it's really square!"[120] With her lilting attack, I contend, Suzuki found a way to bring more curves to the song, even without changing the rhythms as written per se. In the windup to song's end, performing live, she throws her hands out on either side of her body and braces with her shoulders, belting out a money note and sliding down from it into the song's final phrase of extended long tones. Her body nearly square to the audience, slightly angled upstage, upper torso braced, arms extended, Suzuki gives us the classic physicality of the Broadway belter, with the "brash" sound to match.

An Exercise from Pat Suzuki: Curve Attack

Tap out 4/4 time with your foot—one, two, three, four / one, two, three, four (keep going). We are going to use a syncopated rhythm that hits two notes, the first on the downbeat of one and the second on the upbeat midway between two and three, that is: *one*, two, *and* three, four / *one*, two, *and* three, four. Keep going. For a lyric we'll use the word "honey" on the notes where the *one* and the *and* in this dotted-quarter rhythm hit. Pitch the notes on the same note, midway in your range, somewhere that feels powerful but not astronomically high. Sing *hon* [ˈhʌn] on the *one* and *ney* [ni], on the *and*: *hon* (two) *ney* (three, four). Again: *hon* (two) *ney* (three, four). Go straight to the *n* at the end of the first syllable and use it to bounce up into the second. It feels kind of like you're punching the second syllable: *hon-NEY, hon-NEY*. Now, in between singing *hon* [ˈhʌn] and *ney* [ni]—right where you go to the *n* sound, add a dip in pitch (a third down), then hop back up to the original note with a good, strong *n* on *ney*. Do it again. Seems too complicated on the page? Listen to Suzuki's original cast recording of "I Enjoy Being a Girl" and sing along with her "honey" line at 1:11. And lilt when she lilts. That's it.

Eartha Kitt: *Haïtien, français, ou américain . . . un bal est un bal*

It is remarkable that Eartha Kitt is not better known for her work as a performer in US musical theatre. But with her scratchy, sinuous voice and catlike magnetism, Kitt resists easy categorization and her work as a recording artist and screen actress have often eclipsed her status as a Broadway star. Her quirky set of hit songs includes "C'est Si Bon," "I Want to Be Evil," the Turkish tune "Uska Dara," and the original rendition of "Santa Baby." Onscreen, in addition to a slew of variety show spots, she appeared opposite Sidney Poitier in *The Mark of the Hawk* (1957), filmed in Nigeria, and with Nat King Cole in *St. Louis Blues* (1958) before bringing her famous purr to the television role of Catwoman in *Batman* in the late 1960s; late in her career she was featured as the libidinous senior business exec Lady Eloise in Eddie Murphy's *Boomerang* (1992) and provided the voice of villainess Yzma in Disney's *The Emperor's New Groove* (2000) franchise. But before all that, Kitt began her career as a dancer in Katherine Dunham's company and in the Dunham Broadway revues *Blue Holiday* (1945), *Carib Song* (1945), and *Bal Nègre* (1946), in which she also performed vocally before touring to Mexico and throughout Europe with the dance company. In 1949 she began a solo career as a cabaret artist in Paris nightclubs and shortly thereafter appeared in Paris as Helen of Troy in Orson Welles's stage adaptation of the Faust myth, a show that also toured in Germany and Belgium. Her fame throughout Europe—where in the early 1950s she performed her acclaimed cabaret act in Istanbul, London, and Athens, as well as Paris—secured her return to New York nightclubs and breakout Broadway performance in the revue *Leonard Sillman's New Faces of 1952*. She toured across the United States with this musical and reprised her performance, expanded to include more of her hit songs, in the 1954 film adaptation *New Faces*. Her other Broadway credits comprise multiple musicals and plays with music including *Mrs. Patterson* (1954), *Shinbone Alley* (1957), *Timbuktu!* (1978), and *The Wild Party* (2000).

The profoundly internationalist space of the Dunham School of Dance provided the pedagogical framework for Kitt's girlhood performance training. The school paid the living expenses of scholarship students like Kitt and provided them with a small stipend. From 11 a.m. to 11 p.m., between classes, rehearsals, and performances, Kitt was plunged into an educational environment of prestigious black accomplishment and intellectual training as well as interracial and international collaboration. The school was established to deliver on Dunham's vision that dance education should "train the whole person, or 'total dancer.'"[121] Students in the certificate program were required to study a language among other requirements; in addition to Spanish, Russian, and French, courses were offered in anthropology, music appreciation, comedy techniques, dramatic history, psychology, and philosophy. Scholars and artists from all over the world with impressive credentials taught within its classrooms. In addition to Dunham's aim to provide a corrective to the antiblack bent of US public schools, the student body included students from all over the world. "Cuban, Palestinian, Haitian, and Irish students took classes from teachers who hailed from Haiti, Trinidad, Mexico, Austria, and elsewhere."[122] Stephanie Batiste contends that, as she stepped carefully through imperial and objectifying perspectives around her work, Dunham anticipated postmodern anthropological approaches, deploying "ethnography as performance" and positioning herself "as a *participant* in ethnographic exchange as observer and observed."[123] As a teenage student at the school, Kitt saw Dunham as a role model and sought her rarely bestowed approval. She envied Dunham's elegant rehearsal clothes, remembering, "She always looked like the essence of success to me."[124] Further, Kitt's cabaret performance aesthetics can be understood as carrying forward Dunham's aspiration to nonhierarchical cultural exchange.

The scorching intensity of Eartha Kitt's voice, like her gaze, transfixes the audience. Her performances and star persona have frequently been described as "fascinating," and in performance she also projects the sense of being fascinated by the world around her.[125] Like Dunham, Kitt is both "observer and observed," like Lena Horne she withholds even as she appears to proffer herself, requiring the audience to seek her approval more than they may imagine she seeks theirs.[126] In international travels with the Dunham Company prior to the launch of her solo career as a singer, Kitt learned that in 1947 Mexico City black performers could reside close to the performance venue rather than commuting in from the segregated areas of town some distance away as in the United States. She learned that New York was less economically depressed than 1948 London, an impoverished city still reeling from World War II where meat, butter, and sugar were hard to come by. And soon, I imagine, she was able to conclude for herself that, regardless of its country of origin, *un bal est un bal* . . . A fancy party is a fancy party, whether dancing in Haitian exotica costume on Broadway in Dunham's 1946 revue *Bal Negre* or singing the lighthearted Parisian chanson "Bal Petit Bal" on Broadway in producer Leonard Sillman's revue *New Faces of 1952*.

When I began writing about Kitt for this chapter, it seemed inevitable that the vocal detail I would write about is her trademark seductive purr. After all, she is known for the feline grace of her stage presence, was called

Kitty by her friends throughout her life, and literally played Catwoman on the 1960s *Batman* series. Her vocal technique of the purr is a striking sound, what Royster hears as "the growl that some say is the purr of a kitten but you know it is the growl of hunger barely held back."[127] I also hear Kitt's purr as akin to mambo king Pérez Prado's emphatic grunt as an "indexical noise, or as that which makes possible a space of reprieve," a sound that escapes language and music notation to propel mobile and fugitive performance.[128] As a dancer trained in Dunham technique, the embodied technical facility in which she grounds her vocal production is virtuosic. Perhaps in an iteration of the Dunham hinge position exercise, her body arched backward across so many chaise lounges, singing from "a state of extravagant repose," we might hear Kitt's voice as the swivel of a refusal to be confined to expected cultural geographies.[129] As Farah Jasmine Griffin incises, black female voice is itself "like a hinge, a place where things can both come together and break apart."[130]

In her landmark article on black female vocality, Griffin theorizes that black women's voices may provoke national crisis as well as heal them.[131] Famous for chewing out First Lady "Lady Bird" Johnson with a critique of the Vietnam War at a White House luncheon, Kitt's voice falls more on the side of fascinating provocation. It is perhaps in this way that her voice as a black woman is most American. In one of her many autobiographies, *Confessions of a Sex Kitten*, Kitt writes of her first transatlantic travels: "Where and to whom do I belong? Here? There? Everywhere? Nowhere?"[132] But Chita Rivera, Kitt's understudy on the 1957 Broadway musical *Shinbone Alley*, when asked to comment on her experience working with Kitt, all but rolled her eyes and laughed, "I loved Eartha but she was a trip. She was a round-trip."[133] Kitt's globetrotting life and career, whether dining with Indian prime minister Jawaharlal Nehru and politely declining a marriage proposal from soon-to-be-president of Nigeria Nnamdi Azikiwe, simply return her to her own Americanness. The travels and the feelings they sparked in her, she writes, "made me realize how valuable my American passport was"—but, importantly, on terms that she negotiated for herself.[134] I contend that a major way she negotiated her Americanness is via her vocal practice of multilingual singing. Throughout her career, Kitt sang in ten different languages—including French, Spanish, Turkish, Tagalog, Japanese, and Swahili—and by the early 1950s her cabaret repertoire already included songs in seven of these. Below I listen to Kitt's vocal performances of the French-language songs "Bal Petit Bal" and "Toujours Gai" from cast recordings and the film *New Faces*.

In the revue *New Faces*, the 1952 stage production as in the 1954 film version, Kitt's number "Bal Petit Bal" is introduced by a faux Frenchman whistling a carefree tune and speaking a few lines about how the French like to celebrate, "You know, in France we usually celebrate our fourth of July by having what you call a block dance!" While his comments may be meant to justify this black woman's presence within the imagined Parisian landscape, her own accent and vocal performance do that work much more effectively as he translates her initial sung lines into English before turning over the space and exiting. But his introduction is meaningful for the whistle of admiration; as in Suzuki's *Flower Drum Song* number, it is implied that Kitt's character must "know the whistle is meant for me!" In the film the set is full of festive red and white balloons rising high with long, curlicued ribbons streaming down. When Kitt enters, dressed in a red and white striped capri jumpsuit with halter top bodice, she presses one palm against a scenic flat, leans slightly, and sings. Her sound is full of tremulous vibrato, a sweet sound, what is often called a "mix" voice because of its place in a certain vocal netherland between the full-bodied belt and the floated "head voice." This is a little girl's voice, but a French one, and there are moments where she treads with the hush of a whispered sound, the sighed release of opening phrases. On the word "grand" there is the uvular fricative r [ʁ], the French "r" that hints gently at the purr to come in future years. It's an easy-paced song about falling in love with a boy at a party and she swings through a lyric about a French officer who is there coolly talking politics, the praise of a blue- or green-eyed lover. "Bal Petit Bal" is a chanson by French songwriter Francis Lemarque that Kitt used in her cabaret repertoire in Paris and is now interpolated into this Broadway revue. By singing in the original French, Kitt has reclaimed the chanson on Broadway from its translation into American torch song, leveraging its language as the sound of chic cosmopolitanism. The moment that really stands out to me is when she sings the lyric "air de fête," not simply because this really is a light and festive tune, but because of the way she slips in a blue slide on the word "air" and the "r" [ʁ] becomes the guttural sound that is half a hard "g" [g]. It is the texture of these consonants, it occurs to me, that allow her to reconceive the terms of her citizenship.

How did Eartha Kitt come by this world-traveled, continental sound, a far cry from her roots in a sharecropping family in South Carolina? The Tony-winning Broadway orchestrator Daryl Waters, who music directed for Kitt early in his career, commented to me that for years, "Every time I was in a restaurant and heard an Edith Piaf or Marlene Dietrich song in the background, it confirmed that those two had left an indelible impression on [Kitt] during her formative years in Europe."[135] It is also sometimes suggested that Kitt was coached (onstage and off) by sophisticated performer Josh White. Cited in chapter 1 as the speculative teacher-to-a-teacher of Ethel Merman, White was the accompanist and coach for singer Libby Holman and known for his sexy stage presence and seductive finesse as a showman.[136] White traveled the line between bluesman, cabaret act, and downtown nightclub performer, and this fluidity may well have inspired Kitt who blurred the line between her cabaret repertoire and Broadway appearances. Where the "air de fête" discussed above was a song from Kitt's Parisian club repertoire that she saw added to a Broadway revue, the song "Toujours Gai" traveled the opposite direction—from a Broadway score into her cabaret act and related recordings. And if with "Bal Petit Bal" in the early 1950s she approached a Lolita-esque ingénue (if Lolita were a self-styled Parisian girl), by the latter part of the decade with the musical *Shinbone Alley* Kitt played a much more worldly wise character in the role of the sexy alley cat Mehitabel. In a production photo from the 1957 musical (figure 3.6), she lounges on the bare stage against a dark background, wearing a leotard under a cropped shirt fringed with pom poms. Kitt props herself up on one arm with legs stretched out to the side, eyes fixed on the audience as she sips milk from a bottle through a long straw. She seems to stare but the comic feline pose absolutely invites the audience to stare back at the length of her dancer's body.

Shinbone Alley was a fascinating musical, barely-if-at-all remembered today. The show was scored with jazz verve in the vein of a Bernstein or Weill with the occasional tiptoe into boogie-woogie by composer George Kleinsinger, known for his 1940s children's concert score *Tubby the Tuba*, and with skillful lyrics by Joe Darion some years ahead of his penning an immortal impossible dream for *Man of La Mancha* (1965). Its book was by a young Mel Brooks, who had also contributed sketches for *New Faces of 1952*. *Shinbone* was a musical adaptation of the fanciful newspaper column "archy and mehitabel" by Don Marquis that ran in the *New York Herald Tribune* in the 1910s and 1920s.[137] The central characters are Archy, a free-verse writing cockroach poet, and the sleek alley cat Mehitabel, whom novelist E. B. White described as "this dissolute feline, who was a dancer and always the lady, toujours gai."[138] Archy and Mehitabel are improbably but nonetheless the best of friends, although their relationship is constantly threatened by Mehitabel's propensity to run off with the dashing tomcat admirer *du jour*. The reviews for the show were mostly positive, if view-

3.6 Eartha Kitt as alley cat Mehitabel in *Shinbone Alley* (1957). Courtesy of the Billy Rose Theatre Division, New York Public Library for the Performing Arts.

ers emerged a bit perplexed by the show's unusual format—as a series of loosely linked poems ostensibly written by Archy the cockroach, it lacked the throughline of a narrative book musical—and all were complimentary of Kitt's performance within the multiracial cast. Walter Kerr at the *New York Herald Tribune* disliked the show but wrote admiringly of Kitt: "She writhes and wriggles to a dozen insinuating tunes, rasps out her metallic staccato at the ends of long, liquid lines, and flips a trailing boa over a saucy shoulder with thoroughly fetching impudence."[139] For the *New York Times*, Brooks Atkinson observed:

> Despite the bluntness of her given name, Miss Kitt is an unearthly actress with an elusive and insinuating style all her own. Her singing voice is husky and flat, but it is electric with personality. She is not beautiful in any conventional way, but she is alert, alive and magnetic. . . . It should be pointed out that Miss Kitt and Mr. Bracken contribute something positive to the production by accepting the fact that they are not playing musical comedy lovers, but a cat and a cockroach, respectively. . . . There is a lot of fresh and amusing stuff in "Shinbone Alley," particularly notable in a stale season like this one. But the basic problem of how to make a theatre piece out of a book of random verse has not been solved.[140]

The show closed after a month and a half and barely rates a mention in Kitt's autobiography *Confessions of a Sex Kitten*, where she refers to it by the slightly inaccurately title *Archy and Mehitabel* and says it had a "short run" before she resumes discussing her thrilling nightclub engagements in gowns designed by Pierre Balmain.[141] The *Baltimore Afro-American* bemoaned the show's rapid closing, lamenting that it "marked the second heartbreak venture for the internationally famous star." Only somewhat exaggerating the positive reviews from "every newspaper critic in New York," the journalist questioned what could have dimmed the lights of a Broadway show that had seemed destined for bright prospects, regretfully concluding, "One explanation is that the theater as now constituted, is unwilling to accept a colored star in a dramatic production—nor in any other for that matter."[142]

Although no cast album was recorded for *Shinbone Alley*, the audio recording from the house microphones from a performance during the run in 1957 was released as a double CD on Legend Records in 1993, providing a fascinating portal into the production, its sound, and Kitt's vocal presence in the show. On the recording, Kitt's voice is piercingly clear, mostly straight tone (no vibrato) and cuts cleanly across the brassy wail and screech of jazzy orchestration. In "What Do I Care," the ensemble struts along behind her blue prancing vocal: "My heart's been broken a million times / and I've been through the mill . . . but I'm a lady still." All this is interspersed with the shouts and hollers of a cast doing it up to the dance music. The numbers really swing; these are musical theatre song-and-dance numbers conveying the light charm of easygoing show tunes, and the brightness of Kitt's forward-placed sound seems to operate almost in spite of the whimsy of the show's premise. "Flotsam and Jetsam" is a song that makes use of her comic timing, a sequence of Kitt singing Mehitabel's blue response to the rapid-fire spoken word calls of Eddie Bracken as Archy. In "Come to Mee-ow," a comedy number with a vocal exercise literally written into it, Kitt as Mehitabel encounters an operatically inclined suitor who is, as the dialogue quips, both a seducer and producer of cats.[143] In Mehitabel's anthem, whose title is sometimes given as "Cheerio, My Deario" and sometimes as "Toujours Gai," the phrases adjacent in the song's chorus, Kitt is heard comforting a weeping sister alley cat, encouraging her not to cry. This is a whimsical waltz yet it feels somehow wistful. Again there is that tremulous vibrato of hers, itself one degree away from the tremor of weeping. No longer the young girl with her air de fête, Kitt plays the alley cat who is limping and scared, has been through a lot and yet still "I sing and I dance, toujours gai!" Bells sparkle in the orchestration as she delivers this song of hope whose tone, in the colors of Kitt's voice, reminds that hope travels with sadness. The final sung note, the treble proffered in pianissimo promises that, quite often, Kitt-as-Mehitabel is in fact *not* toujours gai. It is an un-"Everything's Coming Up Roses." In that legendary number from *Gypsy* Ethel Merman delivers bravado to insist things will come out right by the sheer force of her will; here, Kitt is melancholic from the start. Royster, writing after Anne Anlin Cheng, theorizes, "Kitt presents her life as one of racial melancholia—and this melancholy in turn informs the tense, high-energy contrariness of her performance aesthetic."[144] I submit it is because Kitt's project is melancholic from the start that she is able to secure her triumph as a black singer within the racially melancholic space of the musical-theatrical stage, with its "desperately insistent tone."[145] It is the linguistic texture of French chanson that gives her license to sing this truth on that most American of spaces, Broadway, with the suede-soft zh [ʒ] and trilling uvular r [ʁ]: *toujours gai!*

An Exercise from Eartha Kitt:
Luxury of Consonants

Spend some time studying a language that is unfamiliar to you. (The best way is to ask for help from someone who speaks the language, but there are all kinds of apps and online resources nowadays, so no excuses.) Then, learn a popular song in this language. Listen carefully to the vocal performance by a fluent speaker. Pay attention to this singer's inflections, timbre of voice, use of vibrato, and, especially, texture of consonants. Sing along with this singer, and then return to singing the song alone. Taste the consonants, especially those that feel different from consonants in other languages you speak and luxuriate in their sound.

Another Exercise (Just Because) from
Eartha Kitt: Lounge Purr

Hinge your body backward, arching your back over a chaise lounge or cushioned footstool. Roll a guttural (uvular voiced fricative) r [ʁ] deep in your throat. (For English-as-a-first-language speakers, it may be closer to a g than what you think of as an r). Make sure the rolling has voice, is a voiced consonant. Pull the breathpower for the sound from deep in your gut as you insinuate your body this way and that, like a cat stretching in the sun. Bonus points if you fix your gaze unflinchingly on a listener while you purr.

Conclusions

It would have been easy to seek a repertoire of vocal secrets to serve up in this chapter. As I examine in the chapter that follows, this is precisely what is widely understood as the necessary material for teaching and studying singing, whether popular or classical techniques—a set of secrets of the voice. Diagnosing this proposition for what it is—a singing teacher's sales pitch, the advisement to hire a guide against hidden dangers—I have offered instead a set of whimsical exercises to invite the reader to participate in joyful and, I hope, fearless singing practice. Like the details to which Alexandra T. Vazquez attends in scholarship that takes shape as aesthetic practice rather than the demarcation of stable regions of knowledge, the vocal exercises distilled here operate via minutiae to interrupt supposedly coherent narratives of song and story. They are perhaps a productive distraction: not-song, not the thing itself, not what anyone would pay to hear. And like other compendiums of vocal exercises, when executed, they also push against stable boundaries of what the singing voice is and can be, a particular form of what Mladen Dolar calls "non-voice" that disrupts both the symbolic nature and the propriety of the well-behaved voice to present new vocal-possibles in the process.[146]

In combination with the vocal exercises gathered here, the analyses of critical duets in this chapter yield an understanding of musical theatre history that not only allows for the presence of black women but also invites an ethic of care for the young black woman artist and her "girlish art of yearning" on the musical stage. The simple fact of recognizing that black women have been (and continue to be) people in the process of growing and changing, rather than "natural" artists presumed to never have had a childhood, is an act of care. In this way, grappling with the hurts and refusals, performances of both dissemblance and charm, careful withholdings as well as strategic seductions, my revisionist musical theatre history responds to what Daphne Brooks has called "a crisis in care for the lives and work of Black women musicians as well as the women who love them."[147] As discussed in chapter 1, singing is not modulated by an "on/off" switch mechanism but is a practice that emerges over time as singers move through girlhood and different chapters of expressive life.

In listening to and singing along with Lena Horne, Mary Martin, Diahann Carroll, Leslie Uggams, Pat Suzuki, and Eartha Kitt, I have studied the ways these artists' voices expressed girlish yearnings by means of the careful smolder, hoydenish mischief, ladylike elegance, righteous confidence, brash sexiness, and tremulous multilingualism, respectively. Along the way they navigated—or appeared somewhat oblivious to—particular kinds of unfreedom in spaces, situations, and experiences marked by the intermingling of melancholy and hope. As I will examine in the next chapter, the ability to freely assume particular affective postures has often been thought of as either the result of or the route to technical proficiency in singing, across the history of vocal pedagogy in the long twentieth century.

4 Secrets of Vocal Health

Voice Teachers and Pop Vocal Technique

The first three chapters of *Blues Mamas and Broadway Belters* argued for early and mid-twentieth-century black women singers of the musical stage as highly trained and effective voice teachers who sounded and transmitted the vocal techniques heard over decades on into Broadway belting today. This chapter locates black women singers in the continuum of voice pedagogy as it is more typically delineated and uncovers how popular singing techniques such as those honed by the blues shouters have been pathologized in the modern voice studio.

Over the course of the twentieth century, within pedagogical and clinical circles in Europe and the United States, the language around the vocal apparatus shifted from the discussion of vocal organs to a greater emphasis on voice production. Terminology that classified the various registers of the voice, understood at the turn of the century to be chest, head, and falsetto, expanded to refer to voice quality and voice color defined in terms of anatomical configuration. And the terms "vocal hygiene" and "vocal health" came into general use among voice teachers. During this period, I ask in this chapter, how did vocal technique come to be synonymous with vocal health in such a way that, for teachers of classical voice, popular singing epitomized *un*health?

I begin with the vocal examples of two renowned, operatically trained singers at the turn of the twentieth century, the African American star of concert hall and vaudeville stage, Sissieretta Jones, and the German opera diva Lilli Lehmann. I then explore the way that Manuel Garcia II, inventor of the laryngoscope, established the much-imitated modern archetype of the singer and voice teacher as voice scientist, and in whose footsteps turn-of-the-twenty-first-century voice teachers such as Oberlin Conservatory professor Richard Miller sought to follow. In Miller's writings and classes, and in those of other US pedagogues featured in the *Journal of the National Association of Teachers of Singing*, how did twentieth-century voice teachers listen to, write about, and theorize the popular singing voice? From the 1970s on, female singers and voice teachers Jo Estill and, later, Jeannette LoVetri advocated for the inclusion of the popular voice in the singing studio: How, I ask, do their methods implicitly theorize the voice and race? I draw on my own study of the Estill method, as a singer and student participant-observer in voice training workshops, to delve into the implications of a technique that theorizes all voices as available to all people. Working through the theorizing of Abbey Lincoln, I arrive at an understanding of vocal sound as shaped by techniques of affective expression that derive from historical context. The promise inherent in the open secret of *singing along with* black women singers, I conclude, lies in the black feminist erotics and politics of self-knowledge.

Sissieretta Jones and the Flexed Voice

At the turn of the twentieth century, the most famous black woman singer in the United States was Sissieretta Jones, billed as "the greatest singer of her race." Jones toured the Caribbean, Latin America, and Europe to great acclaim, singing in celebrated concert halls and before royal and presidential audiences.[1] Images of her such as a 1900 photograph (figure 4.1) show Jones with a nonchalant smile and a dozen gold and bejeweled medals pinned to the bodice of her elegant, corseted dress—these medals were gifts from international dignitaries and fans of her concerts garnered during her travels. A lyric soprano, she was lauded in the press for a voice that was sweet, powerful, and well trained, and given the nickname "Black Patti" after her contemporary, the renowned European opera singer Adelina Patti. Jones's repertoire included operatic works by Giuseppe Verdi and Gioachino Rossini alongside popular songs by Stephen Foster and compositions by African American composer Will Marion Cook and his mentor, Antonin Dvořák. When concert engagements were not forthcoming, she performed extensively on the vaudeville stage, touring the country as the star of her own troupe, the Black Patti Troubadours. Jones had grown up in Providence, Rhode Island, where as a child she sang in the Pond Street Baptist Church and studied voice with Ada Baron Lacombe at the Providence

4.1 Sissieretta Jones portrait (1900). Schomburg Center for Research in Black Culture, New York Public Library Digital Collections.

Academy of Music. As a young woman she pursued conservatory studies in Boston and additional vocal training in New York with a range of teachers including Luisa Cappiani. After a long and successful career in which she supported herself, a spendthrift husband, and her mother, she retired to her home in Providence and sank into relative obscurity, although she reportedly sang in the church choir even in the last years of her life. When she died in 1933, the *Baltimore Afro-American* newspaper paid tribute to the memory of Jones performing music from composer Giacomo Meyerbeer's opera *L'Africaine (The African Woman)* at the height of her fame: "a queenly black singer in a dress of shimmering green, a leopard's skin over her shoulder," a singer whose combined gifts included a "divine voice," "robust body" and "strong will."[2]

In 1900, when she was thirty-two years of age, Jones was in the midst of a forty-five-week tour with her company, in which she gave nearly five hundred performances at theatres across North America. She had expressed to an interviewer a few years earlier that she preferred the concert hall to the vaudeville stage and hoped to return to it and to Europe, but these dreams never materialized.[3] Instead, her company became the most successful African American touring theatre troupe of her time.[4] Some years after her passing, Salem Tutt Whitney, a vaudevillian and former member of the Black Patti Troubadours, recalled Jones's particular practice of preshow vocalization:

> Patti was always early at the theatre. When the opening chorus began, she would come from her dressing room fully dressed, stand in the wings and sing with the chorus until time for her specialty near the close of the show. She said the exercise cleared her throat and flexed her vocal chords [*sic*].[5]

This description of vocalizing attributed to Jones is evocative for the ways in which it both aligns with and revises notions of the classical singer maintaining her technique. The conventional image of an operatically trained singer warming up presents the singer alone, or with an accompanist, moving through scales and arpeggios, exercising sound through the pedestrian acts of walking or hopping the voice through successive arrays of pitches and vowels. In contrast, Tutt's recollection conjures an image of Jones's practice as a vocal warm-up shaped by collectivity and the singer's gesture of authority or even threat. Here, the vocal cords are comparable to biceps, elements of the body that are flexed in a show of strength and latent power. The "clearing" of her throat is the act that creates space for the flexing of vocal cords that keys the assertion of vocal authority. At the same time, the context in which this flexing takes place is one of relative disempowerment, spatially, as the singer waits in the wings. The wings of the theatre are the hidden, liminal space through which the performer must pass to arrive on stage, but also a space from which her voice still carries. While she cannot make herself seen in the wings, she can make herself heard. In the case of Sissieretta Jones's vocal warm-up, she makes herself heard for her own purposes, rather than for the immediate appreciation of the audience. From her position in the shadows, she maintains her voice, asserts its potential to claim the spotlight and command the audience's attention from center stage. At the same time that she remains hidden, in the dark, in the wings, this singer does not conduct her warm-up alone. The collectivity of the choir takes over the lone figure of the singer's piano accompanist, its members engaged onstage in a double performance for both the audience and the backstage star whose flexed voice ultimately secures their own livelihood.

To the description of Sissieretta Jones flexing her vocal cords, I compare the guidance from another distinguished nineteenth-century soprano, the German singer and voice teacher Lilli Lehmann. The performer of some 170 operatic roles ranging from the flexible, agile coloratura to the forceful, dramatic Wagnerian soprano, Lehmann continued performing into her seventh decade. For her disciples, the example of Lehmann's voice itself attested to the viability of her techniques in promising vocal longevity. In 1902, when she was fifty-four years old, her book *How to Sing* was published. In it, she sets forth the secrets of her own technique which, she writes, "seem to be secrets only because students so rarely pursue the path of proper study to the end."[6] Advocating for regular, serious practice to build up endurance, the importance of self-control even in emotive performance, the development of a well-exercised, fluid upper register (head voice), and ongoing study, she observes, "One is never done with learning; and that is especially true of singers."[7] Supported by numerous medical diagrams of the larynx, vocal tract, and lungs, her text pronounces its recommended technique according to the science of the day and encourages singers to draw pictures of the vocal apparatus themselves to internalize this knowledge. Her treatment of the vocal cords is cautionary:

> It can now be seen how easily the vocal cords can be injured by an uncontrolled current of breath, if it is directed against them in all its force. One need only see a picture of the vocal cords to understand the folly of exposing these delicate little bands to the explosive force of the breath.

They cannot be protected too much; and also, they cannot be too carefully exercised. They must be spared all work not properly theirs.[8]

In this formulation the vocal cords that source vocal sound are, far from the locus of threat and power themselves, rather threatened by the "explosive" potentiality of airflow and the unnecessary "work" it may induce. The instruments of voice are "delicate little bands" instead of analogues for biceps. Accordingly, Lehmann's medicalized ways of knowing and understanding the voice position the singer as conservationist and protector of bodily fragility rather than authoritative deployer of bodily strength. For Lehmann, vocal technique is secured not simply through consistent vocal practice—on which point both she and Jones seem to agree—but through cautious exercise that guards against vocal injury. In the event of vocal malfunction, what the singer needs is the great patience of "the singing teacher (the only proper physician for this disease)."[9] As laid out in more dire terms by Lehmann's contemporary Luisa Cappiani, whom Sissieretta Jones cited as the best of several voice teachers with whom she studied in New York, "The student whose voice has been injured . . . must not attempt to cure himself, nor should he go to any but a teacher whose skill is unquestionable, for the slightest imperfection in the cure may ruin the voice permanently."[10] The figure of the voice teacher as diagnostic listener who assesses and prescribes technical measures for bodily healthfulness—protection against vocal ruin—is one with a long history that extends to the present day. By the early 1900s, the idea of voice teacher as medical practitioner was firmly established in both conservatory and clinical circles in the person of Manuel Garcia II, singer, voice teacher, and inventor of the laryngoscope.

The Originary Voice Teacher-Scientist?

Garcia was born in Spain to a respected musical family and grew up in Italy where he trained as a singer. As a young man he traveled to the United States with his family's opera troupe, performing baritone and bass roles, but the operatic stage was not for him, and in later years by his own evaluation it was the fact that he had been pushed to sing too hard too early that caused "the ruin of his voice."[11] Withdrawing from performance, he joined his father in Paris where both were important voice professors at the Paris Conservatoire. Garcia remained in Paris until the French Revolution, at which point he moved to London and accepted an appointment at the Royal College of Music. Perhaps his most famous student was the Swedish soprano Jenny Lind, the nineteenth-century opera superstar whose voice he is said to have saved when in the 1840s he prescribed for her three months of absolute vocal rest followed by a series of lessons.[12] Two of his other students, Mathilde Marchesi and Julius Stockhausen, went on to become the leading voice pedagogues of their era in France and Germany, respectively. As noted in chapter 1, his son Gustave Garcia also went on to teach the Jamaican singer and voice teacher Louis Drysdale, who taught Ethel Waters, Marian Anderson, Florence Mills, and Alberta Hunter, alongside many other performers of various races from Broadway and the West End.

On his one hundredth birthday in 1905, Garcia was celebrated over the course of two days in London. As a detailed article in the *British Medical Journal* recounts, the great man himself, "venerable but by no means decrepit," was subjected to extensive ceremony—speeches, a luncheon, a meeting of the Laryngological Society of London, a banquet with four hundred guests, a reception, and countless toasts.[13] Garcia had just been knighted by King Edward VII of England, and King Alfonso XII of Spain was not to be outdone; the Spanish monarch sent a deputy to invest Garcia as a knight of the Spanish Royal Order. And the German emperor awarded him the "Great Gold Medal for Science." A statement was read from the University of Koenigsberg in Prussia, which had awarded Garcia an honorary doctorate of medicine some decades prior. Addresses were also read from the British Royal Academy of Music, the Royal College of Music, and from laryngology societies in Belgium, Canada, Denmark, Italy, Japan, Poland, Sweden, the United States, and Russia. Beyond his achievements as a singer and voice pedagogue, Garcia won his position as an honored member of the medical world with his 1854 invention of the laryngoscope—a device that used a hand mirror to shine light on a dentist's mirror pressed against the uvula, thereby affording, for the first time in history, a view of the human larynx and its inner workings during vocal use.

The British medical journalist summarizing the events of Garcia's centenary goes to great effort to show that Garcia was no charlatan but truly worthy of long overdue honors bestowed upon him as a man of science: "The invention of the laryngoscope was not a happy accident, but the outcome of long thought, observation, and experiment, and the researches which he made with it were in the truest sense scientific."[14] To this point, in his 1855 paper "Observations on the Human Voice," Garcia detailed, to the subsequent excitement of the medical world, how the larynx looked and moved. From the intake of breath, he tracked the movements of the arytenoid cartilages that draw apart and bring together the ligaments (vocal cords) within the glottis that encases them, such that they resist air pressure until this resistance gives way to the "explosion" of air that Lehmann later referenced as both the source of and threat to vocal sound. Garcia writes, "A series of these . . . explosions, occasioned by the expansive force of the air and the reaction of the glottis, produces the voice."[15]

From a young age, Garcia conducted experiments with animal windpipes as part of studies in vocal anatomy that led to his development of the laryngoscope. Specifically, "his sister, Madame Viardot, tells how he would demonstrate to her the function of the organs of voice by means of bellows inserted into the larynx of a sheep or a cow," and Garcia attended carefully to the different kinds of sounds that resulted.[16] For media studies scholar Jacob Smith, these experiments anticipate Alexander Graham Bell's 1870s experiments with the ear phonautograph—a machine constructed using human ears sourced from Harvard medical school cadavers. In this machine, the partially dissected ear was connected to a stylus that made tracings on a glass plate. Jonathan Sterne explains the ear phonautograph as "a machine for 'writing' sound waves . . . [it] used an excised human middle ear as a transducer, and the functioning of the tympanic membrane (also known as the diaphragm or the eardrum) in the human ear was the model for the diaphragms in all subsequent sound-reproduction technologies."[17] While Garcia's explorations with animal larynxes resulted in the laryngoscope, a device for observation of the vocal mechanism rather than recording of its sound, Smith contends that the laryngoscope must nonetheless be understood as an important theoretical model for sound reproduction: "a modern tool that could be useful for displays of correct technique."[18] Luisa Cappiani, Sissieretta Jones's effusive voice teacher, emerges more skeptical of its usefulness in the voice studio. While she concedes the laryngoscope's usefulness for surgery and the medical field, she points out that it only affords a view of the vocal cords on a few low pitches, hardly the full extent of the singer's range: "Hence, the idea to learn singing by using the laryngoscope is an absurdity."[19] In any case, my project is less concerned with Garcia's relevance for sound recording as it is typically understood than for his mode of medicalized engagement with the voice that lay the groundwork for voice teaching practice for generations to come. The sound recording that interests me, that is to say, is the kind carried and transmitted by voice teachers. Among voice pedagogues, Manuel Garcia II remains revered to this day for his research into, in his words, the "intimate processes of the vocal organs which produce the sounds," and, I argue, he serves as the archetype for the modern voice teacher as medical practitioner.[20]

Voice Studio as Clinic

Within the US context, there are multiple contenders for the role of twenty-first-century heir to Manuel Garcia II's legacy as foremost voice pedagogue and scientist. To some, Robert Sataloff would be the obvious choice. An otolaryngologist and surgeon who has served since 1989 as chair of the board of directors of the Voice Foundation—the leading professional organization of voice scientists—as well as editor-in-chief of its influential *Journal of Voice*, Sataloff has authored and edited sixty-three books and nearly 800 articles on voice science and otolaryngology in addition to his work as a professional singer and singing teacher. His research interests include techniques for the rehabilitation of vocal fold scarring, the development of clinically useful objective voice measures, and the molecular composition of vocal folds. Another strong candidate is Ingo Titze, president of the National Center for Voice and Speech, an electrical engineer turned acoustician who wrote his dissertation in physics on vocal fold modeling, and whose output includes some 450 refereed articles as well as numerous workshops for voice practitioners in the field of vocology, a term of his own coinage that encompasses voice habilitation, therapy, and training. A slightly more left-field entry is Jeannette LoVetri, the Manhattan School of Music-trained singer and proponent of nonclassical singing techniques she groups under the category of "contemporary commercial music." This is a category that is now in wide use among practitioners but, as I discuss below, problematic in its engagement with race and culture. LoVetri is the author of a select number of scientific articles, most jointly researched with Sataloff and other otolaryngologists, on topics including laryngeal musculature and comparative characteristics of opera and musical theatre singing. She is also a teacher of pop singers, Broadway performers, and avant-garde vocalists including Meredith Monk and Theo Bleckmann. LoVetri's contributions to the teaching of nonclassical singing stand in relationship to those of Jo Estill, a late twentieth-century voice pedagogue who also embraced popular song in her voice teaching methods and influential scientific papers and whose work is continued by her students Kimberly Steinhauer and Mary McDonald Klimek. While I will address LoVetri and

Estill later in this chapter, for the role of Garcia heir, I nominate Richard Miller, respected author and longtime professor of performance at Oberlin Conservatory, where he directed a pioneering voice science research laboratory. Until his death in 2009, Miller was a noted figure in voice pedagogy circles in the United States and abroad—following in Garcia's footsteps, he was knighted by European royalty and named a Chevalier in the French Order of Arts and Letters for his contributions to the study of vocalization. At a Voice Foundation of America gala at which he was honored in 2006, Miller's junior colleague Sataloff enthused:

> Richard Miller's contributions to voice pedagogy and science have been extraordinary. He has served as a key bridge between music and science, translating medical and scientific research into practical musical knowledge and translating musical tradition and teaching into incisive foci for scientific research. His interdisciplinary vision, passion, and scholarship have been invaluable to the evolution of modern voice medicine, science, and pedagogy.[21]

For more than twenty years, Miller's column in the National Association of Teachers of Singing (NATS) *Journal of Singing* addressed various topics in voice science and made practical suggestions for their incorporation into the voice teacher's studio. Nearly a hundred of these short essays were gathered together and published in revised form as a book, titled *On the Art of Singing*, in 1996. Writing as one practitioner to another, Miller's prose is conversational, direct, and lucid. A shrewd observer of trends in the field, he is not above skewering his voice-teaching colleagues—referenced anonymously, of course—and he offers an opinionated critique of teachers who rely on outmoded or disproven methods while investing their practice with an aura of mystique and, in his view, unfounded authority. By his own admission, he was not a teacher of popular singing techniques or Broadway belting, about which he remained uncertain and cautious. In his book *Solutions for Singers*, a compendium of answers to questions selected from among 1,500 posed to him by student participants in the many weeklong singing workshops he taught over the course of his career, Miller includes an entry on the topic—controversial among singing teachers—of the healthfulness of belting. In it, he articulates his concerns about the way such a laryngeal position must tax the vocal folds, then defers to other teachers who specialize in the technique before adding, "I remain unconvinced that unmitigated belting does not take a toll on the singing voice. . . . I must also objectively note that some popular belters seem to enjoy long performance careers. Most do not." In concluding, true to form, he adds, cheekily, "Are we still friends?"[22]

As a whole, Miller's work has been celebrated among his peers for the way in which it encourages a standard of assessment based on efficiency and function rather than simply a tone that "sounds beautiful." In contrast to the convention of his time, as another colleague wrote, "Richard has asked us to consider the function first, assuring us that a voice that is functioning well will indeed produce the best possible sound."[23] Mediating between the language of voice scientists and that of historical voice pedagogy, Miller was one of the first teachers to employ a dedicated voice lab in his pedagogy, using and teaching the analysis of singers' vocal spectrograms—visual plots of the spectrum of sound frequencies against time. In addition, he conducted field research on the voice teaching methods currently in use in Europe and mapped the way that twentieth-century teachers of singing in England, France, Germany, and Italy subscribed to and perpetuated differing aesthetic ideals and techniques all under the umbrella of *bel canto* singing. The specificity of this analysis held special relevance for singers in the United States, which is not generally understood to have developed a national style of *bel canto*, and where many students of classical singing have tended to lump together all European techniques without attention to regional nuance. Miller's book offered guidance and clarification to American singers operating within a sphere where "[i]t is quite possible for a student to engage the services of a teacher in Boston or in Oklahoma without knowing that his teacher is advocating methods normally associated with teaching in France or Germany . . . [and which] could provide difficulty if the student is attempting to produce a way of singing that is associated with the Italian tradition."[24] A consistent theme of Miller's oeuvre as a voice pedagogue is his assertion that the voice teacher's role is to be an analyst of vocal performance, which he articulates in medical terms: "Diagnosis and prescription [are] the two chief requirements of teaching the technique of singing."[25] In the clinical mode of observation that Miller applies to voice pedagogy, deeply grounded in scientific studies of laryngology and the bioacoustics of human vocal sound, I discern a clear example of the medical regard that Michel Foucault theorized as definitive of knowledge and discourse in the modern era.

In *The Birth of the Clinic*, Foucault theorizes the way that the modern mode of medical perception has shaped discourse and the history of ideas. Coming into fullness in the nineteenth century, this kind of "medical regard" now in widespread use has to do with the doctor's authority to perceive and describe things that had long been invisible and inexpressible. For Foucault, the doctor's gaze and perceptual mode is what defines the clinical encounter, a way of seeing and speaking about what is seen that emerged just when the European hospital became a multifunctional clinic—a space where doctors both healed patients and taught medicine. Where previously medicine had relied on a classificatory logic, with modern medicine disease was understandable not in terms of class but in terms of its anatomical location. No longer could the physician be imagined as the mythological Greek doctor who interviewed his patients and divided them into four groups, with each group prescribed one of four different treatments—bleeding, induced vomiting, enema, or fresh air.[26] Instead, the clinical encounter focused on determining the way in which disease lodged precisely in human organs. In other words, the clinical encounter was no longer about how different diseases related to one another, but about how each disease related to the specific anatomy of the individual body: "The notion of *seat* has finally replaced that of *class*."[27] Language and description were claimed as the most effective ways of rendering the physician's perception; more efficacious than, for example, the drawing of maps and symptoms that chart body parts in relation to pain. For Foucault, medical perception manifests in the clinician's silent gaze that perceives, within the body's hidden depths, language that precedes what is seen.[28]

To Foucault's important discourse analysis on the medical regard, I must offer a corrective extension, via feminist philosopher Adriana Cavarero.[29] Conventions of metaphysical thought and cultural theory notwithstanding, the voice—the sound that expresses the physician's descriptive language as it is bound up with the medical gaze and the penetration of unseen interiors—sustains meanings beyond those pertaining to speech and language. Cavarero critiques the way that voices have long been understood as subservient to what they signify, and she articulates how this devocalization of *logos* results in a pronounced bias in European philosophical thought. When speaking is subordinated to the gaze and to thinking, she expounds, "The voice thus becomes the limit of speech—its imperfection, its dead weight."[30] Consequently, vocal sound is figured as a threat and disturbance to thought, the extralinguistic excess taken as feminine and irrational distraction to the masculine domain of rational thought. With Cavarero, I contend that in the voice studio in particular, it is vital to attend to the sound of the clinician's spoken description, the evidence and mode of medical perception, as part of the clinical encounter. If any voice pronounces the interior of the body, the voice clinician's voice does so to an even greater degree, as it pronounces both the interior of the teacher's body from which it emanates and that of the singer's body to which the teacher listens.

For Foucault, the medical gaze is all about the hiddenness of secret interiors. Medical description is, in summary, "a revealing gesture" that discloses the anatomy of the body's insides.[31] The listening regard of the twentieth-century voice teacher, necessarily shaped by the mode of medical perception set up by the modern clinical encounter, departs from the listening practice of previous pedagogues who sought to hear first and foremost "the beautiful sound" of the singing voice, in Italian, literally, *bel canto*. In his writing and teaching, Richard Miller explicitly sought to reverse a longstanding formula of vocal expression. Rather than positioning the voice's beautiful sound as revelatory of the artist's feeling—the emotive interior—he taught that what was principally required was instead the healthful functioning of the artist's anatomical interior, and that this would in turn result in the desired beautiful sound. For Miller, the voice is not merely a beautiful sound poised to create organization in the exterior world, a sound with which listening becomes, after Jean-Luc Nancy, "straining toward a possible meaning."[32] Rather, he teaches, the singer's interior world must be well-organized and the beautiful voice will then emerge as its byproduct. By his own account, what Miller purports to teach is not singing but a practice of listening:

> I have personally never taught anyone to sing, nor did anyone ever teach me to sing. Yet I am eternally grateful to four or five people who were trainers who taught me what to listen for in my voice, who pointed to the causes that make one kind of timbre different from one another. . . . They trained me to hear my voice so that I could teach myself. That is what I would like to do with my students. . . . Teaching someone to *hear* the voice and to discriminate among timbres and the physical and acoustic maneuvers that produce the differences among them is to allow each individual singer to do his or her own self-teaching.[33]

In the teaching hospitals Foucault analyzed, physicians engaged with both patients and students, but in the voice clinic these latter two are united in one body. Thus, within the clinical encounter of the voice studio, the singer in search of a lesson is both the patient whose body is the site of potential pathology as well as the student of medical regard. The student-singer's bodily interior must be revealed to both the teacher's *and* the student's perception. What does this encounter open up? If the physician's perception detects the anatomical locations of disease, what the voice clinician's regard opens up is a space of the secret causes of vocal sounds. As Foucault writes, the clinical encounter is about "the medicine of organs, sites, causes"; it opens up "the tangible space of the body, which at the same time is that opaque mass in which secrets, invisible lesions, and the very mystery of origins lie hidden."[34] For Miller and the teachers he encouraged to follow in his example, the vocal pedagogue's medical regard divines the bodily interior by listening not to sound as expressive effect but as revelation of cause. Timbres are heard for the ways they flow from "physical and acoustic maneuvers," and what the voice clinician needs to teach the student is how to hear the various causes that pronounce each of these timbres in the anatomy of her singing body.

The Accidental Voice

What, then, is meant by vocal health? The construct of health is, as critical public health scholars and medical sociologists have articulated, a fraught terrain. On the one hand, it would seem to be, simply, the absence of disease. In this accounting, the medical regard that localizes disease in anatomical isolation seeks to render *unhealth* as a purely biological phenomenon—disease, the bodily dysfunction of "disorder"—absolved of all relation to or consequence from social context. Yet social contexts, such as the conditions of poverty or imperialism, have produced both the violence of diseases and the violence of their stigma for a range of populations at numerous points in history. At the same time that health is generally posited as a neutral ideal, it nonetheless assumes postures that are inherently moralizing and medicalizing. As Jonathan Metzl articulates, "health is a concept, a norm, and a set of bodily practices whose ideological work is often rendered invisible by the assumption that it is a monolithic, universal good."[35] Health promotion discourses valorize and seek to produce white, middle-class, rational subjects with regulated, contained bodies, resulting in widespread understandings of health throughout the United States that have "revolved around the notion of health as self-control, encompassing concepts of self-discipline, self-denial and will power . . . achieved by intentional actions. . . . Health is what one does, as well as the condition one is in."[36] Health thus emerges as an achievement and a status symbol; with the invisibilizing of social and political frameworks that shape the conditions of possibility for health, its opposite, unhealth, presents as the shameful result of indolence and irresponsibility.

Within the voice studio as clinic, Richard Miller invokes vocal health in terms of conserving the voice, combating pathologically breathy phonation, maximizing the effects of an "orderly lifestyle," generating "healthy vocalism through nondestructive techniques," and engaging in visits to the laryngologist's office.[37] He remains firmly convinced that the best singing voice is the classical one:

> There is no reason there cannot be many strands of artistic vocalism from many sources, and there is no need to subject them to aesthetic criteria that do not pertain to them. But it is safe to predict that future research into their function will support the Western ideal, stemming from our Greek heritage, that that which is *the most efficient vocalism is the healthiest vocalism*, and that what we call "beautiful timbre" is its logical result.[38]

For Miller, health derives from efficiency, which ideal he posits will continue to be upheld by scientific research. Timbre, the color of the vocal sound itself, is merely the result of healthful efficiency—a physiologically efficient voice will have "beautiful timbre" and an inefficient voice will not. Miller's emphasis on the efficiency of vocal function echoes theories of the productive body advanced by Frederick Winslow Taylor, whose 1911 text *The Principles of Scientific Management* launched the business field of management science. Taylor proffered numerous mathematical formulas and methods to regulate workers' bodily movements and thereby increase productivity, whether the bodies being regulated were those of burly men hauling pig iron in steel mills or deft young women sorting ball bearings in bicycle-building factories. Central to his theme is the contention that bodily efficiency is the result of systematic training, and "every single act of every workman can be reduced to a science."[39] Similar to the medical regard that localized disease in the individual body, Taylorism sought to "develop each individual man to his highest state of efficiency and prosperity."[40] Yet as dance historian Mark Franko observes in his lucid analysis of the 1930s chorus girl's precision dancing as Taylorized movement, for the performing artist from whom efficiency is demanded, a further demand arises—she must not only dance according to the principles of industrial capitalism, but she must also conceal the extent to which her performance is, in fact, work. In Miller's pedagogical texts, this theme emerges in the problematic impulse to somehow claim the trained, efficient body's health-fulness as a "natural" ideal. This requires a number of logical contortions that position the bodily control that is prized elsewhere as, here, generative of technical error: "the singing student is constantly confronted with errone-ous techniques that diminish the natural processes of body function in the hope of achieving controls that actually upset natural coordination."[41] But who determines what counts as natural and what counts as erroneous technique?

Despite all appeals to the natural and objectively biological grounds of health, it is clear that many kinds of ideological assumptions are bound up in determinations about which kinds of bodies are normal and well-ordered and which are taken to be riddled with disorder. In his writings, Miller maintains that popular singing techniques such as belting fall under the category of erroneous technique and inefficient unhealthfulness. Miller pathologizes the popular voice, repeatedly asserting that most of the patients seen by otolaryngologists are pop singers who lack training and consequently abuse their voices. By contrast, he contends that the trained classical singer whose voice difficulties tend to be relatively minor is a wel-come relief for the beleaguered throat doctor.[42] In this assessment he was far from alone.

In a 1966 statement directed to its readership, the National Association of Teachers of Singing published a strongly worded, cautionary statement titled, "The 'Pop' Singer and the Voice Teacher." Its opening lines sketch the scope of the danger that its authors suggested pop music presented for midcentury vocal pedagogues: "In recent years, the extraordinary devel-opment of communications and the commercial manipulation of public taste by the mass media have posed new and serious problems for the sing-ing teacher."[43] But the issue at hand was more serious than the supposed degeneration of aesthetic taste. The statement traces the impact of folk singers, crooners, jazz singers, Broadway, Tin Pan Alley, and film musicals, through to that of rock music, the target of its sharpest invective. Rock, with its roots in blues, gospel, soul, and country, was amplifying audio to unnecessary, "overpowering" degrees and, sending the young singers who succumbed to its lure to the otolaryngologists in droves to seek healing after the self-inflicted "vocal abuse" they incurred. While I cannot endorse the accusations of poor taste ascribed to aficionados of nonclassical music, I do agree that microphones and amplification led to the development of vocal techniques that are markedly distinct from those prized by singers working in the twentieth-century tradition of *bel canto* voice.[44]

Whether in the radio broadcast room or the recording studio, when by the mid-1920s microphones and amplifiers pervaded both spaces, it was immediately apparent that operatically trained voices neither recorded nor traveled the airwaves well. The classical voice teachers and the radio producers agreed—the microphone exaggerated the flaws of voices trained for large acoustic spaces, where the distance between the singer and audience served, helpfully, to obscure any vocal shortcomings.[45] In short, stars of opera and the concert hall were not commercially successful on the radio or in the burgeoning recording business. At the same time that it was seen as a magnifier of flaws in the classical voice, teachers of classical singing have often scorned the microphone as a kind of "vocal crutch" or trick for the weak singer who lacks the robust, healthful technique for acoustic performance. Yet, as music critic Henry Pleasants observes, the vocal reality that singers had to adapt to with the microphone was the way that "a singer could no longer get any payoff from high notes. Everyone could sound loud and everyone could sound big. The singer was required to phrase and look for effects from his phrasing rather than from his big voice."[46] And so, in the singing of jazz artists like Billie Holiday and crooners like Bing Crosby, the payoff of the big note is traded in for the intimate effects of expressive phrasing.

Music technology, including the microphones that have impacted popular singing techniques, may be understood as not just gizmos or devices but also an environment within which music happens and a set of practices that contribute to music making.[47] In rock, practices of both miking and amplification layer with practices of singing, as the aesthetics of loudness and distortion begin to overlay and mix with voice in specific ways. Accordingly, the rock voice is a particular manifestation of the "mixed voice" that Steven Connor has theorized every voice to be, a vocal sound that ventriloquizes the context around it as it becomes encrusted with other sonic and affective ephemera. Connor writes, "Like flypaper, the voice gathers things on the way, lilts, leanings, aches, eccentricities, accents."[48] Music technology also contributes to mixed voices: "The microphone reveals, in intimate detail, every nuance of the performer's vocal style. But it does not do so in a transparent fashion: every microphone has its own characteristics and colours the sound in subtle yet unmistakable ways."[49] With the microphone, vocal sound yields both the graininess of the singer's body and the graininess of the singer's microphone. And yet, despite the various ways that technological distortion and mediation color and "mix" with vocal sound, rock voices are lauded among their fans for the sincerity that such singing is thought to render in making "real experience" audible.[50] Musicologist Richard Middleton hears in this sincerity a practice of vocal constriction he maps as common to many rock singers and inherited from blues and country traditions, a technique and sound in which "emotional tension tightens the throat."[51] In this hearing, it is the affective charge that delivers the honest, authentic, good voice. This is a far cry from the acoustic honesty advocated by the *bel canto* cohort, free from the trickery of microphones and speakers. Yet it does align with some classical voice pedagogues' investment in emotional sincerity, the belief that emotion is the definitive factor in producing good vocal tone—precisely the view that voice scientists such as Garcia and Miller sought to combat with modern teachings grounded in anatomy instead of vague musical "feeling."[52] Nonetheless, the rock singer's "tightening" of the throat as a means of accessing emotional honesty was certainly not understood by classical voice teachers—whatever their persuasion—to align with notions of vocal healthfulness. Rather, it was precisely the kind of technique against which they railed.

After having taken to task microphone singing and rock amplification, the authors of the 1966 circular "The 'Pop' Singer and the Voice Teacher" unload substantial frustration against Broadway musical theatre. It is true that "foot mikes," low microphones placed on the stage floor by the footlights, were in use on the musical stage by the 1950s, and the body microphones that are taken to be typical for Broadway today made their first appearance with *Funny Girl* in 1964. But these were not used widely until decades later; the rock musicals of the 1960s and 1970s, which were in the distinct minority of Broadway shows, used handheld microphones.[53] Thus when this article was published, the source of irritation at the Broadway voice could not have been the extent to which it encouraged "abusive" vocalization due to amplification. However, the Broadway vocal sound is singled out in a pathologizing tirade that emphatically categorizes singers working in this genre as not only deficient in adequate vocal technique, but lacking technique altogether:

> Many of our profession have long been engaged in training singers whose preferences or professional goals are related solely to the demands of Broadway composers, producers and directors. Unfortunately these demands often include such styles as "belting," "graveling or rasping," glottal attacks and cut-offs, and absence of and/or excessive use of vibrato. These

vocal "sound effects," often produced accidentally by the total *lack* of technique, result in characteristics which become stylistically acceptable and then imitated regardless of potential damage to the performer.[54]

This passage is remarkable for the nuance it provides about just why the acoustic popular voice was heard by pedagogues as so unhealthful to singers, that is, capable of inflicting heavy vocal "damage." First, the sounds that are produced by the Broadway voice are taken to be essentially so grotesque that they cannot even be considered singing at all, but rather a motley collection of "sound effects." Second, the sounds of this voice are modeled by the demands and requirements of composers, producers, and directors—unlike the dynamic of the concert hall or operatic stage where the singer reigns supreme, here the needs of the singing diva are perceived as subordinate to the interests of nonsinging others who, unlike the well-trained classical conductor or accompanist, must have no knowledge about what constitutes proper vocal technique. Third, and most provocatively, the sounds that Broadway singers make that are the absence of technique, its unhealthful negative, are understood here to have been produced without any training whatsoever—accidentally. The popular singing voice is then, in contrast to the functional, efficient classical voice, the aberration of an *accidental* voice. One cannot train for an accident. What's more, and even more threatening to the classical voice teacher as advised by Miller, its causes cannot be divined. The medical regard that listens authoritatively to the bodily interior and brings forth language that precedes and manifests its hiddenness has no play with the voice that is accidental. In this hearing, the singer who wields the accidental voice cannot lay claim to the self-will and self-control with which the vocally healthful individual molds her sound; she does not have the secret of healthful technique. But if she is simply running around in search of accidents and the "sound effects" of nonvoice, she does not seek the voice teacher who will help her hear the way forward. The teachers of singing who write this article emerge as both bewildered and afraid for their livelihoods. In the end, the accidental voice is both so rare that its cause is bafflingly indiscernible, and so commonplace that anyone may encounter it, accidentally, without undertaking careful (and expensive) vocal study of its secrets. Significantly, this assessment maps the precise contours of how black singers' voices have often been figured by conservatory authorities—inexplicable, untrained, and dangerous.

"Contemporary Commercial Music" and Its Noise-Gates

When I began my research for this project, I sensed that a key component of the unhealthy popular voice lay in its racialization; that is, that it was the very blackness of the jazz or blues voice to which white classical singing teachers objected and managed through the category of unhealth. The ongoing separation of jazz and classical voice in today's conservatories presented to me as an obvious residue of the history of racial segregation in the United States. The fear that pure, healthy classical voices will become contaminated by contagious popular voices seems to echo narratives about racial containment and health in this country—consider white America's Jim Crow-era fears around white and black people drinking from the same water fountains or swimming in the same pools that trace this history. What I have encountered in the course of my research, further complicating this notion, is that once popular singing styles such as jazz or blues shouting-turned-belting were taken up by white singers, from the perspective of white listeners the racial origins of these techniques were quickly effaced. I have explored aspects of this movement that apply to vocal sound on the US musical stage throughout *Blues Mamas and Broadway Belters*, and specifically in chapter 1 on blueswomen, shouters, and belters. As a result of this whitewashing, what classical voice teachers protested against was, if not overtly the presence and bodily proximity of black people in singing, instead a "something else" that the popular voice presented and within which blackness was subsumed. As mapped above, a key aspect of this was the extent to which popular singing voices were seen to be obtained, as it were, by accident—not through conscious study. Yet the means by which the most prominent teacher of popular singing in US pedagogical circles has sought to overcome this challenge is highly problematic and profoundly undertheorized.

Jeanette LoVetri, a research colleague of Robert Sataloff, and on the Advisory Board for the Voice Foundation, is a proponent of a teaching method for several nonclassical singing styles she groups together under the title "Contemporary Commercial Music (CCM)." LoVetri has created an institute at Shenandoah University in Virginia dedicated to the study of nonclassical singing, which has prompted the creation of a related graduate program, and where her trademarked Somatic Voicework™, the LoVetri Method curriculum, is taught. The term "CCM" has gained significant traction in pedagogical and research circles, and appears increasingly in voice science publications as well as academic contexts. However, as I explore below, the term is vastly insufficient to the kinds of singing voices it strives to contain and is predicated on an array of troubling assumptions about race and racialized voices. Furthermore, the logic by which it seeks to index particular kinds of music under its umbrella—temporally bounded, performed in for-profit contexts, US-based—emerges as full of grave inconsistencies.

First, the temporal bounds of contemporaneity, the first "C" in the acronym, are applied with great unevenness across the category of CCM music. Within LoVetri's rubric, turn-of-the-twentieth-century blues music is considered contemporary while-turn-of-the-twentieth-century opera is not. Thus, Ma Rainey's vocal sound is heard as existing in an entirely different time from that of opera singers performing in Puccini's *Tosca*, which premiered in Rome in January 1900. Of course, the periodization of music and musical style are often the topics of academic discussion and dispute. It is also true that European and US-based composers and artists across many eras have sought to claim that their particular forms of expression encapsulated newness. The "contemporary" voices performing contemporary classical musical repertoire in today's concert halls certainly wield the term to different ends than those LoVetri intends. Nonetheless, because CCM as a category seeks not to name one mode of vocal contemporaneity amid a proliferation of such expressions, but rather to filter out the contemporary from the noncontemporary to include certain kinds of singing in its purview while excluding others, the delineations that the method pronounces effect a stark violence. If the goal is to claim the mantle of the contemporary for a specific set of vocal sounds and the techniques by which they are produced, then, I argue, it is vital to consider the extent to which such sounds carry across historical musical styles and genres. My concern here is the way in which the antecedents of Ma Rainey's blues shout are entirely effaced in this model. Even if blues singers began to sing particular kinds of tunes called "blues songs" in turn-of-the-twentieth-century United States contexts, their vocal sound did not spring forth fully formed in a burst of spontaneity. Reverberating in the blues singers' voices, one must also listen for the "calls, cries, and hollers" of African Americans performing the ring shout during enslavement as well as black voices bent in the expression of spirituals.[55] Yet through the act of name-branding as CCM, once again blackness is subsumed and its history disavowed. Even for a voice pedagogue who sharply critiques the stigma that popular singing has borne within the conservatory, the black popular voice remains an accidental voice, the sound into which history has merely stumbled of late, contrasted with the carefully trained "noncontemporary" classical voice of whose storied tradition the voice pedagogue is well aware.

Second, the blanket designation of a wide range of musical genres and the voices within them as "commercial"—the second "C" in CCM—produces further distortions. For example, the notion that all gospel music should be comprehended in purely commercial terms mishears and effaces, again, the roots of gospel vocal performance in blues and spirituals which, as James Cone has taught, express "the power of song in the struggle for black survival."[56] The question is, again, about listening, and *for whom* a singer is understood to be performing. By hearing the gospel voice as only-ever the slick and facile sound performed for financial reward, CCM as a formulation misses the point entirely. Black theorists like Cone have made a persuasive and painstakingly constructed case for the importance of attending to how certain kinds of music are "cultural expressions of black people, having prime significance for their community."[57] Yet, although key interventions by leading black studies scholars like Cone emerged many decades ago, LoVetri's increasingly accepted category demonstrates that their import has yet to reach the US voice teaching studio—even a studio that prides itself on rejecting misguided truisms of classical training. The very fact that such an undertheorized idea of race and voice has been able to proceed unchecked underscores just how segregated the domains of voice pedagogy and popular music studies remain. Like the audio engineer's noise-gate, there is much that the door of the CCM teacher's voice studio filters out—more than simply the noncontemporary sounds for which it purports to control. And beyond gospel, this marker of commerciality is also misapplied to other kinds of singing within the CCM category. The creative output of avant-garde performers such as Theo Bleckmann and legendary composer/vocalist Meredith Monk—who are both students of LoVetri and her method—would hardly be considered "commercial" music by most. Despite the acclaim she has received over the course of her innovative career, Monk is described in a 2014 *New York Times* article as a "survivor" of the downtown arts scene; she herself is quoted acknowledging the fact that, although her work has not always been celebrated ("I've been in fashion, out of fashion"), she has continued to create musical and vocal works according to her own "inner necessity."[58] The violence of the second "C" in LoVetri's acronym of contemporary commercial music, then, is that it negates the ways in which singers performing sounds lumped together under the umbrella of CCM produce voice for reasons related to spiritual, racial, and artistic survival. The logic of the market, certain to be the driving force behind a trademarked voice pedagogy method, drowns out the lived experience of the singers whose sounds created the conditions of possibility for the method in the first place.

Third, in a confusing and problematic contortion that also compounds the problems of the first two points above, LoVetri claims that all of the CCM singing styles "arose from untrained singers in various parts of the United States."[59] LoVetri then pivots to insist that a vocal technique such as belting "can be found in diverse multinational music, because it arises from speech (generally, male speech), and as such, does not belong to one culture or time."[60] In addition to the fact that it directly contradicts her prior assertion of the US-based origins of her singing category, this latter claim is bizarre for a number of reasons. To begin with, it is unclear why "male speech" but not, apparently, whatever might be considered "female speech" would be considered intrinsic to belting. But the greater difficulty lies in the fact that this statement contradicts the hold that LoVetri seeks to make the "contemporary" maintain, in now describing this male-derived vocal sound as belonging to many different times as well as to different cultures. When LoVetri describes music outside of the musical theatre and pop worlds, she is especially unsteady on her rhetorical feet, as when she states that CCM styles such as belting are heard in music sung by "Africans, or Native Americans, who did not have any formal musical or vocal training."[61] Beyond the fact that this statement locates "Africans, or Native Americans" firmly in the past, failing to attend to the contemporary ways in which individuals who pertain to those categories still, in fact, sing today, the suggestion that singers from these groups did not and do not engage in musical and vocal training across a range of musical styles is entirely untenable. Despite her best efforts, LoVetri's formulation of the popular voice opposes but nonetheless reifies *bel canto* singing, evidenced by statements such as, "Many kinds of sounds that are not beautiful are perfectly healthy and viable, but it requires skill to negotiate them."[62] In the context of this book, I am interested in the popular singing instructor's move to include a wide range of musical and vocal styles in the academy— or, more accurately, to broaden the understanding of what the academy may be. However, the means by which teachers of singing such as LoVetri enact a potentially inclusive move are built on exclusionary premises that deny the historicity of music created by people of color and sustain the *bel canto* instructor's mythology that the qualifier of "beautiful sound" is a universally accepted given.

The ideas about race and voice on which the CCM method is built have gone largely uncritiqued within voice pedagogy circles, where this topic deserves greater consideration. At the same time, while I take issue with the sweeping and misguided assumptions about race upon which she positions her method, I also wish to point out that the scientific knowledge that LoVetri leverages on behalf of her students' voices is substantial and highly effective—an accomplishment made more impressive by the fact that she has acquired this knowledge outside of the formal avenues of graduate study in laryngology and voice science.[63] And I can certainly recognize some of the contours within the voice pedagogical scene that have prompted this type of approach to teaching popular singing. As James Stark writes in his history of *bel canto* pedagogy, "Despite the disagreements in the pedagogical literature, we cannot ignore the common theme that runs through so many works—namely, that there is something special, perhaps even 'secret,' involved in singing according to *bel canto* principles."[64] The savvy voice teacher cannot allow for the existence of an accidental voice, or she is out of a job. Failing to perceive the popular singing voice as one with its own historicity and pedagogical traditions, she can only figure it as a voice with a new and different kind of hiddenness that she will take on the task of explicating. A voice is only worthy of being taught in the academy, it seems, if it can be taught via its hidden secrets, probed by the listening ear of the voice clinician. For Stark, any "secrets" of the voice that the old masters professed to guard were laid bare long ago by laryngoscope-enabled research.[65] But, as Richard Miller knew, evidenced in his patiently explaining voice science terminology to classical voice pedagogues in his column for more than twenty years, scientific discourse carries its own secrets and esotericism. Foucault teaches:

> Description, in clinical medicine, does not mean placing the hidden or the invisible within reach of those who have no direct access to them; what it means is to give speech to that which everyone sees without seeing—a speech that can be understood only by those initiated into true speech. . . . Here, at the level of theoretical structures, we encounter once again the theme of initiation . . . a form of the *manifestation* of things in their truth, a form of *initiation* into the truth of things.[66]

In short, what Garcia's writings disclose is merely another kind of secret, the enclosedness of medical and anatomical language, ready to be taught by the teacher of popular singing who takes up the task of initiating others into its mysteries.

In conversation with the popular singing method proffered by Lo-Vetri stands another pedagogical approach, the Estill voice model. Devised by US-born singer, voice researcher, and laryngologist Jo Estill and gaining currency from the 1970s on, the Estill method of voice training is also grounded deeply in anatomy and physiology as well as acoustics. As a student of the Estill voice method over the past several years in a number of different contexts including dedicated workshops like the one I describe below, I have noted firsthand the ways that even in a secret-bearing, "scientific" pedagogical approach, the vocal interior is invoked and accessed in affective as well as anatomical terms. Ultimately, with Estill the route to healthy technique is mapped both in how one feels the sensations of vocal sound in one's body and in the affective feelings or emotions one has about and with that sound.

Affective Exercises in the Estill Method

It is early on a chilly fall Saturday morning. We are in a studio in the Music Department at the Campus Notre-Dame-de-Foy on the outskirts of Quebec City, Canada. I arrived on campus late last night—after taking three subway trains, one bus, two planes, and a taxi—at which point I managed to speak enough French to ask the student on duty for a key to my room in the dorm and slept for a brief five hours. I woke to a view of yellow and golden trees, green lawns, a distant lake, and an extensive blue sky—far more nature than I have been accustomed to see on a daily basis in New York City. Breakfast was a granola bar I had stashed in my bag, and, after a short, bleary-eyed walk across campus, here I am at Pavillon De La Salle. There is coffee, tea, and fruit set out in the second-floor hallway as students gather for the course—they are familiar with the routine, as this is the second of two weekends in Estill Voice Training® being offered here on campus. I already took the Level One course in Boston over the summer, so I'm just here for the second weekend: Level Two.[67] I'm recognized and hugged by some of the workshop organizers whom I met in Boston—Lynn, a speech and language pathologist; Michelle, a professor of classical voice and choral music here at Notre-Dame-de-Foy; and Julie, a professor of *chant pop* here and the mastermind behind the event's logistics. Julie is effusive and impressively organized, both a tough taskmaster and a sympathetic encourager of her students, and deeply dedicated to this method.[68] She and Lynn encountered the Estill method a few years ago, and Julie has become a strong devotee, taking lessons with American teachers via Skype, traveling abroad to workshops, and bringing Kimberly Steinhauer, founding partner of Estill Voice International, here to Quebec City for the past several years to teach these two workshops annually.[69] The room is filled with about forty-five students, from Notre-Dame-de-Foy and beyond, including some from as far afield as Montreal and Toronto. I am the only student from the States, and, it appears, the only student of color.

The course was advertised on the Estill website as being taught in English, with French workbooks also available. From the start I find, however, that there is more instruction in French than I anticipated. While I haven't studied the language formally, I can generally track the flow of conversation, thanks in large part to time spent with my Francophone extended family members. I soon catch on as Steinhauer, a.k.a. Kim, peppers her explanations with the French terms for key vocal figures: *le langue élevé . . . le sphincter ary-épiglottique étroit . . .* Slim and bright-eyed, Kim seems to have boundless energy. Her words fly quickly—there is a lot to cover in two days—and her thoughts seem to flow even faster. She has taught this material many times before, and despite its nuances and technicalities, it all comes very easily to her. Whether singing with a kazoo to one nostril to differentiate oral and nasal vocalization, or producing the stentorian tones of a Wagnerian operatic voice, she masterfully performs the full range of Estill voice qualities, isolating small differences in sound and vocal placement as she demonstrates. My fellow classmates appear as awed by this display as I feel. A bilingual Powerpoint presentation is projected on two screens at the front of the room, French on the left and English on the right. Practice sessions, which alternate with the full-group time and are led by teachers working toward certification as Estill Master Teachers, are conducted almost entirely in French. I am grateful for the detailed, eighty-page English-language workbook that supplements the formal presentation, and I cover it with scribbled notes during the ensuing two days. In that time, we move through the flat affect and "nothing special" sense of *speech* quality; the breathy, "blowing over a soda bottle" feel of *falsetto* quality; the low-larynx, low-airflow, whimper of *sob* quality; the low-effort, bright tone of *twang* quality; the complicated, seven-part figure for Estill *opera* quality; and the full-body, low-airflow, high-larynx sound of Broadway or pop *belting*.

Estill technique consists of a series of "vocal figures"—a term inspired by the compulsory figures that ice skaters are required to master, and the idea that singers should take a similar approach to vocal mastery. The Level

One course I completed previously, "Figures for Voice Control," covered a range of different movements singers may use for structures of the larynx, vocal tract, and overall physical support, or "anchoring."[70] This work requires a deep attention to minute motions of the vocal apparatus—are your false vocal folds (folds of mucous membrane above the actual vocal folds) simply chilling out or are they retracted as when you are laughing silently? And can you maintain that retraction once you stop your silent laugh? Can you invoke it at will, as an ingredient ready at hand to be added to your vocal performance? In Level Two, we are here to learn the "Figure Combinations for Six Voice Qualities," what Kim describes not as prescriptions but rather as "recipes" for putting together sets of figures to create the voice qualities detailed above.

Each day, after hours of exercises, audio, and video clips, we close with an open coaching session—students bring songs with which they are having difficulty and Kim coaches them through trouble spots. For French Canadian students singing American pop songs, often part of the trick is to place the vowels in a different way. There is a warmth and calmness to these singers' everyday speech, and repackaging it into the brassy tones of American lyrics requires some effort, shifting vowel placement from the back of the mouth to the front, adjusting body posture from the laidback to a more fully engaged, even aggressive stance. At the end of the last day, Kim works with two young women who want to sing belt songs. She has them stand at opposite ends of the small stage at the front of the room, and shout greetings back and forth to one another. "Hey, Dominique!" "Hey, Marie!" It is clear how much full-body effort is needed to produce this sound in comparison to the singers' expectations. It's not about "trying to make a sound." Instead, Kim urges, you have to "listen to your body more than to the sound."

One morning, there is great excitement among participants about the live endoscopy session to which we will be treated as a part of the course. The entire group is asked to walk down the hall to a different classroom, where the white lines of an empty music score are etched against a green blackboard. At the front of the room, two screens frame a cart bearing a shiny set of medical equipment with various dials and wires. We file, chattering, into the rows of seats. The lights are dimmed. Lynn, the fearless speech and language pathologist, is being prepared for an endoscopy session. The Estill training workshops feature numerous endoscopy videos of footage filmed by small cameras attached to tubing and positioned at the back of the throat just above the vocal folds. A key aspect of the Estill training is a rigorous education in the anatomy and physiology of the larynx. From endoscopy videos, students are taught to identify the epiglottis, flopping around at the edge of the frame like a flexible shoehorn, the triangular arytenoids that are attached to the vocal folds and help to puppet them, as well as the relative thickness and slackness of the pale, rubber band-like vocal folds themselves. When the whole apparatus moves closer to the camera, we are taught, this is because the larynx is rising higher; when the folds slide farther away from the camera, it is because the larynx is lowered in the singer's throat. Yet these teaching videos have all been recorded previously, sometimes decades ago, in unidentified laboratories. By contrast, in the room now we are witnesses to and participants in endoscopy as a live event.

There is a sense that this procedure involves the precarious health of the one who subjects herself to it—whether that precarity may be the impetus or the result of the examination. This is medical equipment, after all, which we are told runs to the tens of thousands of dollars and was brought to Quebec all the way from Toronto by a young woman in the medical equipment company's marketing department. The proceedings require expert facilitation, and so a venerable laryngologist has been invited to do the honors. He stands at the front, adjusting the tubing in Lynn's nose and throat. What would it be like to be the one sitting in her chair—wouldn't it be painful or, at a minimum, irritating? She is coughing. There is a delay and technical adjustments are made. Kim extemporizes, filling the time with details of recent research about how fruit pectin can work to moisturize vocal folds. An image appears onscreen and we have started. The image shows two indeterminate masses of flesh with a dark canyon between them. These must be the sides of the nostril. With the camera, we begin tunneling into the body, the lighted camera illuminating the blood vessels and cartilage as we go. Suddenly uncertain, the camera sharply reverses its direction. Now we are in front of the face, here is the distinct image of a nostril. Abruptly the camera resumes its approach. The screen flashes white, then pink again. We move past nose hairs, and past landmarks of tissue I am unable to identify. The flesh we are seeing is lumpy, red-lined, slick with mucus. The woman seated to my right makes noises of disgust, others laugh nervously. The camera moves unreliably, and the screen flashes through mottled orange, blue, and white images as the laryngologist shifts the medical equipment in search of the view for which we are all waiting expectantly. Then it is as if we are peering over the edge of a precipice, the lolling epiglottis welcomes, and the puffed arytenoids and glistening vocal folds hove into sight. The cause of voice revealed, the class is fully complicit in the project of the medical gaze. The room is suffused with oohs and aahs. This is a rare view, a performance whose liveness substantiates the lectures in a way that diagrams and explanations never can. And yet there is something discomforting about the live endoscopy session, even as it fascinates—discomforting both for the viewer/listener and for the vocalizer, whose bouts of coughing continue through the session. The moisture that lines the cartilage, membranes, and tissue of the singer's larynx sparkle onscreen. In the stroboscopic view, where the image switches from color to black and white, the vocal folds shimmer and glisten—the rippling wave of mucous that encases them is clearly visible. The singer laughs. Watching the corresponding tremor in the vocal folds onscreen, it occurs to me that they look as if they are applauding.

....

In the Estill workshops I have taken, there is an explicit effort to embrace and rearticulate medical understandings of the voice in order to replace vague imagery in teaching directives with specific anatomical descriptions. This aligns with Richard Miller's voice science-infused teaching approach that increasingly defines voice pedagogy in this country, although what is new here, as with LoVetri's work, is the legitimization of the study of the popular voice within the medicalized singing clinic. However, I am struck by the extent to which, in the written texts that accompany Estill workshops, vocal direction is often stated in terms of assuming a particular affective posture. The Estill method advises that contouring one's body and vocal tract into the shape that goes along with a certain emotion, and a corresponding emotional sound, will facilitate a specificity of minute physical adjustments that might otherwise remain inaccessible. According to Estill instructors:

> Many of the [voice] qualities are elicited from basic, primal, and universal emotional prompts that are practiced throughout the model. Estill began her journey explaining the anatomy and physiology behind the emotion; still presently, singing in the Estill Voice Model may be defined as *emotion on pitch*.[71]

For example, a singer may not be able to feel exactly where her false vocal folds are, or her true vocal folds for that matter, but she knows how to laugh, and she knows how to put her throat into the shape of a laugh. Through repeated study, she learns to link the physical feeling of laughing to a technical term, "retraction of the false vocal folds," and a technical implication, "this will help me avoid constriction in my voice." This is but one of many examples, which also include the following vocal-affective directives and corresponding physiological adjustments: A whimper leads to the tilted thyroid cartilage that brings sweetness of tone; the larynx will rise into a position useful for belting if the singer will only "Scream silently as we all might like to do from time to time, just to 'let off steam.'"[72] The prompt to tilt the cricoid cartilage into a position for a more powerful belted sound is to tell a child quietly in the grocery store, "Don't you dare embarrass me."[73] A playground taunt (Nyae, nyae, nyae, nyae, nyae!) will result in the narrowed aryepiglottic sphincter that results in a an acoustical illusion that makes the voice seem louder to the listener yet requires little effort to produce. While I cannot agree that the affective imaginary in place here is "primal and universal" as its teachers assert, I take note of the ways that the Estill theory of the voice proposes an interiority that is not only anatomical but also psychological.[74] This represents a particular broadening of an understanding of the Foucauldian clinical encounter as more than purely physiological; the emotive and anatomical causes of sound exist not in opposition but in combination.

In addition to the embeddedness of a specific affective imaginary in its teaching constructs, the Estill voice model is notable for the way that, via its proposed spectrum of affective and anatomical postures, it aims to develop performance abilities that are applicable to any and all vocal styles—classical, popular, and beyond. This is worth considering in comparison to LoVetri's method of CCM whose stylistic focus is limited to directly opposing classical training. Ultimately the Estill vocal figures, like a system of affects, function as a lexicon not of voice but of voices. Similar to the affect theories of Silvan Tomkins and Baruch Spinoza, there is no underlying structure of morality here. With Estill, although some ways of singing are recognized as more or less effortful than others, ultimately the lesson is about how the vocal apparatus consists of complex relations among parts that the singer can arrange in any number of different ways whether she elects to sing pop songs or cantatas.

In the Estill classroom at the Campus Notre-Dame-de-Foy, at the end of the second and final day we reach the section of the course dedicated to belting. I am physically exhausted but belting is not something you can phone in. I am struck by the assertion that a majority of vocal problems are caused by pushing air. Singers try to get louder by pushing air, Kim contends, when really what is needed is the appropriate vocal setup. She observes that pushing air can cause major problems with belting as well as with operatic singing.[75] In the practice session, following the advice and example of an actress from Saskatchewan, I find it can really help to whfffff out the air before starting to sing. As discussed above, there is a great deal of anxiety, among classically trained singers and teachers, about the belt sound and fear that it will cause vocal problems. Belters are often told, Kim notes, to "be careful." But that is a counterproductive piece of advice. To belt well and healthily, she advises, you have to give it your all, throw your whole body into the effort, engaging the muscles across the upper back, head, and neck—and that is not something you can do when you are trying to be cautious. "Be careful" is very different, she counsels, from "Be strong." Trying to shrink, to have less body and less affect, will not help here. "Listen to your body more than to the sound," Kim coaches the student belters. "Your body should be louder than your voice." A student shouts across the stage at her fellow classmate and then shouts on pitch through a phrase of her chosen song, throwing in a bit of vibrato. Her sound has kicked into a different gear; perhaps, she has found the practiced "accident" of a particular mode of popular voice. The classroom breaks into cheers and applause.

Abbey Lincoln
Learning to Scream

Being careful, as the Estill voice teacher points out, is a caution, a directive to protect against hidden causes of vocal harm. To access a powerful belted voice, the singer must decide, she is told, to forgo an investment in protecting the "delicate little bands" of her voice. But for black people vocalizing in the lives and afterlives of enslavement, this is a decision that has generally not even been on the table. The idea that one's body was something it was even possible to protect was simply not a given. For the careful, ladylike comportment required by the Jim Crow-era double bind existed in direct contrast to what was possible for black girls and women prior.[76] Vocal sounds carry histories. And if US blackness has an originary voice and an originary affective expression, the two are often heard together in the sound of a scream.

For Fred Moten, writing after Frederick Douglass, the originary black voice is the scream of the enslaved woman subjected to violence. This is a particular inversion of the psychoanalytic tradition in which the originary voice is the newborn baby's scream or cry that launches subjectivity.[77] In this case it is not the infant but the maternal figure who screams; subjectivity is cued in the act of listening. Alongside the scream of Frederick Douglass's Aunt Hester, Moten listens to Abbey Lincoln's screamed vocals in the "Protest" section of "Tryptych: Prayer, Protest, Peace" on the 1960 album *We Insist! Max Roach's Freedom Now Suite*. I wish to consider this performance, in the theatricality of its surplus emotion, along the terms laid out by another pivotal protest song. As Nina Simone said of her own scathing indictment of American racism delivered with devastating, up-tempo verve, "Mississippi Goddam" "This is a show tune. But the show hasn't been written for it yet."[78]

For Moten, Lincoln's vocal presents "the echo of Aunt Hester's scream," sign of the scream's unavoidable reproducibility that also bears "a sexual overtone."[79] Farah Jasmine Griffin writes, "In her scream I can hear the beaten slave woman, the mourning black wife or mother, the victim of domestic abuse and the rage and anger of contemporary black Americans."[80] In Scott Saul's hearing, "Lincoln screams with uninterrupted fury and at high volume, in an act of aggression that doubles as the sound of hurt"; he also quotes album producer Nat Hentoff as saying the sound represents "all forms of protest, certainly including violence."[81] In these auditions, the affective tonalities of the sound manifest variously as lusty, mournful, raging, furious, hurt, violent. What might it mean to listen for technique in Lincoln's scream? Binding it to Aunt Hester's shriek would seem to imply that the only possible technique resides in the act of feeling itself. Yet I wish to contrast this assessment to what may be learned from Lincoln's own account of her voice:

> I learned from Max that I should always sound how I feel and that whatever I do, I should do it definitely. . . . Having to scream did a lot for me. It freed me up . . . it deepened my voice and made it more melodious. I'm not the kind of woman that screams. I tried, and I couldn't scream. Then my nephew showed me how. He screamed for me. Babies can scream even louder than we can. It's part of the protection of the woman that she can scream. I know that I've been screaming ever since.[82]

I am struck by the way that Lincoln speaks of how learning intersects with feeling and sounding. Screaming was something that she had to learn, and she cites both a grown man and a baby as voice coaches. What's more, she points to an effect unaddressed by other hearers, and one that invokes unmentioned sister-teachers who surely shared this knowledge: "It's part of the protection of the woman that she can scream." In this sentence she asks us to hear the sonic citation of a different screamer—not only Aunt

Hester, but also the woman who uses her voice as defensive measure. Heard this way, Lincoln's twice-heard scream is not only the sound wrenched from the suffering black woman's body, but also a voicing of the black woman's survival strategy in the face of her sexual and psychic vulnerability. This singing lesson with Abbey Lincon teaches that to speak of affect and vocal technique, then, means speaking variously about feelings that are exhorted, exerted, and perhaps both simultaneously. Vocal sound can be both that which is exhorted—resulting from the felt need, and that which is exerted—resulting from the technical or strategic cause. Both reverberate in the space of voice.[83] As Moten synthesizes elsewhere, "Cause and need converge in the bent or marginal church in which we gather together to be in the name of being otherwise."[84]

The Black Singer-Actress and the Vocal-Possible

To return to the question that opened this book: *What kinds of voices are presently believed to be possible for a black woman on the musical stage?* For me this is an urgent, practical question with concrete implications for black expressive life, and for performing the fullness of a black, female self. The work to dwell in the vocal-possible is ongoing, begun anew with each offset and then onset, each release and fresh attack of vocal sound. Imagine a voice that is expansive, unconstrained. If the voice is a metonym of self, then it matters tremendously what and how vocal sound is allowed to be. As I have sought to show over the course of these chapters, any lesson about the voice is a theory about what voice can be. The promise the Estill vocal model seems to hold out is the exciting possibility of the capacious, multiple voice—the singer is promised that she can sing in any number of ways. But what is to be made of the assertion, implicit but certainly present, that all vocal styles are thus equally available to all people? How do I wrestle with the visceral, felt experience that white singers working to perform certain popular singing styles are seeking to perform blackness, or even, to usurp the black woman's voice, and that routes of vocal possibility do not necessarily flow both ways?

In a group interview published in *Studies in Musical Theatre*, a set of early twenty-first-century black Broadway and off-Broadway musical theatre professionals mapped for me the ways that black vocality remains defined by industry professionals in conflicting terms.[85] As these artists detailed, black singing is taken as something that supposedly may be detached from racial context and widely available (Everyone can riff!) and also something that, when produced by actual black people, is generally expected to be delivered within the tight spaces of profoundly limited terms (You must always riff when you belt!). When casting directors, musical directors, and producers are speaking to black musical theatre performers, the group suggested, the word "belting" often seems to be used interchangeably with "riffing"; the two vocal practices are understood to be interwoven in a way that is hardly the case for performers of other racial backgrounds, and that, further, defies historical accuracy. Individuals in the room observed that, despite the vastly different time periods in which these shows are set, performers in "black shows" such as *Dreamgirls* (1981) to *The Color Purple* (2005) to *Ain't Misbehavin'* (1978) to *Ain't Too Proud: The Life and Times of the Temptations* (2019) are expected to voice blackness in uniform ways. This is the case despite the fact that, as the group pointed out, "Diana Ross is not Aretha Franklin." The mournful question, "Why can't we have period shows?" was raised. Consider the following exchange between singer-actor Zonya Love with music director John Bronston and performer/voice coach Elijah Caldwell:

ZONYA: Well, hold up. Can I say, as a riffer, we get a bad rap. You know what I'm saying? There's too many perpetrators out there that give us a bad rap. *(Laughter in the room.)* No, I'm serious. Because that's what I do.

JOHN: Yeah, but there's a place for riffing.

ZONYA: And that's what I'm saying. People like me, who know *when* to do it. . . . I remember when riffing was like, "Oh my God, you're doing too much." And I thought at the time it had a lot to do with the kind of people who *could* riff. And when Mariah Carey came out? It was like, oh, okay. And so now—this what I think, this is my personal opinion—now that white people can do it, they have the ability to do it, it's like, oh, let's run towards that rather than understanding where it came from, right? Because riffing was, what? The church, blues. That wasn't mainstream. Now that it's mainstream, it's like, let's just do the riff. Let's not learn where it came from.

VARIOUS: Right.

ZONYA: So there's this girl who teaches people how to riff. Okay, you're just playing the notes! But where is the riff coming from?

ELIJAH: Numbers.

ZONYA: You know, it's not attached to anything. And I think, growing up in the church, the riff came out of like a moan, or, it came *from* someplace.[86]

So while present-day black musical theatre performers are expected to perform the "authentic" and "natural" sparkle of riffing whenever they sing, musical theatre performers of other races are increasingly adding riffing to their singing but first, without being required to do so at all times in all time periods, and second, without necessarily understanding, beyond the musical math of how to riff, the deeper artistic and even spiritual necessity for such expressivity in a given piece of music as it flows from the lived experience of black people in America. I take note of the way that Zonya Love points to the *history* within the vocal sound that industry professionals often fail to take into consideration while yet capitalizing on its currency: "It came *from* someplace." For black women singers, the fullness of the vocal-possible comes into the air by means of an awareness of where it comes from and who it comes with.

Black Feminist Voice Lessons
The Open Secret of *Singing Along With*

In this chapter, I have engaged voice teachers and their training methods as objects of analysis in order to examine the way that US vocal pedagogy has constructed singing technique as bodily healthfulness in the twentieth and early twenty-first centuries. In this analysis, singers and voice pedagogues have emerged as thinkers proffering distinct theories of race and vocal sound, often pathologizing or fetishizing the popular singing voice, as the case may be. Returning to the turn of the twentieth century with African American operatic talent and vaudeville star Sissieretta Jones, I have attended to Jones's articulation of the voice as that which is flexed to create sound. And I have argued that the modern era of voice teaching was characterized by a Foucauldian medical regard in which the voice teacher becomes the medicalized listener who diagnoses vocal ills and prescribes technical measures for bodily healthfulness. Against popular singing pedagogies that frame vocal sounds produced by racialized bodies as absurdly ahistorical and profoundly nonspecific, I interposed teachings from singers Abbey Lincoln and Zonya Love to suggest that the vocal sounds of black women must be heard, in all their virtuosity and force, in terms of affect, technique, and history in complement. Through Jones, and the preceding chapters' studies of and with black Broadway singers, I hear an alternate theory of ongoing singing study—learning to sing by *singing along with* . . . the possibility of technique as the pleasure in sharing an open secret.

....

The black feminist practice and theory of *singing along with* refuses to deliver on the voice teacher's expensive, hired-out initiation into the hidden mysteries of the voice. Instead, its practitioners demonstrate that vocal technique may operate as an open secret. Even when mobilized through in-the-open acts of dissembling, black feminist voice is shared knowledge. Those who sing along in flexed and flexible unison may also stumble into the practiced accidents of its technique and touch the vibrations of its histories. Throughout this book I have dwelled with the ways that black women on the musical stage from the turn of the century through the 1960s sang with one another, and what it might mean for us, now, to sing along with them. The singers who are heard, if never captured, within these pages enact the practice of singing along with one another in various ways. Black women like Ma Rainey, Bessie Smith, and Ethel Waters sing along with one another in the scenarios of historical singing lessons. A black performer like Pearl Bailey sings along with her own inviolable, subvocalized sound. And we ourselves may sing along with black women singers like Lena Horne, Diahann Carroll, Leslie Uggams, and Eartha Kitt, exercising vocal techniques in their excellent company.

The politics of singing along with black women singers, for me, lies in the extent to which it is both about performing vocal technique and about performing with an awareness of the historical context that has had a hand in shaping the particular colors of a woman's voice. I work to listen and sing through these textures. After Audre Lorde, it is an act of feeling one's way through technique, stretching hidden parts of the body toward the sonic, and finding interiors that move a woman into new feelings and sounds that are, ultimately, both pleasurable and shared. Singing is a profoundly sensual and erotic act. Why else would its lessons so often be hidden behind layers of secrecy? Perhaps I could have stated this more explicitly earlier. But black women's bodies and sounds have been so over-determined by hypersexualization, so often taken as destined to provide sexual pleasure that I worried it could have been easy to miss my greater points. As Maureen Mahon writes in her study of black women artists in rock, "I am aware of the risk of overemphasizing sexuality and physical appearance in a discussion of women performers, but it is essential to examine these issues since they accompany women onto the public stage. Their impact is heightened for black women."[87] In the case of the voice studio, as compared to the rock concert, perhaps there are more (or different) pitfalls. Of course it is true that the best lovers are also our teachers, but difficulties arise in conflating the two in the scenario of the voice lesson. In the present-day US vocal classroom where litigious and puritanical impulses commingle in complicated ways with the very real need to protect students from harm, I cannot quite put on my syllabus that I expect we will engage in the erotics of singing. How then can I communicate here the openness of the open secret in such a way that it does not reinforce the idea of open as in perpetually available, the black woman's inner sound as ever-open for anyone to take? I must emphasize that this lesson has especial meaning for black women singers ourselves.

As Lorde teaches, the erotic's usefulness has to do with its function as a key site of the political: "Recognizing the power of the erotic within our lives can give us the energy to pursue genuine change within our world, rather than merely settling for a shift of characters in the same weary drama. For not only do we touch our most profoundly creative source, but we do that which is female and self-affirming in the face of a racist, patriarchal, and anti-erotic society."[88] Vocalization that moves through a Lordean black feminist politics requires the joyful engagement of "deep participation," a direct act of the senses that "cannot be felt secondhand." In the act of singing together I attend to "the way my body stretches to music and opens into response."[89] And I draw inspiration from the way that Hortense Spillers has lucidly framed the radical ability of the black woman singer to teach us about what is beautiful about our sexuality: "Black women have learned as much (probably more) that is positive about their sexuality through the *practicing* singer as they have from the polemicist."[90] For Spillers, the impact of this teaching lies in the way that the vocalist is able to sing into the clear knowledge of her own spirit on her own terms. In this way the promise of *singing along with* Sissieretta, Ma, Bessie, Ethel W, Pearl, Juanita, Lena, Diahann, Leslie, and Eartha can be, if we are open to it, the ability to know the fullness of who it is that we really are. Spillers elucidates:

> The Burkean pentad of fiction—agent, agency, act, scene, and purpose as the principal elements involved in the human drama—is compressed in the singer into a living body, insinuating itself through a material scene, and in that dance of motives, in which the motor behavior, the changes of countenance, the vocal dynamics, the calibration of gesture in relationship to a formal object—the song itself—is a precise demonstration of the subject turning in fully conscious knowledge of her own resources toward the object. *In this instance of being-for-self, it does not matter that the vocalist is "entertaining" under American skies because the woman, in her particular and vivid thereness, is an unalterable and discrete moment of self-knowledge.*[91]

Ultimately, for those of us committed to working on the contemporary musical stage, the pedagogical practice of *singing along with* can equip us to hear and voice the condition of greater expressive possibility for black women musical theatre artists across the histories and futures of the art form. This condition is, simply, prizing a vocal-possible that celebrates and manifests a black woman singer-actor's deep self-knowledge.

Coda

Of the hundreds of singing lessons I have taught in more than two decades, nearly all have been recorded, by the singers whom I coached, and yet they constitute an archive to which I no longer have any real access—dispersed across audio recorders, phone apps, and yes, even cassette tapes the country over. But while researching this book, I went in search of any recordings of my own coachings—whether lessons I taught or those in which I studied with other teachers. Perhaps, I thought, dwelling with the ways I have mobilized particular repertoire and vocal exercises in the studio could help to clarify why I sense the voice lesson may be understood as such a fruitful figure for performance analysis. The one set of recordings that I did unearth points up yet another side of my impulse to expand the definition of what counts as a voice lesson in musical theatre singing.

Wedged in a dusty space between the back of my piano and the exposed brick wall of my living room, on the hardwood floors of my Brooklyn apartment, I found a small digital voice recorder bought more than a decade ago. Its recordings are in the now annoyingly unwieldy .WMA format, not easily converted to .MP3s, and so it is a device I no longer use (hence its forgotten location behind the piano) despite its sliding USB connector that once seemed fancy. I acquired this recorder in a presmartphone era to take with me on a specific set of voice lessons that I hear, in my own way, as lessons in musical theatre singing. In the summer of 2011, I spent a week studying Akan classical vocal music—in particular, musical forms sung by all-women ensembles from the Ashanti region—in Accra, Ghana, in preparation for a musical play I was in the process of writing and composing. When I plug my headphones into the recorder now, I hear tracks taped in the University of Ghana performing arts complex, with the sounds of a percussion ensemble rehearsing in the next room bleeding into the space of my private voice lesson taught by Mercy Ayetteh, senior instructor of the Ghana National Dance Ensemble. On the recording, I am singing in Twi, my father's language but one I do not fully understand. I am learning by listening to phrases and repeating back. There are no vocal warm-ups or exercises to start the session. We simply sing each song, phrase by phrase. Listen, repeat back. Listen, repeat back. Discuss as needed. Clarify trouble spots. Listen, repeat back. Sing the phrase again together. The sound we pursue is a straight tone (vibrato-free), a kind of authoritative speaking on pitch, heightened declamation full of what my American ear hears as blue notes; what we are voicing is the call to which others will respond. Ayetteh coaches me on how to stand, how to enter, how to seat myself, how to clap and sway while singing—these movements are a key part of how to perform the sought-after vocal sound. And so the lesson is not only about producing a certain timbre of the voice, the diction of the specific words, nor a particular song in nnwonkoro style. The lesson is also about how to carry, physically, the sense of occasion in which this singing arises.[92]

The research, writing, and revision of my musical play *The Family Resemblance*, for which I took these singing lessons, was intercut with the research, writing, and revision of this book. (The same is true of another musical, *Paradise Square*, which I touch on in the following section, the Playoff to this book.) Songs from *The Family Resemblance* feature prominently among those I have most often coached other singers to perform in recent years. The show has a score where musical style serves explicitly as a function of character; singer-actors move across US folk and popular song, West African highlife, and Akan classical music. I bring up this musical here not only because its sound is part of the underscoring that has, for me, reverberated through *Blues Mamas and Broadway Belters*, but also because it points toward a set of lessons that I hope for as I imagine the future of US musicals. Writings on "the American musical," similar to those on jazz, are often predicated on and work to trumpet notions of American exceptionalism. Yet so many theatre forms around the world sustain long histories of presenting dramatic works that include music and dance. For US-based writers of musicals who seek new ways to tell stories of racial identity onstage beyond the well-worn path of minstrel tropes, such transnational practices are vital objects of comparative study. If we are to have new stories and new songs, new lessons will need to be learned—by writers and singers alike. Because, once again, "new" singing does not simply spring forth from nowhere, there is always another singer, whether in the distant past or across contemporaneous distance, from whom one can learn.

Playoff

The playoff is the music that comes in after the number is over. It holds you rapt while it gets you smoothly to the next thing since, as industry knowledge holds, musicals live and die by their transitions. Let the show keep clicking along, let the moments melt into each other on waves of scored sound. And let the blare of horns and keys and winds carry, supported by the sly cool of the bass line and the razzle dazzle of the drums, the residue of what made the just-heard song so pleasurable—the singer's vocal sound that brought it to life. Where the overture at the top of the show (when there is such a thing anymore) anticipates the voices to come, the playoff music, like the underscoring for the curtain call at show's end, recapitulates voice's contours, reminds us of lingering vocal presence even as it compels us forward. On that note. . . .

. . . .

Twice in the span of three weeks during an omicronious winter, approaching the third year of the COVID-19 pandemic, I pressed my mask firmly over mouth and nose and took the subway from the depths of Brooklyn to the only slightly haggard sparkle of midtown Manhattan and the persistent lights of Times Square. I went to see not a Broadway musical but a Broadway play, *Trouble in Mind* (1955) by the late playwright Alice Childress, a black woman. The fact that the play starred black Broadway icon LaChanze was enough of a draw the first time I hurried along 42nd Street for the evening curtain. LaChanze is a singer and actress who has inspired me for decades.[1] As a teen I took refuge in the basement of my family's Pennsylvania home where I could explore raucous, shouty vocal sounds (okay, squawks) relatively undisturbed, and sang Sondheim's "Another Hundred People" along with her sweet, breathy-but-steely belt voice on the 1995 *Company* revival cast album over and over. I could never quite sound like her—and still don't—but that singing along with her brought me to new colors in my voice that I use to this day. In Childress's backstage drama, LaChanze is delightfully cast as Wiletta, an experienced musical comedy star who is getting her first shot at a serious play. Set during the midcentury rehearsal process of a modern anti-lynching play, *Trouble in Mind* dramatizes the conflict that arises between the various members of the multiracial cast and the white director, a self-proclaimed liberal. For me in the audience, freshly emerged from my own intense rehearsal process of a new musical (about which more below) with complicated themes oscillating between racial harmony and racial violence, the relevance and sharp insights of the charged rehearsal room dynamics in Childress's play were breathtaking. The second time I sat myself down in the audience of Roundabout Theatre Company's American Airlines Theatre on 42nd Street, I had a copy of the play in my bag and leaned forward in my seat as if in a class I'd been hoping to attend for a very long time.

A world where black women's voices hold intellect and authority is a world that we are told, again and again, does not exist and cannot be heard. As Daphne Brooks teaches it in her beautiful exegesis *Liner Notes for the Revolution: The Intellectual Life of Black Feminist Sound*, black women in musical performance "have been overlooked or underappreciated, misread and sometimes lazily mythologized, underestimated and sometimes entirely disregarded, and—above all else—perpetually undertheorized by generations of critics for much of the last one hundred years."[2] So although everybody is ready to celebrate music that makes use of (and money from) black women's voices, few people are ready to fully address what black women's voices *do* in the theatre, or in the world. And that is what, in the course of *Trouble in Mind*, Wiletta fights for. Central to the drama is a disagreement between Wiletta and the white director about how her character in the show-within-a-show should sing. Initially, she vocalizes briefly through "a snatch of an old song" in the first scene as she is alone in the theatre, recalling her glory days as a star in the fictitious but aptly named *Brownskin Melody*. Downstage center in her smart yellow suit, LaChanze as Wiletta stretches out her arms, bevels graciously, and launches into two lines of a jazzy melody, "Oh, honey babe."[3] Here she is singing along with her past self, a self that solidified her present love for the theatre but from whom she now hopes to move on with this role in a serious drama. Sadly, the joke is on her, because even in serious drama, Wiletta comes to realize, black women are still expected to doggedly keep on singing, along sharply prescribed routes.

The part Wiletta has secured in the fictitious anti-lynching play *Chaos in Belleville*, her supposed exit ramp from the confines of musical comedy, is none other than the part of a weary-bluesy mother. This is a character who by the close of the play-within-a-play (impossibly!) sadly and prayerfully resigns herself to the fact that she must send her teenage son off to face a lynching mob and stands by helplessly singing a spiritual. Because she lacks training in the dramatic academy compared to her younger-generation castmates, Wiletta carries her own anxieties—which are fanned by the not-entirely-competent, erratic director—that she doesn't know enough about the actor's work of "justifying" her character's actions. But as she grows more attuned to tracing the truth of characterization, the more starkly she realizes the profound *un*truth of the character, Ruby, she is scripted to play. A pivotal moment in this journey of realization is the scene late in the first act of both *Trouble in Mind* and *Chaos in Belville* where, as the director puts it, Ruby is "alone on the porch, worried, heartsick" and starts to sing. [4] The director recites a litany of all the sorrows weighing on the character that the singing, another old song that Wiletta has known for years, should contain. "I know exactly what you want," she returns. And in the role of Wiletta, in the theatre now, LaChanze bends her back, emitting a husky, heavy belt sound sprinkled with dropped-third riffs punctuated with gesticulations—the weary-bluesy church lady. (Childress's script gives the direction that Wiletta "sings a mournful dirge of despair.")[5] Unsatisfied, the director, Mr. Manners, puts Wiletta through a punishing word association exercise in the vocabulary of racial trauma and when she sings in the wake of this work, her voice is a force newly unleashed. Onstage, LaChanze stands upright; she has moved from an uncertain position farther upstage to now hold stage down left, and she pulls the sound from the depths of her body, bright and full and confident and ready to lead the charge with these words, although they are exactly the same lyrics she sang in her first pass.

WILETTA: [*sings a song of strength and anger*]:

Come and go with me to that land
[*The song is overpowering; we see a woman who could fight the world.*]
Come and go with me to that land
Come and go with me to that land—
where I'm bound.

JUDY: Bravo! Magnificent!

MANNERS: Wiletta, if you dare! You will undo us! Are you out of your senses? When you didn't know what you were doing . . . perfection on the nose. I'll grant you the first interpretation was right, without motivating. All right, I'll settle for that.

WILLETTA: [*feeling very lost*]: I said I *knew* what you wanted.[6]

But the damage has been done. Now that Wiletta continues to have trouble "justifying" her character's behavior, she takes it up repeatedly with the director. He doesn't listen to her, she insists, because she lacks the formal education of her fellow actors. Yet she, too, has been enlightened by her studies of the script—not at drama school but with her neighbor Miss Green, who "puts on shows at the church" and "also conducts the church choir."[7] However, this mode of study, two black women in their domestic space, reading and discussing the play together, voice to voice, is received with skepticism by the director. Sitting in the audience, I can tell that Miss Green was on to something, that Wiletta was wise in her choice of teacher/collaborator, and that the theorizing of these black women together is vivid and powerful. In Childress's deft hands and LaChanze's unflinching voice and presence, the entire play cracks on the pressure point of this theorizing and the careful force that Wiletta steadily applies to the white director regarding the play's dramaturgy. I am grateful that Childress held fast to her vision and refused to allow her play to appear on Broadway rewritten and retitled along less racially incendiary lines. At the same time, this refusal meant forgoing a hoped-for, historic Broadway credit in 1955, four years before playwright Lorraine Hansberry's triumph with *A Raisin in the Sun*. When black women have refused to play the parts others would assign to them, or when their strategic refusals or dissemblances have been misinterpreted, the pernicious narrative that they remain "untrained," uneducated, and unqualified persists unchecked.

During the same season as *Trouble in Mind*, 2021–2022, Broadway saw several more black women singer-actresses take the stage in unprecedented roles. The land of Oz as portrayed in *Wicked* permanently cast a black actress, Brittney Johnson, in the role of Glinda the good witch for the first time. *The Phantom of the Opera* similarly cast its first black woman in the leading role of Christine Daaé, Emilie Kouatchou. In Michael R. Jackson's *A Strange Loop*, trans singer-actress L Morgan Lee broke barriers with her meltingly sweet soprano. It was announced that in an upcoming production, six-time Tony Award winner Audra McDonald, whose career may be heard in a meaningful duet with her contemporary LaChanze especially given the significant differences in their sounds, would appear in the first Broadway production by another leading black playwright, Adrienne Kennedy, with *Ohio State Murders*. And over at the Ethel Barrymore Theatre on West 47th Street, an epic Civil War-era megamusical opened for which I served as a lyricist, shaping the score with my wonderful collaborators, co-lyricist Nathan Tysen and composer Jason Howland.

What a time this was, the first season on Broadway since its historic, nearly eighteen-month shutdown due to the COVID-19 pandemic. From March 2020 to August 2021, theatres on Broadway and throughout the United States could not hold performances due to the challenge posed by ethically and safely bringing together large casts of actors in a world where airborne vocal melodies and lovers' kisses onstage—not to mention the simple copresence of audience members breathing side by side in close proximity—carried the danger of a life-threatening virus. When *Paradise Square* rehearsed in the James M. Nederlander Theatre for its pre-Broadway tryout in Chicago in the fall of 2021, it was the first show to perform in that theatre since the start of the pandemic. It felt to me like we were waking up that historic, ornate theatre from its long nap, from the fluorescent-lit rehearsal rooms in the bowels of the building to the uppermost balcony lobby where I went one day to write a new lyric during tech. For many of the artists involved, it was the first time working in a theatre in eighteen months since our 2020 projects were cut short. Like all of us in the rehearsal room the cast wore KN95 masks, somehow executing the intricate, athletic choreography of the dance-heavy show and one power anthem after another while breathing and singing through dense, synthetic polymer material.[8] I will never forget a comment made during these rehearsals by our luminous leading lady Joaquina Kalukango. This was before she went on to win the 2022 Tony Award for Best Leading Actress in a Musical for her tour-de-force performance as Nelly, a free Black woman who owns the show's titular dance hall and is a force in her community (figure P.1). A Juilliard-trained actress, previously a Tony nominee for her performance in the controversial *Slave Play* and who had also appeared on Broadway in three earlier musicals including a turn as Nettie in the hit 2015 revival of *The Color Purple*, Kalukango certainly was technically skilled in how to use her voice. But, she said, she was having a hard time feeling her voice the way she always had, "getting it under her" while wearing the face mask. Certainly, even once a singer knows "how to sing"—and you'd better believe Ms. Joaquina knows how to sing; six thousand people who leapt to

P.1 Joaquina Kalukango performing as Nelly from *Paradise Square* at the 75th Annual Tony Awards (2022). Photo by Theo Wargo via Getty Images.

their feet after her searing performance at Radio City Music Hall during the 2022 Tony Awards can attest to that fact—there is always something new to learn. I don't think any of us could have imagined the singing lessons we would have to learn in the wake of the pandemic, but here we were.

I include below a few thoughts on *Paradise Square* to bear witness to another way that I have experienced the theory and practice of black women's twice-heard singing in the musical theatre. I will speak about two places where our Broadway musical *Paradise Square* stages the black feminist practice of *singing along with*, and which I worked to shape as a co-lyricist with my collaborators on the creative team.[9] Both arise in the second act.

The first instance is in the number "Breathe Easy," an anthem for the show's black ensemble created in the spring and early summer of 2021 by Howland, Tysen, and I together with our bookwriter collaborator, Christina Anderson.[10] As a writing team we decided to add a new number celebrating the moment when Angelina and Washington, two people who are very much in love and who escaped enslavement together but became separated while traveling north, are finally reunited. For the entire show prior Washington has been singing about how amazing his girl Angelina is and—spoilers—how, together, they had to kill the slave master who was sexually abusing her. It's important to note that Angelina is the show's ingénue; once again, for our black ingénues, it's often such an uphill battle to be an innocent and hopeful young woman.[11] Christina wrote a beautiful monologue for Angelina about how on her journey north she was welcomed in by two black women who lived on their own land in the Carolinas and showed her what it truly meant to live in freedom. A rehearsal photo from the Chicago tryout of *Paradise Square* (figure P.2) shows Hailee Kaleem Wright and Kayla Pecchioni, who originated the roles of these women, in rehearsal clothes, with face masks slipped off of faces and looped around their arms for the run-through. Pecchioni rests her hand on the small of Wright's back as they warmly bid farewell to the runaway they have sheltered. It's because of this loving, content black lesbian couple, Sarah and Blessed, that Angelina says to Washington when they finally reunite: "I want what *they* have for us." The black queer couple is the epitome of and model for living in love and freedom. I read this monologue and said, *Wouldn't it be beautiful to hear these three black women singing together?*[12] And that is what we wrote.

Late in Act 2, Angelina is alone in a safehouse in New York, repeating the mantra that Sarah and Blessed taught her, the reminder to breathe and trust that she will get to freedom. In her memory the two women appear

P.2 Hailee Kaleem Wright and Kayla Pecchioni as Sarah and Blessed in rehearsal for *Paradise Square* in Chicago, 2021. Photo by Drew Shade. Used by permission.

and sing with her. "Breathe easy, breathe easy / you will reach freedom one day / and breathe easy, breathe easy / in sweet freedom one day." The song goes on, it's an extended sequence; Washington arrives and sings a duet section with Angelina, and then the ancestors and underground railroad conductors who have helped them both on their way appear in dim lighting and form a chorus that supports and blesses their love and their journey. All sing the refrain: "Breathe easy, you *will* reach freedom one day." As Angelina and Washington embark on the final phase of their journey north to Canada, they follow the path laid out by—and they sing along with—Sarah and Blessed and all who have prayed and believed them to this point. The black feminist act of *singing along with* secures the promise of black survival and black joy. And this is grounded in the Spillersian radical approach to affirming black female sexuality as self-knowledge.

The second incidence occurs in the show's finale. The show's central character, Nelly O'Brien, proprietor of the gritty saloon Paradise Square in lower Manhattan, has broken down in trying to narrate the musical to its close. The losses at this point in the show have been too steep (more spoilers). She has lost her Irish husband on the battlefield, and she has lost her generational wealth to a racist mob. How to go on in the face of this? How to deliver any kind of nontrite message of hope to today's audience? She cannot. Her direct address to the audience falters and breaks off. And what happens is that the ensemble takes up her song, music that she sang at the top of the show about the spirit and self-determination that characterize their community. "There's a song that fills the air." In taking up her music, the ensemble comforts and sings along with her even when she is silent in grief, until she can come back into voice as they all sing to close out the number and the show. Together in song, Nelly and the company hold out the potential, through personal action and accountability, for a brighter future. "Though the battle rages on / in a world in disrepair / The door is always open . . ."

What is at stake in the theory and practice of *singing along with* black women's theatre voices? It is the possibility of knowingly participating in a world definitively shaped by the artful sound that comes from the throat of a black woman. Let's sing!

Appendix

More Exercises for Voice Practice

An Exercise from Sissieretta Jones: Wings Flex
after the Black Patti Troubadours on tour

Stand just outside the playing space in the rehearsal room or in the wings of the theatre. Know that you are the star of the company (even if only in your own mind) and carry yourself accordingly. Sing along with the ensemble rehearsing or performing onstage in a group choral number. Pay attention to how it feels to stretch out your vocal sound while you are vocally part of, and yet physically apart from, the group.

An Exercise from Gertrude "Ma" Rainey and Bessie Smith: Blue It Up On the Road
after their song "Don't Fish in My Sea"

Meet up with a singer you love or admire. Write a song together that has some blue notes in it. (If you don't know what a blue note is, ask somebody!) Sing the song you've written together three ways, moving to different locations (even if in the same room) each time:

1 Sing it together in more or less unison.
2 Sing it for each other, each taking a turn. Whoever is not singing at the time should "talk back" in the spaces between musical phrases. You can encourage the other singer, or emphasize what the lyrics are saying.
3 Sing it for each other, each taking a turn. Whoever is not singing the main melody should again "talk back" but this time by *singing* in the spaces between musical phrases. It's a little call

and response. The responses might need to be short and percussive. If there's not enough space in the song for this, the two of you might need to do a little rewriting!

An Exercise from Sophie Tucker: Play Innocent
after her coachings to a young Mary Martin and other aspiring musical theatre singers

Find a new-to-you song that has some double entendre in it—funny lyrics that are at least a little dirty or could be interpreted that way. Listen around in unusual places while song-hunting—perhaps go to concerts you might not usually attend or listen to recordings of artists you don't know well. (If you perform this song in a moneymaking venue, be sure you have permission from the artist and/or purchase the published sheet music beforehand.) Practice the song with a trusted coach. Each time you get to an innuendo-laden lyric, raise your eyes to the heavens innocently. Subtext: "This song? Dirty? Heavens, what's running through *your* filthy little mind?"

An Exercise from Ethel Waters: Find Your Pearl
after her coachings with accompanist Pearl Wright

Seek out a new musical accompanist to practice with, someone you trust and identify with; perhaps this is a person with whom you share one or more identity categories. Bonus points if you had to look a little harder to learn about and connect with this musician . . . ask around in the not-so-usual places. Work on a new song with this accompanist. Ask for their feedback and incorporate some of their suggestions in your singing as you practice. Take note of what feedback they may be giving you, or the way they are communicating it, that is different from what you usually experience in learning and rehearsing a new song.

An Exercise from Ethel Merman: Silent Shout
after a song about having rhythm

Plant your feet and square your shoulders. Bend your elbows away from your body, hold your hands in loose fists and feel how this activates your arms and torso. Take a breath. (I recommend a high breath. Gasp in.) Drop your jaw and *silently* shout "Aw" [ɔ] while you count to sixty-four (or as high as you can). The key will be not to flood the air but let it out slowly. (I also recommend that you think about laughing while you do this to avoid clenching/constricting your larynx.)

An Exercise from Juanita Hall: Cracked Diphthong
after travels from Juilliard to Bali Ha'i to the Blues

(Note: I give this exercise without costume or makeup.)

Begin low in your range on the vowel *ah* [ɑ], a round sound with a gently aspirated attack—let the vibrato roll, almost exaggerated, "operatic" in caricature if need be—and glide up to a pitch an octave higher. On this higher note, maintain the volume and let the vowel open into the diphthong, shifting to *ee* [ɪ]. Feel how the quality of your voice enters a certain precarity, with the steadiness of your speaking voice threatening to crack. Edge upward chromatically and repeat the octave leap: *ah-ee* [aɪ]. As you rise higher, *let the voice crack* and/or find its way into a muscular-sounding falsetto. Let the vibrato continue to ring in this new voice color. Edge higher, half-step by half-step. Notice how the vibrato stabilizes and/or destabilizes your voice as you dip out of your speaking register and into the cracked tone of lighter, wispier sound. Also, don't push it; this can tire out your voice. Do the exercise, see what you notice, and move on.

An Exercise from Pearl Bailey: Listen to Yourself
after her nightclub act

Sing a song you know well. Stop in the middle and say whatever comes to your mind—not for an outside listener, but talking to yourself, whatever comes to mind that interests you. Where do your thoughts lead? Find a way to bring them back to the next part of the song and launch back into singing again. Repeat the exercise. The trick is to sing the entire song for yourself, keeping your inner monologue going, so that when you stop singing and start speaking, you know what to say. Because you've been listening to the sound of your own thoughts, in between singing, all along.

. . . .

NOTE A set of exercises inspired by the vocal performances of Lena Horne, Mary Martin, Diahann Carroll, Leslie Uggams, Pat Suzuki, and Eartha Kitt can be found in chapter 3.

Notes

Acknowledgments

An early version of chapter 1 of this book was published as "Vocal Colour in Blue: Early Twentieth-Century Black Women Singers as Voice Teachers," in *Performance Matters* 6, no. 2 (2020): 52–66; and portions of chapter 4 are published in "The Black Broadway Voice: Calls and Responses," in *Studies in Musical Theatre* 14, no. 3 (2020): 343–59.

Introduction

1   This is not a question about what kinds of voices *are* possible, which implies an assumption that the range of vocal sounds available to black women is necessarily limited because such sounds emanate from racialized bodies. This kind of thinking drifts far too easily to the logic of nineteenth-century pseudosciences that insinuate absurd racial classification systems, wielding measurements of skulls and bones and bodies to assert the relative capabilities, intellectual or otherwise, of individuals of different races. See Eidsheim, "Race and Aesthetics of Vocal Timbre," 338–65.

2   Asare, "The Black Broadway Voice," 343–59.

3   There have of course been many lauded black women singers of classical music, but the extant literature on voice pedagogy largely presumes their absence or glosses over their presence. As I discuss in what follows, "voice pedagogy" as a category is presumed to be classical voice pedagogy unless otherwise marked. Where I have found blackness invoked, generally it has been in the nascent literature on popular voice pedagogies.

4   I grew up in a religious space that posited an iterated form of Black Atlantic black churchiness that tends toward the illegible in the US context. As a child and teenager, my mixed-race family attended a church

in central Pennsylvania where the congregation's full-bodied, four-part hymn-singing in the Germanic and Anabaptist tradition reminds my west African father of the choral music from his Presbyterian missionary upbringing in Ghana, where his father was a choir director and church organist.

5 Asare, "The Black Broadway Voice."

6 Sood, "Neither Here Nor There," 337, 340. "When I first moved to New York I was an actor and no one knew how to cast me. I remember one of my first big callbacks for a Broadway show was *Bombay Dreams*. It really threw me because I was not South Asian and yet that was the way I was reading to casting directors. I think it was part of why I started writing. I felt like [as an actor] you can be judged at such a surface level, and there was, especially at that time, the idea that if you look something, you can just do it. If the mainstream audiences coming to the show would buy you in a role, then you should get up there. There's something wrong about that. I only made it through a couple callbacks and it kind of faded away. But I stopped auditioning soon after because it was really disorienting for me. I got into the BMI workshop and started being more of a writer."

7 This tradition of self-referential musical theatre by writers of color includes a series of Broadway and beyond-Broadway musicals, not only Jackson's Pulitzer Prize and Tony Award–winning *A Strange Loop* (2019), but also Kirsten Childs's Obie Award–winning *The Bubbly Black Girl Sheds Her Chameleon Skin* (2000), and *Invisible Thread* by Griffin Matthews and Matt Gould—also titled *Witness Uganda* in various iterations beyond the Second Stage production in New York in 2015—as well as my own musical play *The Family Resemblance*, workshopped at the Eugene O'Neill Center in Waterford, Connecticut, in 2018. With the commercial theatre production of *In the Heights* (2008), Lin-Manuel Miranda literally wrote his person and presence onto the Broadway stage.

8 Hartman, *Wayward Lives, Beautiful Experiments*, 345.

9 Brooks, *Liner Notes for the Revolution*, 3.

10 Wolf, *Changed for Good*, 18. Wolf asserts this project of focusing in on women and how they perform and relate also makes space for projects that are "undeniably queer." I celebrate the queer textures of listening to and singing along with other women, and specifically, with black women. Wolf's first book on musical theatre feminisms is also an important inspiration for this work. See Wolf, *A Problem Like Maria*.

11 Cavarero, *For More Than One Voice*, 118.

12 Similarly, in writing about gender and voice in Puerto Rican popular music, Licia Fiol-Matta strategically animates and reclaims the disparaging way that women singers are lumped together as somehow extraneous to the grand trajectory of genius, male-authored music. See Fiol-Matta, *The Great Woman Singer*.

13   As Heather Williams details in her book *Self-Taught*, black Americans, historically denied access to education, have sought lessons by illicit or unorthodox means. See Williams, *Self-Taught*.

14   At the same time, the kind of musical education studied here stands in meaningful relation to the "egalitarian, nonhierarchical vision of pedagogy" George Lewis has painstakingly documented within the experimental work of black musicians in the Association for the Advancement of Creative Musicians School in Chicago, founded in 1967. There, Richard Muhal Abrams articulated a view of musical training in the form of "collaboration between the so-called teachers and so-called students." See Lewis, *A Power Stronger Than Itself*, 177.

15   The way that I understand techniques of vocal practice has much to do with the notion of "techniques of the body" theorized by French sociologist Marcel Mauss, which has been so useful to dance studies. In assessing actions of the body and their particular quality as learned techniques, Mauss works through a litany of observations around walking, running, squatting, sleeping, swimming, marching, digging, spitting, dancing, climbing, having sex, breathing, laughing, and giving birth. He carefully notes that these behaviors, far from being somehow "natural" or inherent, are learned—the result of education and the imitation of those in positions of authority. Many of the techniques Mauss describes, such as laughing and breathing, implicate the voice directly; Mauss, "Techniques of the Body" (1934).

16   The understanding of voice as something that may be easily and permanently ruined pervades voice pedagogy, including that of two renowned nineteenth-century teachers, Garcia and G. B. Lamperti. Garcia asserts, "Freshness and steadiness are the most valuable properties of a voice, but are also the most delicate, easily injured, and quickly lost. When once impaired, they are never to be restored; and this is precisely the condition of a voice which is said to be 'broken' . . . [which] may be attributed to injudicious vocal education . . . the result . . . being, utterly to destroy the voice"; Garcia, *Garcia's New Treatise on the Art of Singing*, 8. And for his part, Lamperti cautions, "When the chest-voice is forced up too high, the head-voice loses in mellowness and carrying-power; how many beautiful alto voices have been ruined—caused to break—by this unnatural method!" See Lamperti, *The Technics of Bel Canto*, 24.

17   Meizel, *Multivocality*, studies what singers do to navigate multiple vocal identities in the act of singing across stylistic, cultural, geographic and bodily difference has much to offer for the study of voices in musicals.

18   I understand vocal styles, sounded via techniques of the body, as certainly engaged with the social yet neither a stable field within which layers and textures of musical expression happen nor an externalized object plucked from the wardrobe of social context. Stephen Feld has written about

style, in the context of playing in the groove, as a "musical order" in the process of being sustained. From the practitioner perspective, instructor of popular voice Donna Soto-Morettini describes musical styles as one or another suit of clothing that the vocalist puts on or takes off—style as vocal attire, or a sort of cosplay of the voice that veers uncomfortably close to the minstrel impulse to "black up." See Feld, "Aesthetics as Iconicity of Style," 107; and Soto-Morettini, *Popular Singing and Style*.

19   My analysis builds on the germinal work of leading performance studies scholars. Richard Schechner theorizes ritual and theatre performance practices as "twice-behaved behavior." The twoness that interests him arises from the dynamism of the space between the performer's embodied self and symbolic other, and from the fact that any ritual performance necessarily restages past performances. Similarly, Diana Taylor establishes the "scenario" as a unit of the repertoire that effects a "once-againness" and stages "the generative critical distance between social actor and character." I extend this work by noting that songs take shape not only via theatrical repertoires but also in the context of the musician's set of tunes. The itinerant blues singer's repertoire manifests its particular textures of once-againness in a series of renditions which, after Christine Bacareza Balance, are ever in the process of being remade. Songs in the act of being resung again and again, Balance shows, unseat miraculous and hegemonic notions of origin and discovery. See Schechner, *Between Theater and Anthropology*; Taylor, *The Archive and the Repertoire*, 30, 32; and Balance, *Tropical Renditions*.

20   DuBoisian double consciousness famously invokes the kind of critical distance that operates as a dynamic, even resonant, gap between inner, affective experience—the way one feels oneself to be—and outer, visual aspect—the way one is taken to appear. As evidenced in writings spurred on by African American spirituals, what he called the "sorrow songs," for DuBois this critical distance clearly keys an attunement to song. See DuBois, *The Souls of Black Folk*.

21   I engage musical theatre singing as a form of the critical performance practice Eidsheim advocates and models in her work. See Eidsheim, *The Race of Sound*.

22   Moten, *In the Break*.

23   Moten, "Comparing Domains of Improvisation," April 23, 2021.

24   Moten, "Comparing Domains of Improvisation," April 23, 2021.

25   Moten, "Comparing Domains of Improvisation," April 23, 2021.

26   Morrison, "Black Studies Center Public Dialogue. Pt. 2." I thank Michael R. Jackson for directing me to this Morrison quote in the spring of 2021.

27   Eidsheim, *Sensing Sound*.

28   Osseo-Asare, *Bitter Roots*, 2.

29   E. Patrick Johnson writes, regarding the slipperiness that adheres to notions of authenticity: "And yet human commingling necessarily entails

the syncretism whereby cultures assimilate and adopt aspects of each other. Indeed, as 'white always seems to attract stains,' black similarly seems to absorb light." See Johnson, *Appropriating Blackness*, 5.

30   Tagaq, *Tanya Tagaq—Retribution*.

31   Robinson, *Hungry Listening*.

32   Throughout this book I include the year in which a given musical first appeared on Broadway as the parenthetical following its first mention in the text. In many cases, of course, a show had a production history prior to arriving on Broadway, whether in London or regionally in the United States. Despite all the ways that I feel in my bones that Broadway should not be taken as the only, nor the best, site of meaningful musical theatre, I have followed this convention for the sake of consistency and in the interest of providing an at-a-glance sense of the timeframe in which each of these musicals emerged. In several cases the year that the show opened on Broadway is different from the year in which a Tony Award for its star was awarded; the Tony Awards ceremony generally takes place in the spring of a given year in recognition of all the plays and musicals that have opened during the prior season, which extends across two calendar years.

33   Hatch, "A White Folks Guide to 200 Years of Black and White Drama," 18.

34   See especially chapter 1 of Poulson-Bryant, "Strollin' through Broadway History," 155–73.

35   Donatella Galella expertly maps this history. See Galella, *America in the Round*. See in particular chapter 4, "Cultivating *Raisin* and the Popular Black Musical."

36   As Nadine George-Graves observes, studies of 1920s black theatre have long privileged the Harlem Renaissance movement yet the circuits and reach of black vaudeville constitute a vibrant space within which to consider the impactful work of black women artists. See George-Graves, *The Royalty of Negro Vaudeville*, 2. George-Graves studies the influence of the celebrated Whitman Sisters in performance, pedagogy, and arts management.

37   Woll, *Black Musical Theatre*, xii.

38   Harold Wheeler won a Lifetime Achievement Tony Award in 2019.

39   Southern, *The Music of Black Americans*, 563–64.

40   Henry T. Sampson writes mournfully of "the demise of the black producer," observing that: "By the early 1930s, almost all of the black musical comedy shows that played on Broadway were produced by whites. . . . By the mid-1930s, musical comedy shows and revues produced by, owned by, and performed by blacks were well on the road to decline." See Sampson, *Blacks in Blackface*, 35.

41   Jessica Sternfeld and Elizabeth Wollman have critiqued the indiscriminate use of the term "Golden Age" in musical theatre studies, highlighting its inconsistencies and the way it seems to devalue what transpired in its wake. I find these critiques compelling yet would also note that it

remains in wide use among practitioners and musical theatre training programs, where the requirement to have "Golden Age" song repertoire in one's book still stands. Additionally, it seems a bit unjust to me that we would entirely dispense with the term and the prestige it carries without having first allowed black women artists to share in some of that prestige. At the same time, remembering Moten's injunction to avoid the simple aim of seeking honor for black artists, perhaps the fact that so few black artists are recognized as shaping Broadway's golden heyday should form a greater part of the critique for jettisoning the moniker. See Sternfeld and Wollman, "After the Golden Age," 111–24.

42 Perhaps this is part of why musical theatre fans can be so fiercely insistent, to the point of delusion, in denying the various racisms in many "great shows"—out of a fear that the beloved art object will be excised from the canon.

43 Possible exceptions include Ethel Waters and Audra McDonald.

44 My intent is not to reify the awards ceremony in an act of unreserved endorsement. However, assembling the list of black women who were the first to win Tony Awards for performances in musical theatre provides one means of tracking and listening to those whose performances, even if largely forgotten today, were deemed outstanding in their own time.

45 This project stands in conversation with works by Christine Bacareza Balance, *Tropical Renditions*; Angela Davis, *Blues Legacies and Black Feminism*; Jayna Brown, *Babylon Girls*; Daphne A. Brooks, *Bodies in Dissent* and *Liner Notes for the Revolution*; Farah Jasmine Griffin, *If You Can't Be Free, Be a Mystery* and "When Malindy Sings"; Shana Redmond, *Anthem*; Elena Elias Krell, "Contours through Covers," 476–503; Licia Fiol-Matta, *The Great Woman Singer*; Tavia Nyong'o, "Afro-Philo-Sonic Fictions," 173–79; Alexandra T. Vazquez, *Listening in Detail*; and Shane Vogel, "Performing 'Stormy Weather,'" 93–113, and *Stolen Time*.

46 Moten, *In the Break*; Lewis, *A Power Stronger Than Itself*.

47 Kajikawa, "Leaders of the New School?" 45.

48 Johnson, "Building the Broadway Voice"; Macpherson, "Sing"; Wollman, *The Theater Will Rock*.

49 Stacy Wolf's analysis of *West Side Story*'s "A Boy Like That," the iconic duet between ingénue Maria and secondary lead Anita, can be extended by a deeper consideration of vocal sound. Beyond the dramatic or the compositional, an attention to the sound of singers' voices has much to add to the analysis. Noting that Anita is an alto and Maria is a soprano is not precisely sufficient and may in fact be a bit misleading. These descriptions of vocal range, or *fach*, are drawn from the classical world and of limited use in the musical theatre context. More specifically, Maria's classical, lyrically written sound brings the value system of the composer and casting director to bear on her character as more European and evolved,

where Anita's low-to-the-ground belt voice carries the legacy of the blues shouters and a host of ideas around the earthiness (or "fieriness") and pragmatism of women whose voices sound like that. Here audiences are presented with two kinds of Puerto Ricanness and two kinds of femininity, and the fact that both resolve in tragedy by the show's end seems to foreclose a field of vocal possibility. Yet even within the tight spaces of such sonic parameters, one can listen in detail for the ways that singers of color move through sound to execute choices about the musical-theatrical vocal-possible. This attention to technical practice brings into hearing further dimensions of what a voice—and a dramatic character—is, means, and does in full potentiality.

The casting of white actress Carol Lawrence as ingénue Maria, and Puerto Rican actress Chita Rivera as Anita in the original Broadway production of *West Side Story* in 1957 has much to do with the vocal sound the producers wanted for each character. The implication is that the idealized Puerto Rican woman, love interest for white American male lead Tony, had a voice that could be performed only by a white singer. Additionally, I must note that triple threat Broadway legend Chita Rivera's *vocal* performances, although beyond the scope of this book, deserve greater scholarly consideration. As a Tony Award–winning woman of color star from Broadway's "Golden Age" who sustained a remarkable career on Broadway over six decades, Rivera's performances stand in conversation with African American and Asian American artists like Diahann Carroll, Pat Suzuki, and Leslie Uggams, whose Broadway careers were, by comparison, much more short-lived.

50 A key aim of the book is to unsettle ideas of history and genre as stable, fixed entities, and to point up the ways that historical sound travels—often across musical genres—in vocal practice, including in contemporary practice. Alexandra T. Vazquez's approach to writing on Cuban popular music via detailed, interruptive "interaction" rather than "account" is instructive here. See Vazquez, *Listening in Detail*, 8.

51 The bird with an egg in its beak that reaches back toward the feathers it already carries is not engaging a distant, externalized past but an embodied reality, a "behindness" that is already part of its corporeal being. For more on sankofa and theatre practice, see Yeboah, "All the Nation's a Stage," 147–68.

52 Davis, "The Context Problem," 208.

53 My upbringing in central Pennsylvania has connected me to a line of voice teachers that traces directly to Jo Estill, founder of the Estill pedagogical model. Specifically, Kimberly Steinhauer, president of Estill Voice International and director of the Estill workshop in Quebec City, which I discuss in chapter 4, grew up in a town only twelve miles from my hometown of State College, Pennsylvania. Steinhauer's high school choir director,

Jessica McNall, taught throughout the central Pennsylvania region and led a local children's choir I sang in when I was five years old, where she taught warm-ups and vocalizations from the Estill method that I remember today; McNall later came to teach at my high school, where I studied with her and served as a piano accompanist for her private voice teaching practice. McNall was a student of Jo Estill's at the University of Pittsburgh in the 1980s and traveled internationally with Estill leading workshops of her method. For these reasons, my Pennsylvania roots and lineage of voice study grant me a particular insider access to this method and its teachers that I acknowledge and benefit from as I engage the theoretical implications of singing practice.

54 Steinhauer, "Estill Workshop (Level Two)"; Sussuma, "Estill Workshop (Level Two), 'Figuring Out the Figures." Since the time of this workshop, Sussuma has parted ways with the Estill orthodoxy and continues teaching voice in a personalized method that also draws on his training as a certified Feldenkrais® practitioner.

55 This approach to listening has points of intersection with the materialisms proposed by feminist scholars, and elucidated for the voice by Nina Eidsheim, in which perception determines and coconstitutes reality. Deborah Kapchan's work on the sound body as porous and in the process of transformation—a context in which music functions as just one of the "prostheses and technologies that extend the body"—is also relevant here. See Kapchan, "Body," 39.

56 Ahrens, ASCAP/Disney Musical Theatre Writing Workshop.

57 McMillin, *The Musical as Drama*.

58 These are as follows: chapter 1: "Poor Man's Blues" (Bessie Smith); "Don't Fish in My Sea" (Ma Rainey and another interlocutor, possibly Bessie Smith); "The International Rag" (Sophie Tucker); "The Bully Song" (May Irwin); "St. Louis Blues" (Ethel Waters); and "I Got Rhythm" from the musical *Girl Crazy* (Ethel Merman). In chapter 2: "Stormy Weather" (Ethel Waters); "Supper Time" from *As Thousands Cheer* (Ethel Waters); "Bali H'ai" from *South Pacific* (Juanita Hall); "So Long, Dearie" from *Hello, Dolly!* (Pearl Bailey); and "Tired" (Pearl Bailey). In chapter 3: "Can't Help Lovin' Dat Man" from *Show Boat* (Lena Horne); "My Heart Belongs to Daddy" from *Leave It to Me* (Mary Martin); "I'm Gonna Wash That Man Right Outa My Hair" from *South Pacific* (Mary Martin); "A Sleepin' Bee" from *House of Flowers* (Diahann Carroll); "My Own Morning" from *Hallelujah, Baby!* (Leslie Uggams); "Being Good Isn't Good Enough" from *Hallelujah, Baby!* (Leslie Uggams); "I Enjoy Being a Girl" from *Flower Drum Song* (Pat Suzuki); "Bal Petit Bal" from *Leonard Sillman's New Faces of 1952* (Eartha Kitt); and "Cheerio, My Deario (Toujours Gai)" from *Shinbone Alley* (Eartha Kitt).

59 For more on the way that singing voices function technically in relation to songwriting practice, see Asare, "The Singing Voice." I must also note that in the musical theatre we cannot speak of a vocal performer's "interpreta-

tion" in quite the same terms as is often the case with other genres of recorded popular song. Here, musical choices such as phrasing must also be understood as acting choices, interpretation that is in service of character.

60 Musical theatre performers often speak of the songs in their repertoire and in the binder they carry to auditions as songs that are in their "book."

Chapter 1: Vocal Color in Blue

1 Miller, *Place for Us*, 108.

2 On the "twice-behaved" nature of performance, see Schechner, *Between Theater and Anthropology*.

3 On this point, Eidsheim writes: "By shifting our assumption of the singer from pure producer to producer and listener, we can recognize that he or she is listening to and also assigning meaning to or withholding it from a given labeling of his or her vocal timbre." Eidsheim, *The Race of Sound*, 180.

4 Eidsheim, *Sensing Sound*.

5 Herrera, Marshall, and McMahon, "Sound Acts."

6 On black women classical singers and their training, see Story, *And So I Sing*; and Eidsheim, *The Race of Sound*.

7 Taylor, *The Archive and the Repertoire*, 30, 32. Taylor posits the "scenario" as a unit of the repertoire that effects a "once-againness" and stages "the generative critical distance between social actor and character."

8 Work, *American Negro Songs*, 32.

9 Lott, *Love and Theft*, 53.

10 Miller, *Segregating Sound*, 14.

11 Miller, *Segregating Sound*, 14–15.

12 At the same time I do not want to dismiss the very real ways that the contributions of black musicians have been systematically erased in histories of popular and recorded music. See for example Maultsby, "The Politics of Race Erasure in Defining Black Popular Music Origins," 61–79.

13 Work, *American Negro Songs*, 29.

14 Cone, *The Spirituals and the Blues*, 122.

15 Barthes, "The Grain of the Voice," 508.

16 Connor, *Beyond Words*, 28.

17 Moten, *In the Break*, 107.

18 Waters and Samuels, *His Eye Is on the Sparrow*, 91.

19 Albertson, *Bessie*, 14.

20 McGinley, *Staging the Blues*.

21 Daphne Brooks has pointed up the fact that present-day listeners are trained by television reality shows to exercise a certain vigilance against supposed intonation problems, standing ready to apply the damning critique of "pitchy-ness" to singers whose performance disappoints. See Brooks, "'Sister, Can You Line It Out?'" 617–27.

22 Davis, *Blues Legacies and Black Feminism*, 213.

23 Davis, *Blues Legacies and Black Feminism,* 256.

24 Davis, *Blues Legacies and Black Feminism,* 76.

25 Peterson, *The African American Theatre Directory,* 6, 116; Lieb, *Mother of the Blues*, 1.

26 Sampson, *Blacks in Blackface.*

27 "Bessie Smith Star of Fast Revue at Gibson's Next Week," *Philadelphia Tribune*, October 27, 1927.

28 Southern, *The Music of Black Americans*, 299.

29 Southern, *The Music of Black Americans*, 373.

30 Block, et al., *American Musical Theater.*

31 See Sampson, *Blacks in Blackface*, 1636; Albertson, *Bessie*, 27–28; Hischak, *Broadway Plays and Musicals*, 208.

32 Sampson, *Blacks in Blackface*, 1711–12.

33 Hill and Barnett, *The A to Z of African American Theater*, 225. In 1972, Hopkins won a Tony Award for Best Featured Actress in a Musical for her performance in *Inner City*, a short-lived revue of social protest-infused nursery rhymes. Trained on the 1950s gospel music circuit, she transitioned later to singing blues and jazz and, in the 1970s, to acting.

34 Lacking this gloss, the term "coon shouter" itself is one that Lynn Abbott and Doug Seroff take as an evolution of the earlier "jubilee shouter" and "camp meeting shouter."

35 Jess, "Coon Songs Must Go! Coon Songs Go On . . . ," 317–18.

36 Brooks, "To Be Black Is to Be Funny," 13.

37 Trevathan, Irwin, and White-Smith Music Publishing, "May Irwin's 'Bully' Song."

38 Niles, "Shout, Coon, Shout!," 517. Niles was later credited with helping to launch the American folk music revival in the 1950s and 1960s.

39 Niles, "Shout, Coon, Shout!," 522.

40 Niles, "Shout, Coon, Shout!," 530.

41 Irwin was also one of the few women songwriters in Tin Pan Alley. See Brooks, "'To Be Black Is to Be Funny,'" 9.

42 Tucker, *Some of These Days*, 48, 114.

43 Tucker, *Some of These Days*, 59.

44 On May Irwin's method of vocal study: "Her first 'rag-time' was "The Bully," in which she made great sport by bringing a little coloured boy on the stage with her. Miss [May] Irwin says the way to learn to sing "rag-time" is to catch a negro and study him." See Strang, "Famous Actresses of the Day in America," 185.

45 Melnick addresses this underdiscussed trajectory in *A Right to Sing the Blues*, 85.

46 Brooks, "'To Be Black Is to Be Funny,'" 2; Abbott and Seroff, *Ragged but Right*, 5; and Knapp, *The American Musical and the Formation of National*

Identity, 73–74. I claim the subsumption of "coon shouting" within ragtime as a dirty secret of musical theatre origins given how rarely it is mentioned in depth in musical theatre histories and the extent to which ragtime almost completely eclipses all consideration of "coon shouting." Raymond Knapp does devote space to the topic, however, in his near-encyclopedic writings on the origins of musical theatre song.

47 Sophie Tucker and Al Jolson *"International Rag."*

48 Berlin, *The International Rag.*

49 Most, *Making Americans.*

50 I refer here to the "mixed voice" theorized by Steven Connor: "Like flypaper, the voice gathers things on the way, lilts, leanings, aches, eccentricities, accents." See Connor, *Beyond Words*, 29.

51 See Brown Lavitt, "First of the Red Hot Mamas," 253–90; and Merwin, *In Their Own Image.*

52 Albertson, *Bessie*, 21–22. In her biography *Alberta Hunter*, blues diva Hunter also narrates a specific incident in which she was asked to give a singing lesson to Sophie Tucker but declined. See Taylor, *Alberta Hunter*, 39.

53 Waters and Samuels, *His Eye Is on the Sparrow*, 135.

54 Waters also appeared on Broadway in the nonmusical plays *Mamba's Daughters* (1939) based on the book by Dubose Heyward, and *The Member of the Wedding* (1950) by Carson McCullers. Chapter 2 of this book considers two of her most famous songs and Waters's impact as a torch singer.

55 Waters and Samuels, *His Eye Is on the Sparrow*, 87. Donald Bogle contends that she was actually twenty-one years old by this time. See Bogle, *Heat Wave.*

56 In 1914, the composer of "St. Louis Blues," W. C. Handy, performed regularly with his band at Dixie Park in Memphis, which boasted an action-packed dance floor that could accommodate a thousand dancers at a time. "St. Louis Blues" was written specifically as dance music, and the composer deemed it a success when it was a hit on the dance floor. Handy had noticed how dancers were responding to the tango rhythm in the song "Maori" by William H. Tyers: "I began to suspect there was something Negroid in that beat, something that quickened the blood of the Dixie Park dancers. . . . Later, because of this conviction, I introduced the rhythm into my own compositions." See Handy, *Father of the Blues*, 98. In his 1930 survey of the Harlem Renaissance, James Weldon Johnson notes that the tango was a greater American dance craze than even the Charleston at its height. See Johnson, *Black Manhattan*, 191.

57 "Command Performance #22," *Armed Forces Radio Network*, July 14, 1942.

58 Waters and Samuels, *His Eye Is on the Sparrow*, 91.

59 Waters and Samuels, *His Eye Is on the Sparrow*, 91.

60 Waters and Samuels, *His Eye Is on the Sparrow*, 91.

61 Welch was a singer of black, Native American, and Scottish heritage who appeared on Broadway in the black revues *Runnin' Wild* (1928) and

various *Blackbirds*, also performing in Paris (where she met Waters) before relocating to London in the 1930s where she starred in cabaret, film, and West End musical theatre over the next five decades. See Bourne, *Elisabeth Welch*, 14–15.

62 Fisher, "The Caucasian Storms Harlem," 394.

63 Waters and Samuels, *His Eye Is on the Sparrow*, 227.

64 Waters and Samuels, *His Eye Is on the Sparrow*, 184.

65 Waters and Samuels, *His Eye Is on the Sparrow*, 198, 220.

66 Waters and Samuels, *His Eye Is on the Sparrow*, 238.

67 "Operated on Throat of Ethel Waters," *The Baltimore Afro-American*, November 30, 1929, 3. In *His Eye Is on the Sparrow*, Waters identifies the Parisian throat doctor by whom she was treated as a Dr. Weisart and does not speak of receiving surgery until she left Paris for London and treatment by Dr. Horsford.

68 Waters and Samuels, *His Eye Is on the Sparrow*, 236.

69 "European Makes Splendid Offer: Scholarship to American Girls by Professor Drysdale Sponsored by Florence Mills," *New York Amsterdam News*, February 9, 1927, 11.

70 "Miss Marion [*sic*] Anderson, the beautiful contralto of Philadelphia, is now doing some coaching with the noted Prof. Louis Drysdale. Miss Anderson, who has had lots of experience with teachers, speaks in glowing terms of Prof. Drysdale's method. Prof. Drysdale has been unusually busy this season. Besides his regular pupils, which are indeed many, he is teaching three or four West End musical comedy stars." Browning, "Browning's London Letter," 7, col. 7.

71 "Ethel Waters Returns to U.S.; May Star in Broadway Revue," *Chicago Defender*, March 22, 1930, 7, col. 3.

72 I have not come across any examples of black women blues singers taught by white women in the research for this chapter.

73 Hughes, "The Negro Artist and the Racial Mountain," 57.

74 Davis, *Blues Legacies and Black Feminism*, 153.

75 Reece, "A Performance Biography of Ethel Waters (1896–1977)," 34.

76 Vogel, "Performing 'Stormy Weather,'" 97.

77 Waters and Samuels, *His Eye Is on the Sparrow*, 261.

78 Merman and Eells, *Merman*, 39.

79 "Ethel Merman, 1978 Interview and 'Annie Get Your Gun' Medley," accessed May 23, 2020, https://www.youtube.com/watch?v=vaoFW _ij9I0. In this clip, Merman performs and discusses her career with interviewers Tony Randall and Mike Douglas.

80 "Ethel Merman Performing 'I Got Rhythm'" (1931), YouTube, 2016.

81 The term "rhythm singer" came into use in the 1940s and 1950s and is perhaps closest to what we would now think of as "jazz singer," but it is interesting that Ella Fitzgerald at least felt there was a difference between

the two. See interview with drummer/composer Terri Lyne Carrington in Enstice and Stockhouse, *Jazzwomen*, 55.

82 Merman and Eells, *Merman*, 44.

83 Wolf, *A Problem Like Maria*, 97.

84 See Wald, *Josh White*, 95; Kellow, *Ethel Merman*, 17. Kellow describes several vocalists whose influence he hears in Merman's voice, including Helen Morgan, Ruth Etting, and Helen Kane, as well as Al Jolson and Harry Richman. In Chapter 3 I also address White's influence on Eartha Kitt in his movement between blues, cabaret, and nightclub spaces.

85 "Origin of the Musical Verb 'Belt,'" *A Way with Words Radio Show*, 2014.

Chapter 2: Beyond the Weary-Bluesy Mammy

1 AAPAC's report on diversity in the 2018–2019 New York theatre season notes that, "at 61.5% of available roles across the industry, white actors continue to be the only race to overrepresent by almost double their respective population size in NYC." See Bandhu and Achacoso, "The Visibility Report." In 2022 the AAPAC was awarded a Tony Award for "Excellence in Theatre" for their significant advocacy work.

2 Catanese, *The Problem of the Color[blind]*; Pao, *No Safe Spaces*; Herrera, "'But Do We Have the Actors for That?,'" 23–35. See also Banks and Syler, *Casting a Movement*.

3 Notable work in musical theatre and type includes that of Brian Herrera (see previous footnote) and Donatella Galella on casting Latinx roles and contemporary practices of yellowface, respectively. Ryan Donovan's work on female musical theatre performers and sizist assumptions is also relevant here, as well as Stacy Wolf's categorizing of female roles in musicals, although this work is built primarily around white women performers. See Galella, "Artists of Color/Cross-Racial Casting"; Donovan, "'Must Be Heavyset,'" 1–17; and Wolf, *Changed for Good*. Focusing on early twentieth century black women performers at the intersection of dance, music, and comedy, Jayna Brown's *Babylon Girls* is essential reading about black women performers and type. *Blues Mamas and Broadway Belters* follows this pathbreaking work by considering how racial types on the musical stage are constructed, and exacted, through song.

4 Bailey, *The Raw Pearl*, 123.

5 Vogel, "Performing 'Stormy Weather.'"

6 warholsoup100, *Ethel Waters—Stormy Weather*.

7 Raymon, "'Rhapsody in Black' Still Has Ethel"; "Ethel Waters, Hubby Separate"; "Torch Singer, Ethel Waters in N.Y. Church"; "Ethel Waters, Weld, 1:30 P. M."; and Shalett, "Harlem's Ethel Waters."

8 Decker, *Show Boat*, 65; Moore, "'The Hieroglyphics of Love,'" 32.

9   almonkitt, "My Man Mon Homme 1920."

10 Grossman, *Funny Woman*. Brice quoted in Grossman, 3. Grossman also offers a comparison of the French- and English-language versions of "Mon Homme," 127.

11 Stratton, *Jews, Race and Popular Music*, 14, 18–19.

12 Grant and Akst, "Am I Blue?"; preservationhall01, *Ethel Waters—Am I Blue–1929 Film*. There is a reason that so many black performers of his time adored singing Harold Arlen's bluesy music; I can't quite put my finger on it, but this may be more a question of felt experience and spirit than dispassionate musical analysis. I can't escape the sense that, different from another undeniably talented composer (George Gershwin), Arlen got something right about the feeling that the blues music wanted to bring into the world, when he put pen to paper.

13 Bogle, *Toms, Coons, Mulattoes, Mammies, and Bucks*, 137, 145.

14 Glover, "Joy and Love in Zora Neale Hurston and Dorothy Waring's 1944 Black Feminist Musical Polk County," 52.

15 Glover specifically detects this dynamic in the Arena Stage production of *Polk County*. Re the female pedagogical duet, see Wolf, *Changed for Good*.

16 Brooks, *Liner Notes for the Revolution*, 130.

17 Hurston, "Zora Neale Hurston Collected Songs."

18 Hurston and Waring, "Polk County," 294. Throughout the musical play, the extent to which Leafy's fairness is celebrated as an undisputed quality of beauty is unsettling, balanced only by the equal adoration the community heaps on the "handsome" darker-skinned and "physically strong" Big Sweet, whose character description also notes that she "sings well" (271).

19 Hurston and Waring, "Polk County," 303–11. Big Sweet's reference to "sure enough blues" is earlier in her first scene with Leafy (298).

20 Westtoledoguy, *Careless Love—Ethel Waters, Herman Chittison Trio*, RCA Victor Records #20-2459, 2020.

21 These lyrics are however different from the version printed in Hurston's script, although both appear to be iterations of the song by W. C. Handy, whose lyrics are printed in Davis, *Blues Legacies and Black Feminism*, 269.

22 Baraka, *Blues People*, 129.

23 Asare, "The Black Broadway Voice," 357.

24 Asare, "The Black Broadway Voice," 357.

25 "Radio: $115,000 for a Copy Act."

26 Decker, *Show Boat*, 65.

27 Moore, "'The Hieroglyphics of Love,'" 33.

28 In this way the languid torch singer making money for Florenz Ziegfeld on the Broadway stage—whether of the various Ziegfeld Follies or *Show Boat*, which Ziegfeld also produced—performs a certain kind of resonance with the efficiency of the Taylorized chorus girl. As Mark Franko notes, "Her role in the figuration of this totality obscures, not surpris-

ingly, the status of her own performance as work." See Franko, *The Work of Dance*, 22.

29 Bogle, *Toms, Coons, Mulattoes, Mammies, and Bucks*, 51.

30 Berlin, "Supper Time"; Waters, *Supper Time*, "Am I Blue?"

31 Floyd, *The Power of Black Music*, 76.

32 This speech is impressively delivered by Viola Davis—with the gravelly whisper of guarded but joyful wisdom—in the George C. Wolfe-directed Netflix film *Ma Rainey's Black Bottom* (2020).

33 Wilson and Stewart, *Ma Rainey's Black Bottom*, 83. In the Netflix film, Davis speaks the first line as, "The more music you have in the world."

34 In an interview with Wilson scholar and Howard University professor Sandra Shannon, Wilson observed: "Blues is the best literature we have. If you look at the singers, they actually follow a long line all the way back to Africa, and various other parts of the world. They are carriers of the culture, carriers of ideas . . . blues and music have always been at the forefront in the development of the character and consciousness of black America, and people have senselessly destroyed and stopped that. Then you're taking away from the people their self-definition—in essence, their self-determination." See Shannon, "Blues, History, and Dramaturgy," 540–41.

35 Koritha Mitchell has written powerfully about the ways that black Americans leveraged performance practices (in ways that exceed the reductive frame of "protest art") to find means of living with the violent murder of thousands of black people by white mobs. See Mitchell, *Living with Lynching*.

36 Waters, *Supper Time*.

37 Grossman, *Funny Woman*, 125; Clements, "Sighing, a French Sound Endures."

38 Eidsheim, *The Race of Sound*, 152; Frith, *Performing Rites*, 185.

39 Bogle, *Heat Wave*, 27.

40 Eichler, *Ethel Waters, Person to Person*. I am grateful to Kelly Kessler for directing me to this interview.

41 Griffin, "When Malindy Sings."

42 Petty, *Stealing the Show*, 22.

43 Bogle, *Heat Wave*.

44 "News of the Stage."

45 "Deny Lena Horne's Movie Career Is Halted."

46 As early as 1932 the *Chicago Defender* had reported that "a new musical comedy" adaptation of the Bontemps novel titled *God Sends Sunday* was on its way to a New York premiere, with a score by Will Marion Cook. A decade later when the retitled project manifested as *St. Louis Woman*, Cook had evidently been replaced by Harold Arlen. See Bearden, "Around New York."

47 Lee, "'St. Louis Woman' Has Phony Plot."

48 See Bailey, *The Raw Pearl*, 65; "Hit Show Will Tour Nation"; Holt, "Trouble Stalks 'St. Louis' Woman"; Boozer, "Script Proves Lena's St. Louis Woman' No Reflection on Race"; Nichols, "The Play"; "La Horne Quits Cast of Backwards Musical"; Lees, *Portrait of Johnny*, 237; "News of the Stage."

49 For an excellent study of Horne's performance in this musical as a replacement for Harry Belafonte's starpower, see Vogel, *Stolen Time*.

50 Todd Decker has argued persuasively that *Show Boat* should not be excised from studies of black-cast musicals. See Decker, *Show Boat*, 5.

51 Lee, "'St. Louis Woman' Has Phony Plot."

52 "News of the Stage," 1946; Boozer, "Script Proves Lena's St. Louis Woman' No Reflection on Race."

53 Nichols, "The Play."

54 The distinction between the two different categories of awards could be compared to the Academy Awards' Best Actress versus Best Supporting Actress. Similar to how the Academy of Motion Picture Arts and Sciences has separate awards for best actress in a drama and in a comedy, the American Theatre Wing's Antoinette Perry (Tony) Awards has separate categories for best actress (and actor) in a play and in a musical.

55 To call her Vietnamese per se is a tiny bit historically incorrect, but only slightly, and I think evocative for today's readers. Bloody Mary is described in the script of *South Pacific* as Tonkinese, having relocated to the islands in which the play is set in the company of a French planter; Tonkin is a northern province of what is now Vietnam. Her status as a colonial subject is written multiply in her destiny as shaped by French colonists as well as white American authors, first by author James Michener and then bookwriter Joshua Logan, lyricist-bookwriter Oscar Hammerstein II, and composer Richard Rodgers who placed broken words in her mouth. See Rodgers, Hammerstein, and Logan, *South Pacific*.

56 The term "high yellowface" is of my own coinage. But while the absurd embarrassment of racist riches it calls forth makes me laugh, I recognize there is no great honor in coining a new phrase that, however accurate, encapsulates multiple offensive terms within its formulation.

57 *South Pacific* won the 1950 Pulitzer Prize for Drama and continues to be widely produced. Many present-day iterations are amateur and regional productions in schools and community theatres, and until very recently few have showcased Asian American actresses in the role of Bloody Mary; it has long been acceptable, even expected, for the role to be played by a black woman. As recently as 2001–2002, a US touring production of *South Pacific* cast the late Armelia McQueen, an alumna of the original cast of the all-black musical *Ain't Misbehavin'* (1978) and also known for her screen role as Whoopi Goldberg's sister in the movie *Ghost* (1990), in the role of Bloody Mary. The 2008–2010 Broadway revival at

Lincoln Center did take care to cast Filipina singer-actress Loretta Sayres Able, a longtime performer in Hawaiian theatre and nightclub venues, in the role. Interestingly, Able's performance credits include a turn as Effie White in *Dreamgirls*, perhaps the most famous black woman character in the Broadway musical canon, at the Hawaii Theatre earlier in her career. The 2009–2011 US touring production of *South Pacific* featured Keala Settle, a Hawaiian performer of mixed Maori and British descent, in the role of Bloody Mary. For a thoughtful critique of *South Pacific* as racialized musical drama, see Most, "'You've Got to Be Carefully Taught,'" 307–77.

58 See Lewis, *Flower Drum Songs*, 37–48; and Rodgers, *Musical Stages*, 295.

59 "Juanita Hill Signed." Page unknown; clipping included in the New York Public Library for the Performing Arts Research Collection. *Flower Drum Song* is discussed in detail in chapter 3, via Hall's castmate Pat Suzuki.

60 Sources for this biographical sketch include: Bracks and Smith, *Black Women of the Harlem Renaissance Era*; Hischak, "Hall, Juanita"; "Juanita Hall, 'Bloody Mary' of Stage, Screen, Dies," 59; Simpson, *Hall Johnson*.

61 During my research, I found that the Registrar's Office at The Juilliard School was unable to confirm her matriculation, noting that she may have studied with Juilliard faculty members privately (email correspondence with The Juilliard School). I also found that multiple sources claim Hall performed on Broadway in Florenz Ziegfeld's production of *Show Boat*, whether in the original 1927 production or the 1932 revival (it was sometimes stated that she appeared specifically in the tragic mulatta role of Julie, other times noted that she was in the chorus), although I was unable to find any evidence in support of this claim. In several newspaper articles from the 1950s she is described as having appeared in *Show Boat* at the age of fourteen; the fact that Hall would have been twenty-seven years old in 1928 suggests to me that the story may have been the apocryphal invention of a journalist—or a mythology actively cultivated by Hall herself—that was then kept in newspaper files and trotted out every time an article about Hall went to press.

62 See Hawkins, "Jose 'Happy Talks' to Juanita Hall"; and Morehouse, "Broadway After Dark," 26.

63 Simpson, *Hall Johnson*, 25; *Bessie Smith—St. Louis Blues (1929)*.

64 This program is reprinted in Dietz and E. T. S., "Marc Blitzstein and the 'Agit-Prop' Theatre of the 1930's," 63.

65 See Rampersad, *The Life of Langston Hughes*, 121.

66 Bald, "Bloody Mary of 'South Pacific' Talks Genially of Love."

67 "Juanita Hall," page unknown.

68 Rodgers and Hammerstein II, *South Pacific*.

69 Andrea Most makes this observation. See footnote 20 in Most, "'You've Got to Be Carefully Taught,'" 313: "The choice of dialect makes clear that

Rodgers and Hammerstein see little difference between varieties of racial otherness. All are figured in terms of American black/white relations."

70 Clément, "Through Voices, History," 24.

71 Shimakawa, *National Abjection*, 31. In *Miss Saigon*, Shimakawa elaborates, Kim is aestheticized and rendered what theatre audiences call "sympathetic," due to the beauty and pathos of her maternal instinct as that which drives her to suicide. By comparison, I contend that Bloody Mary's maternal role—remembering that Juanita Hall considered her "an invincible mother" in newspaper interviews—renders her, however, distinctly not beautiful. Perhaps if her love of her daughter Liat drove her to suicide, rather than merely to entice an officer into her daughter's arms, presumably for her own material gain, Bloody Mary would have been a musical theatre heroine rather than comic character role. But that would have been a different *South Pacific* altogether.

72 Atkinson, "Flower Drum Song Opens at St. James," 30.

73 Hawkins, "Jose 'Happy Talks' to Juanita Hall." The article is so titled because it details how Jose Ferrer came to see *South Pacific* and complimented Hall on her acting. Of note, the actress Chin Yu whom Hall mentions in this quote was in the ensemble of *South Pacific* on Broadway and went on to appear in international productions of the musical, playing the role of Liat (Bloody Mary's daughter) in London and Australia. In Australia she fell in love with and married the local actor (David Williams), who played opposite her as Lieutenant Cable, the young officer love interest to whom Mary Sings "Bali Ha'i." The two married in London in 1954, where Yu was performing in the hit American play *Teahouse of the August Moon* (the show in which Broadway singer-actress Pat Suzuki, considered in chapter 4, got her start in its US touring production). Chin Yu Williams then relocated to Australia where she continued performing on stage and screen. See Solomon, "South Pacific"; and "Sydney Singer Weds Actress."

74 In the intervening years, Hall also appeared in 1954 in the Harold Arlen/Truman Capote musical *House of Flowers*, which featured both Pearl Bailey and a breakout performance by Diahann Carroll, considered later in this chapter.

75 Logan, *Movie Stars, Real People, and Me*, 129.

76 Eugene Thamon Simpson, August 10, 2017. Simpson worked in New York City as a voice coach and accompanist in the 1950s and 1960s, although he did not cross paths with Hall. A distinguished African American musician, he worked frequently as an accompanist for opera diva Leontyne Price on recordings and in televised performances.

77 Middleton, "Rock Singing," 31.

78 "Earle, Philly," page unknown.

79 "Paramount Reviews," 16.

80 Feather, *Liner Notes*.

81 Lamm, "Juanita Hall Looking beyond 'Bloody Mary.'"

82 Luther Henderson was a leading black music director, conductor, arranger, and orchestrator whose Broadway credits included *Flower Drum Song* (1958), *Funny Girl* (1964), *Hallelujah, Baby!* (1967), *Purlie* (1970), *Ain't Misbehavin'* (1978), *Lena Horne* (1981), and *Jelly's Last Jam* (1993).

83 Bald, "Bloody Mary of 'South Pacific' Talks Genially of Love."

84 Mishkin, "Juanita Hall Sings Blues on Mondays."

85 *What's My Line?—Pearl Bailey; February 6, 1955.*

86 *What's My Line?—Pearl Bailey; Panel: Allen Ludden, Betty White, August 28, 1966.*

87 Bailey, *The Raw Pearl*, 9.

88 Bailey, *The Raw Pearl*, 26.

89 Strang, "St. Louis Woman."

90 Bailey appeared on Broadway in the following musicals: *St. Louis Woman* (1946), *Arms and the Girl* (1950), *Bless You All* (1950), *House of Flowers* (1954), *Hello, Dolly!* (1964; 1975). See "Pearl Bailey," in *Internet Broadway Database*.

91 Bailey, *The Raw Pearl*, 105.

92 Bailey, *The Raw Pearl*, 95.

93 Bailey, *The Raw Pearl*, 94; emphasis original.

94 Channing, *Just Lucky I Guess*, 7–8.

95 Channing, *Just Lucky I Guess*, 21.

96 MrPoochsmooch, *Hello Dolly! Pearl Bailey 1968 Tony Awards*.

97 Wolf, *Changed for Good*.

98 Kessler, *Broadway in the Box*, 60; emphasis original.

99 Bailey, "Tired." In different recordings, different monologues can be heard here, on entirely different themes.

100 A close friend of Bailey's once commented, "Strange, how they all think you ad lib the whole show." We were getting ready to go down and do the show at the Shoreham, in D. C. I said, touching my noodle, "I'm prepared. I prepare above my neck [use my head]. When I go out there it looks like it's all newly made up." See Bailey, *The Raw Pearl*, 109.

101 Bailey, *The Raw Pearl*, 123.

102 *New York Times* critic John S. Wilson quoted in Pao, *No Safe Spaces*, 179.

103 Clive Barnes quoted in Ragni Lantz, "HELLO, DOLLY," 89.

104 Lantz, "HELLO, DOLLY!" 89.

105 Pao, *No Safe Spaces*, 183.

106 Bailey, *The Raw Pearl*, 1968, 105; emphasis added.

107 Krell, "Contours through Covers," 494.

108 Derrida, "The Voice That Keeps Silence," 495–503; 498.

109 Wojcik, "Typecasting," 243. Race does not even become a category in Hollywood's official listing of actors, *The Academy Players Directory*, until the 1930s, by which point Wojcik notes that the compendium "includes separate sections labeled 'Colored' and 'Oriental,' which list all African

American and Asian actors and actresses, adults and children, together while it classifies white men (without identifying them as such) as leading men, younger leading men, characters and comedians; white women as leading women, ingénues, characters and comediennes; and white children as boys and girls. . . . By 1945, possibly in response to NAACP calls for better representation in Hollywood, actors of color are included among the regular categories but are *indexed* separately. Initially, there seems to be an unwritten rule that an African American or Asian actor cannot be a lead. Lena Horne, for instance, is listed as a 'character or comedienne' in the 1945 *Academy Players Directory*, despite her groundbreaking star contract" (243).

110 Vargas, *Dissonant Divas in Chicana Music*, xv.

Chapter 3: "A Little Singer on Broadway"

1 Wald, "Afterword," 284. Wald is listening here to Judy Garland performing youthfulness in the Harold Arlen/E. Y. "Yip" Harburg song "Over the Rainbow" from *The Wizard of Oz*.

2 Shane Vogel also names Diahann Carroll and Eartha Kitt, among other black women performers of the screen, as heirs to Horne's vocal practice.

3 It is important to me to include the Japanese American powerhouse belter Suzuki in this study alongside young black women such as Kitt, Carroll, and Uggams singing on "Golden Age" Broadway. First, beyond the fact that her vocal belt is incredible and should be more widely known, Suzuki's voice and presence as a performer talk back to imperialist representations purveyed by black women like Juanita Hall, discussed in the previous chapter. The inclusion of her voice also allows for striking comparative nuances in studying the at-times questionable, are-they-aren't-they appropriative moves of Eartha Kitt, what Collen Kim Daniher terms Kitt's "racial modulations" and Daphne Brooks calls the "sonic cosmopolitanism" of a "gorgeously unruly transnational self." Additionally, I want to unsettle the oft-perceived fixity of the black/white binary as primary organizational framework for discussions about race on the US musical stage. Suzuki's voice allows for deeper analysis of this chapter's central focus—the way that youthful feminine glamour has been voiced on Broadway beyond the figure of the white ingénue. See Daniher, "Yella Gal," 16–33; Brooks, "Planet Earth(a)," 118.

4 *How Diahann Carroll's Broadway Sound Set Her Apart.*

5 Vazquez studies popular music as a means to access the flows between the United States and Cuba, and between race and empire. She writes: "To listen in detail calls into primary question the ways that music and the musical reflect—in flashes, moments, sounds—the colonial, racial, and geographic past and present of Cuba as much as the creative traditions

that impact and impart from it. . . . Listening in detail ignores those accusations of going too far, of giving too much time to a recording of seemingly
little significance." See Vazquez, *Listening in Detail*, 4.

6 Albertson, *Bessie*, 8, 11.

7 Waters and Samuels, *His Eye Is on the Sparrow*, 74–87. Bogle, however, suggests that Waters booked this gig on her birthday in 1917, which would
have made her twenty-one. See Bogle, *Heat Wave*, 19.

8 Wilson, "Pearl Bailey, Cabaret Trouper and Musical Star, Dies at 72."

9 "Juanita Hall Hailed as Nightclub 'Find'"; "Eye to Eye with Juanita Hall."
As noted in the previous chapter, Hall's birth date is widely reported as
1901, which would have made her closer to twenty-six years old when the
original production of *Show Boat* (in which she claimed to have been cast)
premiered. But she may very well have graduated from or departed high
school in her early teens to begin performing.

10 Simmons, *Crescent City Girls*.

11 Horne specifies, "The North has always had a history of prejudice just as
the South has had. It's a little more finely drawn and sharper." See Feinstein, "Lena Horne Speaks Freely on Race, Marriage," 61. See also Purnell,
Theoharis, and Woodard, *The Strange Careers of the Jim Crow North*.

12 Simmons, *Crescent City Girls*, 3.

13 Simmons, *Crescent City Girls*, 29.

14 Horne, *In Person*, 13.

15 Cox, *Shapeshifters*.

16 Carby, *Reconstructing Womanhood*, 39.

17 Hine, "Rape and the Inner Lives of Black Women in the Middle West," 912.

18 Vogel, *The Scene of Harlem Cabaret*, 178.

19 Fiol-Matta, *The Great Woman Singer*.

20 Baker, *Modernism and the Harlem Renaissance*, 33.

21 I have opted to forgo an analysis of "Stormy Weather," although it is a signature song of both Ethel Waters and Lena Horne. Vogel gives a fantastic
reading of Horne's performances of this song early and late in her career
via the way the hit Broadway musical she shaped, *Lena Horne: The Lady
and Her Music* (1981), encompassed both interpretations. Horne won a
special Tony Award in the wake of this performance. See Vogel, *The Scene
of Harlem Cabaret*, 185–87.

22 Asare and Decker, "The Enduring Relevance of *Show Boat*"; Decker, *Show
Boat*.

23 In both instances the role was given to white women, Carol Bruce in the
1946 Broadway revival and Ava Gardner in the 1951 film; for the film
Gardner's vocals were dubbed by Annette Warren.

24 Feinstein, "Lena Horne Speaks Freely on Race, Marriage, Stage," 64.

25 I thank writer and historian of black fashion Jonathan Square for helping
me describe this truly fabulous dress in more precise terms (Jonathan

Square, personal email correspondence, January 29, 2022). A 1940s take on a late nineteenth-century dress, it was designed by MGM's Helen Rose, who also designed Grace Kelly's wedding gown.

26 Martin, "The Day I Found Me."

27 Woolf, *A Problem Like Maria*, 62.

28 Schmidt quoted in Kaufman, *Some Enchanted Evenings*, 4. Harvey Schmidt was the composer of the long-running hit off-Broadway musical *The Fantasticks* (1960) and the last Broadway musical in which Martin appeared, *I Do! I Do!* (1966).

29 Horne, *In Person, Lena Horne*, 7.

30 Silas Green was a stage persona created by Salem Tutt Whitney, who is quoted in chapter 4 regarding the vocal practice of turn-of-the-century black musical theatre diva Sissieretta Jones, with whom he toured. This story about being warned of danger ahead by a furtive black figure on the road to the Green tent show is related in Horne, *In Person, Lena Horne*, 19.

31 Cahoon quoted in Kaufman, *Some Enchanted Evenings*, 9.

32 Horne, *In Person*, 49. I truly regret that I have been unable to find any further detail on the mysterious, first nameless Mr. Jerrahol.

33 The Ward-Belmont School for Girls in Nashville later became Belmont University, which boasts several successful country singers among its alumni and continues to educate excellent musical theatre belters to this day. It became coeducational in 1951 although it was not until 1965 that the school accepted nonwhite students, some thirty-five years after Martin was a student.

34 Kaufman, *Some Enchanted Evenings*, 16.

35 Fanchon Simon and her brother Marco Wolf were a vaudeville dance duo on the Orpheum circuit in the 1920s who went on to become Los Angeles theatre managers, producers of lavish stage shows, and choreographer/arrangers of Hollywood musical and dance sequences. They also operated a talent school whose students included the likes of Judy Garland, Shirley Temple, and Cyd Charisse. See Fanchon and Marco, "Fanchon and Marco."

36 Martin, "The Day I Found Me."

37 Buckley, *The Hornes*, 185. And Buckley quoted in Irvin, *Kay Thompson*, 97.

38 For more on Thompson, who was the vocal arranger on Arthur Freed's musicals, appeared in the musical film *Funny Face*, and also authored the "Eloise" series of children's books, see Irvin, *Kay Thompson*. It is interesting to note that Buckley comments Thompson coached Horne to open her mouth more fully when in Horne's autobiographical revue, *The Lady and Her Music*, "a disembodied director's voice instructs her midsong: 'Now Miss Horne, try not to open your mouth so wide when you sing. Remember the screen is different from the stage. Try to sing with a pretty mouth.'" See Vogel, *The Scene of Harlem Cabaret*, 185.

39   In a 1970 interview Horne said, referencing the blues-to-gospel sounds she long felt she did not have access to, "I'm still trying to learn how to sing. But I say, inside every black woman, there's an Aretha screaming to come out." See "The Black Woman." In this episode, Horne is interviewed by a young Nikki Giovanni, who reads to her the poem she has written in honor of Horne.

40   Moss, "Great Voices Are Born—Not Made." Ads for Humphrey's studio in the late 1940s into the 1950s hawked "private lessons in Vocal Technique, Coaching, Styling, Class instruction in Haromny, Sightsinging, Showmanship, Microphone Technique, etc." and listed Martin among his star pupils along with Gordon MacRae and Shirley Temple. "Display Ad 25—No Title," *Los Angeles Times (1923–1995)*, March 30, 1947, 25; "Display Ad 86—No Title," *Los Angeles Times (1923–1995)*, May 21, 1950, 86.

41   "Her 'Strip-Tease' Stopped the Show."

42   "Her 'Strip-Tease' Stopped the Show."

43   Porter quoted in Kaufman, *Some Enchanted Evenings*, 30.

44   Martin, *My Heart Belongs*, 74; Kaufman, *Some Enchanted Evenings*, 30.

45   Wolf, *A Problem Like Maria*, 54.

46   Wolf, *A Problem Like Maria*, 62.

47   "Her 'Strip-Tease' Stopped the Show." The fact of her already having been married once is tactfully not mentioned, sustaining the image of the naive and innocent girl.

48   Rodgers and Hammerstein, *South Pacific*; and *South Pacific—I'm Gonna Wash That Man Right Out Of My Hair—Mary Martin*.

49   For the characterization of "I'm Gonna Wash" as un-blue, see Mast, *Can't Help Singin',* 208.

50   Brown, *Babylon Girls*, 244. The internationally acclaimed black starlet who could have figured as Horne's voice teacher, Harlem it-girl and *Shuffle Along* (1921) Broadway lead Florence Mills, passed away in 1927 when Horne was but ten years old; journalists continued to compare Horne to Mills into the 1960s. See Feinstein, "Lena Horne Speaks Freely on Race, Marriage, Stage."

51   Regarding the expected vocal expression of this type, Alexandra Appolloni writes, "The ingénue is a white archetype of feminine youth that emerges time and again in Western art and performance. She occupies a liminal space between girl and woman, and that liminality is audible when she sings." See Appolloni, "Authority, Ability, and the Aging Ingenue's Voice," 145.

52   Stanislavski, "Types of Actors," 17, 18.

53   Simmons, *Crescent City Girls*, 52.

54   "He had mentioned at some point during our awkward meeting that no silent-screen stars were black. And I told him there was no Norma Desmond, either. 'She's a fictional character,' I said. But I still don't know

to this day why he was so keen on maligning me at that audition when he saw me becoming so anxious in his presence." See Carroll, *The Legs Are the Last to Go*, 21.

55 Carroll continues: "She told Rodgers she was certain he'd hired tutors to teach me diction and manners, and that I was a fabricated black character who was designed to startle white audiences. Did Rodgers, who wrote 'You've Got to Be Carefully Taught' about prejudice for *South Pacific*, argue with this racist hostess or give her a dressing-down? Did he tell her to cancel her party? No, he did neither." See Carroll, *The Legs Are the Last to Go*, 30.

56 Brooks, "Bold Soul Ingenue" and "Roundtable." Brooks's roundtable presentation was given at the EMP Pop Conference *From A Whisper to a Scream*.

57 She observes, "The Motown sound is, of course, famously clean and straightforward . . . and girl group music from Motown is arguably the most polished of all." See Warwick, *Girl Groups, Girl Culture*, 153.

58 Warwick, *Girl Groups, Girl Culture*, 161.

59 Again, as a result of "the demise of the black producer" during the 1930s, the men in positions of power whom black Broadway ingénues had to prove entrancing were overwhelmingly white men. See Sampson, *Blacks in Blackface*, 35.

60 In the years (1907–1936) when impresario Florenz Ziegfeld was preparing his Follies stage for the languid, willowy white woman torch singer, he also drove a lasting shift in marketing the sex appeal of women onstage in the figure of the chorus girl. Unlike the powerful and imposing physicalities of female burlesque performers, the svelte, small-framed young white women in Ziegfeld's choruses were selected precisely because their nudity onstage could be artfully framed as nonthreatening. Broadway's subsequent ingénues may have remained fully clothed, but the impact of this shift persisted. See Allen, *Horrible Prettiness*, 245.

61 Despite the coldness with which she speaks of him in her autobiography, Rodgers was reported by some contemporaries to have been desperately in love with Diahann Carroll throughout the rehearsal period and run of his musical *No Strings*. Rodgers's biographer Meryl Secrest writes: "Photographs taken during rehearsals show that Rodgers is always in close proximity to his leading lady. He is holding her hand, or giving her a neck rub, or his hands are on her shoulders or around her waist. [Bookwriter] Samuel Taylor energetically denied the idea that there was anything between them. . . . On the other hand, Jerry Whyte, who worked on the show, had confided in Dania Krupska that Rodgers was deeply in love and that Carroll was the great love of his life. 'Jerry told me that Dick would stand there and beg her to go out with him with tears in his eyes. Whatever it was, she possessed him. I can't remember all the details, but there was something pathetic and sad about his behavior; he would go

and stand outside her door.' Although apparently charmed and flattered by Rodgers's attentions, [Carroll] kept him at arm's length." See Secrest, *Somewhere for Me*, 358–59.

62 Ealey, "Young, Bubbly, and Black," 55–64. Ealey looks to the work of early twenty-first century black female musical theatre writer-composer Kirsten Childs to examine how the affective armor of the "bubbly" black ingénue character operates as a nuanced intervention.

63 Appolloni, "Authority, Ability, and the Aging Ingenue's Voice," 145.

64 Uggams quoted in Reed, "Baby Learned Never Learned to Cry," 135.

65 "N.Y. Singer Diahann Carroll Finds Cinderella-Like Fame," 60–61.

66 "N.Y. Singer Diahann Carroll Finds Cinderella-Like Fame."

67 *Tony-Winning Star Leslie Uggams on InnerVIEWS with Ernie Manouse.*

68 Oblender, "Leslie Uggams," 197–200; *Tony-Winning Star Leslie Uggams on InnerVIEWS with Ernie Manouse*. However, *Sing Along with Mitch* was not aired in some parts of the South because Miller refused to isolate Uggams's performances into sections that could have been excised from the show in specially cut versions more palatable to white Southerners' tastes, as had been done for films in which Lena Horne appeared.

69 Rodgers, *Musical Stages*, 307.

70 *Tony-Winning Star Leslie Uggams on InnerVIEWS with Ernie Manouse.*

71 "Diahann Stars in Tailor-Made Musical," 65; "Diahann Carroll Is the New Toast of Broadway," 55.

72 *Diahann Carroll: My Grandmother.*

73 *Deleted Scene: Why Diahann Carroll Doesn't Sing the Blues.*

74 "Words of the Week," 32.

75 Rodgers, *Musical Stages*, 307.

76 Carroll, "Richard Rodgers Is Calling," 223. Interestingly, as noted above, Kwan was also tapped to play the vampish Linda Low in the 1961 film version of *Flower Drum Song.*

77 "Diahann Carroll Honored at House of Flowers."

78 *How Diahann Carroll's Broadway Sound Set Her Apart.*

79 For example, the bulk of her main number from *No Strings*, "The Sweetest Things," is in the key of A-minor, with A4 as the top note. By comparison, the title song of "The Sound of Music" is pitched in the key of D-major as Martin sings it in the original cast album, rising only as high as B4. It is true that Audra McDonald's rendition of the song "A Sleepin' Bee" from *House of Flowers*, the version of this song to which I was first introduced, is pitched one full step higher than Carroll's version in the original cast recording, shifted from the original key of E to F-sharp. See Carroll, "A Sleepin' Bee"; Carroll and Kiley, "The Sweetest Sounds"; Martin, "The Sound of Music."

80 Carroll, "A Sleepin' Bee"; *Diahann Carroll—"Love Comes A-Calling on You" (1953)*. Note that vintage video clips misdocument the title of the song.

My research indicates that this televised performance of the song "A Sleepin' Bee" aired on the television show *Coke Time with Eddie Fisher* in 1955. (Despite the fact that multiple online sources cite this episode as having aired in 1953, Fisher introduces Carroll by noting that she is stopping the show nightly on Broadway with *House of Flowers*, which did not open until December 30, 1954.)

81 Jefferson, "The Negro on Broadway, 1954–1955," 304–5.

82 Oblender, "Leslie Uggams," 197.

83 *Tony-Winning Star Leslie Uggams on InnerViews with Ernie Manouse.*

84 Rosen, "Frank Sinatra and Billie Holiday." "Sinatra made no secret of his debt to Holiday: 'It is Billie Holiday . . . who was, and still remains, the greatest single musical influence on me,' he said in 1958."

85 *Leslie Uggams on Controversy about Her Being on "Sing Along with Mitch."*

86 *Leslie Uggams on Controversy about Her Being on "Sing Along with Mitch."*

87 Jones, *Black Music*, 213; emphasis in original.

88 Hollywood, "Lena Horne."

89 Reed, "Baby Learned Never Learned to Cry."

90 In his review, *New York Times* critic Walter Kerr cited Hayman's performance as Uggams's mother in *Hallelujah, Baby!* as "a bandanna-bound mammy played with palm-cracking smartness by Lillian Hayman." See Kerr, "'Baby' Bets a Kiss." Hayman had an extensive television career on the show *One Life to Live* and appeared in a number of Broadway musicals including *Kwamina* (1961), an interracial romance set in an African village, in which she played the role "Mammy Trader," and the Kander and Ebb musical *70, Girls, 70* (1971)—both of which were extremely short-lived. See "Lillian Hayman," *Internet Broadway Database*.

91 Mordden, *Open a New Window*, 236.

92 Woll, *Black Musical Theatre*, 247.

93 Mordden, *Open a New Window*, 236.

94 Uggams, "'My Own Morning' and 'Being Good Isn't Good Enough.'"

95 *Hallelujah, Baby!* My research indicates that the footage in this video is from an episode of the *Ed Sullivan Show* that aired May 14, 1967.

96 Cheng, *The Melancholy of Race*, 34.

97 Royster, *Sounding Like a No-No*, 44.

98 Even into adulthood Suzuki's small stature has often been commented on—often by white listeners—as seemingly at odds with the big sound of her voice. See Glover, "Tiny Oriental Ball of Fire Has Broadway Bedazzled," 1.

99 Leonard, "The Girl Who's 1,000 Times Good," 1–d5.

100 Royster, *Sounding Like a No-No*, 45.

101 Turner, "Pat Suzuki," 10.

102 Glover, "Tiny Oriental Ball of Fire Has Broadway Bedazzled," 1.

103 Crosby, *The Many Sides of Pat Suzuki.*

104 "Song belter" is the way Richard Rodgers refers to her in the one sentence in which Suzuki appears in his autobiography. See Rodgers, *Musical Stages*, 295. The musical *Flower Drum Song* is an adaptation of the book by the same title by C. Y. Lee, published in 1957. The nightclub in which the character Linda Low performs is called in the stage musical the Celestial Bar (in the film, Celestial Gardens); it is inspired by the actual, famed San Francisco Chinatown venue the Forbidden City. The Forbidden City might be fruitfully considered as an analogue to Harlem's Cotton Club, not least in the display of racialized bodies and performance for consumption by white patrons.

105 See Oja, *Bernstein Meets Broadway*.

106 Hall also appeared in this role in the 1961 movie version of *Flower Drum Song*, a replacement for Anna May Wong. See Metzger, "Part 2 Introduction," 106. For an overview of Juanita Hall's performance and the response from the black press, see Edney, "'Integration through the Wide Open Back Door,'" 261–72; and Koster, *Flower Drum Song*. A clip of just this number is viewable via blingnetzwork, *Chop Suey—Flower Drum Song*.

107 Cheng, *The Melancholy of Race*, 41.

108 Glover, "Tiny Oriental Ball of Fire Has Broadway Bedazzled," 1.

109 Tynan, "Tiny Chinese Minds," 104; Atkinson, "Flower Drum Song Opens at St. James," 44 and "Flower Drum Song," 1; Dash, *Women's Wear Daily*, 56.

110 In his scathing critique of the original production of *Flower Drum Song*, the *New Yorker*'s reviewer Kenneth Tynan took authors Richard Rodgers and Oscar Hammerstein II to task for casting two actresses of Japanese ancestry in a show purportedly set in San Francisco's Chinatown, and for essentially reproducing the Orientalism they had hitherto created in their shows *The King and I* and *South Pacific*: "It seems to have worried neither Mr. Rodgers nor Mr. Hammerstein very much that the behavior of wartorn Pacific Islanders and nineteenth-century Siamese might be slightly different from that of Chinese residents of present-day California, where 'Flower Drum Song' is fictionally sung. So little, indeed, has it worried them that they have entrusted the principal female roles to Japanese actresses. The assumption, which may be justified, is that the audience will not notice the difference." See Tynan, "Tiny Chinese Minds," 104.

111 In the 2002 revival of the musical with a new book by David Henry Hwang, the role of Linda Low was played by Taiwan-born Sandra Allen, with the Filipina *Miss Saigon* star Lea Salonga in the ingénue role of Mei-Li.

112 Chang, "I Dreamed I Was Wanted," 150.

113 Thank you to Nathan Lamp for bringing Jorgensen's performance of this song to my attention.

114 In addition to the scholars named above, see Chang, "I Dreamed I Was Wanted"; Kim, "Asian Performance on the Stage of American Empire in

Flower Drum Song," 1–37; Ma, "Rodgers and Hammerstein's 'Chopsticks' Musicals," 17–26. Because most of the scholarship on *Flower Drum Song* focuses on the film, critical commentary on Pat Suzuki remains limited.

115 Galella, "Feeling Yellow," 67–77.

116 Lewis, *Flower Drum Songs*, 85.

117 *Pat Suzuki I Enjoy Being a Girl* and *Flower Drum Song—Ed Sullivan Show*.

118 That is, she sings with more *ee* [ɪ] than *eh* [e] in a vowel sound within the word "race" that combines them both: *reh-ees* [reɪs].

119 Rodgers, *I Enjoy Being a Girl*.

120 Lewis, *Flower Drum Songs*, 54.

121 Das, *Katherine Dunham*, 108.

122 Das, *Katherine Dunham*, 117. Das notes (107): "Basil Matthews, a Catholic priest from Trinidad with a doctorate in sociology from Fordham University, taught philosophy. He was not the only PhD on staff. Ben Frederic Carruthers, who taught Spanish, had a PhD from the University of Havana. . . . José Limón (born in Mexico) was an instructor of modern dance. The ballet instructor had danced with international companies including the Ballet Russe de Monte Carlo."

123 Batiste, *Darkening Mirrors*, 175.

124 Kitt, *Thursday's Child*, 79.

125 In a quote circulated proudly throughout Kitt's body of interviews and writings, Orson Welles is said to have proclaimed her, "The most exciting woman in the world."

126 In Horne's theorization, "Usually performers seek the audience's approval, but in my appearances they, in a sense, had to seek mine." See Horne, *Lena*, 197.

127 Royster, *Sounding Like a No-No*, 34.

128 Vazquez, *Listening in Detail*, 153.

129 Williams, *America's Mistress*, 171. "State of extravagant repose" is a quote from theatre critic Kenneth Tynan writing on Kitt's appearance at the Cafe de Paris in London. Tynan also effuses, "Miss Kitt is the vocal soul of every Siamese cat who ever lived."

130 Griffin, "When Malindy Sings," 104.

131 Griffin, "When Malindy Sings," 104.

132 Kitt, *Confessions of a Sex Kitten*, 57.

133 *Chita Rivera Chats West Side Story, Eartha Kitt, Advice.*

134 Kitt, *Thursday's Child*, 133.

135 Daryl Waters, personal communication, February 19, 2019.

136 Josephine Premice, who also appeared in the Dunham revue that was Kitt's Broadway debut, *Blue Holiday* (1945), and was nominated for a Tony Award alongside her castmate Lena Horne for her performance as Ginger in *Jamaica* (1957), recalled of Josh White: "He was a marvelous

showman, and one clever thing he did was he would come on stage and take about five minutes tuning his guitar, but the tuning was all flexing his muscles. Every muscle rippled, and that's why he did it, because you know he had tuned his guitar before he left his dressing room. But he'd do this whole thing, and then everybody would applaud the tuning! He had all those white ladies chasing and putting gold watches on him far and wide." See Wald, *Josh White*, 113. Biographer Elijah Wald refers to Josh White as "the sophisticated star who became the model for Harry Belafonte" (*Society Blues*, x). White performed in cabaret and blues venues and on Broadway, appearing with Paul Robeson in the musical *John Henry* (1940) in the role of Blind Lemon Jefferson. His son John White Jr. was a Tony-winning child performer who went to the Professional Children's School in Manhattan with Leslie Uggams.

137 The collected volumes of the *archy and mehitabel* column, published in the late 1920s and 1930s, were illustrated by white-passing black cartoonist George Herriman, the New Orleans creole creator of the *Krazy Kat* comic. The stage musical was preceded by a Columbia Masterworks recording in 1954 with Carol Channing as Mehitabel and Eddie Bracken as Archy. There was a later 1970 film titled *Shinbone Alley* with Channing again playing Mehitabel. Additionally, the musical is licensed through Music Theatre International with the title *archy and mehitabel*. Of note, the character names are given in lowercase, as in Marquis's original column, because they are ostensibly being written into existence by archy the cockroach, who types everything in lowercase as he cannot reach the shift key.

138 "Archy and Mehitabel: A Back Alley Opera—1954," E. B. White's liner notes for this 1954 recording, which preceded the stage musical, are beautifully written, a heartfelt homage to Marquis and the pathos and depth of his comic poetic contribution.

139 Kerr, "'Shinbone Alley.'"

140 Atkinson, "Shinebone Alley." The wry critique of a stage full of animals, primarily cats, whose text is a book of verse, speaks for itself, a quarter-century prior to Andrew Lloyd Webber's megamusical *Cats* (1981).

141 Kitt, *Confessions of a Sex Kitten*, 188. In the same section, Kitt also mentions leveraging her international connections to help raise funds for the production: "One night the producer called me at home (I was living in my house on East 92nd Street) and told me he was running out of money and might not be able to open the show. I sent a telegram to the Aga Khan, who sent the money needed within twenty-four hours, no questions asked."

142 "Eartha Kitt 'Shinbone Alley' Flops, Closes." The article's author also anxiously considers what effect this closure may have for another upcoming Broadway musical with black actress headliner, Lena Horne's *Jamaica*.

143 This tomcat du jour promises to make a star out of Kitt as Mehitabel: "I will work with you, I will mold you, and in a short time you will

become . . ." Archy the cockroach prompts, "a mother." Elsewhere in the show, Lillian Hayman plays a mother cat to black soprano Reri Grist. Hayman, as noted earlier would go on to win a Tony in the role of Leslie Uggams's mother in *Hallelujah, Baby!* (1967). The cast also included Chita Rivera, who was Kitt's standby, and Mexican dancer Carmen Gutierrez, who would go on to perform alongside Rivera in the ensemble of *West Side Story* (1957) and whose eclectic repertoire also included Broadway appearances in *Finian's Rainbow* (1947) and *The King and I* (1951) as a royal child. The ballet dancers Allegra Kent and Jacques D'Amboise were also noted by many reviewers as standouts.

144 Royster, *Sounding Like a No-No*, 42.

145 "But at the edge of the musical's celebration of intermixing, the discordant note of racial difference (and the potential threat of miscegenation) has always introduced a tragic key, or at least lent a desperately insistent tone, to the radiance of its songs." Cheng, *Melancholy of Race*, 42.

146 Dolar, *A Voice and Nothing More*, 29. As noted above, the act of laughing is itself a vocal exercise that I regularly teach and practice.

I also find the notion of a vocal exercise as that which exceeds the symbolic useful also for the ways in which it reverberates between and across the *detail* that can be listened to and the *gesture* that can be taken up. Where Mladen Dolar insists that "singing is bad communication" (Dolar, *A Voice and Nothing More*, 30), for Giorgio Agamben, a gesture operates as "communication of a communicability." See Agamben, "Notes on Gesture," 60. It is a gag in the sense of impeding speech, something that must be understood as more than either the merely instrumental or the single-pointed telos of aesthetic experience. Hearing the vocal exercise as gesture with Agamben means hearing it beyond the particular vocalise or posture prescribed to "solve" a particular vocal problem—neither for the extent to which it elicits nor manifests a beautiful, pleasing sound. As a gag, the gesture, like Dolar's hiccupping nonvoices, produces a break in intelligibility while foregrounding the human experience of communicating, or more nearly, of stumbling in the act of communicating. The vocal exercise as gestural gag, then, hinders speech if not sound, producing a break in meaning while calling up the political relationality of a communicative act.

147 Brooks, *Liner Notes for the Revolution*, 45.

Chapter 4: Secrets of Vocal Health

1 Kristin Moriah analyzes how Jones recorded her vocal sound in scrapbooking practices, especially the way the singer leveraged documentation of her performances in Germany. See Moriah, "On the Record," 26–42.

2 "Black Patti."

3   "A Chat with Black Patti."

4   Riis, *Just before Jazz.*

5   "Black Patti's Husband Threw Her Money into the Streets."

6   Lehmann, *How to Sing,* 4.

7   Lehmann, *How to Sing,* 8.

8   Lehmann, *How to Sing,* 173.

9   Lehmann, *How to Sing,* 179.

10 Cappiani, *Practical Hints and Helps for Perfection in Singing,* 65. Jones cites Cappiani as her preferred voice teacher in "A Chat with Black Patti."

11 "The Garcia Centenary," 681–89.

12 "Memoirs of Jenny Lind."

13 "The Garcia Centenary."

14 "The Garcia Centenary," 684.

15 Garcia II, "Observations on the Human Voice," 404.

16 "The Garcia Centenary," 682.

17 Sterne, *The Audible Past,* 22.

18 Jacob Smith, "Rough Mix," 133.

19 Cappiani, *Practical Hints and Helps for Perfection in Singing,* 74.

20 Garcia II, "Observations on the Human Voice," 405.

21 "Renowned Vocal Pedagogue Richard Miller, Emeritus Professor of Singing, Dies at 83." Miller was more than twenty years older than Sataloff.

22 Miller, *Solutions for Singers,* 151.

23 Kiesgen, "How Richard Miller Changed the Way We Think about Singing," 261–64.

24 Kiesgen, "How Richard Miller Changed the Way We Think about Singing," 262.

25 Miller, *On the Art of Singing,* 7.

26 Foucault, *The Birth of the Clinic.* G. Zimmerman's description of Aescalapius's practice is quoted on page 15.

27 Foucault, *The Birth of the Clinic,* 140.

28 "The observing gaze manifests its virtues only in a double silence: the relative silence of theories, imaginings, and whatever serves as an obstacle to the sensible immediate; and the absolute silence of all language that is anterior to that of the visible. Above the density of this double silence things seen can be heard at last, and heard solely by virtue of the fact that they are seen." Foucault, *The Birth of the Clinic,* 108.

29 Cavarero's theory of vocal uniqueness, however, has been compellingly critiqued by Nina Sun Eidsheim, among others. See Eidsheim, *The Race of Sound.* The notion of sonic citation and the practice of singing along with others that I advance also unsettles the idea of voice as an unassailably singular marker of identity.

30 Cavarero, *For More Than One Voice,* 42.

31 Foucault, *The Birth of the Clinic,* 196.

32 Nancy, *Listening,* 5.

33 Miller, *On the Art of Singing*, 46.

34 Foucault, *The Birth of the Clinic*, 122.

35 Metzl and Kirkland, *Against Health*, 9.

36 Lupton, *The Imperative of Health*, 138.

37 Miller, *On the Art of Singing*, xiii, 81, 158, 306.

38 Miller, *On the Art of Singing*, 121; emphasis added.

39 Taylor, *The Principles of Scientific Management*, 64.

40 Taylor, *The Principles of Scientific Management*, 43.

41 Miller, *On the Art of Singing*, 205.

42 See Miller, *On the Art of Singing*, 306; and Miller, *Solutions for Singers*, 152.

43 "The 'Pop' Singer and the Voice Teacher," 1.

44 It is important to note that, of course, Italian *bel canto* itself moved through its own trajectory of technical shifts, as classical voice pedagogy historians including Berton Coffin and James Stark have documented. *Bel canto* in its early iterations was heard in sixteenth-century salons before shifting to the sound needed to carry in eighteenth-century tiered auditoriums that seated many thousands of audience members. By the time Manuel Garcia II wrote his definitive nineteenth-century texts on voice technique, he felt it important to detail the ways that the "dark" vocal sounds demanded by dramatic singing were growing more widely celebrated than the "clear" tone of lyric singing. See Coffin, *Historical Vocal Pedagogy Classics*, 12.

45 See Smith, *Rough Mix*, 133; and Lockheart, "A History of Early Microphone Singing, 1925–1939," 367–85.

46 Pleasants, "Bel Canto in Jazz and Pop Singing," 54–59. Pleasants, an American music critic, wrote extensively in the late twentieth century on operatic and popular vocalists whom he considered "great singers." In this article he makes a recuperative move to celebrate several pop singers, including Ethel Waters, Sarah Vaughan, and Frank Sinatra, but does so, strangely, by mapping the ways in which their performance practices exemplify Baroque singing techniques such as appoggiatura, rubato, and portamento.

47 Théberge, "'Plugged In,'" 1–25.

48 Connor, *Beyond Words*, 29.

49 Théberge, "'Plugged In,'" 5. The "mixed voice" could of course also be analyzed in terms of its production in the engineer's recording mix, although this is an analysis that lies beyond the scope of my project here. Note also that the term "mixed voice" here as used by sound and media scholars is distinct from the way voice practitioners speak of the timbre of the vocal mix sound; neither does it refer to singers of mixed race.

50 Middleton, "Rock Singing," 38.

51 Middleton, "Rock Singing," 31.

52 The author of a well-regarded, early twentieth-century voice pedagogy text asserts, "True tone color does not come as the result of trying by

some physical process to make the tone light or dark but *from the automatic response to musical concept or feeling.*" See Clippinger, *The Head Voice and Other Problems*, 7; emphasis original.

53 See O'Toole, "THEATER," 4; Wollman, *The Theater Will Rock*, 124–27. The body microphone, or radio microphone, came into prominence in the era of 1990s megamusicals on Broadway.

54 "The 'Pop' Singer and the Voice Teacher," 2; emphasis in original.

55 See Floyd, "Ring Shout," 49–70; Stuckey, *Slave Culture*.

56 Cone, *The Spirituals and the Blues*, 27.

57 Cone, *The Spirituals and the Blues*, 3.

58 Woolfe, "A Singular World That Won't Fade Away."

59 Woodruff, "On the Voice," 45.

60 Woodruff, "On the Voice," 45.

61 Woodruff, "On the Voice," 49.

62 Woodruff, "On the Voice," 49.

63 LoVetri does not hold a graduate degree in either science or music, having withdrawn from the Manhattan School of Music midway through her master's degree studies at that prestigious conservatory.

64 Stark, *Bel Canto*, xx.

65 On this point, Stark quotes Hermann Klein, a prominent, London-based early twentieth-century voice teacher: "Many people imagine that there is involved in the Italian method something in the nature of a great secret. . . . The true answer to that suggestion is that if trade secrets of the kind ever existed they were divulged by Manuel Garcia years ago." Klein quoted in Stark, *Bel Canto*, 225.

66 Foucault, *The Birth of the Clinic*, 115.

67 Estill Voice Training® Level Two Workshop, Quebec City, Canada, October 12–13, 2013. I have participated in additional Estill Voice Training® Workshops in Boston in August 2013, in New York City in August 2015, and in Kenosha, Wisconsin, in September 2019.

68 Since the time I attended this Estill course in 2013, Julie Cimon Racine founded her own company, La Voix Dynamique (https://lavoixdynamique .com) and continues to be a respected leader in the Estill community, where she now holds one of the highest teaching and mentoring certifications (EMCI-TP).

69 In contrast to several women teachers of popular singing, Steinhauer holds a PhD in Communication Science and Disorders and has held research scientist positions at healthcare and medical centers as well as performed as a singer, music director, and conductor in opera and musical theatre venues. In addition to serving as president of Estill Voice Training® leading workshops in the Estill method around the world, she has served on the voice faculty of the performing arts conservatory at Point Park University in Pittsburgh. Jo Estill, with whom Steinhauer

studied directly, never completed her own doctoral studies, although late in her life she was awarded an honorary doctorate from the University of Anglia in Norwich, UK. Credentials play a significant part in the extent to which singing teachers, especially women singing teachers, are taken seriously within voice science circles.

70 Structures of the larynx in the Estill method include figures for the true vocal folds in terms of onset and offset, the degree of body-cover (or mass, although this term is deemed less scientifically and anatomically accurate) of the vocal folds brought together in making sound, the degree of constriction or retraction of the false vocal folds, the relative tilt of the thyroid and cricoid cartilages, and the narrowing of the aery-epiglottic sphincter. Structures of the vocal tract include figures for the position of the larynx, velum (nasal port), tongue, jaw, and lips; support structures include figures for anchoring the sound with the head, neck, and torso.

71 Steinhauer and Estill, "The Estill Voice Model."

72 *Estill Voice Training Workbook—Level One*, 68.

73 This direction was given by Kim Steinhauer in the Level Two workshop in Quebec City, Canada, in October 2013.

74 The embodied expression of emotions, in voice or otherwise, is necessarily conditioned by culture, not a universal given. The affective and emotional imaginary of Estill as it is heard variously in Estill Voice Training® workshops around the world could be a fruitful area of future research.

75 The Estill method downplays the importance of the breath to the production of vocal sound, in marked contrast to more traditional vocal pedagogies. In fact, the breath is often figured as more of a villain than a generous collaborator—the tendency to push breath being pointed up as the cause of numerous vocal problems. In this general dismissal of the breath, Estill training recalls Roland Barthes's adroit critique: "How many singing teachers have we not heard prophesying that the art of vocal music rested entirely on the mastery, the correct discipline of breathing!" See Barthes, "The Grain of the Voice," 506.

76 Again, I refer to the double bind of white supremacy and expectations of ladylike virtue that LaKisha Simmons has theorized, and which I discuss in detail in chapter 3. See Simmons, *Crescent City Girls*.

77 See Cavarero, *For More Than One Voice*, 169; Dolar, *A Voice and Nothing More*, 27–28; and Nancy, *Listening*, 17.

78 Simone quoted in Redmond, *Anthem*, 183. Joshua Chambers-Letson also notes that Nina Simone worked as a vocal coach until "she got hip to the fact that you could make even more money playing music in local bars than teaching private lessons." See Chambers-Letson, *After the Party*, 51. For Chambers-Letson, minoritarian performance is the very matter of survival. The work of performers like Simone refutes a particular fiction

of equivalence that capitalism enforces, instead enacting a commons of incommensurability that takes shape as a sharing out, redistribution, being together in difference. The notions of black feminist voice training as open secret and performance of self-knowledge, discussed later in this chapter, have resonances with Chambers-Letson's elegant theorizing.

79 Moten, *In the Break*, 22.

80 Griffin, *If You Can't Be Free, Be a Mystery*, 171.

81 Saul, *Freedom Is, Freedom Ain't*, 95.

82 Lincoln quoted in Griffin, *If You Can't Be Free, Be a Mystery*, 172.

83 This awareness that the technical sound of black voice may be exerted as well as exhorted deflects the reductive suggestion that history made a sound and black women stood by, helpless, and opened their mouths to accommodate. The recurring figure of the weary-bluesy mammy type in musical theatre seems predicated on this notion—any technical power of the black woman's voice resides in her capacity to endlessly labor and suffer. On a related note, Daphne Brooks explicates the ways that the Fisk Jubilee Singers, "the world's first African American celebrity vocal group," were heard by white audiences in the late nineteenth century as rendering slavery's traumas audible and even pleasurable. As a group the singers were understood to have a particular, primary access to affect and emotion, as representatives and stand-ins for those who suffered the terrors of plantation life. Brooks notes, "Choosing to focus on the black spirituals singer as mythical tabula rasa, the Jubilees' white audiences and critics repeatedly gravitate toward lauding the effect of the song rather than the performer who interprets and finesses the material." Because the singers' expertise does not feature in such a hearing, audiences are able to extrapolate, if not in so many words, that it was the condition of enslavement itself that carved out such transporting voices from black bodies. In this hearing, racialized bodies become merely passive instruments lacking artistry or technique as such: it is slavery, the horrific affective experience, that is the real singer to be applauded. In other words, historically, for many white listeners the only secret, causal knowledge allowed the black voice in its *a priori* state of unhealth is that of secret pain. This is not what I am suggesting. See Brooks, *Bodies in Dissent*, 294, 300.

84 Moten, "Black Op," 1747.

85 Portions of the below text were previously published in Asare, "The Black Broadway Voice," 343–59.

86 Zonya Love's credits include Celie in *The Color Purple* on Broadway. John Bronston conducted the North American tour of *Hair* and as of this writing is a music directing fellow with Broadway's TINA: *The Tina Turner Musical*. Elijah Caldwell was the swing for multiple roles in the original off-Broadway production of *A Strange Loop* and teaches musical theatre voice at Marymount Manhattan College.

87 Mahon, *Black Diamond Queens*.

88 Lorde, "Uses of the Erotic," 59.

89 Lorde, "Uses of the Erotic," 59, 56.

90 Spillers, "Interstices," 166; emphasis original.

91 Spillers, "Interstices," 165; emphasis added.

92 I am indebted to Dr. Paschal Yao Younge for arranging these lessons for me.

Playoff

1 From *Once on This Island* (1990) to the *Company* revival (1995) and *The Bubbly Black Girl Sheds Her Chameleon Skin* (2000), *The Color Purple* (2004), *Dessa Rose* (2005), *If/Then* (2014), and *The Secret Life of Bees* (2019), to name just a few, LaChanze has originated groundbreaking roles on Broadway and off, and was the quintessential black ingénue that my generation looked up to. It is difficult to overstate how rare this consistent stream of roles has been for black women in the musical theatre. LaChanze has eight Broadway shows to her name and double that number in off-Broadway, regional, and national tour credits. Nearly every one is a musical.

2 Brooks, *Liner Notes for the Revolution*.

3 Childress, "Trouble in Mind," 51.

4 Childress, "Trouble in Mind," 74.

5 Childress, "Trouble in Mind," 74.

6 Childress, "Trouble in Mind," 76.

7 Childress, "Trouble in Mind," 85.

8 Bill T. Jones, Garrett Coleman, and Jason Oremus (Irish and Hammerstep choreography), Chloe Davis and Gelan Lambert (associates), collectively won the 2022 Drama Desk Award for Outstanding Choreography for *Paradise Square*.

9 Sadly, the release of the original Broadway cast album of *Paradise Square*, although fully recorded and mixed, is delayed indefinitely as of this writing due to the producer's outstanding contractual obligations to artists. Video footage of songs from the show, including promotional studio recordings (although these do not always reflect the final version of lyrics), can be found on Youtube.

10 The script of a musical, separate from its songs, is referred to as its "book"; the bookwriter is the playwright. *Paradise Square* had been in development with several talented artists who had mostly rotated off by the time I joined the team; in my process the bookwriter I worked most closely with was the brilliant Anderson. Tysen and Howland are white men; Anderson is a black woman.

11   Christina Anderson and I, the two black women on the writing team, joined the project midstream and inherited these characters and many plot points.

12   These roles were originated on Broadway by Gabrielle McClinton (Angelina), Hailee Kaleem Wright (Sarah), and Kayla Pecchioni (Blessed). Playing the roles of Sarah and Blessed, written by Christina, a black queer woman playwright, meant a great deal to Hailee and Kayla, two black queer women performers.

Bibliography

Abbott, Lynn, and Doug Seroff. *Ragged but Right: Black Traveling Shows, "Coon Songs," and the Dark Pathway to Blues and Jazz*. Jackson: University Press of Mississippi, 2007.

"A Chat with Black Patti." *New York Dramatic Mirror*, January 11, 1896.

Agamben, Giorgio. "Notes on Gesture." In *Means without End: Notes on Politics*. Translated by Vincenzo Binetti and Cesare Casarino, 49–62. Minneapolis: University of Minnesota Press, 2000.

Ahrens, Lynn. ASCAP/Disney Musical Theatre Writing Workshop. New York City, April 2010.

Albertson, Chris. *Bessie*. New Haven, CT: Yale University Press, 1972.

Allen, Robert C. *Horrible Prettiness: Burlesque and American Culture*. Cultural Studies of the United States. Chapel Hill: University of North Carolina Press, 2006.

almonkitt. "My Man Mon Homme 1920." Accessed July 16, 2021. https://www.youtube.com/watch?v=J_43tgFprrY.

Appolloni, Alexandra. "Authority, Ability, and the Aging Ingenue's Voice." In *Voicing Girlhood in Popular Music: Performance, Authority, Authenticity*. Edited by Jacqueline Warwick and Allison Adrian, 143–67. New York: Taylor and Francis, 2016.

"Archy and Mehitabel: A Back Alley Opera—1954." Official Masterworks Broadway Site. https://www.masterworksbroadway.com/music/archy-and-mehitabel-a-back-alley-opera-1954/. Accessed February 2, 2022.

Asare, Masi. "The Black Broadway Voice: Calls and Responses." *Studies in Musical Theatre* 14, no. 3 (2020): 343–59.

Asare, Masi. "The Singing Voice." In *Routledge Companion to Musical Theatre*. Edited by Ryan Donovan and Laura McDonald. London: Routledge, 2022.

Asare, Masi, and Todd Decker. "The Enduring Relevance of *Show Boat*." Rodgers and Hammerstein Organization website, December 2022. https://rodgersandhammerstein.com/the-enduring-relevance-of-show-boat/.

Atkinson, Brooks. "Flower Drum Song." *New York Times*, December 7, 1958.

Atkinson, Brooks. "Flower Drum Song Opens at St. James." *New York Times,* December 2, 1958.

Atkinson, Brooks. "'Shinbone Alley': Eartha Kitt and Eddie Bracken Play Don Marquis' Cockroach and Cat Pivot Characters Showshop Goods the Libretto." *New York Times,* April 28, 1957. Arts and Leisure.

Bailey, Pearl. *The Raw Pearl.* New York: Harcourt, Brace, and World, 1968.

Bailey, Pearl. "Tired." In *Pearl Bailey Entertains.* With Mitchell Ayres and His Orchestra. New York: Columbia Records, 1950.

Baker, Houston A. *Modernism and the Harlem Renaissance.* Chicago: University of Chicago Press, 1987.

Balance, Christine Bacareza. *Tropical Renditions: Making Musical Scenes in Filipino America.* Refiguring American Music. Durham, NC: Duke University Press, 2016.

Bald, Wambly. "Bloody Mary of 'South Pacific' Talks Genially of Love." *New York Post Home News,* June 27, 1949.

Bandhu, Pun, and Alyssa Achacoso. "The Visibility Report: Racial Representation on NYC Stages." The Asian American Performers Action Coalition, June 18, 2021. http://www.aapacnyc.org/2018-2019.

Banks, Daniel. "The Welcome Table: Casting for an Integrated Society." *Theatre Topics* 23, no. 1 (2013): 1–18.

Banks, Daniel, and Claire Syler. *Casting a Movement: The Welcome Table Initiative.* London: Taylor and Francis, 2019.

Baraka, Imamu Amiri. *Blues People: Negro Music in White America.* New York: Morrow, 1963.

Barthes, Roland. "The Grain of the Voice." In *The Sound Studies Reader.* Edited by Jonathan Sterne. New York: Routledge, 2012.

Batiste, Stephanie Leigh. *Darkening Mirrors: Imperial Representation in Depression-Era African American Performance.* Durham, NC: Duke University Press, 2011.

Bearden, Bessye. "Around New York." *Chicago Defender (National Edition) (1921–1967).* July 16, 1932, sec. Stage-Music-Movies.

Berlin, Irving. "Supper Time." Irving Berlin, 1933. Frances G. Spencer Collection of American Popular Sheet Music, Baylor University.

Berlin, Irving. *The International Rag.* New York: Waterson, Berlin & Snyder, 1913.

Bessie Smith—St. Louis Blues (1929). Accessed May 23, 2020. https://www.youtube .com/watch?v=OAchCljBr_Q.

"Bessie Smith Star of Fast Revue at Gibson's Next Week." *Philadelphia Tribune,* October 27, 1927.

"Black Patti." *Baltimore Afro-American,* July 8, 1933.

"Black Patti's Husband Threw Her Money into the Streets." *Chicago Defender,* October 16, 1948.

"The Black Woman." *Black Journal.* New York: WNET, 1970. American Archive of Public Broadcasting (GBH and the Library of Congress). http:// americanarchive.org/catalog/cpb-aacip-512-3t9d50gs73.

Block, Geoffrey, Sandra Jean Graham, Orly Leah Krasner, Todd Decker, Paul R. Laird, Jessica Sternfeld, Garrett Eisler, et al. *American Musical Theater: Grove Music Essentials*. London: Oxford University Press, 2015.

Bogle, Donald. *Heat Wave: The Life and Career of Ethel Waters*. New York: Harper-Collins, 2011.

Bogle, Donald. *Toms, Coons, Mulattoes, Mammies, and Bucks: An Interpretive History of Blacks in American Films*. New York: Bloomsbury Academic US, 2015.

Boozer, Thelma Berlack. "Script Proves Lena's St. Louis Woman' No Reflection on Race: Readers OK Opus for B'way Stage." *The Pittsburgh Courier (1911–1950)*. City Edition. September 22, 1945, sec. Theatrical.

Bourne, Stephen. *Elisabeth Welch: Soft Lights and Sweet Music*. Lanham, MD: Scarecrow Press, n.d.

Bracks, Lean'tin L., and Jessie Carney Smith, eds. *Black Women of the Harlem Renaissance Era*. Lanham, MD: Rowman and Littlefield, 2014.

Brooks, Daphne. *Bodies in Dissent: Spectacular Performances of Race and Freedom, 1850–1910*. Durham, NC: Duke University Press, 2006.

Brooks, Daphne. "Bold Soul Ingenue." In Liner Notes to *Take a Look: Aretha Franklin Complete on Columbia*. NewYork: Sony/Legacy, 2011.

Brooks, Daphne. *Liner Notes for the Revolution: The Intellectual Life of Black Feminist Sound*. Cambridge, MA: Harvard University Press, 2021.

Brooks, Daphne. "Planet Earth(a): Sonic Cosmoplitanism and Black Feminist Theory." In *Cornbread and Cuchifritos: Ethnic Identity Politics, Transnationalization, and Transculturation in American Urban Popular Music*. Edited by Wilfried Raussert and Michelle Habell-Pallán, 118. Tempe, AZ: Bilingual Press, 2011.

Brooks, Daphne. "Roundtable: From A Whisper to a Scream: The Voice in Music." EMP Pop Conference. Seattle, April 14, 2016. unpublished paper.

Brooks, Daphne. "Roundtable: Voicing Girlhood in Popular Music." Audio podcast. EMP Museum. Pop Conference 2016, n.d. Accessed June 17, 2016.

Brooks, Daphne. "'Sister, Can You Line It Out?': Zora Neale Hurston and the Sound of Angular Black Womanhood." *Amerikastudien / American Studies* 55, no. 4 (2010): 617–27.

Brooks, Lori Lynne. "'To Be Black Is to Be Funny': 'Coon-Shouting' and the Melancholic Production of the White Comedienne." *Women and Performance: A Journal of Feminist Theory* 25, no. 1 (January 2, 2015): 1–22.

Brown, Jayna. *Babylon Girls: Black Women Performers and the Shaping of the Modern*. Durham, NC: Duke University Press, 2008.

Brown Lavitt, Pamela. "First of the Red Hot Mamas: 'Coon Shouting'; and the Jewish Ziegfeld Girl." *American Jewish History* 87, no. 4 (1999): 253–90. https://doi.org/10.1353/ajh.1999.0031.

Browning, Ivan H. "Browning's London Letter." *Chicago Defender*.

Buckley, Gail Lumet. *The Hornes: An American Family*. New York: Knopf, 1986.

Cappiani, Luisa. *Practical Hints and Helps for Perfection in Singing*. New York: Leo Faist, 1908.

Carby, Hazel V. *Reconstructing Womanhood: The Emergence of the Afro-American Woman Novelist*. New York: Oxford University Press, 1987.

Carroll, Diahann. "A Sleepin' Bee." In *House of Flowers (Original Broadway Cast Recording)*. Book by Truman Capote; Music by Harold Arlen; Lyrics by Truman Capote and Harold Arlen. New York: Columbia Masterworks, 1955.

Carroll, Diahann. "Richard Rodgers Is Calling." In *Richard Rodgers Reader*. Edited by Geoffrey Block, 217–23. New York: Oxford University Press, 2002.

Carroll, Diahann. *The Legs Are the Last to Go: Aging, Acting, Marrying, and Other Things I Learned the Hard Way*. New York: Amistad, 2008.

Carroll, Diahann, and Richard Kiley. "The Sweetest Sounds." In *No Strings: A New Musical (Original Broadway Cast)*. Music and Lyrics by Richard Rodgers; Book by Samuel Taylor. New York: Columbia Masterworks, 1955.

Catanese, Brandi Wilkins. *The Problem of the Color[blind]: Racial Transgression and the Politics of Black Performance*. Ann Arbor: University of Michigan Press, 2012.

Cavarero, Adriana. *For More Than One Voice: Toward a Philosophy of Vocal Expression*. Translated by Paul Kottman. Palo Alto, CA: Stanford University Press, 2005.

Chambers-Letson, Joshua Takano. *After the Party: A Manifesto for Queer of Color Life*. Sexual Cultures. New York: New York University Press, 2018.

Chang, Juliana. "I Dreamed I Was Wanted: Flower Drum Song and Specters of Modernity." *Camera Obscura: Feminism, Culture, and Media Studies* 29, no. 3: 87 (December 1, 2014): 149–83. https://doi.org/10.1215/02705346-2801551.

Channing, Carol. *Just Lucky I Guess: A Memoir of Sorts*. New York: Simon and Schuster, 2002.

Cheng, Anne Anlin. *The Melancholy of Race*. Oxford: Oxford University Press, 2001.

Childress, Alice. "Trouble in Mind." In *Selected Plays*. Edited by Kathy A. Perkins. Evanston, IL: Northwestern University Press, 2011.

Chita Rivera Chats West Side Story, Eartha Kitt, Advice—BroadwayCon 2017. https://www.youtube.com/watch?v=I_Sj5a-OjrU. Accessed February 7, 2022.

Chop Suey—Flower Drum Song. blingnetzwork. Accessed July 21, 2021. https://www.youtube.com/watch?v=bPwiqmv6Xeo.

Clément, Catherine. "Through Voices, History." In *Siren Songs: Representations of Gender and Sexuality in Opera*. Edited by Mary Ann Smart. Princeton, NJ: Princeton University Press, 2000.

Clements, Marcelle. "Sighing, a French Sound Endures." *New York Times*, October 18, 1998, sec. Theater. https://www.nytimes.com/1998/10/18/theater/music-sighing-a-french-sound-endures.html.

Clippinger, D. A. *The Head Voice and Other Problems: Practical Talks on Singing*. Boston: Oliver Ditson, 1917.

Coffin, Berton. *Historical Vocal Pedagogy Classics*. Lanham, MD: Scarecrow Press, 1989.

"Command Performance #22." *Armed Forces Radio Network*, July 14, 1942.

Cone, James H. *The Spirituals and the Blues: An Interpretation*. New York: Orbis Books, 1972.

Connor, Steven. *Beyond Words: Sobs, Hums, Stutters, and Other Vocalizations*. London: Reaktion Books, 2014.

Cox, Aimee Meredith. *Shapeshifters: Black Girls and the Choreography of Citizenship*. Durham, NC: Duke University Press, 2015.

Crosby, Bing. *The Many Sides of Pat Suzuki*. Liner Notes. LP. Vik, 1958.

Das, Joanna Dee. *Katherine Dunham: Dance and the African Diaspora*. New York: Oxford University Press, 2017.

Dash, Thomas R. *Women's Wear Daily*, December 3, 1958.

Davis, Angela. *Blues Legacies and Black Feminism: Gertrude "Ma" Rainey, Bessie Smith, and Billie Holiday*. New York: Vintage Books, 1998.

Davis, Tracy C. "The Context Problem." *Theatre Survey* 45, no. 2 (2004): 203–9.

Decker, Todd R. *Show Boat: Performing Race in an American Musical*. Broadway Legacies. Oxford: Oxford University Press, 2013.

Deleted Scene: Why Diahann Carroll Doesn't Sing the Blues: Oprah's Master Class. Oprah Winfrey Network. Accessed March 4, 2024. https://www.youtube .com/watch?v=T5NfVEHY9dA.

"Deny Lena Horne's Movie Career Halted: Refusal of 'Mammy' Role Is the Reason; Movie Czar Refutes Truth of Rumors in NAACP Reply." *Cleveland Call and Post*, October 13, 1945.

Derrida, Jacques. "The Voice That Keeps Silence." In *The Sound Studies Reader*. Edited by Jonathan Sterne, 495–503. New York: Routledge, 2012.

"Diahann Carroll Honored at House of Flowers." *Jet*, October 21, 2013.

"Diahann Carroll Is the New Toast of Broadway." *Jet*, March 29, 1962.

Diahann Carroll—"Love Comes A-Calling on You" (1953). Accessed May 23, 2020. https://www.youtube.com/watch?v=rokyVOWKRUk.

Diahann Carroll: My Grandmother. Accessed May 23, 2020. https://www.youtube .com/watch?v=-EZyuFSzrko.

"Diahann Stars in Tailor-Made Musical." *Jet*, February 8, 1962.

Dietz, Robert J., and E. T. S. "Marc Blitzstein and the 'Agit-Prop' Theatre of the 1930's." *Anuario Interamericano de Investigación Musical* 6 (1970): 51–66. https://doi.org/10.2307/779925.

Dolar, Mladen. *A Voice and Nothing More*. Cambridge, MA: MIT Press, 2006.

Donovan, Ryan. "'Must Be Heavyset': Casting Women, Fat Stigma, and Broadway Bodies." *Journal of American Drama and Theatre* 31, no. 3 (Spring 2019): 1–17.

Du Bois, W. E. B. *The Souls of Black Folk*. Oxford: Oxford University Press, 1903.

Ealey, Jordan. "Young, Bubbly, and Black: The Affective Performance of Black Girlhood in Kirsten Childs's *The Bubbly Black Girl Sheds Her Chameleon Skin*." *The Black Scholar* 50, no. 4 (2020): 55–64. https://doi.org/10.1080 /00064246.2020.181038.

"Earle, Philly." *Variety*, August 5, 1951. Page unknown.

"Eartha Kitt 'Shinbone Alley' Flops, Closes." *Afro-American (1893–)*, June 8, 1957.

Edney, K. "'Integration through the Wide Open Back Door': African Americans Respond to Flower Drum Song (1958)." *Studies in Musical Theatre* 4, no. 3 (2010): 261–72. https://doi.org/10.1386/smt.4.3.261_1.

Eichler, Alan. *Ethel Waters, Person to Person, 1954 TV, I Got Rhythm*. Accessed July 9, 2021. https://www.youtube.com/watch?v=2UTUJlT3oyI.

Eidsheim, Nina Sun. "Race and Aesthetics of Vocal Timbre." In *Rethinking Difference in Music Scholarship*. Edited by Olivia Ashley Bloechl, Melanie Diane Lowe, and Jeffrey Kallberg, 338–65. Cambridge: Cambridge University Press, 2015.

Eidsheim, Nina Sun. *Sensing Sound: Singing and Listening as Vibrational Practices.* Sign, Storage, Transmission. Durham, NC: Duke University Press, 2015.

Eidsheim, Nina Sun. *The Race of Sound: Listening, Timbre, and Vocality in African American Music*. Refiguring American Music. Durham, NC: Duke University Press, 2018.

Enstice, Wayne, and Janis Stockhouse. *Jazzwomen: Conversations with Twenty-One Musicians*. Bloomington: Indiana University Press, 2004.

Estill Voice Training® Workbook—Level One. Pittsburgh, PA: Estill Voice International, 2010.

Ethel Merman, 1978 Interview and "Annie Get Your Gun" Medley. Accessed May 23, 2020. https://www.youtube.com/watch?v=vaoFW_ij9I0.

Ethel Merman Performing "I Got Rhythm" (1931). YouTube, 2016. Accessed May 23, 2020.

Ethel Waters—Am I Blue–1929 Film. preservationhall01. Accessed July 16, 2021.

"Ethel Waters, Hubby Separate: Blues Queen Sings 'Eddie Doesn't Live Here Anymore.'" *Pittsburgh Courier*, April 7, 1934.

"Ethel Waters Returns to U.S.; May Star in Broadway Revue." *Chicago Defender*, March 22, 1930.

"Ethel Waters, Weld, 1:30 P. M." *Daily Boston Globe (1928–1960)*, November 22, 1936.

"European Makes Splendid Offer: Scholarship to American Girls by Professor Drysdale Sponsored by Florence Mills." *New York Amsterdam News*, February 9, 1927.

"Eye to Eye with Juanita Hall." *New York Amsterdam News,* January 25, 1958.

Fanchon, Simon, and Marco Wolff. "Fanchon and Marco." Accessed January 27, 2022. https://fanchonandmarco.com/fanchon-and-marco-history.

Feather, Leonard. Liner Notes: *Juanita Hall—The Original Bloody Mary—Sings the Blues*. Counterpoint, 1958.

Feinstein, Herbert. "Lena Horne Speaks Freely on Race, Marriage, Stage," *Ebony*, May 1963, 61.

Feld, Steven. "Aesthetics as Iconicity of Style, or 'Lift-up-over Sounding': Getting into the Kaluli Groove." *Yearbook for Traditional Music* 20 (1988): 74–113. https://doi.org/10.2307/768167.

Fiol-Matta, Licia. *The Great Woman Singer: Gender and Voice in Puerto Rican Music.* Refiguring American Music. Durham, NC: Duke University Press, 2017.

Fisher, Rudolph. "The Caucasian Storms Harlem." *American Mercury,* 1927, sec. 2, 394.

Flower Drum Song—Ed Sullivan Show. Accessed May 23, 2020. https://www .youtube.com/watch?v=jkYQaNHl2K8.

Floyd, Samuel A. "Ring Shout! Literary Studies, Historical Studies, and Black Music Inquiry." *Black Music Research Journal* 22, no. 1 (2002): 49–70.

Floyd, Samuel A. *The Power of Black Music: Interpreting Its History from Africa to the United States.* New York: Oxford University Press, 1995.

Foucault, Michel. *The Birth of the Clinic.* New York: Random House, 1963.

Franko, Mark. *The Work of Dance: Labor, Movement, and Identity in the 1930s.* Middletown, CT: Wesleyan University Press, 2002.

Frith, Simon. *Performing Rites: On the Value of Popular Music.* Cambridge, MA: Harvard University Press, 1996.

Galella, Donatella. *America in the Round: Capital, Race, and Nation at Washington, DC's Arena Stage.* Studies in Theatre History and Culture. Iowa City: University of Iowa Press, 2019.

Galella, Donatella. "Artists of Color/Cross-Racial Casting." In *Casting a Movement.* London: Routledge, 2019.

Galella, Donatella. "Feeling Yellow: Responding to Contemporary Yellowface in Musical Performance." *Journal of Dramatic Theory and Criticism* 32, no. 2 (2018): 67–77. https://doi.org/10.1353/dtc.2018.0005.

"The Garcia Centenary." *British Medical Journal,* no. 1.2308 (1905): 681–89.

Garcia, Manuel, II. *Garcia's New Treatise on the Art of Singing.* Boston: Oliver Ditson Company, 1800.

Garcia, Manuel, II. "Observations on the Human Voice." In *Proceedings of the Royal Society of London,* no. 7 (1854): 399–410.

George-Graves, Nadine. *The Royalty of Negro Vaudeville: The Whitman Sisters and the Negotiation of Race, Gender and Class in African American Theatre, 1900–1940.* New York: St. Martin's Press, 2000.

Glover, Eric M. "Joy and Love in Zora Neale Hurston and Dorothy Waring's 1944 Black Feminist Musical Polk County." *TDR: Drama Review* 65, no. 2 (2021): 45–62. https://doi.org/10.1017/S1054204321000071.

Glover, William. "Tiny Oriental Ball of Fire Has Broadway Bedazzled." *Hartford Courant (1923–1991).* December 21, 1958.

Grant, Clark, and Harry Akst. "Am I Blue?" New York: M. Witmark and Sons, 1919. The Lester S. Levy Sheet Music Collection, Johns Hopkins University. https://levysheetmusic.mse.jhu.edu/collection/155/010a.

Griffin, Farah Jasmine. *If You Can't Be Free, Be a Mystery: In Search of Billie Holiday.* New York: Ballantine, 2001.

Griffin, Farah Jasmine. "When Malindy Sings: A Meditation on Black Women's Vocality." In *Uptown Conversation: The New Jazz Studies.* Edited by

Robert G. O'Meally, Brent Hayes Edwards, and Farah Jasmine Griffin. New York: Columbia University Press, 2004.

Grossman, Barbara Wallace. *Funny Woman: The Life and Times of Fanny Brice.* Bloomington: Indiana University Press, 1991.

Hallelujah, Baby! Accessed May 23, 2020. https://www.youtube.com/watch?v =OC8b-dEsa_s.

Handy, W. C. *Father of the Blues: An Autobiography.* New York: Da Capo Press, 1942.

Hartman, Saidiya V. *Wayward Lives, Beautiful Experiments: Intimate Histories of Social Upheaval.* New York: W. W. Norton, 2019.

Hatch, James V. "A White Folks Guide to 200 Years of Black and White Drama." *TDR: The Drama Review* 16, no. 4 (1972): 5–24.

Hawkins, William. "Jose 'Happy Talks' to Juanita Hall." *New York World-Post,* May 18, 1949.

Herrera, Brian Eugenio. "'But Do We Have the Actors for That?': Some Principles of Practice for Staging Latinx Plays in a University Theatre Context." *Theatre Topics* 27, no. 1 (2017): 23–35.

Herrera, Patricia, Caitlin Marshall, and Marci R. McMahon. "Sound Acts: Unmuting Performance Studies." American Society for Theatre Research (ASTR), Prick Up the Ears Working Group reading, 2019.

Hill, Anthony D., and Douglas Q. Barnett. *The A to Z of African American Theater.* Lanham, MD: Scarecrow Press, 2009.

Hine, Darlene Clark. "Rape and the Inner Lives of Black Women in the Middle West." *Signs: Journal of Women in Culture and Society* 14, no. 4 (1989): 912–20. https://doi.org/10.1086/494552.

"Hint Show Will Tour Nation: Muriel Rahn Also Hit by Its Closing." *Chicago Defender,* July 13, 1946.

Hischak, Thomas S. *Broadway Plays and Musicals: Descriptions and Essential Facts of More Than 14,000 Shows through 2007.* Jefferson, NC: McFarland, 2009.

Hischak, Thomas S . "Hall, Juanita." In *The Oxford Companion to the American Musical: Theatre, Film, and Television.* New York: Oxford University Press, 2008.

Hollywood, Joan Barthel. "Lena Horne: 'Now I Feel Good About Being Me.'" *New York Times,* July 28, 1968.

Holt, Nora. "Trouble Stalks 'St. Louis' Woman": "St. Louis Woman: She's in Opposite Side of The Fence." *New York Amsterdam News (1943–1961),* City Edition. April 6, 1946.

Horne, Lena. *In Person, Lena Horne: As Told to Helen Arstein and Carlton Moss.* New York: Greenberg, 1950.

Horne, Lena. *Lena.* Garden City, NY: Doubleday, 1965.

How Diahann Carroll's Broadway Sound Set Her Apart: Oprah's Master Class. Oprah Winfrey Network. Accessed May 23, 2020. https://www.youtube.com /watch?v=NfDAjoKp9bE.

Hughes, Langston. "The Negro Artist and the Racial Mountain." In *Within the Circle: An Anthology of African American Literary Criticism from the Har-*

lem *Renaissance to the Present*. Edited by Angelyn Mitchell, 57. Durham, NC: Duke University Press, 1993.

Hurston, Zora Neale. "Zora Neale Hurston Collected Songs, Florida Folklife from the WPA Collections, 1937 to 1942." Library of Congress, Washington, DC. Accessed February 5, 2023. https://www.loc.gov/collections/florida -folklife-from-the-works-progress-administration.

Hurston, Zora Neale, and Dorothy Waring. "Polk County." In *Zora Neale Hurston: Collected Plays*. Edited by Jean Lee Cole and Charles Mitchell, 269–362. New Brunswick, NJ: Rutgers University Press, 2008.

Irvin, Sam. *Kay Thompson: From Funny Face to Eloise*. New York: Simon and Schuster, 2010.

Jefferson, Miles. "The Negro on Broadway, 1954–1955: More Spice than Substance." *Phylon* Vol. 16, no 3 (1955): 304–5.

Jess, Tyehimba. "Coon Songs Must Go! Coon Songs Go On . . ." *Callaloo* 35, no. 2 (2012): 317–18.

Johnson, E. Patrick. *Appropriating Blackness: Performance and the Politics of Authenticity*. Durham, NC: Duke University Press, 2003.

Johnson, Jake. "Building the Broadway Voice." *The Oxford Handbook of Voice Studies*. New York: Oxford University Press. July 25, 2019.

Johnson, James Weldon. *Black Manhattan*. New York: Knopf, 1930.

Jones, Leroi [Amiri Baraka]. *Black Music*. New York: Akashic Books, 1968.

"Juanita Hall." *Variety*, May 25, 1949.

"Juanita Hall, 'Bloody Mary' of Stage, Screen, Dies." *Jet*, March 14, 1968, 59.

"Juanita Hall Hailed as Nightclub 'Find.'" *New York Amsterdam News (1943–1961)*. City Edition. July 3, 1948.

"Juanita Hall Signed." *New York Times*, June 2, 1958.

Juilliard School, Registrar's Office. "Juanita Hall." August 16, 2017.

Kajikawa, Loren. "Leaders of the New School? Music Departments, Hip-Hop, and the Challenge of Significant Difference." *Twentieth-Century Music* 18, no. 1 (2021): 45–64.

Kapchan, Deborah. "Body." In *Keywords in Sound*. Edited by David Novak and Matt Sakakeeny, 39. Durham, NC: Duke University Press, 2015.

Kaufman, David. *Some Enchanted Evenings: The Glittering Life and Times of Mary Martin*. New York: St. Martin's, 2016.

Kellow, Brian. *Ethel Merman: A Life*. New York: Viking, 2007.

Kerr, Walter. "'Baby' Bets a Kiss." *New York Times,* May 7, 1967.

Kerr, Walter. "'Shinbone Alley.'" *New York Herald Tribune,* April 15, 1957.

Kessler, Kelly. *Broadway in the Box: Television's Lasting Love Affair with the Musical*. Oxford Scholarship Online. New York: Oxford University Press, 2020.

Kiesgen, Paul. "How Richard Miller Changed the Way We Think about Singing." *Journal of Singing* 62, no. 3 (February 2007): 261–64.

Kim, Chang-Hee. "Asian Performance on the Stage of American Empire in Flower Drum Song." *Cultural Critique* 85 (2013): 1–37.

Kim Daniher, Colleen. "Yella Gal: Eartha Kitt's Racial Modulations." *Women & Performance: A Journal of Feminist Theory* 28, no. 1 (January 2, 2018): 16–33. https://doi.org/10.1080/0740770X.2018.1426200.

Kitt, Eartha. *Confessions of a Sex Kitten.* Fort Lee, NJ: Barricade Books, 1991.

Kitt, Eartha. *Thursday's Child.* New York: Duell, Sloan, and Pearce, 1956. https://hdl.handle.net/2027/uc1.31822013748728.

Knapp, Raymond. *The American Musical and the Formation of National Identity.* Princeton, NJ: Princeton University Press, 2005.

Koster, Henry dir. *Flower Drum Song.* Hollywood: Universal Pictures, 1961.

Krell, Elias. "Contours through Covers: Voice and Affect in the Music of Lucas Silveira." *Journal of Popular Music Studies* 25, no. 4 (2013): 476–503. https://doi.org/10.1111/jpms.12047.

"La Horne Quits Cast of Backwards Musical." *New York Amsterdam News,* City Edition, September 15, 1945.

Lamm, Conrad. "Juanita Hall Looking beyond 'Bloody Mary.'" *New York Herald-Tribune.* May 4, 1958.

Lamperti, G. B. *The Technics of Bel Canto.* Translated by Theodore Baker. New York: G. Shirmer, 1905.

Lantz, Ragni. "HELLO, DOLLY!: Pearl Bailey, Cab Calloway Lend 'Black Magic' to Show." *Ebony,* January 1968.

Lee, John. "'St. Louis Woman' Has Phony Plot." *New Journal and Guide (1916–2003),* April 13, 1946, National Edition.

Lees, Gene. *Portrait of Johnny: The Life of John Herndon Mercer.* Milwaukee, WI: Hal Leonard Corporation, 2004.

Lehmann, Lilli. *How to Sing.* Translated by Richard Aldrich. New York: Macmillan, 1902.

Leonard, William. "The Girl Who' s 1,000 Times Good." *Chicago Daily Tribune,* May 24, 1958.

Leslie Uggams on Controversy about Her Being on "Sing Along with Mitch." emmytvlegends.org. Accessed May 23, 2020. https://www.youtube.com/watch?v=xdhA5tnYHxE.

Lewis, David H. *Flower Drum Songs: The Story of Two Musicals.* Jefferson, NC: McFarland, 2006.

Lewis, George. *A Power Stronger Than Itself: The AACM and American Experimental Music.* Chicago: University of Chicago Press, 2008.

Lieb, Sandra R. *Mother of the Blues: A Study of Ma Rainey.* Amherst: University of Massachusetts Press, 1981.

"Lillian Hayman." In *Internet Broadway Database.* https://www.ibdb.com/broadway-cast-staff/lillian-hayman-89656. Accessed January 3, 2018.

Lockheart, Paula. "A History of Early Microphone Singing, 1925–1939: American Mainstream Popular Singing at the Advent of Electronic Microphone Amplification." *Popular Music and Society* 26, no. 3 (October 1, 2003): 367–85.

Logan, Joshua. *Movie Stars, Real People, and Me.* New York: Delacorte Press, 1978.

Lorde, Audre. "Uses of the Erotic: The Erotic as Power." In *Sister Outsider: Essays and Speeches by Audre Lorde*, 53–59. Berkeley, CA: Crossing Press, 1984.

Lott, Eric. *Love and Theft: Blackface Minstrelsy and the American Working Class.* New York: Oxford University Press, 1993.

Lupton, Deborah. *The Imperative of Health: Public Health and the Regulated Body.* London: Sage Publications, 1995.

Ma, Sheng-mei. "Rodgers and Hammerstein's 'Chopsticks' Musicals." *Literature/Film Quarterly* 31, no. 1 (2003): 17–26.

Macpherson, Ben. "Sing: Musical Theatre Voices from Superstar to Hamilton." In *The Routledge Companion to the Contemporary Musical.* Edited by Jessica Sternfeld and Elizabeth L. Wollman. New York, London: Routledge, 2019.

Mahon, Maureen. *Black Diamond Queens: African American Women and Rock and Roll.* Refiguring American Music. Durham, NC: Duke University Press, 2020.

Martin, Mary. *My Heart Belongs.* New York: Morrow, 1976.

Martin, Mary. "The Day I Found Me." *Detroit Free Press*, October 21, 1956.

Martin, Mary. "The Sound of Music." In *The Sound of Music (Original Broadway Cast Recording).* Music by Richard Rodgers; Lyrics by Oscar Hammerstein II; Book by Howard Lindsay and Russell Crouse. New York: Columbia Masterworks, 1959.

Mast, Gerald. *Can't Help Singin': The American Musical on Stage and Screen.* Woodstock, NY: Overlook Press, 1987.

Maultsby, Portia. "The Politics of Race Erasure in Defining Black Popular Music Origins." In *Issues in African American Music,* 61–79. New York: Routledge, 2016.

Mauss, Marcel. "Techniques of the Body (1934)." In *Incorporations,* 455–77. Edited by Jonathan Crary and Sanford Kwinter. Cambridge, MA: Zone Books, 1992.

McGinley, Paige A. *Staging the Blues: From Tent Shows to Tourism.* Durham, NC: Duke University Press, 2014.

McMillin, Scott. *The Musical as Drama: A Study of the Principles and Conventions behind Musical Shows from Kern to Sondheim.* Princeton, NJ: Princeton University Press, 2006.

Meizel, Katherine. *Multivocality: Singing on the Borders of Identity.* New York: Oxford University Press, 2020.

Melnick, Jeffrey. *A Right to Sing the Blues: African Americans, Jews, and American Popular Song.* Cambridge, MA: Harvard University Press, 2001.

"Memoirs of Jenny Lind." *The Observer,* May 2, 1847.

Merman, Ethel, and George Eells. *Merman: An Autobiography.* New York: Simon & Schuster, 1979.

Merwin, Ted. *In Their Own Image: New York Jews in Jazz Age Popular Culture.* New Brunswick, NJ: Rutgers University Press, 2006.

Metzger, Sean. "Part 2 Introduction." In *Chinese Looks: Fashion, Performance, Race.* Bloomington: Indiana University Press, 2014.

Metzl, Jonathan M., and Anna Kirkland, eds. *Against Health: How Health Became the New Morality.* New York: New York University Press, 2010.

Middleton, Richard. "Rock Singing." In *Cambridge Companion to Singing.* Edited by
    John Potter, 28–41. New York: Cambridge University Press, 2008.
Miller, D. A. *Place for Us: Essay on the Broadway Musical.* Cambridge, MA: Harvard
    University Press, 1998.
Miller, Karl Hagstrom. *Segregating Sound: Inventing Folk and Pop Music in the Age of
    Jim Crow.* Durham, NC: Duke University Press, 2010.
Miller, Richard. *On the Art of Singing.* New York: Oxford University Press, 1996.
Miller, Richard. *Solutions for Singers: Tools for Performers and Teachers.* New York:
    Oxford University Press, 2004.
Mishkin, Leo. "Juanita Hall Sings Blues on Mondays." *Morning Telegraph*, March 30,
    1966.
MissPoochSmooch. *1969 Tony Awards ~ COMPLETE.* Accessed July 17, 2021. https://
    www.youtube.com/watch?v=SevmAKmGkeg.
Mitchell, Koritha. *Living with Lynching: African American Lynching Plays, Performance,
    and Citizenship, 1890–1930.* Champaign: University of Illinois Press, 2011.
Moore, John. "'The Hieroglyphics of Love': The Torch Singers and Interpretation."
    Popular Music 8, no. 1 (1989): 31–58. https://doi.org/10.1017/S02611430
    00003147.
Mordden, Ethan. *Open a New Window: The Broadway Musical in the 1960s.* New
    York: St. Martin's Press, 2015.
Morehouse, Ward. "Broadway After Dark: Bloody Mary Is Her Name." *New York
    Sun*, May 25, 1949, 26.
Moriah, Kristin. "On the Record: Sissieretta Jones and Black Feminist Recording
    Praxes." *Performance Matters* 6, no. 2 (2020): 26–42.
Morrison, Toni. *Black Studies Center Public Dialogue. Pt. 2.* Portland State Univer-
    sity, 1975. https://soundcloud.com/portland-state-library/portland-state
    -black-studies-1.
Moss, N. O. "Great Voices Are Born—Not Made." *Los Angeles Times,* December 24,
    1933.
Most, Andrea. *Making Americans: Jews and the Broadway Musical.* Cambridge, MA:
    Harvard University Press, 2004.
Most, Andrea. "'You've Got to Be Carefully Taught': The Politics of Race in Rod-
    gers and Hammerstein's South Pacific." *Theatre Journal* 52, no. 3 (Octo-
    ber 1, 2000): 307–37. https://doi.org/10.1353/tj.2000.0091.
Moten, Fred. "Black Op." *PMLA* 123, no. 5 (October 1, 2008): 1743–47.
Moten, Fred. "Comparing Domains of Improvisation." Zoom lecture, Columbia
    University. April 23, 2021.
Moten, Fred. *In the Break: The Aesthetics of the Black Radical Tradition.* Minneapo-
    lis: University of Minnesota Press, 2003.
MrPoochsmooch. *Hello Dolly! Pearl Bailey 1968 Tony Awards.* 2012. https://youtu
    .be/d4eSox16v1k.
Nancy, Jean-Luc. *Listening.* Translated by Charlotte Mandell. New York: Fordham
    University Press, 2007.

"News of the Stage: 'St. Louis Woman,' All-Negro Musical, Arriving at the Martin Beck Tonight—Ruby Hill in Lead 'Walk Hard' to Quit Potpourri of the Town." *New York Times*, March 30, 1946.

Nichols, Lewis. "The Play." *New York Times*, April 1, 1946, sec. Amusements.

Niles, John J. "Shout, Coon, Shout!" *Musical Quarterly* 16, no. 4 (1930): 516–30.

Nyong'o, Tavia. "Afro-Philo-Sonic Fictions: Black Sound Studies after the Millennium." *Small Axe: A Caribbean Journal of Criticism* 18, no. 2 (44) (July 1, 2014): 173–79.

"N.Y. Singer Diahann Carroll Finds Cinderella-Like Fame." *Jet*, April 15, 1954.

Oblender, David. "Leslie Uggams." *Contemporary Black Biography*, no. 23:197–200. Detroit: Gale, 2000.

O'Connell, Samuel. "Fragmented Musicals and 1970s Soul Aesthetic." In *The Cambridge Companion to African American Theatre*. Edited by Harvey Young, 155–73. Cambridge Companions to Literature. Cambridge: Cambridge University Press, 2012.

Oja, Carol J. *Bernstein Meets Broadway: Collaborative Art in a Time of War*. Broadway Legacies. New York: Oxford University Press, 2014.

"Operated on Throat of Ethel Waters." *Baltimore Afro-American*, November 30, 1929.

"Origin of the Musical Verb 'Belt.'" *A Way with Words Radio Show*. 2014.

Osseo-Asare, Abena Dove. *Bitter Roots: The Search for Healing Plants in Africa*. Chicago: University of Chicago Press, 2014.

O'Toole, Lawrence. "Theater: Musical Theater Is Discovering a New Voice." *New York Times*, January 22, 1995.

Pao, Angela C. *No Safe Spaces: Re-Casting Race, Ethnicity, and Nationality in American Theater*. Ann Arbor: University of Michigan Press, 2010.

"Paramount Reviews." *Variety*, June 6, 1951, 16.

Pat Suzuki "I Enjoy Being a Girl on the Ed Sullivan Show." Accessed March 13, 2024. https://youtu.be/RxGnM7_1yRI?si=reXBX3xHqfeP8EiZ.

"Pearl Bailey." In *Internet Broadway Database*. https://www.ibdb.com/broadway -cast-staff/pearl-bailey-30650. Accessed January 2, 2018.

Peterson, Bernard L. *The African American Theatre Directory, 1816–1960: A Comprehensive Guide to Early Black Theatre Organizations, Companies, Theatres, and Performing Groups*. Westport, CT: Greenwood Publishing, 1997.

Petty, Miriam J. *Stealing the Show: African American Performers and Audiences in 1930s Hollywood*. Oakland: University of California Press, 2016.

Pleasants, Henry. "Bel Canto in Jazz and Pop Singing." *Music Educators Journal* 59, no. 9 (May 1, 1973): 54–59.

"The 'Pop' Singer and the Voice Teacher." *American Academy of Teachers of Singing. Journal of Singing* 43, no. 1 (September/October 1986): 21.

Poulson-Bryant, Scott. "Strollin' through Broadway History: *Bubbling Brown Sugar* and the Performance of Cultural Citizenship in the 1970s." In "Everybody Is a Star!: Uplift, Citizenship, and the Cross-Racial Politics of 1970s U.S. Popular Culture." PhD diss., Harvard University, 2016.

Purnell, Brian, Jeanne Theoharis, and Komozi Woodard. *The Strange Careers of the Jim Crow North: Segregation and Struggle Outside of the South.* New York: New York University Press, 2019.

"Radio: $115,000 for a Copy Act." *Variety (Archive: 1905–2000).* Los Angeles: Penske Business Corporation, May 13, 1936.

Rampersad, Arnold. *The Life of Langston Hughes: Volume II: 1914–1967, I Dream a World.* New York: Oxford University Press, 2002.

Raymon, Don. "'Rhapsody in Black' Still Has Ethel; Why Ask More?" *Chicago Defender,* January 21, 1933, sec. Stage-Music-Movies.

Redmond, Shana L. *Anthem: Social Movements and the Sound of Solidarity in the African Diaspora.* New York: New York University Press, 2014.

Reece, Dwandalyn. "A Performance Biography of Ethel Waters (1896–1977)." PhD diss., New York University, 2000.

Reed, Rex. "Baby Learned Never Learned to Cry." *New York Times,* May 7, 1967.

"Renowned Vocal Pedagogue Richard Miller, Emeritus Professor of Singing, Dies at 83." May 12, 2009. Oberlin Conservatory website. Accessed July 17, 2017.

Riis, Thomas L. *Just before Jazz.* Washington, DC: Smithsonian Institution Press, 1989.

Robinson, Dylan. *Hungry Listening: Resonant Theory for Indigenous Sound Studies.* Minneapolis: University of Minnesota Press, 2020.

Rodgers, Richard. *I Enjoy Being a Girl.* New York: Williamson Music, 1958.

Rodgers, Richard. *Musical Stages.* New York: Random House, 1975.

Rodgers, Richard. *South Pacific—I'm Gonna Wash That Man Right Out of My Hair—Mary Martin.* Broadway Classixs, 2010. https://www.youtube.com/watch?v=C5DiQsKpEkc.

Rodgers, Richard, and Oscar Hammerstein II. *South Pacific (Original Broadway Cast Recording).* Sony Classical, 1998. Naxos Music Library.

Rodgers, Richard, Oscar Hammerstein II, and Joshua Logan. *South Pacific.* New York: Williamson Music, 1956.

Rosen, Judy. "Frank Sinatra and Billie Holiday: They Did It Their Way." *New York Times,* October 19, 2015, sec. T Magazine. https://www.nytimes.com/2015/10/19/t-magazine/frank-sinatra-and-billie-holiday-bond.html.

Royster, Francesca T. *Sounding Like a No-No: Queer Sounds and Eccentric Acts in the Post-Soul Era.* Ann Arbor: University of Michigan Press, 2013.

Sampson, Henry T. *Blacks in Blackface: A Sourcebook on Early Black Musical Shows.* Lanham, MD: Scarecrow Press, 1980.

Saul, Scott. *Freedom Is, Freedom Ain't.* Cambridge, MA: Harvard University Press, 2003.

Schechner, Richard. *Between Theater and Anthropology.* Philadelphia: University of Pennsylvania Press, 1985.

Secrest, Meryle. *Somewhere for Me: A Biography of Richard Rodgers.* New York: Knopf, 2001.

Shalett, Sidney M. "Harlem's Ethel Waters: Notes on the Lady Who Currently Appears In 'Cabin in the Sky.'" *New York Times*, November 10, 1940, sec. Arts and Leisure.

Shannon, Sandra G. "Blues, History, and Dramaturgy: An Interview with August Wilson." *African American Review* 27, no. 4 (1993): 539–59. https://doi.org/10.2307/3041887.

Shimakawa, Karen. *National Abjection: The Asian American Body Onstage*. Durham, NC: Duke University Press, 2002.

Simmons, LaKisha Michelle. *Crescent City Girls: The Lives of Young Black Women in Segregated New Orleans*. Gender and American Culture. Chapel Hill: University of North Carolina Press, 2015.

Simpson, Eugene Thamon. *Hall Johnson: His Life, His Spirit, and His Music*. Lanham, MD: Scarecrow Press, 2008.

Simpson, Eugene Thamon, Personal correspondence. August 10, 2017.

Smith, Jacob. *Vocal Tracks: Performance and Sound Media*. Berkeley: University of California Press, 2008.

Solomon, Lee. "South Pacific: Return of One of the Greats." Aussietheatre.com. October 18, 2011.

Sood, Jahn. "Neither Here Nor There: Becoming Indian-American in Theater." *Musical Theater Today* 3: (319–63), 2019.

Sophie Tucker and Al Jolson "International Rag." Accessed May 23, 2020. https://www.youtube.com/watch?v=_kptyY_SC_I.

Soto-Morettini, Donna. *Popular Singing and Style:* 2nd ed. London: Bloomsbury Methuen Drama, 2006.

Southern, Eileen. *The Music of Black Americans: A History*. New York: W. W. Norton, 1971.

Spillers, Hortense. "Interstices: A Small Drama of Words." In *Black, White, and in Color: Essays on American Literature and Culture*, 152–75. Chicago: University of Chicago Press, 2003.

Stanislavski, Konstantin. "Types of Actors." In *Stanislavski's Legacy: A Collection of Comments on a Variety of Aspects of an Actor's Art and Life*. New York: Theatre Arts Books, 1968.

Stark, James. *Bel Canto: A History of Vocal Pedagogy*. Toronto: University of Toronto Press, 2000.

Steinhauer, K., and J. Estill. "The Estill Voice Model: Physiology of Emotion." In *Emotions in the Human Voice*. Vol. 2, *Clinical Evidence*. Edited by Krzysztof Izdebski. San Diego, CA: Plural Publishing, 2008.

Steinhauer, Kimberly. "Estill Workshop (Level Two)." Quebec City, October 2013.

Sterne, Jonathan. *The Audible Past: Cultural Origins of Sound Reproduction*. Durham, NC: Duke University Press, 2003.

Sternfeld, Jessica, and Elizabeth Wollman. "After the Golden Age." In *The Oxford Handbook of the American Musical*. Edited by Raymond Knapp, Mitchell Morris, and Stacy Wolf, 111–24. New York: Oxford University Press, 2011.

Story, Rosalyn M. *And So I Sing: African-American Divas of Opera and Concert.* New York: Warner Books, 1990.

Strang, Lewis. "St. Louis Woman." *New York Times,* April 1946.

Strang, Lewis C. "Famous Actresses of the Day in America." Boston: L.C. Page and Company, 1899.

Stratton, Jon. *Jews, Race and Popular Music.* Ashgate Popular and Folk Music Series. Farnham, UK: Ashgate, 2009.

Stuckey, Sterling. *Slave Culture: Nationalist Theory and the Foundations of Black America.* New York: Oxford University Press, 1987.

Sussuma, Robert. "Estill Workshop (Level Two), 'Figuring Out the Figures.'" New York, August 2015.

"Sydney Singer Weds Actress." *Sydney Morning Herald,* July 21, 1954.

Tagaq, Tanya. *Tanya Tagaq—Retribution.* Accessed July 22, 2021. https://www .youtube.com/watch?v=xNYTA6SV6tM.

Taylor, Diana. *The Archive and the Repertoire: Performing Cultural Memory in the Americas.* Durham, NC: Duke University Press, 2003.

Taylor, Frank C. *Alberta Hunter: A Celebration in Blues.* New York: McGraw-Hill, 1987.

Taylor, Frederick Winslow. *The Principles of Scientific Management.* New York: Harper and Brothers, 1911.

Théberge, Paul. "'Plugged In': Technology and Popular Music." In *The Cambridge Companion to Pop and Rock.* Edited by Simon Frith, Will Straw, and John Street, 1–25. Cambridge: Cambridge University Press, 2001.

Tony-Winning Star Leslie Uggams on InnerViews with Ernie Manouse. Accessed May 23, 2020. https://youtu.be/eknh_W4q8qU?si=mhUgn2ZWbTJvoCfs.

"Torch Singer, Ethel Waters in N.Y. Church." *Atlanta Daily World (1932–2003).* September 5, 1934, sec. Theatre Movies Radio.

Trevathan, Charles E. (lyricist), May Irwin (vocalist), and Charles E. Trevathan (composer). *The Bully.* 1907. Audio. https://www.loc.gov/item/jukebox -124996. "May Irwin's 'Bully' Song."

Tucker, Sophie. *Some of These Days: The Autobiography of Sophie Tucker.* New York: Doubleday, Doran, 1945.

Turner, Diane. "Pat Suzuki: A Jet-Propelled Butterfly." *Montreal Gazette,* July 19, 1968.

Tynan, Kenneth. "Tiny Chinese Minds." *New Yorker.* December 13, 1958.

Uggams, Leslie. "'My Own Morning' and 'Being Good Isn't Good Enough.'" In *Hallelujah, Baby! (Original Broadway Cast).* Music by Jule Styne; Lyrics by Betty Comden and Adolph Green; Book by Arthur Laurents. Sony Broadway, 1967.

Vargas, Deborah R. *Dissonant Divas in Chicana Music.* Minneapolis: University of Minnesota Press, 2012.

Vazquez, Alexandra T. *Listening in Detail: Performances of Cuban Music.* Durham, NC: Duke University Press, 2013.

Vogel, Shane. "Performing 'Stormy Weather': Ethel Waters, Lena Horne, and Katherine Dunham." *South Central Review* 25, no. 1 (2008): 93–113.

Vogel, Shane. *The Scene of Harlem Cabaret: Race, Sexuality, Performance.* Chicago: University of Chicago Press, 2009.

Vogel, Shane. *Stolen Time: Black Fad Performance and the Calypso Craze.* Chicago: University of Chicago Press, 2018.

Wald, Elijah. *Josh White: Society Blues.* Amherst: University of Massachusetts Press, 2000.

Wald, Gayle. "Afterword: 'The Art of Yearning.'" In *Voicing Girlhood in Popular Music: Performance, Authority, Authenticity.* Edited by Allison Adrian and Jacqueline C. Warwick, 281–85. New York: Routledge, 2016.

Warwick, Jacqueline C. *Girl Groups, Girl Culture: Popular Music and Identity in the 1960s.* New York: Routledge, 2007.

warholsoup100. *Ethel Waters—Stormy Weather (Keeps Rainin' All the Time) 1933* "The Cotton Club Years." Accessed July 10, 2021. https://www.youtube.com/watch?v=1WUzOkGY7i8.

Waters, Ethel. *Supper Time.* "Am I Blue?" Goldjazzyrecords, 2017. https://open.spotify.com/track/2ccGiib2oDkQNDl4FjlAvH.

Waters, Ethel, and Charles Samuels. *His Eye Is on the Sparrow: An Autobiography.* New York: Da Capo Press, 1992 [1950].

Westtoledoguy. *Careless Love—Ethel Waters, Herman Chittison Trio.* RCA Victor Records #20-2459, 2020. Accessed March 4, 2024. https://www.youtube.com/watch?v=wsckQ-a2aUM.

What's My Line?—Pearl Bailey; February 6, 1955. Accessed May 23, 2020. https://www.youtube.com/watch?v=dBlNO5LlR9o.

What's My Line?—Pearl Bailey; PANEL: Allen Ludden, Betty White (August 28, 1966). Accessed January 3, 2018. https://www.youtube.com/watch?v=MRmy3EIQa94.

Williams, Heather Andrea. *Self-Taught: African American Education in Slavery and Freedom.* John Hope Franklin Series in African American History and Culture. Chapel Hill: University of North Carolina Press, 2007.

Williams, John. *America's Mistress: The Life and Times of Eartha Kitt.* London: Quercus, 2013.

Wilson, August, and Michael Stewart. *Ma Rainey's Black Bottom.* Concord Theatricals, 1985.

Wilson, John S. "Pearl Bailey, Cabaret Trouper and Musical Star, Dies at 72: *New York Times*, August 18, 1990.

Wojcik, Pamela Robertson. "Typecasting." *Criticism* 45, no. 2 (2003): 223–49.

Wolf, Stacy. *Changed for Good: A Feminist History of the Broadway Musical.* London: Oxford University Press, 2011.

Wolf, Stacy. *A Problem Like Maria: Gender and Sexuality in the American Musical.* Ann Arbor: University of Michigan Press, 2002.

Woll, Allen L. *Black Musical Theatre: From Coontown to Dreamgirls*. Baton Rouge: Louisiana State University Press, 1989.

Wollman, Elizabeth Lara. *The Theater Will Rock: A History of the Rock Musical, from "Hair" to "Hedwig."* Ann Arbor: University of Michigan Press, 2009.

Woodruff, Neal W. "On the Voice: Contemporary Commercial Voice Pedagogy Applied to the Choral Ensemble: An Interview with Jeannette LoVetri." *Choral Journal* 52, no. 5 (December 2011): 39–53.

Woolfe, Zachary. "A Singular World That Won't Fade Away." *New York Times*, November 28, 2014, sec. Arts. https://www.nytimes.com/2014/11/30/arts/music/meredith-monk-celebrates-50-years-of-work.html.

"Words of the Week." *Jet*, July 11, 1974.

Work, John W. *American Negro Songs: 230 Folk Songs and Spirituals, Religious and Secular*. New York: Crown, 1940.

Yeboah, Nikki. "All the Nation's a Stage: The Ghana National Theatre as Sankofa Praxis." *Theatre Journal* 73, no. 2 (2021): 147–68.

Index

Association for the Advancement of Creative
　Musicians School, 217n14
As Thousands Cheer (musical), 76–77
Atkinson, Brooks, 88, 158
auditions, for Broadway, 1, 2, 4, 129, 216n6,
　223n60
Aunt Jemima (persona), 73
Ayetteh, Mercy, 200

Bacharach, Burt, 14
"Il Bacio" (song), 123
Bailey, Pearl, 21, 65–66, 81–82, 92–93, 96,
　233n100; on Broadway, 233n90; exercises
　from, 213; in *Hello, Dolly!*, 101–2; Horne
　compared with, 112; as humorist, 100;
　presence of, 99–100; subvocal voice
　protected by, 102–3; Tony Awards performed
　at by, 97–98; Tucker advising, 95
Baker, B. J., 147
Balance, Christine Bacareza, 218n19, 220n45
"Bali Ha'i" (song), 87–89, 232n73
"Bal Petit Bal" (song), 154–55
Baltimore Afro-American (newspaper), 53
Banks, Daniel, 65
Banks, Edith, 144
Baraka, Amiri, 72, 137
Barnes, Clive, 102
Barnet, Charlie, 110
Barthes, Roland, 31, 248n75
Batman (television show), 152, 154
beautiful sound (*bel canto*), 172–74, 177–79,
　184–85, 246n44
"Being Good Isn't Good Enough" (song),
　139–42
bel canto. See beautiful sound
Belinda, Alex, 37
Bell, Alexander Graham, 169
Belmont Theatre, 37
Belmont University, 236n33
belters, Broadway. *See specific topics*
belting, 61, 195; by Carroll, 119; CCM and, 184;
　Estill and, 187, 191–92; Miller and, 171, by
　Suzuki, 145–46; by Uggams, 142; riffing
　and, 195; vocal pedagogues against, 22, 24
Bennett, Michael, 14

Berlin, Edward, 43
Berlin, Irving, 42–45, 58, 79
Beulah (television comedy), 130
The Birth of the Clinic (Foucault), 172–73
Bitter Roots (Osseo-Asare), 12
blackface, 27, 36, 39–40, 73–74
black female vocality, during national crisis,
　154
black feminist study, vocal-possible and, 4–7
black feminist voice lessons, on *singing along
　with*, 196–99
black girlhood, 109–11, 116
black girl singers, double bind faced by,
　110–11
Black Patti Troubadours (troupe), 163
black popular music, African spirit worship
　connected to, 137
Black Studies Center, at Portland State
　University, 11
Black Swan Records, 48
Blake, Eubie, 13
Bleckmann, Theo, 170
Bloody Mary (character), from *South Pacific*,
　21, 83, 86–92, 230n55, 230n57, 232n71
Blue Holiday (musical), 242n136
Blue It Up On the Road (exercise), 211
blues, 31; Arlen composing, 228n12; Broadway
　and, 54, 63; torch songs differentiated
　from, 67–68; Waters influencing, 75; in
　yellowface, 82
blues lyrics, repetition in, 34
blues shouters, Broadway belters influenced
　by, 20
blues shouting, vocal pedagogy against, 22
blues singers: musical theatre impacted by,
　61–62; travel influencing, 34; vaudeville
　and, 37
Blyden, Larry, 149
Bogle, Donald, 68, 74, 235n7
Bombay Dreams (musical), 216n6
Boomerang (film), 152
"A Boy Like That" (song), 220n49
Bracken, Eddie, 159, 243n137
"Breathe Easy" (song), 208
Brice, Fanny, 67, 69, 78

Broadway, 85, 105, 202–6, 219n32, 250n1;
auditions for, 1; Bailey on, 233n90; black
girlhood and, 109–10; black women erased
on, 15–16; blues and, 54, 63; COVID-19
pandemic impacting, 206–7; Horne
on, 107; "The 'Pop' Singer and the Voice
Teacher" expressing frustration toward,
179–80; twice-heard voice of, 24–25; Waters
on, 55, 225n54. *See specific musicals*
Broadway belters. *See specific topics*
Bronston, John, 195, 249n86
Brooks, Daphne, 6, 70, 127, 203, 223n21,
249n83
Brooks, Lori, 40
Brooks, Mel, 156
Brown, Jayna, 125
Bruce, Carol, 235n23
Bubbling Brown Sugar (musical), 14
*The Bubbly Black Girl Sheds Her Chameleon
Skin* (musical), 216n7
"Bully Song" (song), 40

Cabaret (musical), 100
Cabin in the Sky (film), 79–80
Cabin in the Sky (revival), 92
Cahoon, Helen, 118
Caldwell, Elijah, 195–96, 249n86
Call Me Madam (musical), 94
Calloway, Cab, 94, 101
"Camp Amache" (Grenada War Relocation
Center), 144
Campus Notre-Dame-de-Foy, 186, 191–92
"Can't Help Lovin' Dat Man" (song), 74,
114–15
Capote, Truman, 130, 135
Cappiani, Luisa, 163, 167, 169
Carby, Hazel, 111
"Careless Love" (song), 71, 72
Carmen Jones (film), 81, 130
Carroll, Diahann (née Carol Diann Johnson),
15–16, 21, 107, 129–30, 237n54, 238n55;
exercises from, 136; in *House of Flowers*,
133–35; in *No Strings*, 125–27, 131; on
recording industry, 133–34; Rodgers and,
126–27, 131, 133, 238n55, 238n61; "A Sleepin'

Bee" performed by, 135–36, 239n80; "The
Sweetest Things" sung by, 239n79; Tony
Awards won by, 124, 131; Uggams contrasted
with, 131–32
Carroll, Vinnette, 14
Carruthers, Ben Frederic, 242n122
casting, 64–66, 216n6
Catanese, Brandi Wilkins, 65
Cats (musical), 243n140
Cavarero, Adriana, 103, 173–74, 245n29
CCM (contemporary commercial music),
181–86
"C'est Si Bon" (song), 152
Chambers-Letson, Joshua, 248n78
Chang, Juliana, 147
Channing, Carol, 95, 97, 98, 243n137
Chaos in Belville (play), 204
character diva, 103–4
Cheatham, Doc, 91
"Cheerio, My Deario" (song), 159
Cheng, Anne Anlin, 142–43, 159
Childress, Alice, 202, 203, 205
Childs, Kirsten, 216n7, 239n62
"Chop Suey" (song), 146
chorus girls, 238n60
churchiness, black, 1–3, 137, 216n4
church soloist, vocal coaches of, 2–3
citation, sonic, 9–13
classical music, black women singers of,
215n3
classical singing teachers, popular voice
racialized by, 181
Claudine (film), 132
Clément, Catherine, 87
clinic, voice studio as, 170–75
Coffin, Berton, 246n44
Coke Time with Eddie Fisher (television show),
239n80
Cole, Bob, 36
Cole, Nat King, 152
The Color Purple (musical), 206, 249n86
Columbia Records, 52, 137
Columbia University, 9
"Come to Mee-ow" (song), 159
Company (album), 202–3

244n146; from Martin, 124; from Merman, 212–13; from Rainey, 211–12; from Smith, B., 211–12; from Suzuki, 151; from Tucker, 212; from Uggams, 142. *See also* singing along with

Eyen, Tom, 14

Eyes of God (album), 137–38

Faison, George, 14

The Family Resemblance (musical), 200–201, 216n7

The Fantasticks (musical), 236n28

Feather, Leonard, 91

Fernández, Ruth, 23

Ferrer, Jose, 232n73

"Figure Combinations for Six Voice Qualities" (course), 188

"Figures for Voice Control" (course), 188

Find Your Pearl (exercise), 212

Fiol-Matta, Licia, 216n12

Fisher, Rudolph, 51

Fisk Jubilee Singers (vocal group), 249n83

Fitzgerald, Ella, 55, 137, 226n81

flexed voice, Jones, S., and, 163–67, 196

"Flotsam and Jetsam" (song), 159

Flower Drum Song (film), 146–47, 241n106

Flower Drum Song (musical), 65, 83, 133, 142–48, 241n104, 241n110

Floyd, George, 10

Floyd, Samuel A., 75

Forbidden City (venue), 241n104

Foster, Stephen, 163

Foucault, Michel, 172–74, 185, 196

Francis, Arlene, 93

Franko, Mark, 176, 228n28

Freed, Arthur, 80, 236n38

Funny Face (film), 236n38

Funny Girl (musical), 67, 179

Galella, Donatella, 149, 227n3

Garcia, Gustave, 53, 168

Garcia, Manuel, II, 8, 53, 162, 167–68, 217n16, 246n44

Gardella, Tess, 73–74

Gardner, Ava, 235n23

Garland, Judy, 234n1

George-Graves, Nadine, 219n36

Gershwin, George, 56, 58–59

Ghost (film), 230n57

Giovanni, Nikki, 237n39

Girl Crazy (musical), 56

girlhood, black, 109–10, 116

Glover, Eric M., 69

God Sends Sunday (novel), 229n46

"Golden Age," of musical theatre, 15–16, 219n41

Gone with the Wind (film), 79

"A Good Man Is Hard to Find" (song), 45

Gordy, Berry, 128

Gould, Matt, 216n7

Graham, Billy, 55

Grant, Micki, 14

Graphenreed, Timothy, 14

Greene, Silas, 117, 236n30

The Green Pastures (play), 85

Grenada War Relocation Center "Camp Amache," 144

Griffin, Farah Jasmine, 79, 154, 193

Grist, Reri, 243n143

Gutierrez, Carmen, 243n143

Gypsy (musical), 57–58

Hall, Juanita, 65–66, 82, 84–85, 109, 232n74, 235n9; Asian Americans played by, 88–89; "Bali Ha'i" sung by, 87–88; exercises from, 213; Feather on, 91; in *Flower Drum Song* (film), 241n106, 241n110; grandmother of, 90–92; in *Show Boat*, 231n61; in *South Pacific*, 21, 232n73; Tony Award won by, 83

Hallelujah, Baby! (musical), 22, 125, 138–40, 240n90, 243n143

Hall Johnson Negro Choir, 85

Hammerstein, Oscar, II, 83, 150, 230n55, 241n110. *See also specific works*

Handy, W. C., 48–49, 225n56, 228n21

Hansberry, Lorraine, 14, 205

Harlem Renaissance, 219n36, 225n56

Harris, Ben, 36

Harvard (university), 2–3

Harvard Kuumba Singers (gospel choir), 3

Hawkins, Coleman, 91
Hawkins, Jose, 232n71
Hayes, Edgar, 94
Hayman, Lillian, 138–39, 240n90, 243n143
health, 175–77, 196
"Heat Wave" (song), 77
Hello, Dolly! (musical), 65, 94–95, 100–102
Henderson, Luther, 233n82
Henley, Lou, 51
Henry, David, 241n111
Hentoff, Nat, 193
Herman, Jerry, 97, 101
Herrera, Brian, 227n3
Herriman, George, 243n137
Hester, "Aunt," 193
Heyward, Dubose, 225n54
high yellowface, 21, 82, 92, 101, 146, 230n56
Hill, Ruby, 81
Hine, Darlene Clark, 111
"His Eye is on the Sparrow" (Waters), 52, 55
Holiday, Billie, 77, 78, 137, 240n84, 240n90
Holliday, Jennifer, 15
Holman, Libby, 61, 156
Holt, William, 37
honor, thing of, 9–13
Hopkins, Linda, 37, 224
Horne, Lena, 21, 103, 109, 113, 138, 234n2;
    Bailey compared with, 112; on Broadway,
    107; "Can't Help Lovin' Dat Man" sung
    by, 114–15; Cotton Club worked at by,
    118–19; double bind sung from by, 112;
    exercises from, 116; Giovanni interviewing,
    237n39; in *The Lady and Her Music*, 236n38;
    prejudice discussed by, 235n11; *St. Louis
    Woman* refused to be in by, 80–81; "Stormy
    Weather" performed by, 235n21; Tony
    Awards won by, 117; Waters and, 79–80
Horsford, Cyril, 52
House of Flowers (musical), 65, 93–94, 130,
    133–35, 232n74, 239n79
How Come? (musical), 36–37
"How Deep is the Ocean" (song), 90
Howland, Jason, 206, 208, 250n10
How to Sing (Lehmann), 166
Hughes, Langston, 54, 85, 86, 137

humorist, Bailey as, 100
Humphrey, Stetson, 118, 119, 237n40
Hunter, Alberta, 36, 45–46, 53, 225n52
Hunter, Eddie, 36
Hurston, Zora Neale, 21, 69–73, 104, 228n21
Hwang, David Henry, 149, 241n111
Hyers sisters, 36

I Do! I Do! (musical), 236n28
"I Enjoy Being a Girl" (song), 147, 149–51
"I Got Rhythm" (song), 56–57, 60
"I Gotta Right to Sing the Blues" (song), 138
"I'm Gonna Wash That Man Right Outa My
    Hair" (song), 123–24
Indianapolis Freeman (newspaper), 40
ingénue: black women singers as, 106–7, 127–28;
    Martin as, 122; vocal expression of, 237n51
Inner City (musical), 224n33
"The International Rag" (song), 44–45
In the Break (Moten), 9–10
In the Heights (musical), 216n7
Invisible Thread (musical), 216n7
Irwin, May, 39, 40, 224n44
"I Want to Be Evil" (song), 152

Jack Paar Show (*The Tonight Show*) (television
    variety show), 145
Jackson, Michael R., 4, 205, 216n7
Jamaica (musical), 81, 116, 243n142
James M. Nederlander Theatre, 206
Jefferson, Miles, 134
Jerrahol (singing teacher), 118–19
Jerry's Girls (musical), 127
Jess, Tyehimba, 40
Jewish artists, musical theatre platforming, 45
Jewish torch singers, 67
Jim Crow-era, black girlhood during, 116
Jim Crow South, 117
John Henry (musical), 242n136
Johnson, Billy, 36
Johnson, Brittney, 205
Johnson, E. Patrick, 217n29
Johnson, "Lady Bird," 154
Johnson, Zonya Love, 72–73. *See also* Love,
    Zonya

Smiling Open Vowels (exercise), 136

Smith, Bessie, 20, 29–30, 109; Davis, A., speculating on, 33; exercises from, 211–12; in *How Come?*, 36–37; shouting by, 31–37; Waters discussing, 49–50

Smith, Jacob, 169

Smith, Maud, 32

Smith, Muriel, 89

SNCC (Student Nonviolent Coordinating Committee), 138

So in Love! (album), 138

Solutions for Singers (Miller), 171

songs, performance of, 19

songwriting practice, singing voices and, 222n59

sonic citation, 9–13

Soto-Morettini, Donna, 217n18

The Sound of Music (musical), 116, 122, 239n79

Southern, Eileen, 36

South Pacific (movie), 89

South Pacific (musical), 82, 116, 146; Bloody Mary from, 21, 83, 86–92, 230n55, 230n57, 232n71; Hall in, 21, 232n73; Pulitzer Prize won by, 230n57

Spillers, Hortense, 22, 198–99

Spinoza, Baruch, 191

Square, Jonathan, 235n25

Stanislavski, Konstantin, 125

Stark, James, 185, 246n44

Steinhauer, Kimberly, 170, 187, 189, 192–93, 221n53, 247n69

Sterne, Jonathan, 169

Sternfeld, Jessica, 219n41

Stockhausen, Julius, 168

"Stormy Weather" (song), 52, 74–75, 80; "Am I Blue" compared with, 68; Horne performing, 235n21; Waters performing, 66–69

"Strange Fruit" (song), 77

A Strange Loop (Jackson), 205, 216n7

A Strange Loop (musical), 249n86

Stratton, Jon, 67

Street Scene (musical), 85

Streisand, Barbra, 67

Student Nonviolent Coordinating Committee (SNCC), 138

Studies in Musical Theatre (group interview), 194–95

subvocal voice, Bailey protecting, 102–3

Sunset Boulevard (musical), 126

"Supper Time" (song), 66, 75–79

Suzuki, Pat, 21, 142, 234n3, 240n98; belting by, 145–46; childhood of, 143–44; exercises from, 151; in *Flower Drum Song*, 145–48; "I Enjoy Being a Girl" (song) performed by, 149–51; Lee on, 149; Rodgers describing, 241n104

Sweet Charity (musical), 100

"The Sweetest Things" (song), 239n79

Sweet Mama Stringbean (Ethel Waters blues name), 48, 72

Tagaq, Tanya, 13

"Talent '48" (revue), 85

tango, 225n56

Taylor, Breonna, 10, 223n7

Taylor, Diana, 29, 217n19

Taylor, Frederick Winslow, 176

Taylor, Samuel, 238n61

Teahouse of the August Moon (play), 145

techniques of the body, 7–8, 217n15

Tharpe, Sister Rosetta, 94

Theatre Owners Booking Association circuit (TOBA circuit), 35

Thompson, Kay, 119, 236n38

Thoroughly Modern Millie (musical), 127

Till the Clouds Roll By (film), 114

timbre, efficiency resulting in, 176–77

timing, Rodgers emphasized by, 151

Tin Pan Alley (song publisher), 42–43

"Tired" (song), 100–101, 233n99

Titze, Ingo, 170

TOBA circuit (Theatre Owners Booking Association circuit), 35

Tomkins, Silvan, 191

Tony Award. *See* Antoinette Perry Awards for Excellence in Theatre

torch singers, 228n28; black, 66–69, 75; Jewish, 67; Waters as, 65–66; white, 74 torch songs, 67–68, 74–75, 78

Tosca (opera), 182

"Toujours Gai" (song), 154, 156, 159

travel, blues singers influenced by, 34

A Trip to Coontown (musical comedy), 36, 39

Trouble in Mind (play), 202–5

"Tryptych" (song), 193

Tucker, Sophie, 20, 37–38, 40; autobiography
of, 42; Bailey advised by, 95; exercises from,
212; Hunter on, 45–46; "The International
Rag" performed by, 44–45; originality
emphasized by, 43

Twi (language), 200

"twice-behaved behavior," 217n19

twice-heard behavior, singing technique and,
7–9

twice-heard voice, of Broadway, 24–25

Tyers, William H., 225n56

Tynan, Kenneth, 241n110, 242n129

types, 64–65, 104–5, 122, 125, 227n3. *See also*
ingénue; torch singers; weary-bluesy
mammy

Tysen, Nathan, 206, 208, 250n10

Uggams, Leslie, 16, 21, 82, 129–30, 243n143;
"Being Good Isn't Good Enough" sung by,
141–42; Carroll, D., contrasted with, 131–32;
exercises from, 142; in *Hallelujah, Baby!*,
138–40; "My Own Morning" sung by,
139–41; *Sing Along with Mitch* performed
on by, 131, 239n62; Tony Awards winning,
125; Waters compared with, 136

University of Ghana, 200

"Uska Dara" (song), 152

Vandross, Luther, 14

Vargas, Deborah, 103

vaudeville, blues singers and, 37

Vazquez, Alexandra T., 21, 108–9, 160, 221n50,
234n5

Velasco, Vi, 22

Verdi, Giuseppe, 163

via techniques of the body, vocal style, 217n18

Village Vanguard, 94

vocal-affective-racial types, casting and, 64–66

vocal coaches, of church soloist, 2–3

vocal cords, 165–67

vocal exercises. *See* exercises, vocal

vocal expression, of ingénues, 237n51

vocal figures, 187–88

vocal harm, belting and, 192

vocal health, 175–77, 196

vocal instruction, as technique of the body, 7–8

vocalists, Waters influencing, 227n84

vocal pedagogy: against belting, 22; against
blues shouting, 22; health constructed by,
196; popular music studies and, 17

vocal-possible: black feminist study and, 4–7;
black singer-actress and, 194–96, 199; by
singing along with influencing, 22

vocal sounds, 215n1, 244n1

vocal style, 54, 217n18

vocal teachers, pop vocal technique and,
162–63

vocal technique: pop, 162–63; *singing
along with* and, 197–98; singing lessons
teaching, 8–9. *See also* exercises, vocal;
singing technique

Vogel, Shane, 54, 112, 234n2, 235n21

voice: accidental, 175, 180; conserving the ,
176; Derrida on, 102–3; flexed, 163–67, 196;
medical understanding of, 190; mixed, 178,
225n50, 246n49; originary, 192–93;
subvocal, 102–3; twice-heard, 24–25.
See also popular voice

Voice Foundation, 181

voice pedagogy, 25, 215n3, 246n52

voice pedagogy literature, singing technique
policed by, 7

voice practice, 20

voice studio, as clinic, 170–75

voice teachers, belting discouraged by, 24

voice teaching, 20

Wald, Elijah, 242n136

Wald, Gayle, 106, 234n1

Waring, Dorothy, 69

Warren, Annette, 235n23

Warwick, Jacqueline, 127–28

Washington, "Aunt Dinah," 137

Washington, Fredi, 81
Waters, Daryl, 155
Waters, Ethel, 21, 31, 39, 46–47, 130, 212; in
    As Thousands Cheer, 76–77; blues influenced
    by, 75; on Broadway, 55, 225n54; "Careless
    Love" sung by, 72; Davis on, 54; Henley
    teaching, 51; Horne and, 79–80; Hurston
    and, 69–70, 72; musical theatre associ-
    ated with, 48; repertoire extended by, 52;
    "St. Louis Blues" sung by, 48; Smith, B.,
    discussed by, 49–50; "Stormy Weather"
    performed by, 66–67; Sweet Mama String-
    bean (Ethel Waters blues name), 48, 72;
    as torch singer, 65–66; Uggams compared
    with, 136; vocalists influenced by, 227n84;
    vocal surgery undergone by, 52–53; weary-
    bluesy mammy reified by, 104
weary-bluesy mammy, 249n83; *Gone with the
    Wind* celebrating, 79; Hayman playing,
    240n90; torch songs and, 74–75; Waters
    reifying, 104
Webber, Andrew Lloyd, 243n140
Weill, Kurt, 85
We Insist! (album), 193
Welch, Elisabeth, 50–51, 225n56
Welles, Orson, 242n122
West Side Story (musical), 220n49, 243n143
"What Do I Care" (song), 159
"What's My Line?" (television show), 92
Wheeler, Harold, 14
"When I walk that levee road" (song), 41
White, E. B., 156, 243n138
White, George, 36

White, John, Jr., 242n136
White, Josh, 61, 156, 242n136
White, Walter, 80
Whitney, Salem Tutt, 165, 236n30
Whyte, Jerry, 238n61
Wicked (musical), 205
Williams, Heather, 216n13
Wilson, August, 75–76, 229n34
Wings Flex (exercise), 211
Witness Uganda (musical), 216n7
The Wiz (musical), 13, 14, 15
WNYC Radio, 85
Wojcik, Pamela, 103
Wolf, Marco, 236n35
Wolf, Stacy, 6, 58, 69, 100, 122, 216n10, 220n49,
    227n3
Wollman, Elizabeth, 219n41
Work, John Wesley, Jr., 28, 29
The World of Suzie Wong (film), 146–47
Wright, Hailee Kaleem, 208–9, 251n12
Wright, Pearl, 51–52, 66, 212

yellowface: blues in, 82; Galella on witnessing,
    149; high, 21, 82, 92, 101, 146, 230n56
Young, Joe, 68
"You've Got to Be Carefully Taught" (song),
    238n55
Yu, Chin, 146, 232n73

Ziegfeld, Florenz, 37, 67, 228n28, 231n61,
    238n60
Ziegfeld Follies, 39, 67
Zip Coon (minstrel figure), 39